The Pearson Custom Program for

Camden County College

Pearson Learning Solutions

New York Boston San Francisco
London Toronto Sydney Tokyo Singapore Madrid
Mexico City Munich Paris Cape Town Hong Kong Montreal

Senior Vice President, Editorial and Marketing: Patrick F. Boles
Editor: Ana Díaz-Caneja
Development Editor: Christina Martin
Operations Manager: Eric M. Kenney
Production Manager: Jennifer Berry
Art Director: Renée Sartell
Cover Designers: Blair Brown and Kristen Kiley

Cover Art: Jerry Driendl/Getty Images, Inc.; Steve Bloom/Getty Images, Inc.; "Cheetah" courtesy of Marvin Mattelson/Getty Images; "Tabs" courtesy of Andrey Prokhorov/iStockphoto; "Open Doors" courtesy of Spectral-Design/iStockphoto; "Compass" courtesy of Laurent Hamels/Getty Images; "Fortune Teller" courtesy of Ingvald Kaldhussaeter/iStockphoto; "Ladder of Success" courtesy of iStockphoto; "Global Communication in Blue" courtesy of iStockphoto.

This special edition published in cooperation with Pearson Learning Solutions.

Printed in the United States of America.

Please visit our web site at *www.pearsoncustom.com/custom-library/custom-phit.*

Attention bookstores: For permission to return any unsold stock, contact us at *pe-uscustomreturns@pearson.com.*

Pearson Learning Solutions, 501 Boylston Street, Suite 900, Boston, MA 02116
A Pearson Education Company
www.pearsoned.com

ISBN 10: 1-256-03206-9
ISBN 13: 978-1-256-03206-9

Contents

ACCESS

INTRODUCTION TO ACCESS

Finding Your Way Through a Database

CASE STUDY | Managing a Business in the Global Economy

Watch the Set-up Video for this Case Study!

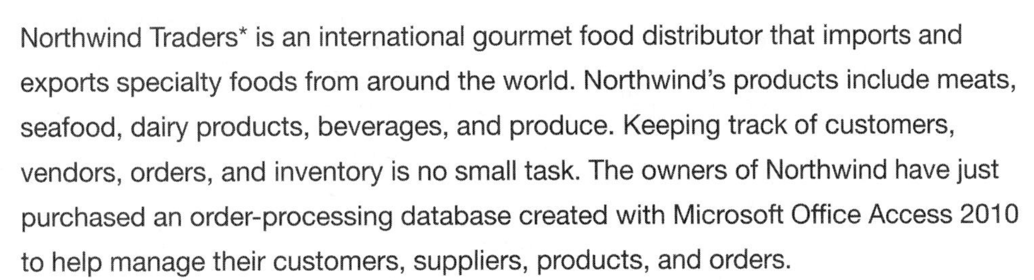

Northwind Traders* is an international gourmet food distributor that imports and exports specialty foods from around the world. Northwind's products include meats, seafood, dairy products, beverages, and produce. Keeping track of customers, vendors, orders, and inventory is no small task. The owners of Northwind have just purchased an order-processing database created with Microsoft Office Access 2010 to help manage their customers, suppliers, products, and orders.

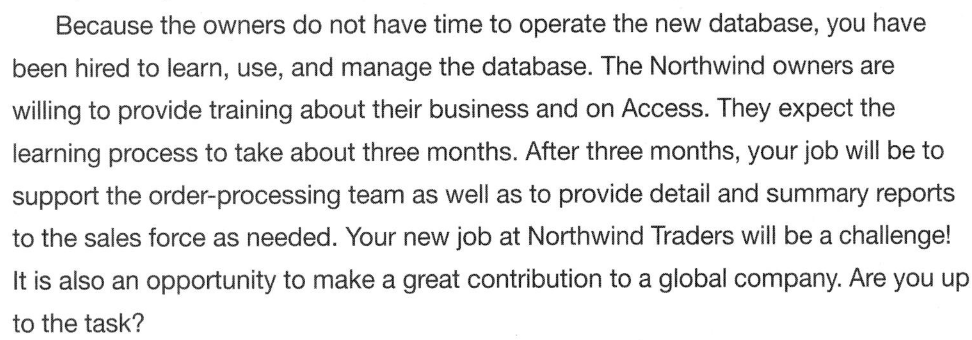

Because the owners do not have time to operate the new database, you have been hired to learn, use, and manage the database. The Northwind owners are willing to provide training about their business and on Access. They expect the learning process to take about three months. After three months, your job will be to support the order-processing team as well as to provide detail and summary reports to the sales force as needed. Your new job at Northwind Traders will be a challenge! It is also an opportunity to make a great contribution to a global company. Are you up to the task?

*Northwind Traders was created by the Microsoft Access Team and is shipped with Access as a sample database you can use to learn about Access. The names of companies, products, people, characters, and/or data are fictitious. The practice database you will use is a modified version of Northwind Traders.

OBJECTIVES

AFTER YOU READ THIS CHAPTER, YOU WILL BE ABLE TO:

1. Navigate among the objects in an Access database
2. Understand the difference between working in storage and memory
3. Practice good database file management
4. Back up, compact, and repair Access files
5. Create filters
6. Sort table data on one or more fields
7. Know when to use Access or Excel to manage data
8. Use the Relationships window
9. Understand relational power

Databases Are Everywhere!

If you use the Internet, you use databases often. When you shop online or check your bank statement, you are connecting to a database. Even when you type a search phrase into Google and click Search, you are using Google's massive database with all of its stored Web page references and keywords. Look for something on eBay, and you are searching eBay's database to find a product on which you might want to bid. Need a new pair of shoes? Log on to the Columbia Web site (see Figure 1), and find the right pair in your style, your size, and your price range. All this information is stored in its products database.

If you use the Internet, you use databases often.

FIGURE 1 Columbia Web Site ➤

You are exposed to other databases on a regular basis outside of Internet shopping. For example, your community college or university uses a database to store the registration data. When you registered for this course, your data was entered into a database. The database probably told you the number of available seats but not the names of the other students who enrolled in the class. In addition, social networking Web sites such as Facebook and LinkedIn are storing data on large database servers.

Organizations rely on data to conduct daily operations, regardless of whether the organization exists as a profit or not-for-profit environment. Organizations maintain data about their customers, employees, orders, volunteers, activities, and facilities. Every keystroke and mouse click creates data about the organization that needs to be stored, organized, and available for analysis. Access is a valuable decision-making tool that many organizations are using or want to use.

In this section, you will explore Access database objects and work with table views. You will also learn the difference between working in storage and working in memory, and you will learn how changes to database objects are saved. Finally, you will practice good database maintenance techniques by backing up, compacting, and repairing databases.

Navigating Among the Objects in an Access Database

An **object** in an Access database is a main component that is created and used to make the database function.

A **field** is the smallest data element contained in a table. Examples of fields are first name, last name, address, and phone number.

A **record** is a complete set of all of the data elements (fields) about one person, place, event, or concept.

A **table**, the foundation of every database, is a collection of related records.

A **database** consists of one or more tables to store data, one or more forms to enter data into the tables, and one or more reports to output the table data as organized information.

The ***objects*** in an Access database are the main components that are created and used to make the database function. The four main object types are tables, queries, forms, and reports. Two other object types, macros and modules, are used less frequently. Throughout this chapter, you will learn how to use each type of object.

To understand how an Access database works and how to use Access effectively, you should first learn the terms of the key object—the table. A ***field*** is the smallest data element contained in a table. Fields define the type of data that is collected, for example, text, numeric, or date. Examples of fields are first name, last name, address, and phone number. A field may be required or optional. For example, a person's last name may be required, but a fax number may be optional. A ***record*** is a complete set of all of the data elements (fields) about one person, place, event, or concept. For example, your first name, last name, student ID, phone number, and e-mail address constitute your record in your instructor's class roster. A ***table***, the foundation of every database, is a collection of related records. For example, all the students in your class would be entered into the Class Roster table during registration.

A ***database*** consists of one or more tables to store data, one or more forms to enter data into the tables, and one or more reports to output the table data as organized information. The main functions of a database are to collect data, to store data logically, to manipulate data to make it more useful, and to output the data to the screen and printed reports. Databases also export data to files so the files can be imported by other databases or other information-processing systems.

TIP Data Versus Information

Data and *information* are two terms that are often used interchangeably. However, when it comes to databases, the two terms mean different things. *Data* is what is entered into the tables of the database. *Information* is the finished product that is produced by the database in a query or in a printed report. Data is converted to information by selecting, calculating, sorting, or summarizing records. Decisions in an organization are usually based on information produced by a database, rather than raw data.

Examine the Access Interface

Figure 2 shows the Access Interface for the Northwind Traders database, which was introduced in the Case Study at the beginning of this chapter. The top section, known as the Ribbon, remains the same no matter which database is open. Below the Ribbon, you find all the objects that are needed to make the current database function; these objects are stored in the Navigation Pane (on the left). To the right of the Navigation Pane, the currently open objects are displayed and are delimited with tabs. The title bar at the top of the window contains the name of the application (Microsoft Access), the name of the currently loaded database (Northwind), and the file format (Access 2007) of the loaded database. Because Access 2010 does not have a new file format, you will see Access 2007 in the title bar throughout this textbook. The Minimize, Maximize (or Restore), and Close icons can be found on the right of the title bar. The tab below the Ribbon shows that the Employees table is currently open. When more than one object is open at a time, one tab will be shown for each open object. Click on a tab to view or modify that object independently of the other objects.

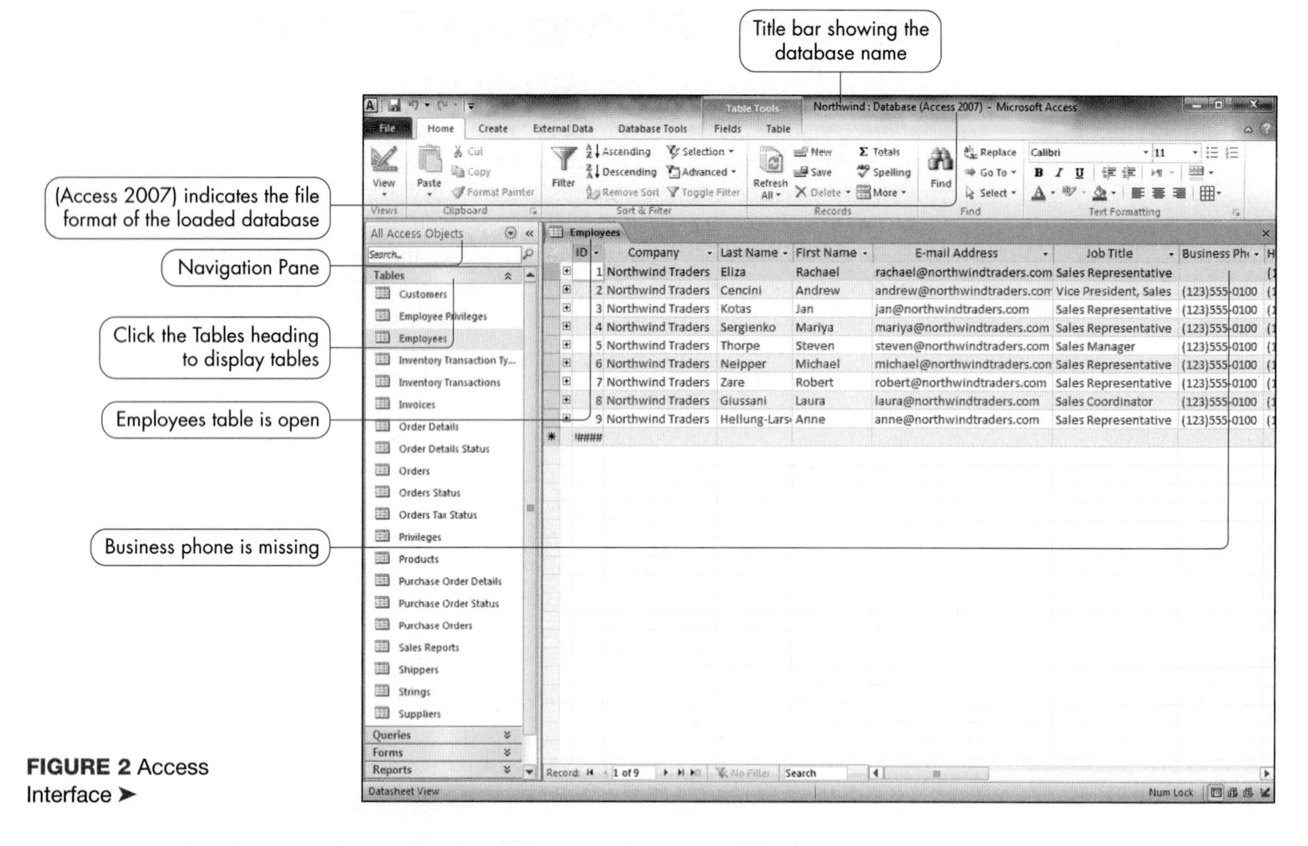
Title bar showing the database name
(Access 2007) indicates the file format of the loaded database
Navigation Pane
Click the Tables heading to display tables
Employees table is open
Business phone is missing

FIGURE 2 Access Interface ➤

Figure 2 shows that the Northwind database contains 20 tables: Customers, Employee Privileges, Employees, etc. Each table contains multiple records. The Employees table is currently open and shows nine records for the nine employees who work for the company. The Employees table contains 18 fields (or attributes) about each employee, including the employee's Last Name, First Name, E-Mail Address, Job Title, and so on. Occasionally, a field does not contain a value for a particular record. One of the employees, Rachael Eliza, did not provide a business phone. The value of that field is missing. Access shows a blank cell when data is missing.

The Suppliers table holds a record for each vendor from whom the firm purchases products; the Orders table holds one record for each order. The real power of Access is derived from a database with multiple tables and the relationships that connect the tables.

The **Navigation Pane** organizes and lists the database objects in an Access database.

The ***Navigation Pane*** organizes and lists the database objects in an Access database. As stated earlier, six types of objects—tables, queries, forms, reports, macros, and modules—can exist in a database. Most databases contain multiple tables, queries, forms, and reports. Tables store the data, forms enable users to enter information into the tables, reports enable users to display data in an organized format, and queries enable users to ask questions about the data. In Figure 2, the Tables group shows all the table objects; the other objects are hidden until you click a group heading to expand the group and display the objects. Click a visible group name to hide the group. To change the way objects are displayed within a group, right-click the group, and select from a list of options. For example, you can right-click the Queries category, point to View By, and then click Details to see when each query was created.

The Access Ribbon contains the icons that help you perform the database functions to maintain a database. These commands are described in detail on the following Reference page. You do not need to memorize every icon, group, and tab; however, it will be helpful to refer to this page as you are learning Access.

REFERENCE Access Ribbon

Tab and Groups	Description
File	The File tab leads to the Backstage view, which gives you access to a variety of database tools such as Compact and Repair, Back Up Database, and Print.
Home Views Clipboard Sort & Filter Records Find Text Formatting	The default Access tab. Contains basic editing functions, such as cut and paste, filtering, find and replace, and most formatting actions.
Create Templates Tables Queries Forms Reports Macros & Code	This tab contains all the create tools, such as create Tables, create Forms, create Reports, and create Queries.
External Data Import & Link Export Collect Data Web Linked Lists	This tab contains all of the operations to facilitate data import and export.
Database Tools Tools Macro Relationships Analyze Move Data Add-Ins	This tab enables you to use the more advanced features of Access. Set relationships between tables, analyze a table or query, and migrate your data to SQL Server or SharePoint.

Work with Table Views

The **Datasheet view** is where you add, edit, and delete the records of a table.

The **Design view** is where you create tables, add and delete fields, and modify field properties.

Access provides two different ways to view a table: the Datasheet view and the Design view. The ***Datasheet view*** is a grid containing columns (fields) and rows (records), similar to an Excel spreadsheet. You can view, add, edit, and delete records in the Datasheet view. The ***Design view*** is used to create and modify a table's design by specifying the fields it will contain, the fields' data types, and their associated properties. Data types define the type of data that will be stored in a field, such as currency, numeric, text, etc. For example, if you need to store the pay rate of an employee, you would enter the field name Pay Rate and select the data type currency. The field properties define the characteristics of the fields in more detail. For example, for the field Pay Rate, you could set a field property that requires Pay Rate to be less than $25 (a higher rate would trigger a manager's approval). To accomplish this, you would set the validation rule to <25 to prevent users from entering a pay rate higher than $25.

Figure 3 shows the Design view for the Customers table. In the top portion, each row contains the field names, the data type, and an optional description for each field in the table. In the bottom portion, the Field Properties pane contains the properties (details) for each field. Click on a field, and the field properties will be displayed in the bottom portion of the Design view window.

Figure 4 shows the Datasheet view for the Customers table. The top row in the table contains the field names. Each additional row contains a record (the data for a specific customer). Each column represents a field (one attribute about a customer). Every record in the table represents a different customer; all records contain the same fields.

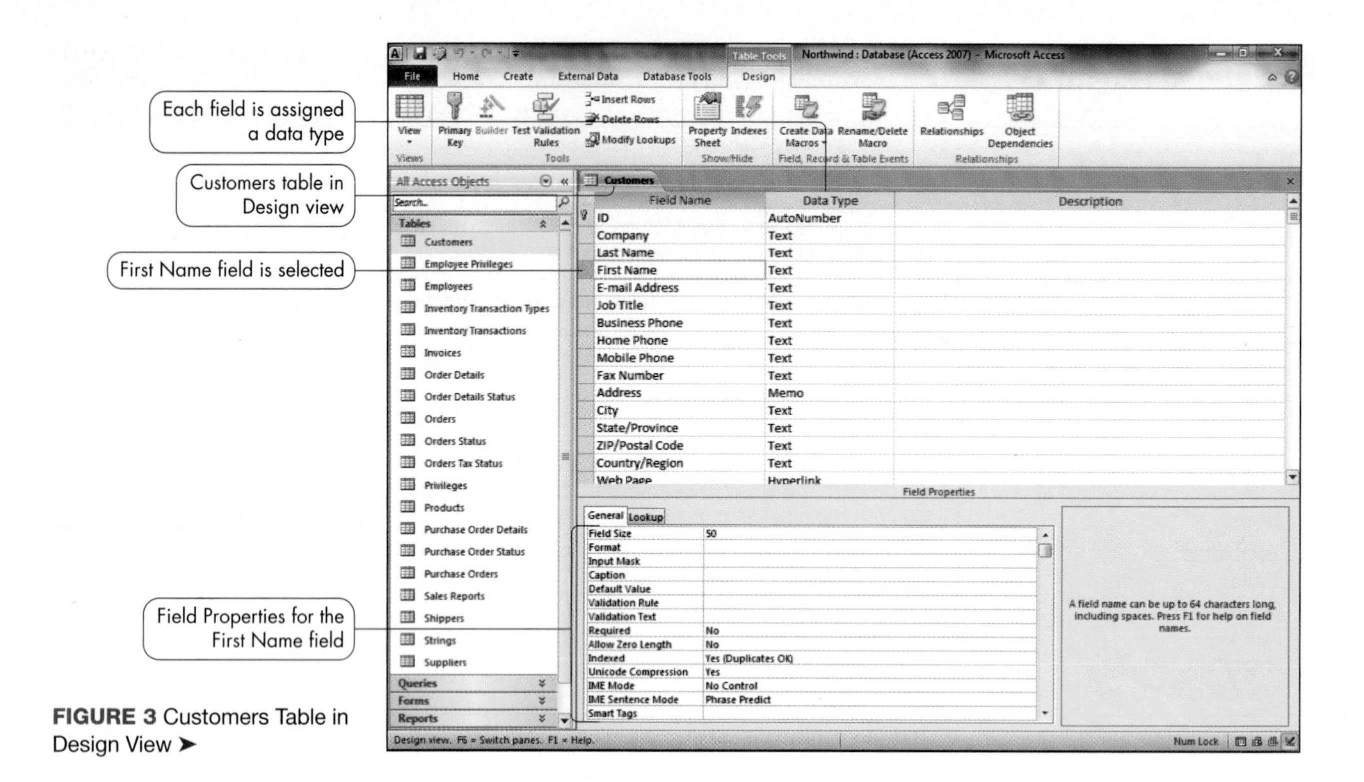
Each field is assigned a data type
Customers table in Design view
First Name field is selected
Field Properties for the First Name field

FIGURE 3 Customers Table in Design View ➤

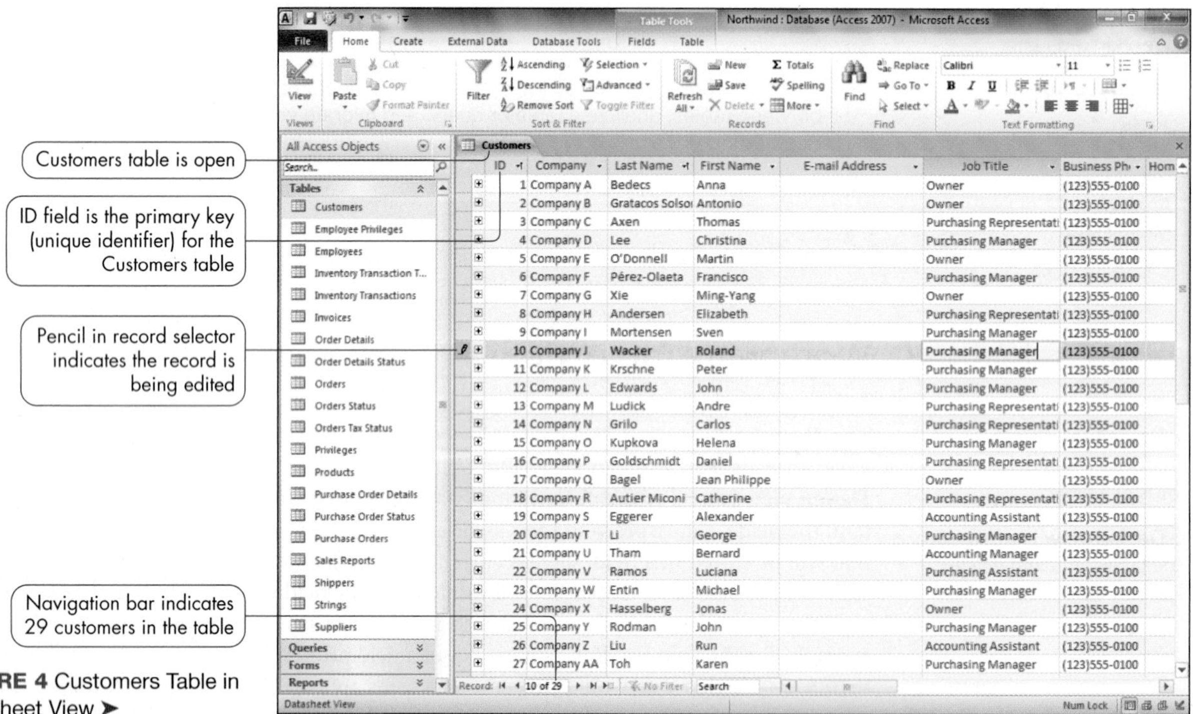
Customers table is open
ID field is the primary key (unique identifier) for the Customers table
Pencil in record selector indicates the record is being edited
Navigation bar indicates 29 customers in the table

FIGURE 4 Customers Table in Datasheet View ➤

The **primary key** is the field (or combination of fields) that uniquely identifies each record in a table.

The ***primary key*** is the field (or combination of fields) that uniquely identifies each record in a table. The ID field is the primary key in the Customers table; it ensures that each record in the table can be distinguished from every other record. It also helps prevent the occurrence of duplicate records. Primary key fields may be numbers, letters, or a combination of both. In this case, the primary key is an autonumber (a number that is generated by Access and is incremented each time a record is added). Another example of a primary key is Social Security Number, which is often used in an employee table.

The navigation bar at the bottom of Figure 4 shows that the Customers table has 29 records and that record number 10 is the current record. The vertical scroll bar on the right side of the window only appears when the table contains more records than can appear in the window at one time. Similarly, the horizontal scroll bar at the bottom of the window only appears when the table contains more fields than can appear in the window at one time.

The pencil symbol to the left of Record 10 indicates that the data in that record is being edited and that changes have not yet been saved. The pencil symbol disappears when you move to another record. It is important to understand that Access saves data automatically as soon as you move from one record to another. This may seem counter-intuitive at first, since Word and Excel do not save changes and additions automatically. With Word and Excel, you must click the Save icon in order to save your work (or set auto-save to save automatically in the background).

Figure 5 shows the navigation buttons that you use to move through the records in a table, query, or form. The buttons enable you to go to the first record, the previous record, the next record, or the last record. The button with the asterisk is used to add a new (blank) record. You can also type a number directly into the current record cell, and Access will take you to that record. Finally, the navigation bar enables you to locate a record based on a single word. Type a word in the search cell box, and Access will locate the first record that contains the word.

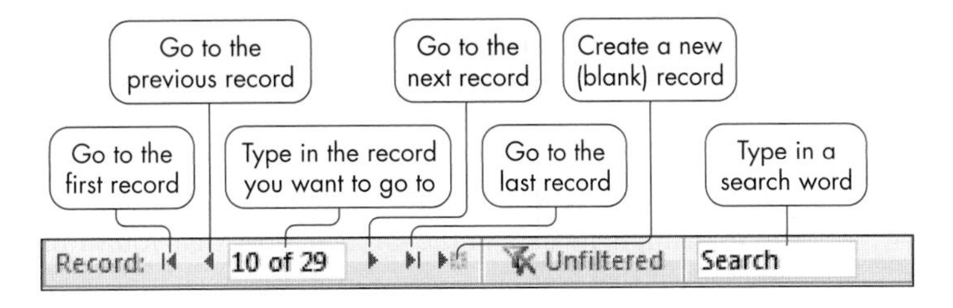

FIGURE 5 Navigation Buttons ➤

No system, no matter how sophisticated, can produce valid output from invalid input. Access database systems are built to anticipate data entry errors. These systems contain table validation rules created to prevent invalid data entry. Two types of validation rules exist: those built into Access and those a developer creates specifically for a database. For example, Access will automatically prevent you from adding a new record with the same primary key as an existing record. Access does not allow you to enter text or numeric data into a date field. A database developer can add validation rules, such as requiring a person's last name or requiring an employee's social security number. A developer can also limit the length of data, such as only enabling five digits for a zip code or two characters for a state abbreviation.

Use Forms, Queries, and Reports

As previously indicated, an Access database is made up of different types of objects together with the tables and the data they contain. The tables are the heart of any database because they contain the *actual* data. The other objects in a database—such as forms, queries, and reports—are based on one or more underlying tables. Figure 6 displays a form based on the Customers table shown earlier.

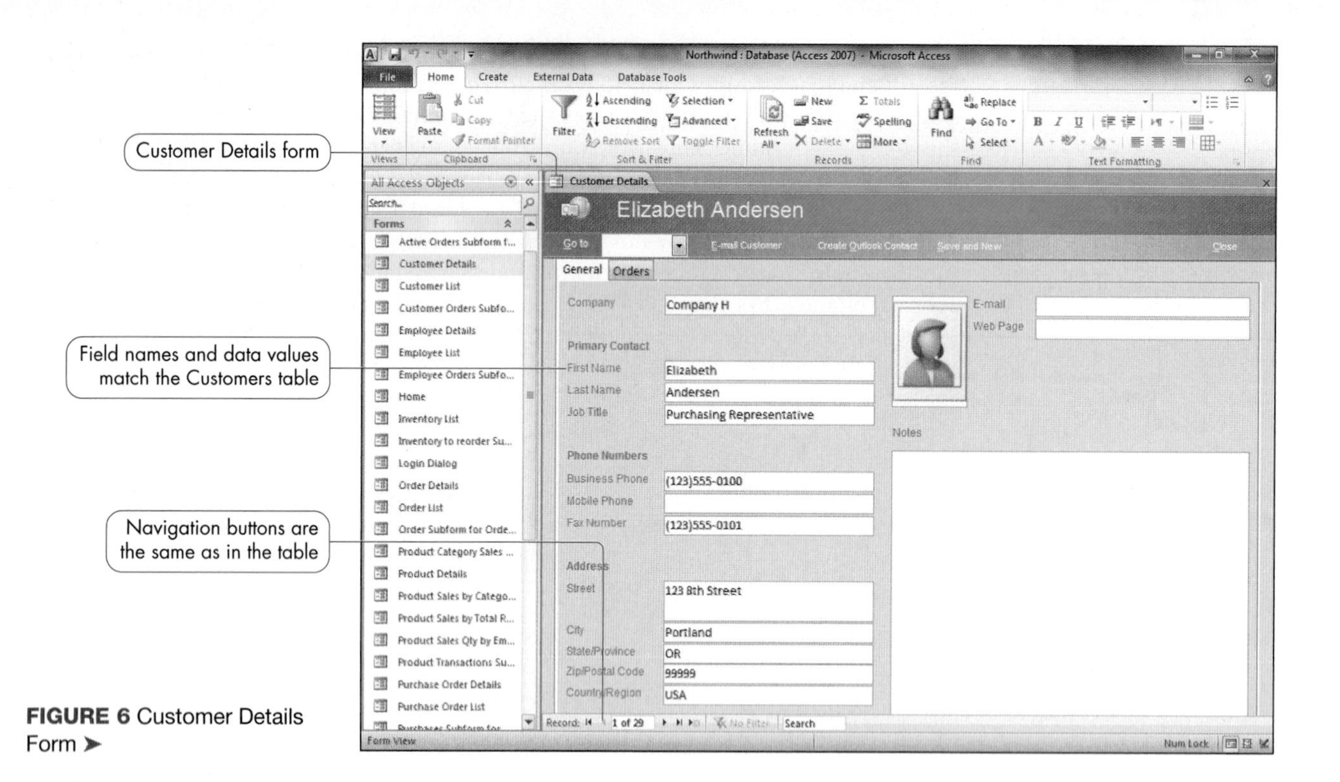

FIGURE 6 Customer Details Form ➤

A **form** is an object that enables you to enter, modify, or delete table data.

A ***form*** is an object that enables you to enter, modify, or delete table data. A form enables you to manipulate data in the same manner that you would in a table's Datasheet view. The difference is that you can create a form that will limit the user to viewing only one record at a time. This helps the user to focus on the data being entered or modified and also provides more reliable data entry. A form may also contain command buttons that enable you to add a new record, print a record, or close the form. The status bar and navigation buttons at the bottom of the form are similar to those that appear at the bottom of a table. As an Access user, you will add, delete, and edit records in Form view. As the Access designer, you will create and edit the form structure in Design view.

A **query** is a question that you ask about the data in the tables of your database.

A ***query*** is a question that you ask about the data in the tables of your database. The answer is shown in the query results. A query can be used to display only records that meet a certain criterion and only the fields that are required. Figure 7 shows the query design for the question "Which products does Northwind purchase from Supplier A?" The Products table contains records for many vendors, but the records shown in Figure 8 are only the products that were supplied by Supplier A. If you want to know the details about a specific supplier (such as Supplier A), you set the criterion in the query to specify which supplier you need to know about.

A **criterion** (**criteria**, pl) is a number, a text phrase, or an expression used to filter the records in a table.

A ***criterion*** (***criteria***, pl) is a number, a text phrase, or an expression used to filter the records in a table. If you need the names of all the suppliers in New York, you can set the supplier's state criterion to *New York*. The results would yield only those suppliers from New York. Query results are in Datasheet view and are similar in appearance to the underlying table, except that the query contains selected records and/or selected fields for those records. The query also may list the records in a different sequence from that of the table.

You also can use a query to add new records and modify existing records. If you open a query and notice an error in an address field, you can edit the record directly in the query results. When you edit a value in a query, you are also updating the data in the underlying table. Editing in a query is efficient but should be used with caution to avoid inadvertently updating the tables. Queries may be opened in Datasheet view or Design view. You use the Datasheet view to examine the query output; you use the Design view to specify which fields to display and what criteria you want.

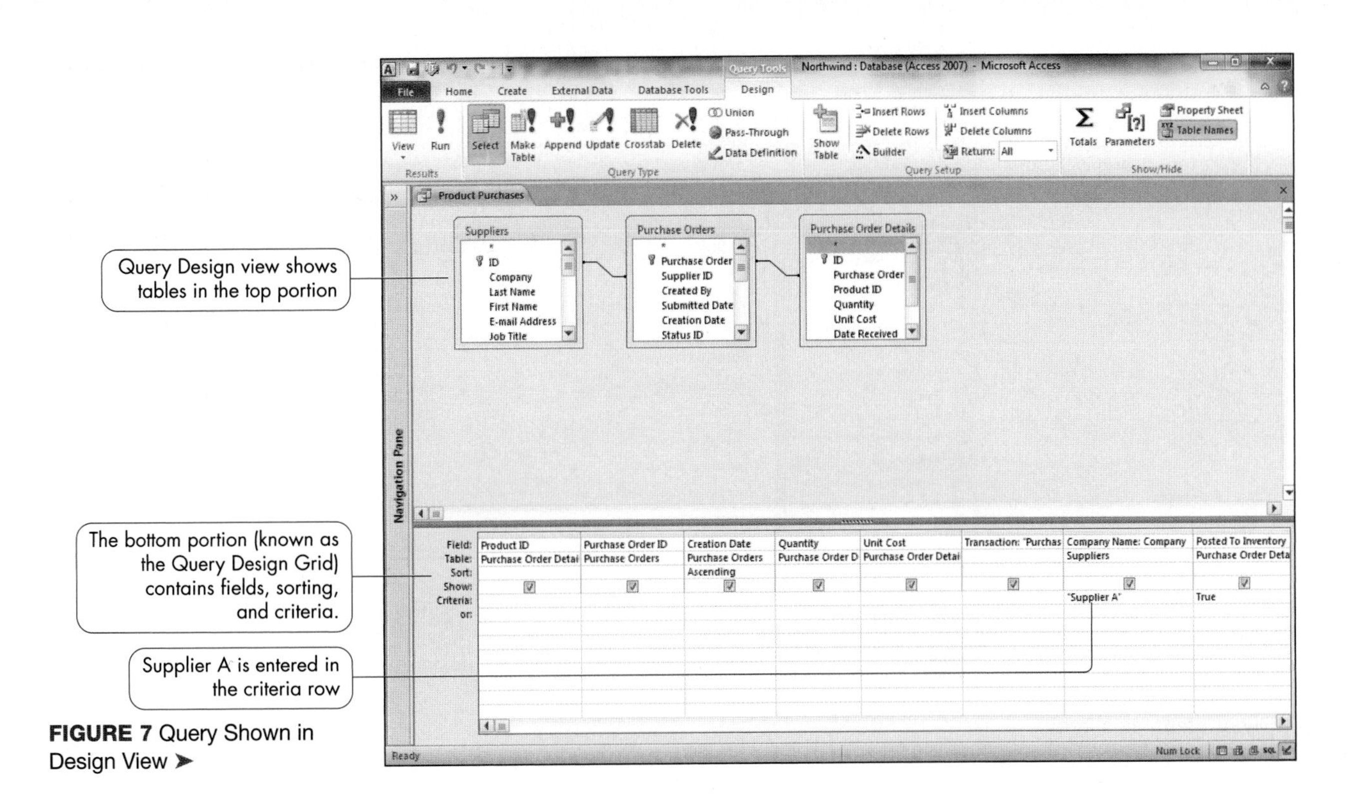
Query Design view shows tables in the top portion
The bottom portion (known as the Query Design Grid) contains fields, sorting, and criteria.
Supplier A is entered in the criteria row

FIGURE 7 Query Shown in Design View ➤

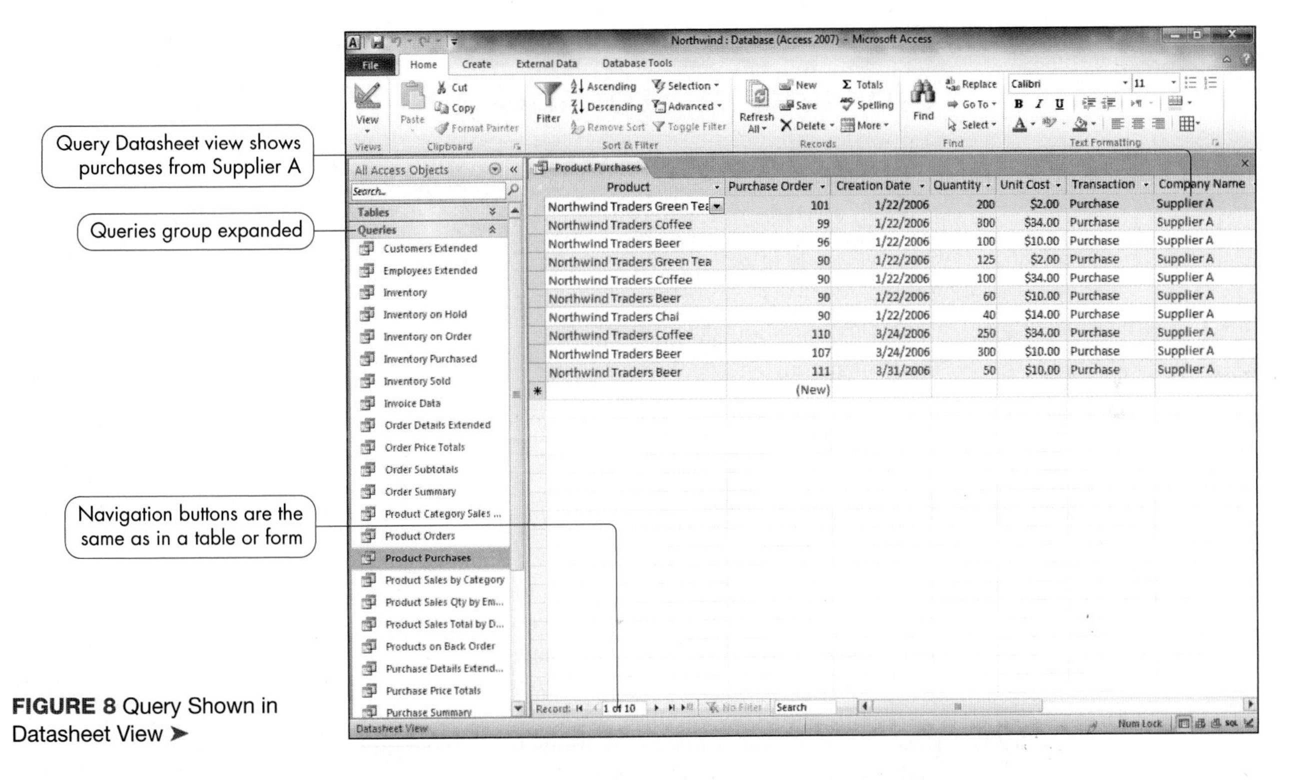
Query Datasheet view shows purchases from Supplier A
Queries group expanded
Navigation buttons are the same as in a table or form

FIGURE 8 Query Shown in Datasheet View ➤

A **report** contains professional-looking formatted information from underlying tables or queries.

A ***report*** contains professional-looking formatted information from underlying tables or queries. Figure 9 displays a report that contains the same information as the query in Figure 8. Because the report information contains a more professional look than a query or table, you normally present database information using a report. Access provides different views for designing, modifying, and running reports. Most Access users use only the Print Preview, Layout, and Report views of a report.

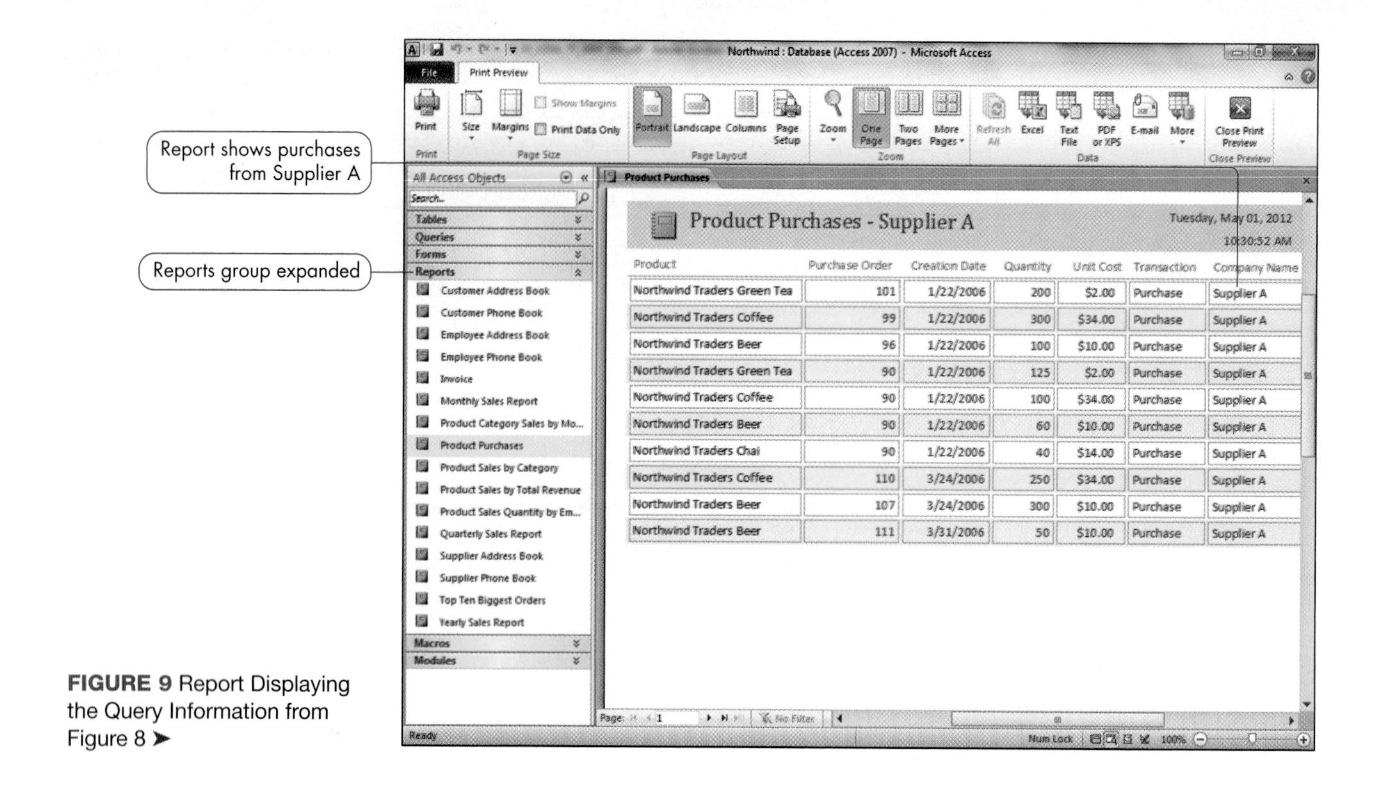

FIGURE 9 Report Displaying the Query Information from Figure 8 ➤

Understanding the Difference Between Working in Storage and Memory

Access is different from the other Microsoft Office applications. Word, Excel, and PowerPoint all work primarily from memory. In those applications, your work is not automatically saved to your hard drive unless you click the Save icon. This could be catastrophic if you are working on a large Word document and you forget to save it. If the power is lost, you may lose your document. Access, on the other hand, works primarily from storage. As you enter and update the data in an Access database, the changes are automatically saved to your hard drive. If a power failure occurs, you will only lose the changes from the record that you are currently editing. Another common characteristic among Word, Excel, and PowerPoint is that usually only one person uses a file at one time. Access is different. With an Access database file, several users can work in the same file at the same time.

When you make a change to a field's content in an Access table (for example, changing a customer's phone number), Access saves your changes as soon as you move the insertion point (or focus) to a different record. You do not need to click the Save icon. However, you are required to Save after you modify the design of a table, a query, a form, or a report. When you modify an object's design, such as the Customers form, and then close it, Access will prompt you with the message "Do you want to save changes to the design of form 'Customers'?" Click Yes to save your changes.

Also in Access, you can click Undo to reverse the most recent change (the phone number you just modified) to a single record immediately after making changes to that record. However, unlike other Office programs that enable multiple Undo steps, you cannot use Undo to reverse multiple edits in Access.

Multiple users, from different computers, can work on an Access database simultaneously. As long as two users do not attempt to change the same record at the same time, Access will enable two or more users to work on the same database file at the same time. One person can be adding records to the Customers table while another can be creating a query based on the Products table. Two users can even work on the same table as long as they are not working on the same record.

TIP Save Edits While Keeping a Record Active

When you want to save changes to a record you are editing while remaining on the same record, press Shift+Enter. The pencil symbol disappears, indicating that the change is saved. Save is optional since Access saves changes automatically when you move to a different record.

Practicing Good Database File Management

Database files are similar to other files (spreadsheets, documents, and images) on your computer. They must be filed in an organized manner using folders and subfolders, they must be named appropriately, and they must be backed up in case of a computer failure. Access files require additional understanding and maintenance to avoid data loss.

Every time you open a student file, you will be directed to copy the file and to rename the copied file. As you are learning about Access databases, you will probably make mistakes. Since you'll be working from the copy, you can easily recover from one of these mistakes by reverting back to the original and starting over.

Access speed measures the time it takes for the storage device to make the file content available for use.

Access runs best from a local disk drive or network disk drive because those drives have sufficient access speed to support the software. ***Access speed*** measures the time it takes for the storage device to make the file content available for use. If your school provides you with storage space on the school's network, store your student files there. The advantage to using the network is that the network administration staff back up files regularly. If you have no storage on the school network, your next best storage option is a thumb drive, also known as a USB jump drive, a flash drive, a pen drive, or a stick drive.

Backing Up, Compacting, and Repairing Access Files

Compact and Repair reduces the size of the database.

Backup creates a duplicate copy of the database.

Data is the lifeblood of any organization. Access provides two utilities to help protect the data within a database: ***Compact and Repair*** and ***backup***. These two functions both help protect your data, but they each serve a different purpose. Compact and Repair reduces the size of the database. Backup creates a duplicate copy of the database.

Compact and Repair a Database

All Access databases have a tendency to expand with everyday use. Entering data, creating queries, running reports, deleting objects, and adding indexes will all cause a database file to expand. This growth may increase storage requirements and may also impact database performance. In addition, databases that are compacted regularly are less likely to become corrupt—resulting in loss of data. Access provides a utility—Compact and Repair Database—in the Backstage view that addresses this issue. When you run the Compact and Repair utility, it creates a new database file behind the scenes and copies all the objects from the original database into the new one. As it copies the objects into the new file, Access will remove temporary objects and unclaimed space due to deleted objects, resulting in a smaller database file. Compact and Repair will also defragment a fragmented database file if needed. When the utility is finished copying the data, it deletes the original file and renames the new one with the same name as the original. This utility can also be used to repair a corrupt database. In most cases, only a small amount of data—the last record modified—will be lost during the repair process. You should compact your database every day.

Back Up a Database

Imagine what would happen to a firm that loses the orders placed but not shipped, a charity that loses the list of donor contributions, or a hospital that loses the digital records of its patients. Fortunately, Access recognizes how critical backup procedures are to organizations and makes backing up the database files easy. You back up an Access file (and all of the objects inside) with just a few mouse clicks. To back up files, click the File tab, and then click Save & Publish from the list of options. From the list of Save & Publish options, double-click Back Up Database, and the Save As dialog box opens. You can designate the folder location and the file name for the backup copy of the database. Access provides a default file name that is the original file name followed by the current date. The default database type is accdb.

In the next Hands-On Exercise, you will work with the Northwind Traders database you read about in the Case Study at the beginning of the chapter. Northwind purchases food items from suppliers around the world and sells them to restaurants and specialty food shops. Northwind depends on the data stored in its Access database to process orders and make daily decisions.

HANDS-ON EXERCISES

1 Databases Are Everywhere!

In your new position with Northwind Traders, you need to spend time getting familiar with its Access database. You will open its database and add, edit, and delete records using both tables and forms. Finally, you will perform management duties by compacting and backing up the database file.

Skills covered: Open an Access File, Save the File with a New Name, and Work with the New File • Edit a Record • Navigate an Access Form and Add Records • Recognize the Connection Between Table and Form, Delete a Record • Compact, Repair, and Back Up the Database

STEP 1 OPEN AN ACCESS FILE, SAVE THE FILE WITH A NEW NAME, AND WORK WITH THE NEW FILE

This exercise introduces you to the Northwind Traders database. You will use this database to practice working with database files. Refer to Figure 10 as you complete Step 1.

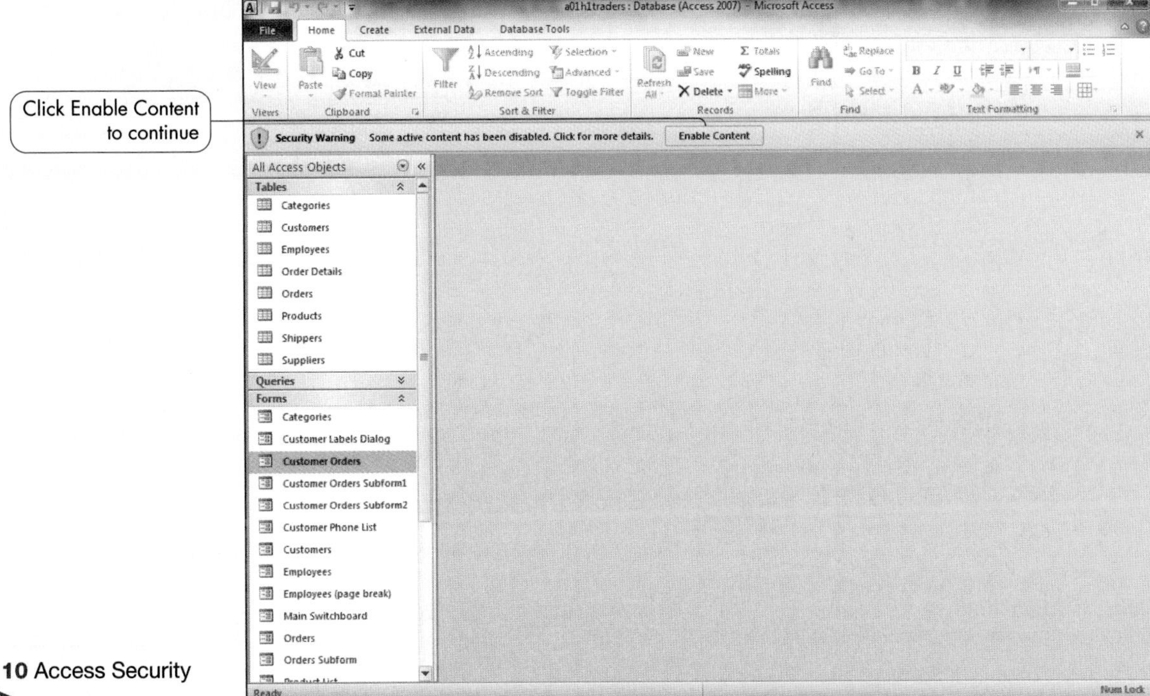

FIGURE 10 Access Security Warning ➤

a. Open the database named *a01h1traders* in the folder location designated by your instructor.

b. Click the **File tab**, click **Save Database As**, and then locate the folder location designated by your instructor.

When you name solution files, use your last and first names. For example, as the Access author, I would name my database a01h1traders_MastKeith.

TROUBLESHOOTING: If you make any major mistakes in this exercise, you can close the file, make another copy of *a01h1traders*, and then start this exercise over.

c. Type **a01h1traders_LastnameFirstname** as the new file name, and then click **Save** to create the new database.

This step creates the new Access database file. The Security Warning message bar may appear below the Ribbon, indicating that some database content is disabled.

d. Click **Enable Content** on the Security Warning message bar.

When you open an Access file from this book, you will need to enable the content. Several viruses and worms may be transmitted via Access files. You may be confident of the trustworthiness of the files in this book. However, if an Access file arrives as an attachment from an unsolicited e-mail message, you should not open it. Microsoft warns all users of Access that a potential threat exists every time a file is opened. Keep the database open for the rest of the exercise.

STEP 2 EDIT A RECORD

You need to modify the data in the Northwind database since customers will change their address, phone numbers, and order data from time to time. Refer to Figure 11 as you complete Step 2.

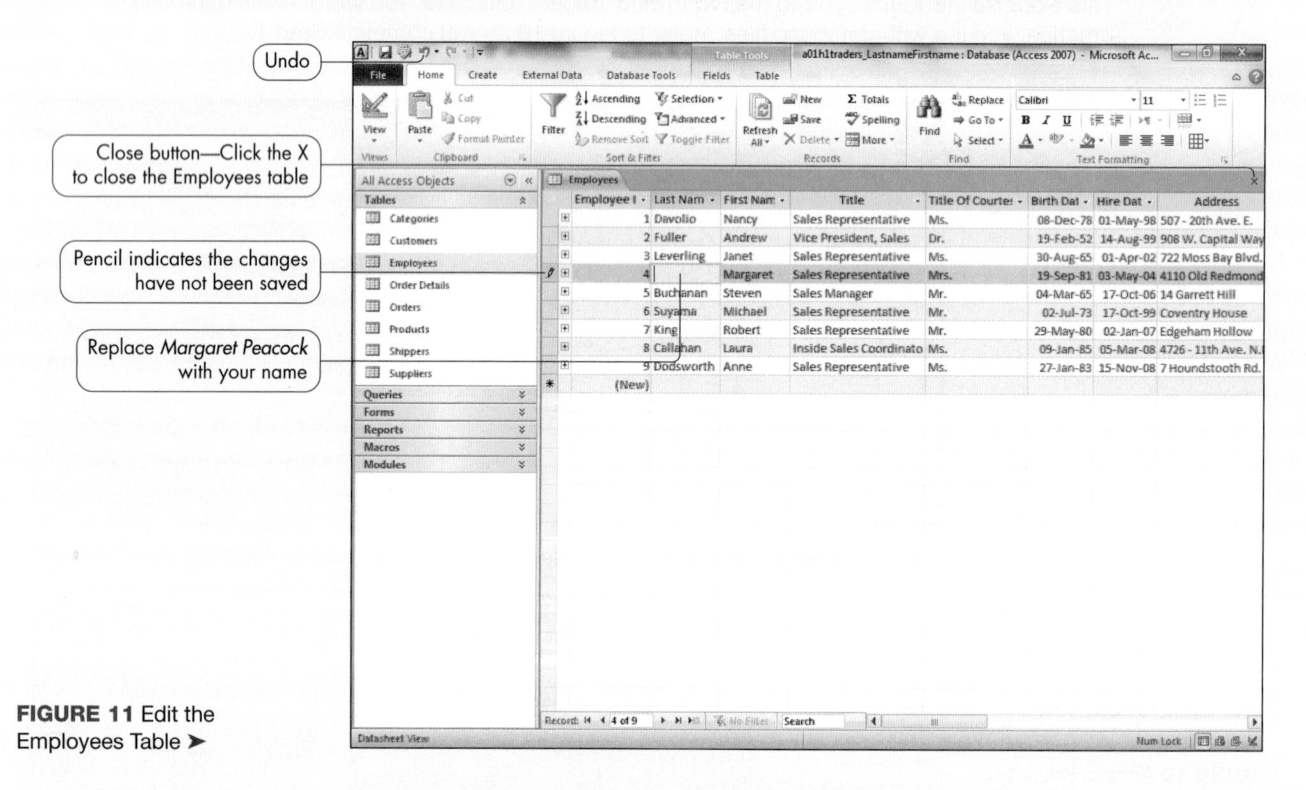

FIGURE 11 Edit the Employees Table ➤

a. Click the **Tables group** in the Navigation Pane (if necessary) to expand the list of available tables.

The list of tables contained in the database file opens.

b. Double-click the **Employees table** to open it (see Figure 11).

c. Click on the **Last Name field** in the fourth row. Double-click **Peacock**; the entire name highlights. Type your last name to replace *Peacock.*

d. Press **Tab** to move to the next field in the fourth row. Replace *Margaret* with your first name, and then press **Tab**.

You have made changes to two fields in the same record (row); note the pencil symbol on the left side in the row selector box.

e. Click **Undo** in the Quick Access Toolbar.

   Your first and last names reverts back to *Margaret Peacock* because you have not yet left the record.

f. Type your first and last names again to replace *Margaret Peacock*. Press **Tab**.

   You should now be in the Title field and your title, *Sales Representative*, is selected. The pencil symbol still displays in the row selector.

g. Click anywhere in the third row where Janet Leverling's data is stored.

   The pencil symbol disappears, indicating your changes have been saved.

h. Click the **Address field** in the first record, the one for Nancy Davolio. Select the entire address, and then type **4004 East Morningside Dr.** Click anywhere on Andrew Fuller's record.

i. Click **Undo**.

   Nancy's address reverts back to *507 - 20th Ave. E.* However, the Undo command is now faded. You can no longer undo the change that you made replacing Margaret Peacock's name with your own.

j. Click the **Close button** (the X at the top of the table) to close the Employees table.

   The Employees table closes. You are not prompted about saving your changes; they have already been saved for you because Access works in storage, not memory. If you reopen the Employees table, you will see your name in place of Margaret Peacock's name.

> **TROUBLESHOOTING:** If you click the Close (X) button on the title bar at the top right of the window and accidentally close the database, locate the file, and then double-click it to start again.

STEP 3 NAVIGATE AN ACCESS FORM AND ADD RECORDS

You need to add new products to the Northwind database since the company will be adding a new line of products to the database. Refer to Figure 12 as you complete Step 3.

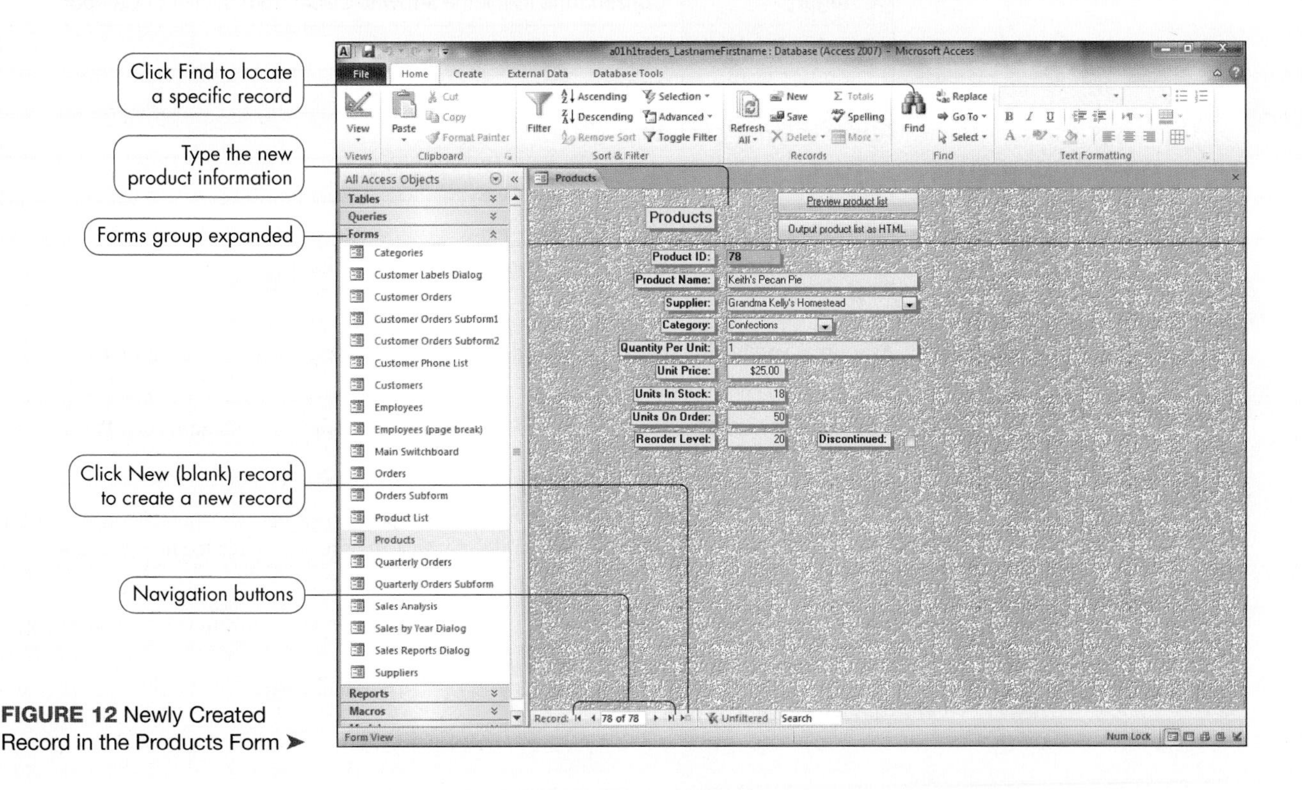

FIGURE 12 Newly Created Record in the Products Form ➤

a. Click the **Tables group** in the Navigation Pane to collapse it.

   The list of available tables collapses.

b. Click the **Forms group** in the Navigation Pane (if necessary) to expand the list of available forms.

c. Double-click the **Products form** to open it.

d. Use Figure 12 to locate the navigation buttons (arrows) at the bottom of the Access window. Practice moving from one record to the next. Click **Next record**, and then click **Last record**; click **Previous record**, and then **First record**.

e. Click **Find** in the Find group on the Home tab.

   The Find command is an ideal way to search for specific records within a table, form, or query. You can search a single field or the entire record, match all or part of the selected field(s), move forward or back in a table, or specify a case-sensitive search. The Replace command can be used to substitute one value for another. Be careful when using the Replace All option for global replacement because unintended replacements are possible.

f. Type **Grandma** in the **Find What box**, click the **Match arrow**, and select **Any Part of Field**. Click **Find Next**.

   You should see information about Grandma's Boysenberry Spread. Selecting the *any part of the field* option will return a match even if it is contained in the middle of a word.

g. Close the Find dialog box.

h. Click **New (blank) record** on the navigation bar.

i. Enter the following information for a new product. Press **Tab** to navigate through the form.

Field Name	Value to Type
Product Name	***your name*** **Pecan Pie**
Supplier	**Grandma Kelly's Homestead** (Note: click the arrow to select from the list of Suppliers)
Category	**Confections** (Click the arrow to select from the list of Categories)
Quantity Per Unit	**1**
Unit Price	**25.00**
Units in Stock	**18**
Units on Order	**50**
Reorder Level	**20**
Discontinued	**No** (the checkbox remains unchecked)

   As soon as you begin typing in the product name box, Access assigns a Product ID, in this case 78, to the record. The Product ID is used as the primary key in the Products table.

j. Click anywhere on the Pecan Pie record you just entered. Click the **File tab**, click **Print**, and then click **Print Preview**.

   The first four records appear in the Print Preview.

k. Click **Last Page** in the navigation bar, and then click the previous page to show the new record you entered.

   The beginning of the Pecan Pie record is now visible. The record continues on the next page.

l. Click **Close Print Preview** in the Close Preview group.

m. Close the Products form.

STEP 4 RECOGNIZE THE CONNECTION BETWEEN TABLE AND FORM, DELETE A RECORD

You need to understand how Access stores data. After you add the new products using a form, you verify that the products are also in the table. You also attempt to delete a record. Refer to Figure 13 as you complete Step 4.

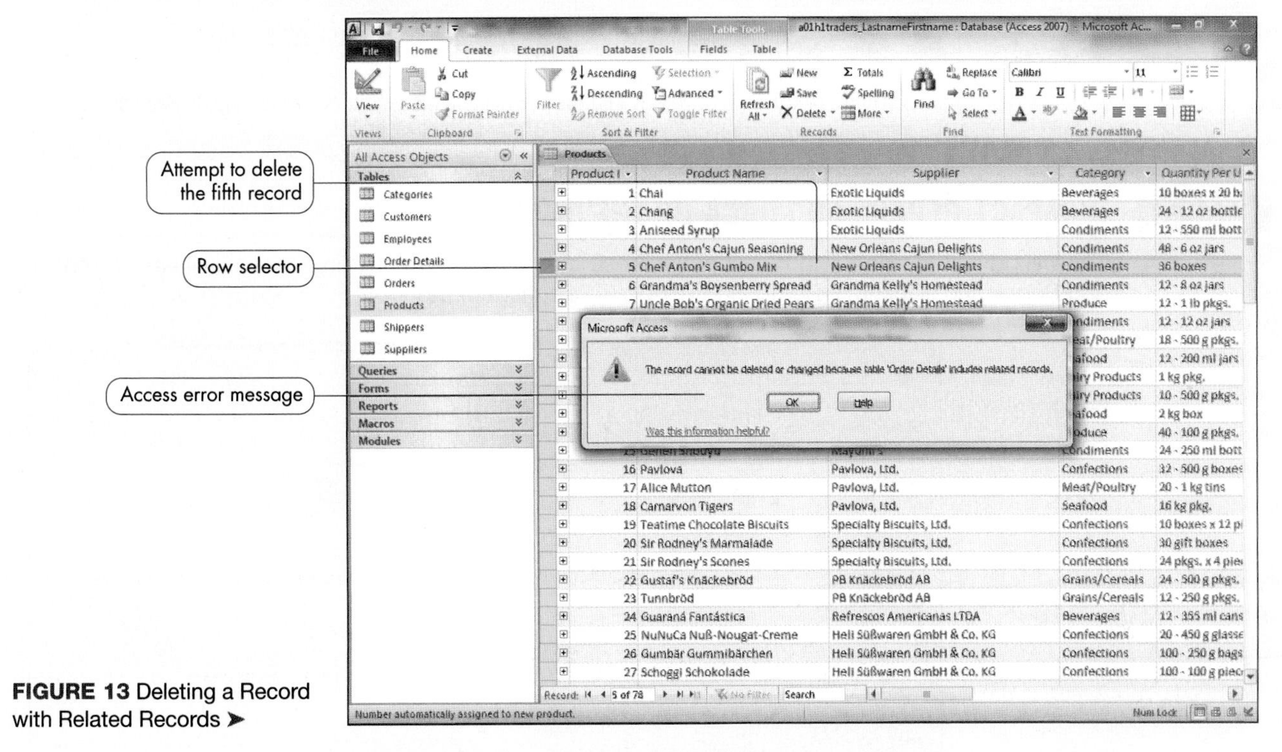

FIGURE 13 Deleting a Record with Related Records ➤

a. Click the **Forms group** in the Navigation Pane to collapse it.

   The list of available forms collapses.

b. Click the **Tables group** in the Navigation Pane to expand it.

   The list of available tables is shown. You need to prove that the change you made to the Products form will appear in the Products table.

c. Double-click the **Products table** to open it.

d. Click **Last record** in the navigation bar.

   The Pecan Pie record you entered in the Products form is listed as the last record in the Products table. The Products form was created from the Products table. Your newly created record, Pecan Pie, is stored in the Products table even though you added it in the form.

e. Navigate to the fifth record in the table, *Chef Anton's Gumbo Mix*.

f. Use the horizontal scroll bar to scroll right until you see the Discontinued field.

   The check mark in the Discontinued check box tells you that this product has been discontinued.

g. Click the **row selector box** to the left of the fifth record.

   The row highlights with a gold-colored border.

h. Click **Delete** in the Records group. Read the error message.

   An error message appears. It tells you that you cannot delete this record because the table Order Details has related records. (Customers ordered this product in the past.) Even though the product is now discontinued and none of it is in stock, it cannot be deleted from the Products table because related records exist in the Order Details table.

i. Click **OK**.

j. Navigate to the last record. Click the **row selector box** to highlight the entire row.

k. Click **Delete** in the Records group. Read the warning.

   A warning box appears. It tells you that this action cannot be undone. Although this product can be deleted because it was just entered and no orders were created for it, you do not want to delete the record.

l. Click **No**. You do not want to delete this record. Close the Products table.

TROUBLESHOOTING: If you clicked Yes and deleted the record, return to Step 3i. Reenter the information for this record. You will need it later in the lesson.

STEP 5 COMPACT, REPAIR, AND BACK UP THE DATABASE

You will protect the Northwind Traders database by using the two built-in Access utilities—Compact and Repair and Backup. Refer to Figure 14 as you complete Step 5.

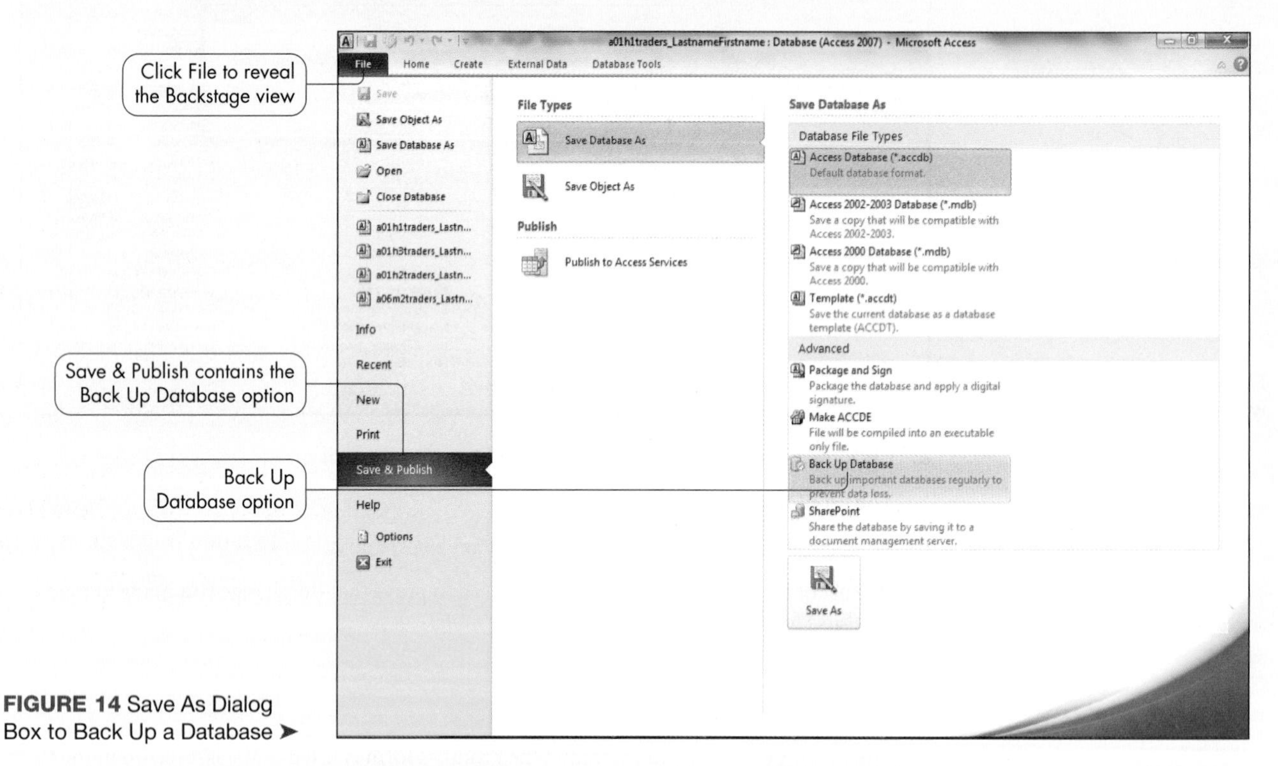

FIGURE 14 Save As Dialog Box to Back Up a Database ➤

a. Click the **File tab**.

   The File tab reveals the Backstage view, which gives you access to a variety of database tools: Compact and Repair, Back Up Database, and Print, to name a few.

b. Click **Compact & Repair Database**.

   Databases tend to get larger as you use them. This feature acts as a defragmenter and eliminates wasted space. Before running this feature, close any open objects in the database.

c. Click the **File tab**, click **Save & Publish**, and then double-click **Back Up Database**.

   The Save As dialog box opens. Verify the Save in folder is correct before saving. The backup utility assigns a default name by adding a date to your file name.

d. Click **Save** to accept the default backup file name with today's date.

   You just created a backup of the database after completing Hands-On Exercise 1. The original database *a01h1traders_LastnameFirstname* remains onscreen.

e. Keep the database onscreen if you plan to continue with Hands-On Exercise 2. If not, close the database and exit Access.

Filters, Sorts, and Access Versus Excel

Access provides you with many tools that you can use to identify and extract only the data needed at the moment. For example, you might need to know which suppliers are located in New Orleans or which customers have outstanding orders that were placed in the last seven days. You might use that information to identify possible disruptions to product deliveries or customers who may need a telephone call to let them know the status of their orders. Both Access and Excel contain powerful tools that enable you to extract the information you need and arrange it in a way that makes it easy to analyze. An important part of becoming a proficient Office user is learning how to use these tools to accomplish a task.

Access provides you with many tools that you can use to identify and extract only the data needed at the moment.

In this section, you will learn how to isolate records in a table based on certain criteria. You will also examine the strengths of Access and Excel in more detail so you can better determine when to use which application to complete a given task.

Creating Filters

In the first Hands-On Exercise, you added Pecan Pie to the Products table with a category of *Confections*, but you also saw many other products. Suppose you wanted a list of all of the products in the Confections category. To do this, you could open the Products table in Datasheet view and create a filter. A ***filter*** displays a subset of records based on specified criteria. A filter works with either a table's datasheet or a query's datasheet. You can use filters to analyze data quickly. Applying a filter does not delete any records; filters only *hide* records that do not match the criteria. Two types of filters are discussed in this section: Filter by Selection and Filter by Form. Filter by Selection selects only the records that match preselected single criteria, whereas Filter by Form offers a more versatile way to select a subset of records, including the use of comparison operators.

A **filter** displays a subset of records based on specified criteria.

Figure 15 displays the Customers table with 29 records. The records in the table are displayed in sequence according to the CustomerID, which is also the primary key (the field or combination of fields that uniquely identifies a record). The navigation bar at the bottom indicates that the active record is the first row in the table. Many times you will only want to see a subset of the customer records—you can accomplish this using a filter. For example, suppose you want a list of all customers whose Job Title is *Owner*.

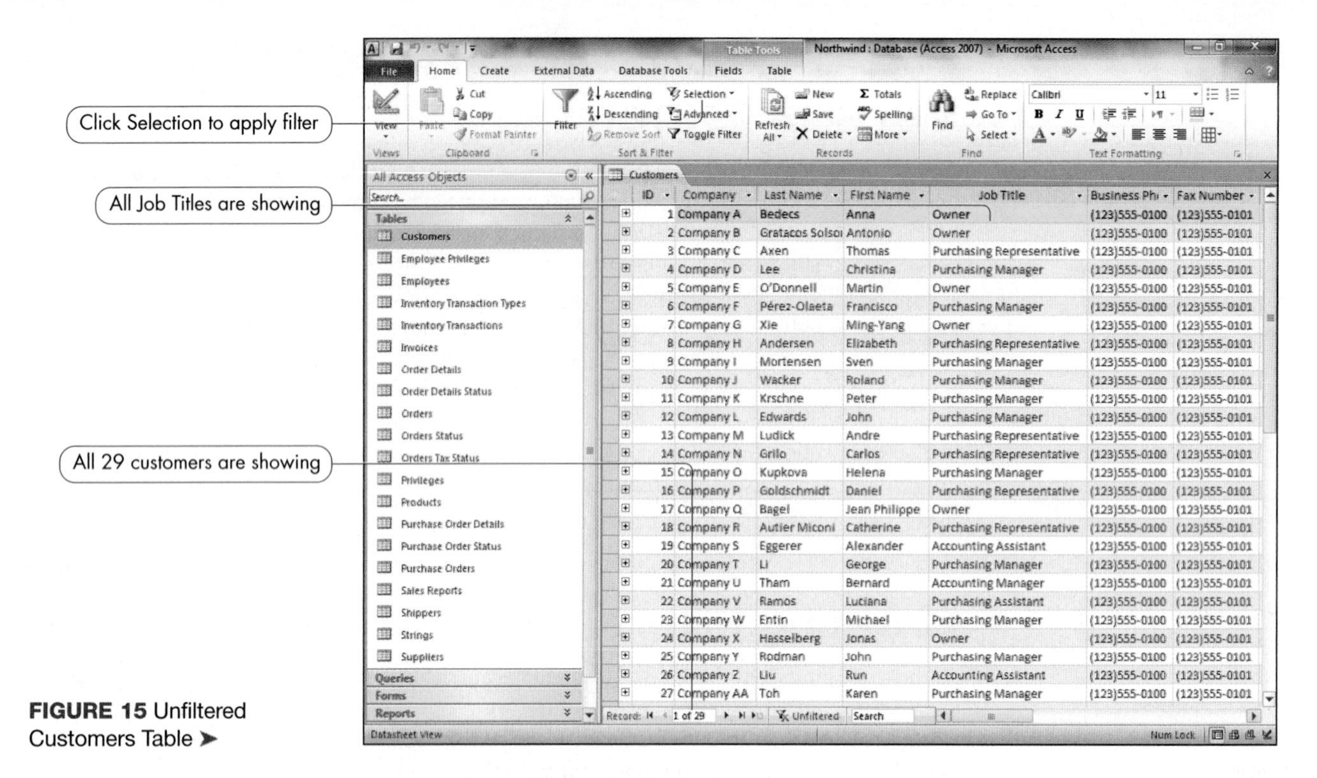

FIGURE 15 Unfiltered Customers Table ➤

Figure 16 displays a filtered view of the Customers table, showing records with Job Title of *Owner*. The navigation bar shows that this is a filtered list containing 6 records matching the criteria. (The Customers table still contains the original 29 records, but only 6 records are visible with the filter applied.)

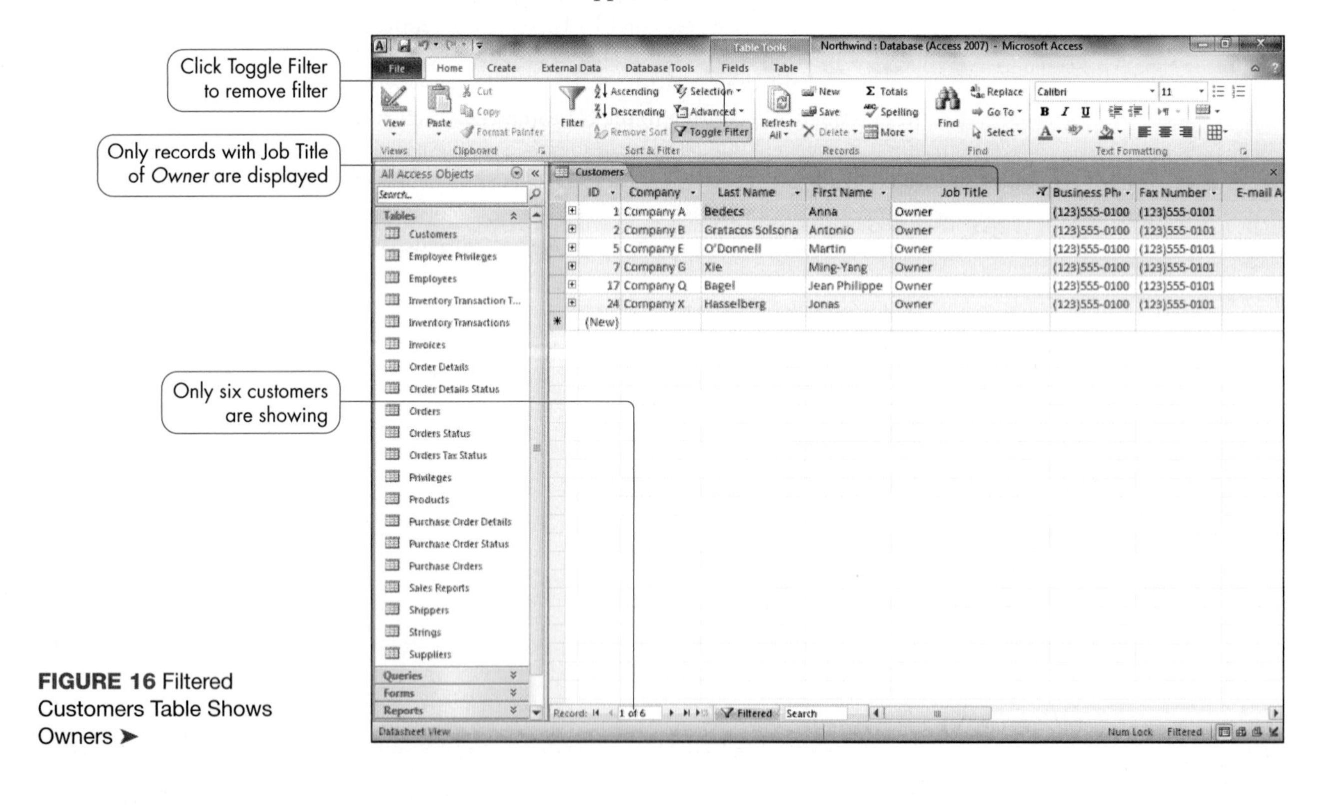

FIGURE 16 Filtered Customers Table Shows Owners ➤

> **TIP** Use Quick Keyboard Shortcuts
>
> Look for underlined letters in Access menus. They indicate the letters to use for the keyboard shortcuts. For example, when you click the Selection arrow in the Sort & Filter group, you can click the Equals "xyz criterion" menu selection or simply type the letter *E*, because the letter *E* in *Equals* is underlined, indicating a shortcut key.

Filter by Selection displays only the records that match the selected criteria.

Filter by Selection displays only the records that match the selected criteria. The easiest way to implement a Filter by Selection is as follows:

1. Click in any field that contains the criterion on which you want to filter.
2. Click Filter by Selection in the Sort & Filter group.
3. Select Equals "criterion" from the list of options.

Only the records that match the selected criterion will be displayed.

Filter by Form displays table records based on multiple criteria. Filter by Form enables the user to apply the logical operators AND and OR.

A **comparison operator** is used to evaluate the relationship between two quantities to determine if they are equal or not equal; and, if they are not equal, a comparison operator determines which one is greater than the other.

Figure 17 illustrates another, more versatile, way to apply a filter, using Filter by Form. ***Filter by Form*** displays table records based on multiple criteria. Filter by Form enables the user to apply the logical operators AND and OR. For the AND operator, a record is included in the results if all the criteria are true; for the OR operator, a record is included if at least one criterion is true. Another advantage of the Filter by Form function is that you can use a comparison operator. A ***comparison operator*** is used to evaluate the relationship between two quantities to determine if they are equal or not equal; and, if they are not equal, a comparison operator determines which one is greater than the other. Comparison operator symbols include: equal (=), not equal (<>), greater than (>), less than (<), greater than or equal to (>=), and less than or equal to (<=). For example, you can use a comparison operator to select products with an inventory level greater than 30 (>30). Filter by Selection, on the other hand, requires you to specify criteria equal to an existing value. Figure 17 shows a Filter by Form designed to select Products with a reorder level of more than 10 units.

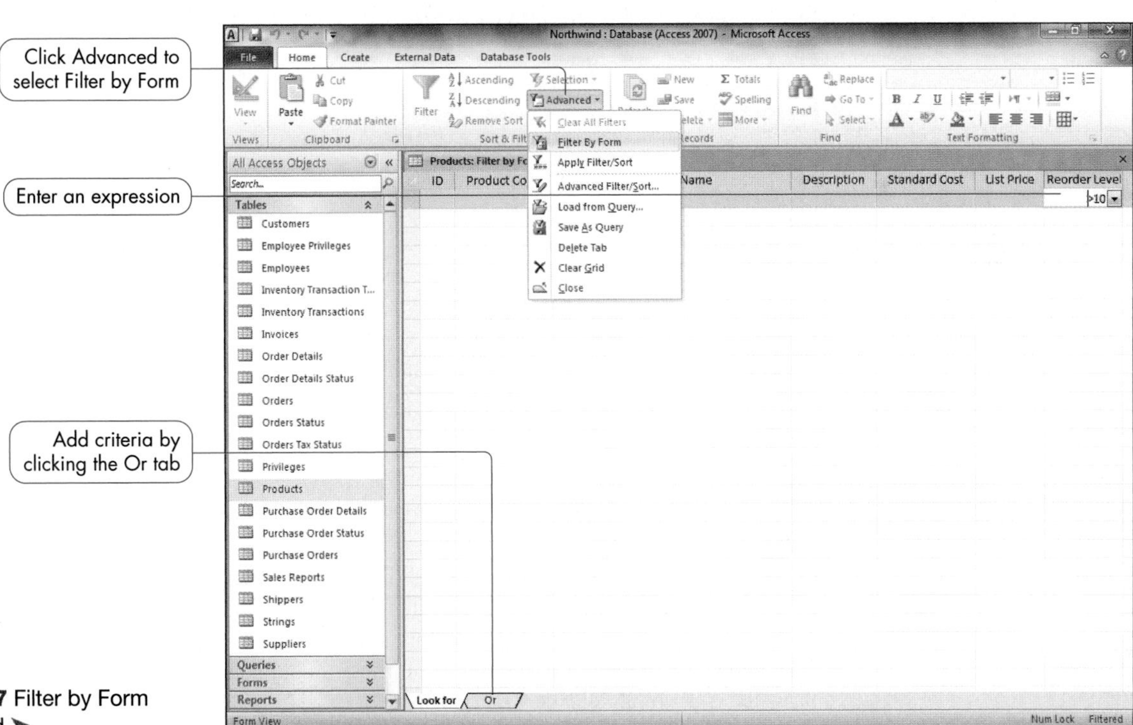

FIGURE 17 Filter by Form Design Grid ➤

To apply an OR comparison operator to a Filter by Form, click the Or tab at the bottom of the window. For example, you could add the criterion *Baked Goods & Mixes* to the category field, which would show all the Products with a reorder level of more than 10 units and all

Products in the Baked Goods & Mixes category. (This OR example is not shown in Figure 17.) Filters enable you to obtain information from a database quickly without creating a query or a report.

Sorting Table Data on One or More Fields

A **sort** lists records in a specific sequence, such as ascending by last name or by ascending EmployeeID.

Ascending sorts a list of text data in alphabetical order or a numeric list in lowest to highest order.

Descending sorts a list of text data in reverse alphabetical order or a numeric list in highest to lowest order.

You can also change the order of the information by sorting by one or more fields. A ***sort*** lists records in a specific sequence, such as alphabetically by last name or by ascending EmployeeID.

To sort a table, do the following:

1. Click in the field that you want to use to sort the records.
2. Click Ascending or Descending in the Sort & Filter group.

Ascending sorts a list of text data in alphabetical order or a numeric list in lowest to highest order. ***Descending*** sorts a list of text data in reverse alphabetical order or a numeric list in highest to lowest order. Figure 18 shows the Customers table sorted in ascending order by state. You may apply both filters and sorts to tables or query results.

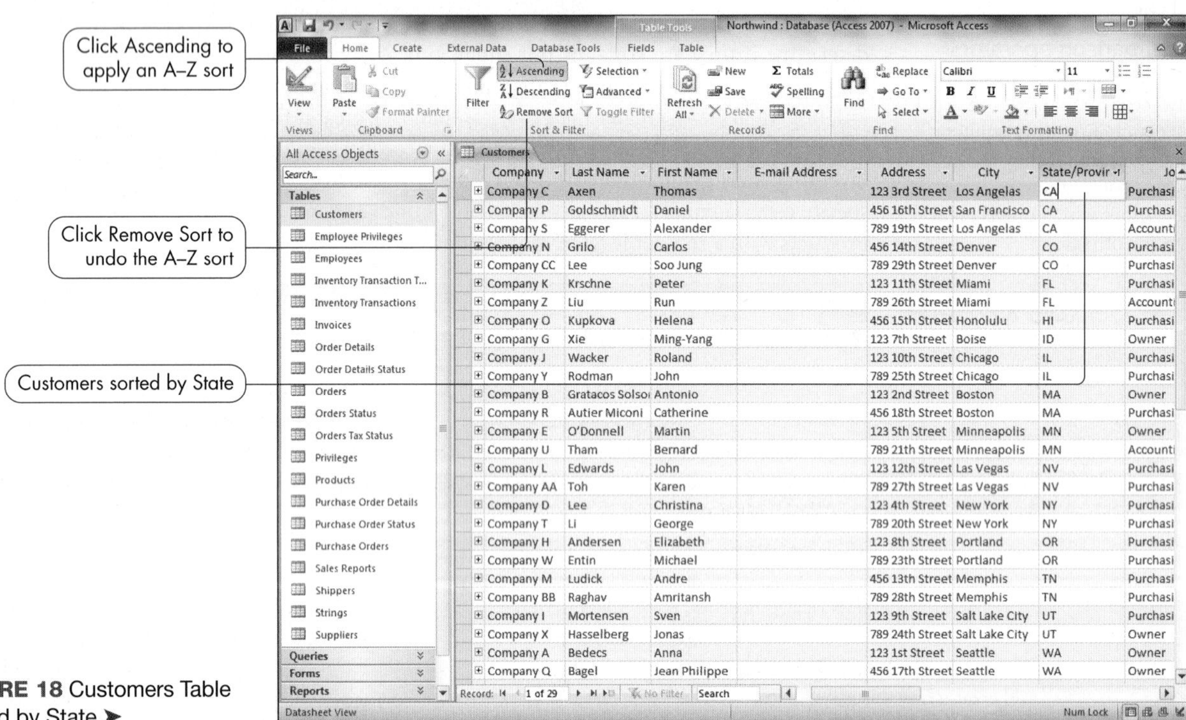

FIGURE 18 Customers Table Sorted by State ➤

The operations can be done in any order; that is, you can filter a table to show only selected records, and then sort the filtered table to display the records in a certain order. Conversely, you can sort a table first and then apply a filter. It does not matter which operation is performed first. You can also filter the table further by applying a second, third, or more criteria; for example, click in a Job Title cell containing *Owner*, and apply a Filter by Selection. Then click *WA* in the State column, and apply a second Filter by Selection to display all the customers from WA. You can also click Toggle Filter at any time to remove all filters and display all of the records in the table. Filters are a temporary method for examining table data. If you close the filtered table and then reopen it, the filter will be removed, and all of the records will be restored.

TIP Use Undo After Applying a Filter by Selection

You can apply one Filter by Selection to a table, and then a second, and then a third to display certain records based on three criteria. If you click Toggle Filter, all three filters will be removed. What if you only want the last filter removed? Click Undo to remove only the last filter. Click Undo again and remove the second-to-last filter. This feature will help you apply *and remove* multiple filters.

Knowing When to Use Access or Excel to Manage Data

You are probably familiar with working in an Excel spreadsheet. You type the column headings, then enter the data, perhaps add a formula or two, then add totals to the bottom. Once the data has been entered, you can apply a filter, or sort the data, or start all over—similar to what we learned to do in Access with filters. It is true that you can accomplish many of the same tasks using either Excel or Access. In this section, you will learn how to decide whether to use Access or Excel. Although the two programs have much in common, they each have distinct advantages. How do you choose whether to use Access or Excel? The choice you make may ultimately depend on how well you know Access. Users who only know Excel are more likely to use a spreadsheet even if a database would be better. When database features are used in Excel, they are generally used on data that is in one table. When the data is better suited to be on two or more tables, then using Access is preferable. Learning how to use Access will be beneficial to you since it will enable you to work more efficiently with large groups of data. Ideally, the type of data and the type of functionality you require should determine which program will work best.

Select the Software to Use

A contact list (e.g., name, address, phone number) created in Excel may serve your needs just fine at first. Each time you meet a new contact, you can add another row to the bottom of your worksheet, as shown in Figure 19. You can sort the list by last name for easier look-up of names. In Excel, you can easily move an entire column, insert a new column, or copy and paste data from one cell to another. This is the "ease of use" characteristic of Excel.

If you needed to expand the information in Excel, to keep track of each time you contacted someone on your contact list, for example, you may need an additional worksheet. This additional sheet would only list the contacts who you contacted and some information about the nature of the contact. Which contact was it? When was the contact made? Was it a phone contact or a face-to-face meeting? As you track these entries, your worksheet will contain a reference to the first worksheet using the Contact Name. As the quantity and complexity of the data increase, the need to organize your data logically also increases.

Access provides built-in tools to help organize data better than Excel. One tool that helps Access organize data is the ability to create relationships between tables. A ***relationship*** is a connection between two tables using a common field. The benefit of a relationship is to efficiently combine data from related tables for the purpose of creating queries, forms, and reports. Relationships are the reason why Access is referred to as a relational database. For example, assume you want to create a Contact Management Database. You would first create two tables to hold contact names and contact notes. You would then create a relationship between the Contact Name table and the Contact Notes table using ContactID as the common field. To create a Contacts Form or Query, you would take advantage of the two related tables.

A **relationship** is a connection between two tables using a common field.

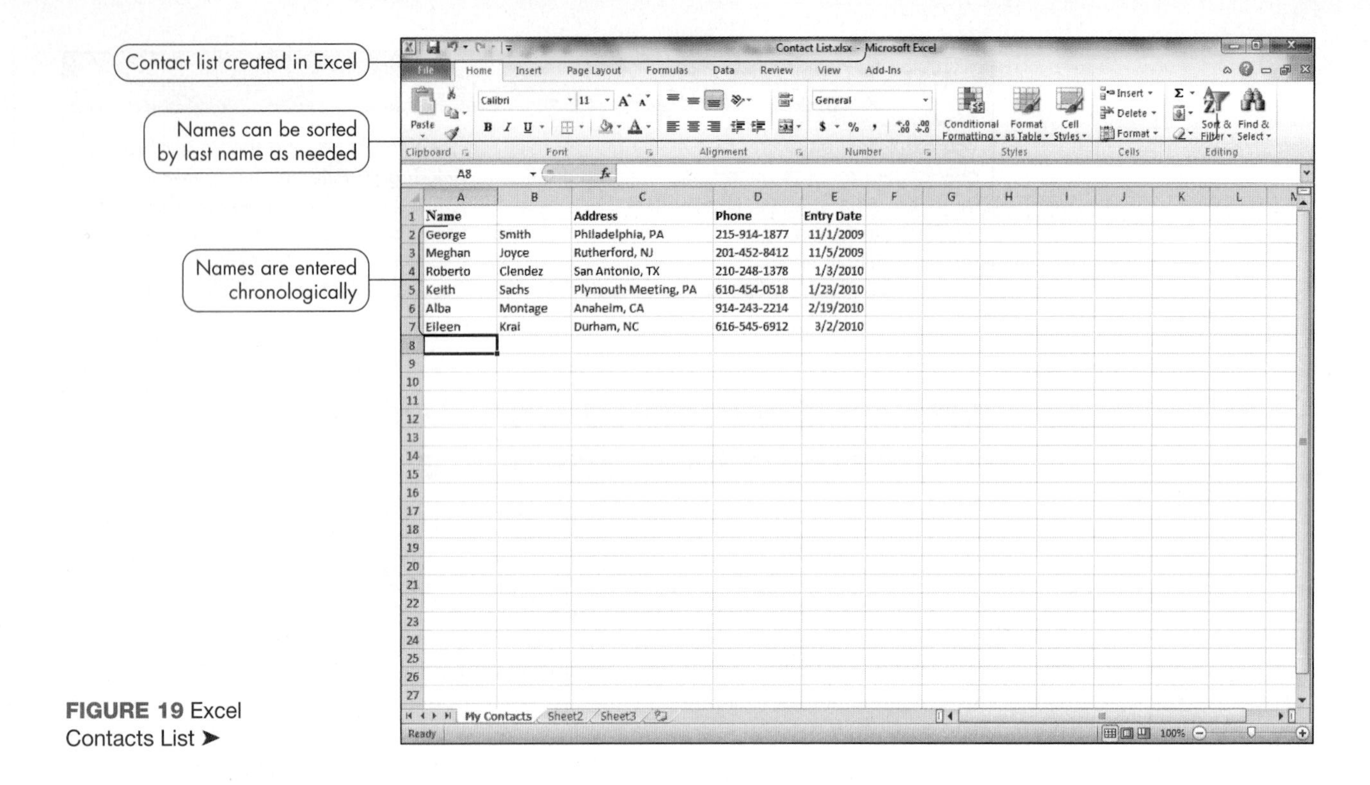

FIGURE 19 Excel Contacts List ➤

Use Access

You should use Access to manage data when you:

- Require multiple related tables to store your data.
- Have a large amount of data.
- Need to connect to and retrieve data from external databases, such as Microsoft SQL Server.
- Need to group, sort, and total data based on various parameters.
- Have an application that requires multiple users to connect to one data source at the same time.

Use Excel

You should use Excel to manage data when you:

- Only need one worksheet to handle all of your data (i.e., you do not need multiple worksheets).
- Have mostly numeric data—for example, you need to maintain an expense statement.
- Require subtotals and totals in your worksheet.
- Want to primarily run a series of "what if" scenarios on your data.
- Need to create complex charts and/or graphs.

In the next Hands-On Exercise, you will create and apply filters, create comparison operator expressions using Filter by Form, and sort records in the Datasheet view of the Customers table.

HANDS-ON EXERCISES

2 Filters, Sorts, and Access Versus Excel

The sales managers at Northwind Traders need quick answers to their questions about customer orders. You use the Access database to filter tables to answer most of these questions. Before printing your results, make sure you sort the records based on the managers' needs.

Skills covered: Use Filter by Selection with an Equal Condition • Use Filter by Selection with a Contains Condition • Use Filter by Form with a Comparison Operator • Sort a Table

STEP 1 USE FILTER BY SELECTION WITH AN EQUAL CONDITION

As you continue to learn about the Northwind Traders database, you are expected to provide answers to questions about the customers and products. In this exercise, you use filters to find customers who live in London. Refer to Figure 20 as you complete Step 1.

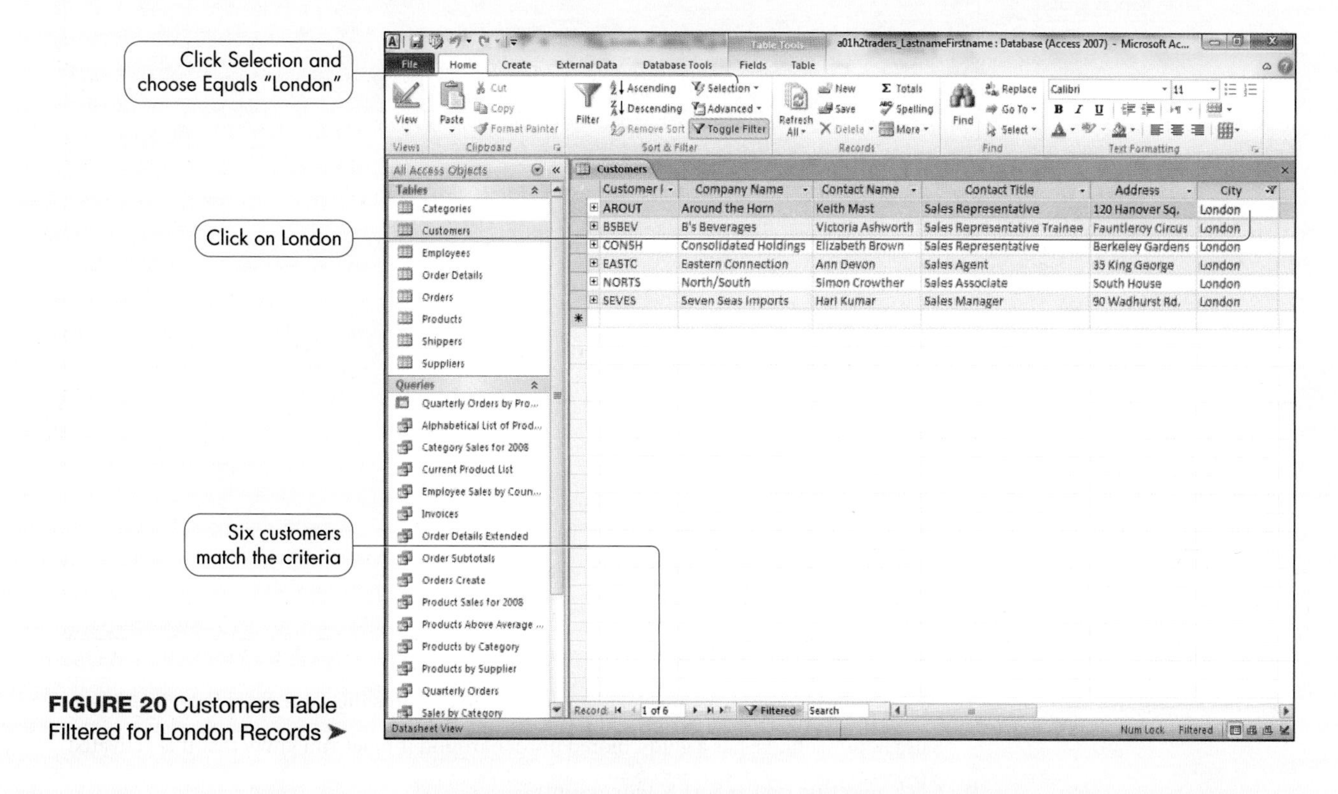

FIGURE 20 Customers Table Filtered for London Records ➤

a. Open *a01h1traders_LastnameFirstname* if you closed it at the end of Hands-On Exercise 1. Click the **File tab**, click **Save Database As**, and then type **a01h2traders_LastnameFirstname**, changing *h1* to *h2*. Click **Save**.

> **TROUBLESHOOTING:** If you make any major mistakes in this exercise, you can delete the *a01h2traders_LastnameFirstname* file, repeat step a above, and then start the exercise over.

b. Open the Customers table, navigate to record four, and then replace *Thomas Hardy* with your name in the Contact Name field.

c. Scroll right until the City field is visible. The fourth record has a value of *London* in the City field. Click on the field to select it.

   The word *London* has a gold-colored border around it to let you know that it is active.

d. Click **Selection** in the Sort & Filter group.

e. Choose **Equals "London"** from the menu.

   Six records should be displayed.

f. Click **Toggle Filter** in the Sort & Filter group to remove the filter.

g. Click **Toggle Filter** again to reset the filter. Leave the Customers table open for the next step.

STEP 2 USE FILTER BY SELECTION WITH A CONTAINS CONDITION

At times, you need to print information for the Northwind managers. In this exercise, you print your results. Refer to Figure 21 as you complete Step 2.

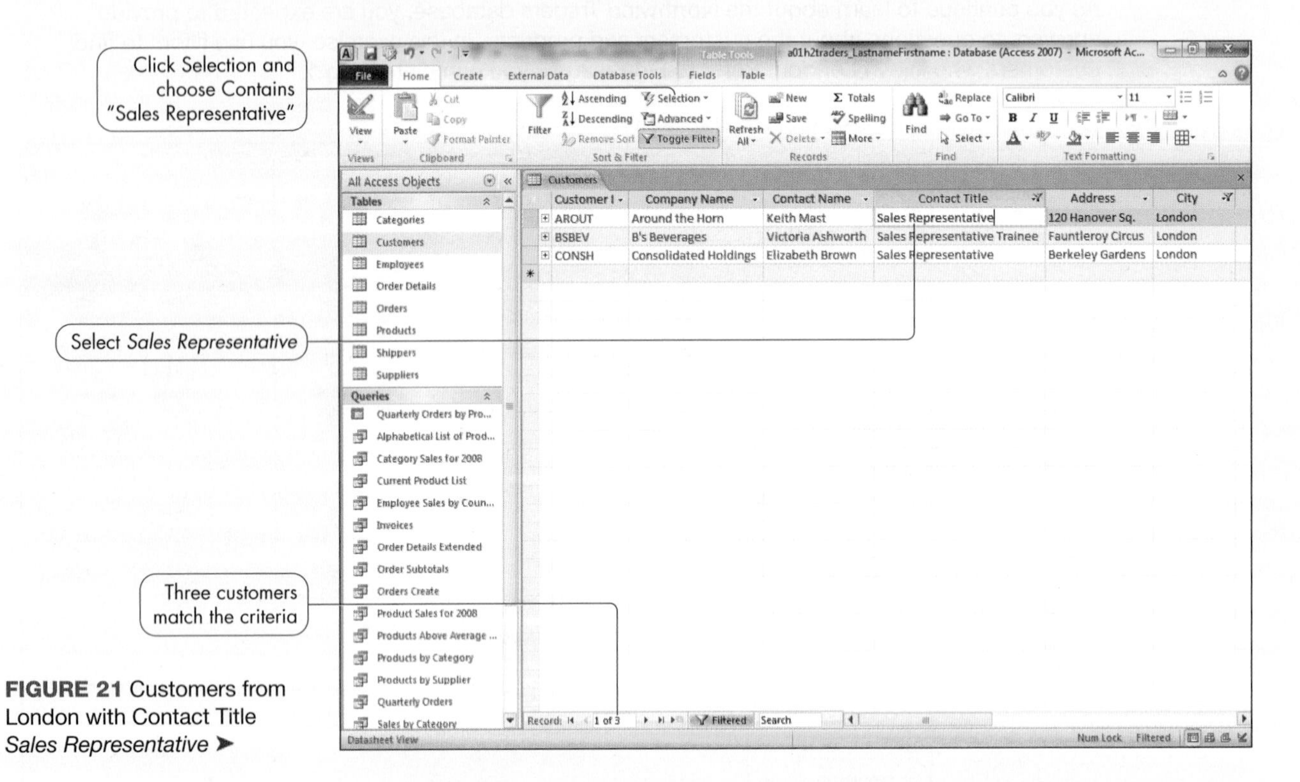

FIGURE 21 Customers from London with Contact Title *Sales Representative* ➤

a. Click in any field in the Contact Title column that contains the value *Sales Representative.*

   Sales Representative has a gold-colored border around it to let you know that it is activated.

b. Click **Selection** on the Sort & Filter group.

c. Click **Contains "Sales Representative"**.

   You have applied a second layer of filtering to the customers in London. The second layer further restricts the display to only those customers who have the words *Sales Representative* contained in their titles.

d. Scroll left until you see your name. Compare your results to those shown in Figure 21.

e. Click **Toggle Filter** in the Sort & Filter group to remove the filters.

f. Close the Customers table. Click **No** if a dialog box asks if you want to save the design changes to the Customers table.

STEP 3 USE FILTER BY FORM WITH A COMPARISON OPERATOR

At Northwind Traders, you are asked to provide a list of records that do not match just one set of criteria. Use a Filter by Form to provide the information when two or more criteria are needed. Refer to Figure 22 as you complete Step 3.

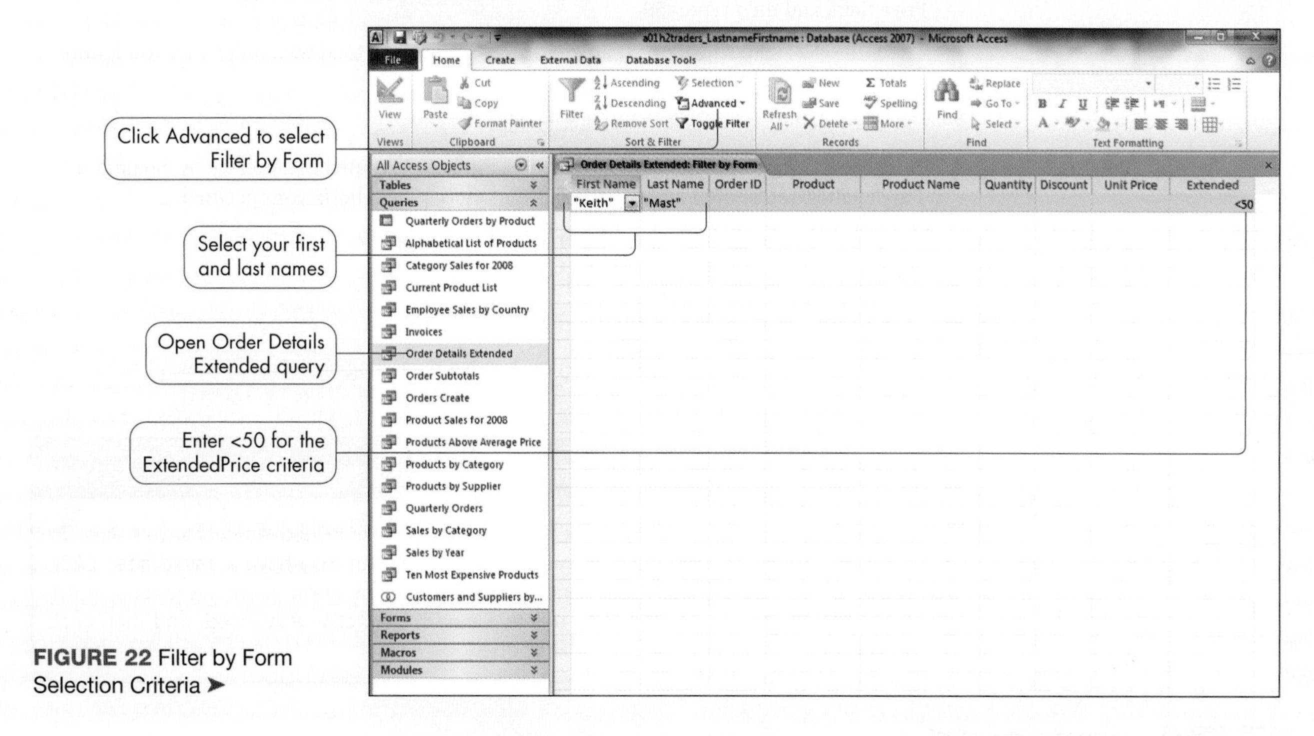
Click Advanced to select Filter by Form
Select your first and last names
Open Order Details Extended query
Enter <50 for the ExtendedPrice criteria

FIGURE 22 Filter by Form Selection Criteria ➤

a. Click the **Tables group** in the Navigation Pane to collapse the listed tables.

b. Click the **Queries group** in the Navigation Pane to expand the lists of available queries.

c. Locate and double-click the **Order Details Extended query** to open it.

This query contains information about orders. It has fields containing information about the salesperson, the Order ID, the product name, the unit price, quantity ordered, the discount given, and an extended price. The extended price is a field used to total order information.

d. Click **Advanced** in the Sort & Filter group.

While you are applying a Filter by Form to a query, you can use the same process to apply a Filter by Form to a table.

e. Select **Filter by Form** from the list.

All of the records are now hidden, and you only see field names with an arrow in the first field. Click on the other fields, and an arrow appears.

f. Click in the first row under the First Name field.

An arrow appears at the right of the box.

g. Click the **First Name arrow.**

A list of all available first names appears. Your name should be on the list. Figure 22 shows Keith Mast, which replaced Margaret Peacock in Hands-On Exercise 1.

TROUBLESHOOTING: If you do not see your name and you do see Margaret on the list, you probably skipped Steps 3c and 3d in Hands-On Exercise 1. Close the query without saving changes, turn back to the first Hands-On Exercise, and rework it, making sure not to omit any steps. Then you can return to this spot and work the remainder of this Hands-On Exercise.

h. Select your first name from the list.

i. Click in the first row under the Last Name field to reveal the arrow. Locate and select your last name by clicking it.

j. Scroll right until you see the Extended Price field. Click in the first row under the Extended Price field, and then type **<50**.

   This will select all of the items that you ordered where the total was under $50. You ignore the arrow and type the expression needed.

k. Click **Toggle Filter** in the Sort & Filter group.

   You have specified which records to include and have executed the filtering by clicking Toggle Filter. You should have 31 records that match the criteria you specified.

l. Click the **File tab**, click **Print**, and then click **Print Preview**.

   You instructed Access to preview the filtered query results.

m. Click **Close Print Preview** in the Print Preview group.

n. Close the Order Details Extended query. Click **No** if a dialog box asks if you want to save your changes.

> **TIP Deleting Filter by Form Criterion**
>
> While working with Filter by Selection or Filter by Form, you may inadvertently save a filter. To view a saved filter, open the table or query that you suspect may have a saved filter. Click Advanced in the Sort & Filter group, and then click Filter by Form. If criteria appear in the form, then a filter has been saved. To delete a saved filter, click Advanced, and then click Clear All Filters. Close and save the table or query.

STEP 4 SORT A TABLE

Your boss at Northwind is happy with your work; however, he would like some of the information to appear in a different order. Sort the records in the Customers table using the boss's new criteria. Refer to Figure 23 as you complete Step 4.

FIGURE 23 Customers Table Sorted by Country and Then City ➤

a. Click the **Queries group** in the Navigation Pane to collapse the listed queries.

b. Click the **Tables group** in the Navigation Pane to expand the lists of available tables.

c. Locate and double-click the **Customers table** to open it.

This table contains information about customers. It is sorted in ascending order by the Customer ID field. Because this field contains text, the table is sorted in alphabetical order.

d. Click any value in the Customer ID field. Click **Descending** in the Sort & Filter group on the Home tab.

Sorting in descending order on a character field produces a reverse alphabetical order.

e. Scroll right until you can see both the Country and City fields.

If you close the Navigation Pane, locating the fields on the far right will be easier.

f. Click the **Country column heading.**

The entire column is selected.

g. Click the **Country column heading** again, and hold down the **left mouse button.**

A thick dark blue line displays on the left edge of the Country field column.

h. Check to make sure that you see the thick blue line. Drag the **Country field** to the left until the thick black line moves between the City and Region fields. Release the mouse and the Country field position moves to the right of the City field.

You moved the Country field next to the City field so you can easily sort the table based on both fields.

i. Click any city name in the City field, and then click **Ascending** in the Sort & Filter group.

j. Click any country name in the Country field, and then click **Ascending.**

The countries are sorted in alphabetical order. The cities within each country also are sorted alphabetically. For example, the customer in Graz, Austria, is listed before the customer in Salzburg, Austria.

k. Close the Customers table. Do not save the changes.

l. Click the **File tab**, and then click **Compact & Repair Database.**

m. Click the **File tab**, click **Save & Publish**, and then double-click **Back Up Database**. Accept *a01h2traders_LastnameFirstname_date* as the file name, and then click **Save.**

You just created a backup of the database after completing Hands-On Exercise 2. The *a01h2traders_LastnameFirstname* database remains onscreen.

n. Keep the database onscreen if you plan to continue with Hands-On Exercise 3. If not, close the database and exit Access.

Relational Database

Access is known as a relational database management system (RDBMS).

Access is known as a **relational database management system** (RDBMS); using an RDBMS, you can manage groups of data (tables) and then set rules (relationships) between tables.

Join lines enable you to create a relationship between two tables using a common field.

A **foreign key** is a field in one table that is also the primary key of another table.

In the previous section, we compared Excel worksheets to Access relational databases. Access has the ability to create relationships between two tables, whereas Excel does not. Access is known as a ***relational database management system*** (RDBMS); using an RDBMS, you can manage groups of data (tables) and then set rules (relationships) between tables. When relational databases are designed properly, users can easily combine data from multiple tables to create queries, forms, and reports.

Good database design begins with grouping data into the correct tables. This practice, known as normalization, will take time to learn, but over time you will begin to understand the fundamentals. The design of a relational database management system is illustrated in Figure 24, which shows the table design of the Northwind Traders database. The tables have been created, the field names have been added, and the data types have been set. The diagram also shows the relationships that were created between tables using join lines. ***Join lines*** enable you to create a relationship between two tables using a common field. When relationships are established, three options are available to further dictate how Access will manage the relationship: Enforce referential integrity, Cascade update related fields, and Cascade delete related records. Later in this section, you will learn more about enforcing referential integrity. Using the enforce referential integrity option will help keep invalid data out of your database. Examples of invalid data include (1) entering an order for a customer that does not exist, (2) tagging a new product with a nonexistent category, and (3) entering a person's address with an invalid state abbreviation.

Figure 24 shows the join lines between related tables as a series of lines connecting the common fields. For example, the Suppliers table is joined to the Products table using the common field SupplierID.

When the database is set up properly, the users of the data can be confident that searching through the Customers table will produce accurate results about their order history or their outstanding invoices.

In this section, you will explore relationships between tables and learn about the power of relational data.

Using the Relationships Window

The relationships in a database are represented by the lines between the tables, as shown in Figure 24. Relationships are set in the Relationships window by the database developer after the tables have been created but before any sample data is entered. The most common method of connecting two tables is to connect the primary key from one table to the foreign key of another. A ***foreign key*** is a field in one table that is also the primary key of another table. For example, the SupplierID (primary key) in the Suppliers table is joined to the SupplierID (foreign key) in the Products table. As you learned before, the primary key is a field that uniquely identifies each record in a table.

To create a relationship between two tables, follow these guidelines:

1. Click Relationships in the Relationships group on the Database Tools tab.
2. Add the two tables that you want to join together to the Relationships window.
3. Drag the common field (e.g., SupplierID) from the primary table (e.g., Suppliers) onto the common field (e.g., SupplierID) of the related table (e.g., Products).
4. The data types of the common fields must be the same.
5. Check the Enforce Referential Integrity check box.
6. Close the Relationships window.

Enforce Referential Integrity

Enforce referential integrity ensures that data cannot be entered into a related table unless it first exists in the primary table.

Enforce referential integrity is one of the three options you can select when setting a table relationship. When ***enforce referential integrity*** is checked, Access ensures that data cannot be entered into a related table unless it first exists in the primary table. For example, in Figure 24, you cannot enter an order into the Order table for a Customer with CustomerID 9308 if Customer 9308 has not been entered in the Customer table. This rule ensures the integrity of the data in the database and improves overall data accuracy. Referential integrity also prohibits users from deleting a record in one table if it has records in related tables (i.e., you cannot delete Customer 8819 if Customer 8819 has any orders).

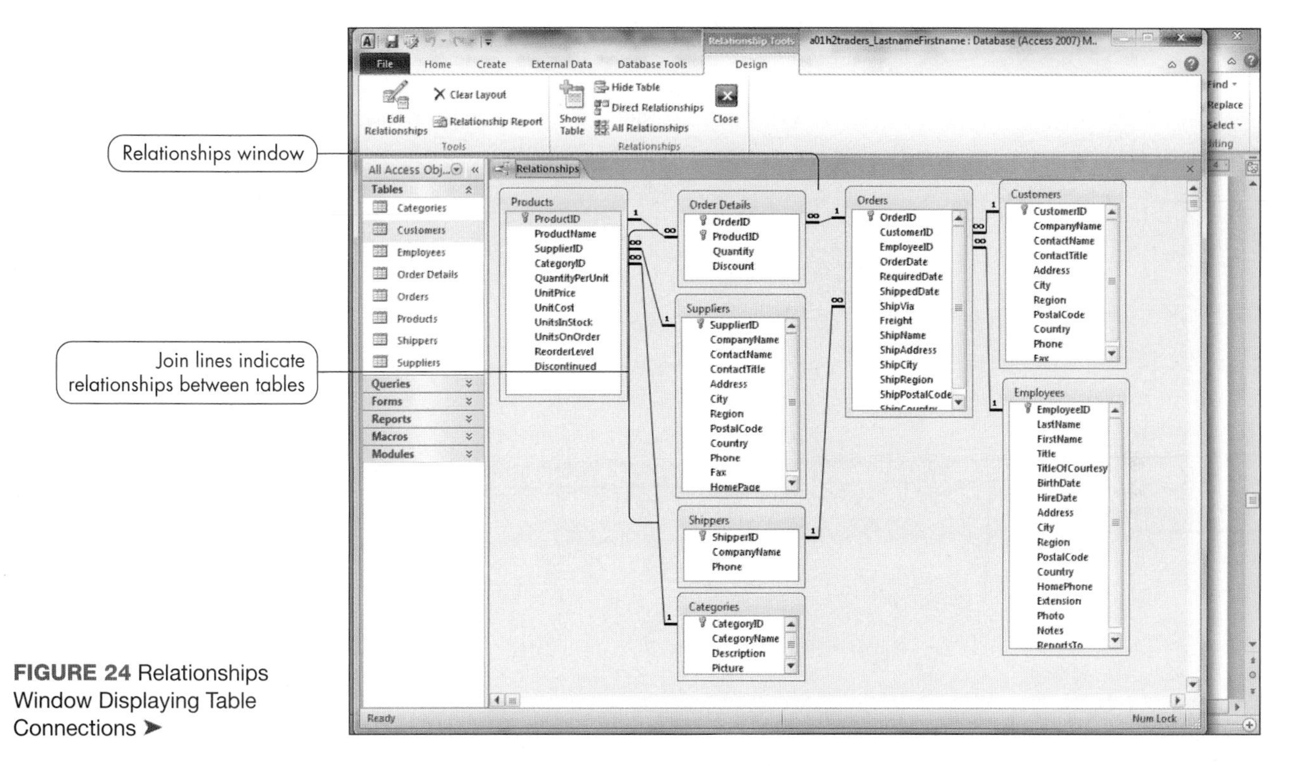

FIGURE 24 Relationships Window Displaying Table Connections ➤

Create Sample Data

When learning database skills, starting with a smaller set of sample data prior to entering all company records can be helpful. The same design principles apply regardless of the number of records. A small amount of data gives you the ability to check the tables and quickly see if your results are correct. Even though the data amounts are small, as you test the database tables and relationships, the results will prove useful as you work with larger data sets.

When learning database skills, starting with a smaller set of sample data prior to entering all company records can be helpful.

Understanding Relational Power

In the previous section, you learned that you should use Access when you have relational data. Access derives power from multiple tables and the relationships between those tables. This type of database is illustrated in Figure 24. This diagram describes the database structure of the Northwind Traders company. If you examine some of the connections, you will see that the EmployeeID is a foreign key in the Orders table. That means you can produce a report displaying all orders for a customer and the employee name (from the Employees table) that entered the order. The Orders table is joined to the Order Details table where the OrderID is the common field. The Products table is joined to the Order Details table where ProductID is the common field. These table connections enable you to query (ask) the database for information stored in multiple tables. This feature gives the manager the ability to ask questions like "How many different beverages were shipped last week?" and "What was the total revenue generated from seafood orders last year?"

Suppose a customer called to complain that his orders were arriving late. Because the ShipperID is a foreign key field in the Orders table, you could query the database to find out which shipper delivered that customer's merchandise. Are the other orders also late? Does the firm need to reconsider its shipping options? The design of a relational database enables us to extract information from multiple tables in a single query or report.

In the next Hands-On Exercise, you will examine the Relationships window, create a filter in a query and a report, and remove a filter.

3 Relational Database

You continue to use the Access database to filter tables and provide answers to the Northwind employees' questions. When the same question is repeated by several employees, you look for a way to save your filter by form specifications.

Skills covered: Use the Relationships Window • Filter a Query • Use Filter by Form with a Comparison Operator and Reapply a Saved Filter • Filter a Report • Remove a Filter

STEP 1 USE THE RELATIONSHIPS WINDOW

In this exercise, you examine the relationships established in the Northwind Traders database to learn more about the overall design of the database. Refer to Figure 25 as you complete Step 1.

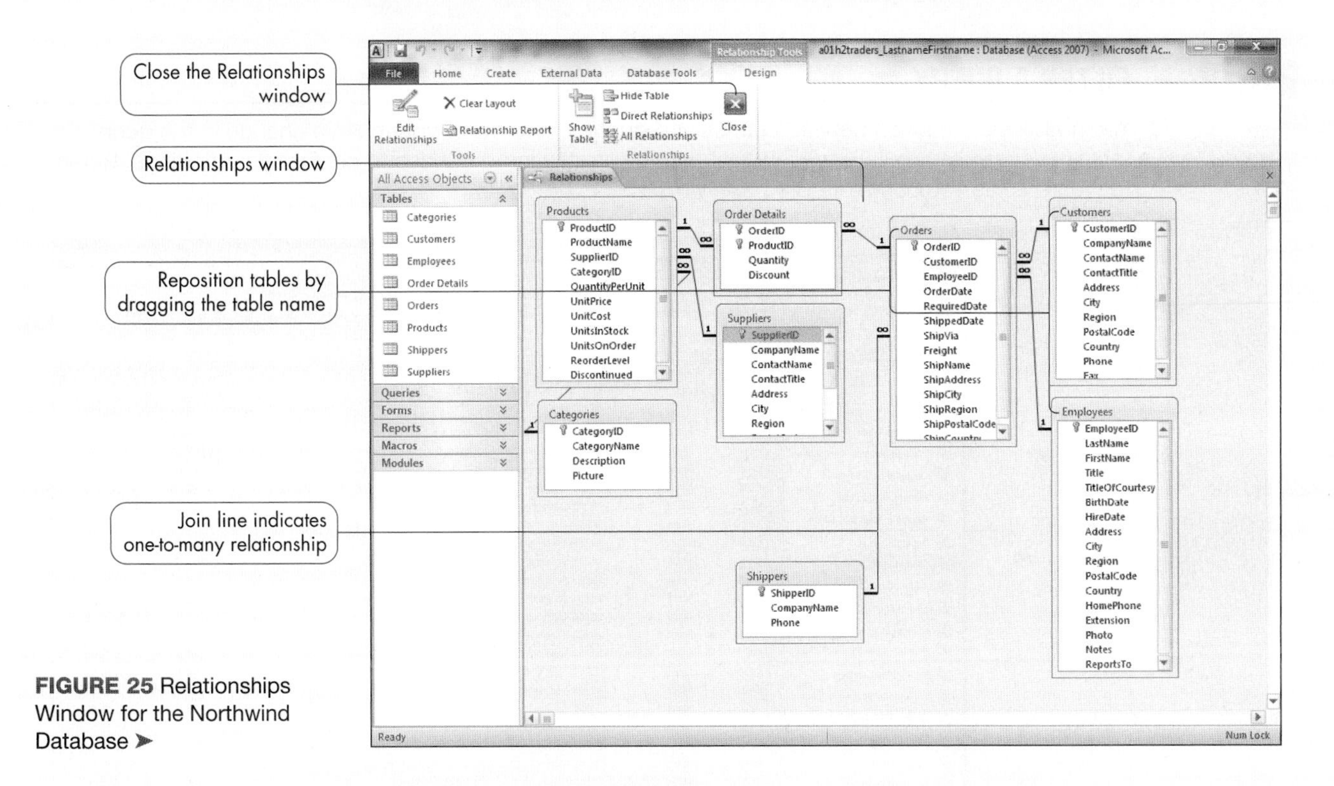

FIGURE 25 Relationships Window for the Northwind Database ➤

a. Open *a01h2traders_LastnameFirstname* if you closed it at the end of Hands-On Exercise 2. Click the **File tab**, click **Save Database As**, and then type **a01h3traders_LastnameFirstname**, changing *h2* to *h3*. Click **Save**.

> **TROUBLESHOOTING:** If you make any major mistakes in this exercise, you can delete the *a01h3traders_LastnameFirstname* file, repeat step a above, and then start the exercise over.

b. Click the **Database Tools tab**, and then click **Relationships** in the Relationships group.

Examine the relationships that connect the various tables. For example, the Products table is connected to the Suppliers, Categories, and Order Details tables.

c. Click **Show Table** in the Relationships group on the Relationship Tools Design tab.

The Show Table dialog box opens. It tells you that eight tables are available in the database. If you look in the Relationships window, you will see that all eight tables are in the relationships diagram.

d. Click the **Queries tab** in the Show Table dialog box.

You could add all of the queries to the Relationships window. Things might become cluttered, but you could tell at a glance where the queries get their information.

e. Close the Show Table dialog box.

f. Click **All Access Objects** on the Navigation Pane.

g. Select **Tables and Related Views**.

You now see each table and all the queries, forms, and reports that are based on each table. If a query is created using more than one table, it appears multiple times in the Navigation Pane.

h. Close the Relationships window. Click **All Tables** on the Navigation Pane, and then select **Object Type**.

STEP 2 FILTER A QUERY

You notice a connection between tables and queries. Whenever you make a change in the query, the table is updated as well. Run a few tests on the Northwind database to confirm your findings. Refer to Figure 26 as you complete Step 2.

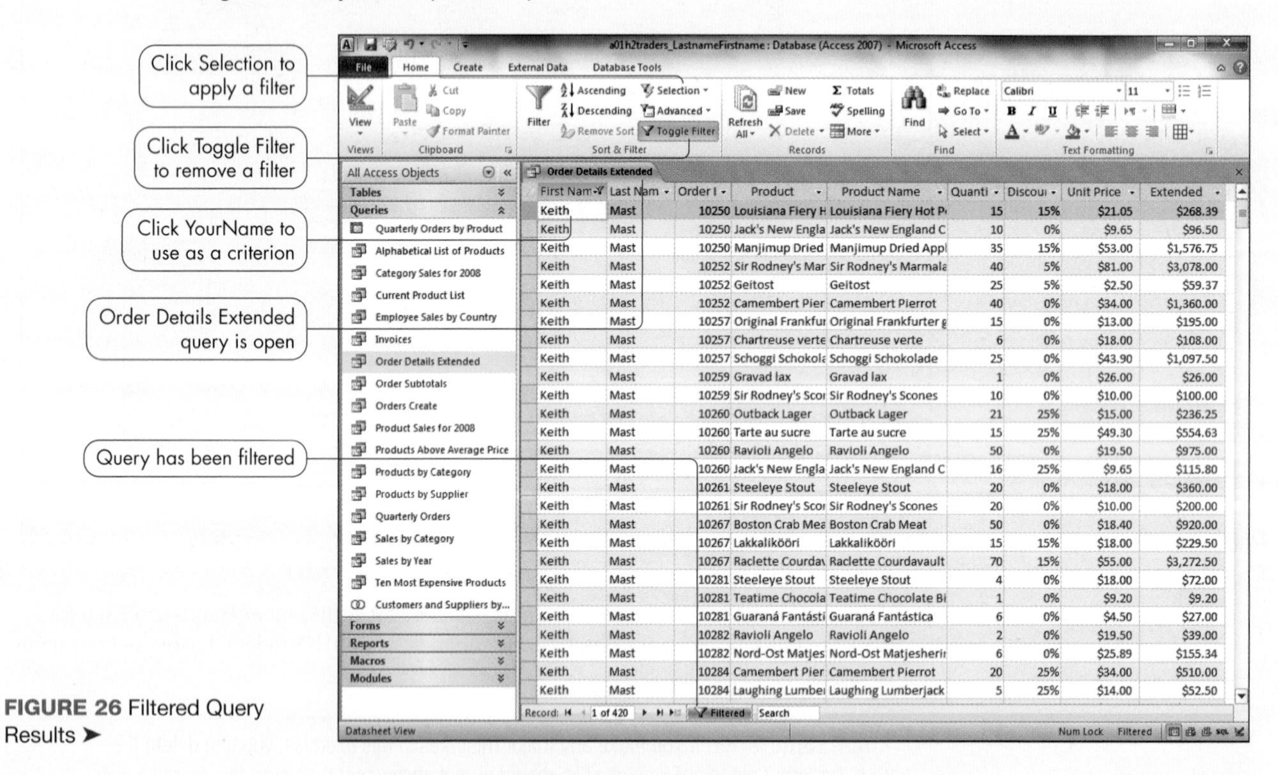

FIGURE 26 Filtered Query Results ➤

a. Collapse the Tables group, and expand the Queries group, and then locate and double-click the **Order Details Extended query**.

b. Find an occurrence of your last name, and then click it to select it.

c. Click **Selection** in the Sort & Filter group. Select **Equals "YourName"** from the selection menu.

The query results are reduced to 420 records.

d. Click **Toggle Filter** in the Sort & Filter group to remove the filter.

STEP 3 USE FILTER BY FORM WITH A COMPARISON OPERATOR AND REAPPLY A SAVED FILTER

Use Filter by Form to solve more complex questions about the Northwind data. After you retrieve the records, you save the Filter by Form specifications so you can reapply the filter later. Refer to Figure 27 as you complete Step 3.

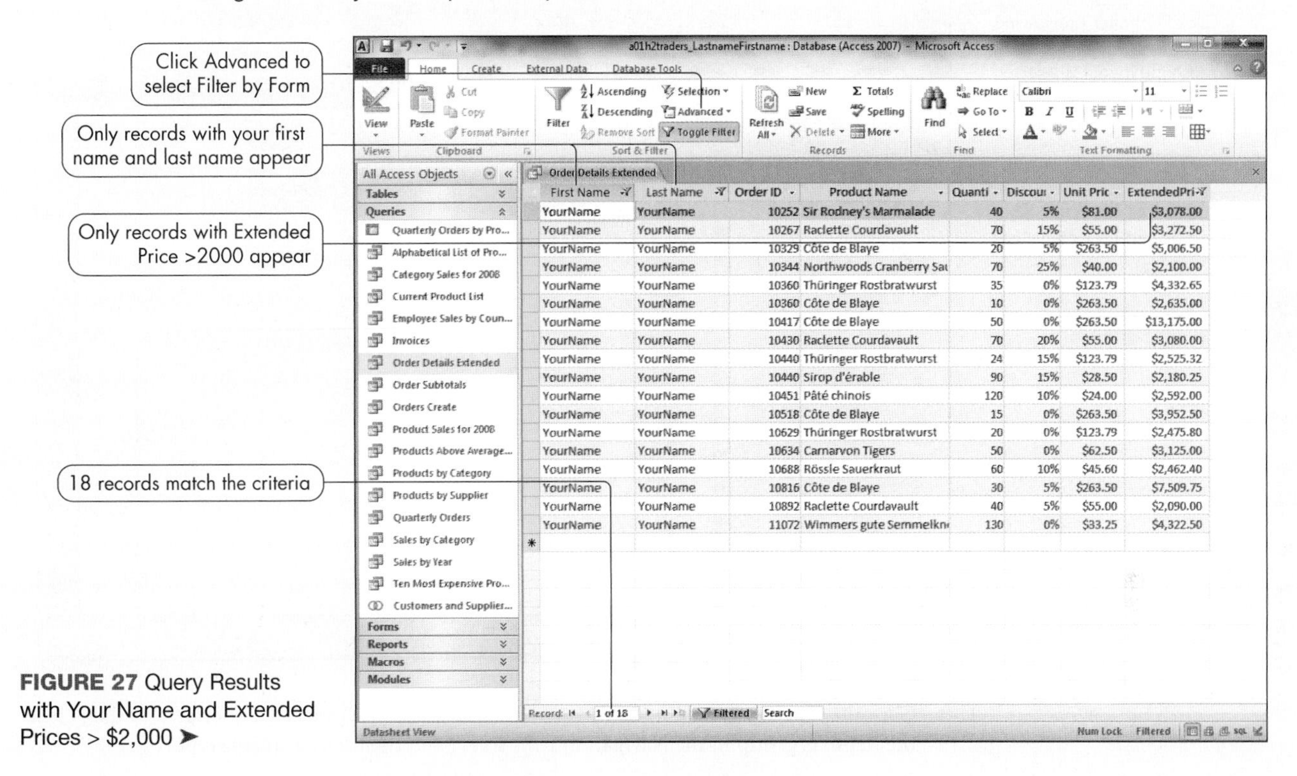
Click Advanced to select Filter by Form
Only records with your first name and last name appear
Only records with Extended Price >2000 appear
18 records match the criteria
a01h2traders_LastnameFirstname : Database (Access 2007) - Microsoft Access
Order Details Extended
Record: 1 of 18
Filtered
Search

First Name	Last Name	Order ID	Product Name	Quanti	Discou	Unit Pric	ExtendedPri
YourName	YourName	10252	Sir Rodney's Marmalade	40	5%	$81.00	$3,078.00
YourName	YourName	10267	Raclette Courdavault	70	15%	$55.00	$3,272.50
YourName	YourName	10329	Côte de Blaye	20	5%	$263.50	$5,006.50
YourName	YourName	10344	Northwoods Cranberry Sau	70	25%	$40.00	$2,100.00
YourName	YourName	10360	Thüringer Rostbratwurst	35	0%	$123.79	$4,332.65
YourName	YourName	10360	Côte de Blaye	10	0%	$263.50	$2,635.00
YourName	YourName	10417	Côte de Blaye	50	0%	$263.50	$13,175.00
YourName	YourName	10430	Raclette Courdavault	70	20%	$55.00	$3,080.00
YourName	YourName	10440	Thüringer Rostbratwurst	24	15%	$123.79	$2,525.32
YourName	YourName	10440	Sirop d'érable	90	15%	$28.50	$2,180.25
YourName	YourName	10451	Pâté chinois	120	10%	$24.00	$2,592.00
YourName	YourName	10518	Côte de Blaye	15	0%	$263.50	$3,952.50
YourName	YourName	10629	Thüringer Rostbratwurst	20	0%	$123.79	$2,475.80
YourName	YourName	10634	Carnarvon Tigers	50	0%	$62.50	$3,125.00
YourName	YourName	10688	Rössle Sauerkraut	60	10%	$45.60	$2,462.40
YourName	YourName	10816	Côte de Blaye	30	5%	$263.50	$7,509.75
YourName	YourName	10892	Raclette Courdavault	40	5%	$55.00	$2,090.00
YourName	YourName	11072	Wimmers gute Semmelkn	130	0%	$33.25	$4,322.50

FIGURE 27 Query Results with Your Name and Extended Prices > $2,000 ➤

a. Click **Advanced** in the Sort & Filter group.

b. Select **Filter By Form** from the list.

   Because Access will save the last filter you created, the Filter by Form design sheet opens with one criterion already filled in. Your name displays in the selection box under the Last Name field.

c. Scroll right (or press **Tab**) until the Extended Price field is visible. Click the first row in the Extended Price field.

d. Type >**2000**.

   The Extended Price field shows the purchased amount for each item ordered. If an item sold for $15 and a customer ordered 10, the Extended Price would display $150.

e. Click **Toggle Filter** in the Sort & Filter group. Examine the filtered results.

   Your comparison operator instruction, >2000, identified 18 items ordered where the extended price exceeded $2,000.

f. Close the Order Details Extended query by clicking the **Close button**. Answer **Yes** when asked *Do you want to save changes?*.

g. Open the Order Details Extended query again.

   The filter disengages when you close and reopen the object. However, the filter has been stored with the query. You may reapply the filter at any time by clicking the Toggle Filter command (until the next filter replaces the current one).

h. Click **Toggle Filter** in the Sort & Filter group.

i. Compare your results to Figure 27. If your results are correct, close and save the query.

STEP 4 FILTER A REPORT

You wonder if one report can serve several purposes. You discover that a report can be customized using the Filter by Selection feature. Refer to Figure 28 as you complete Step 4.

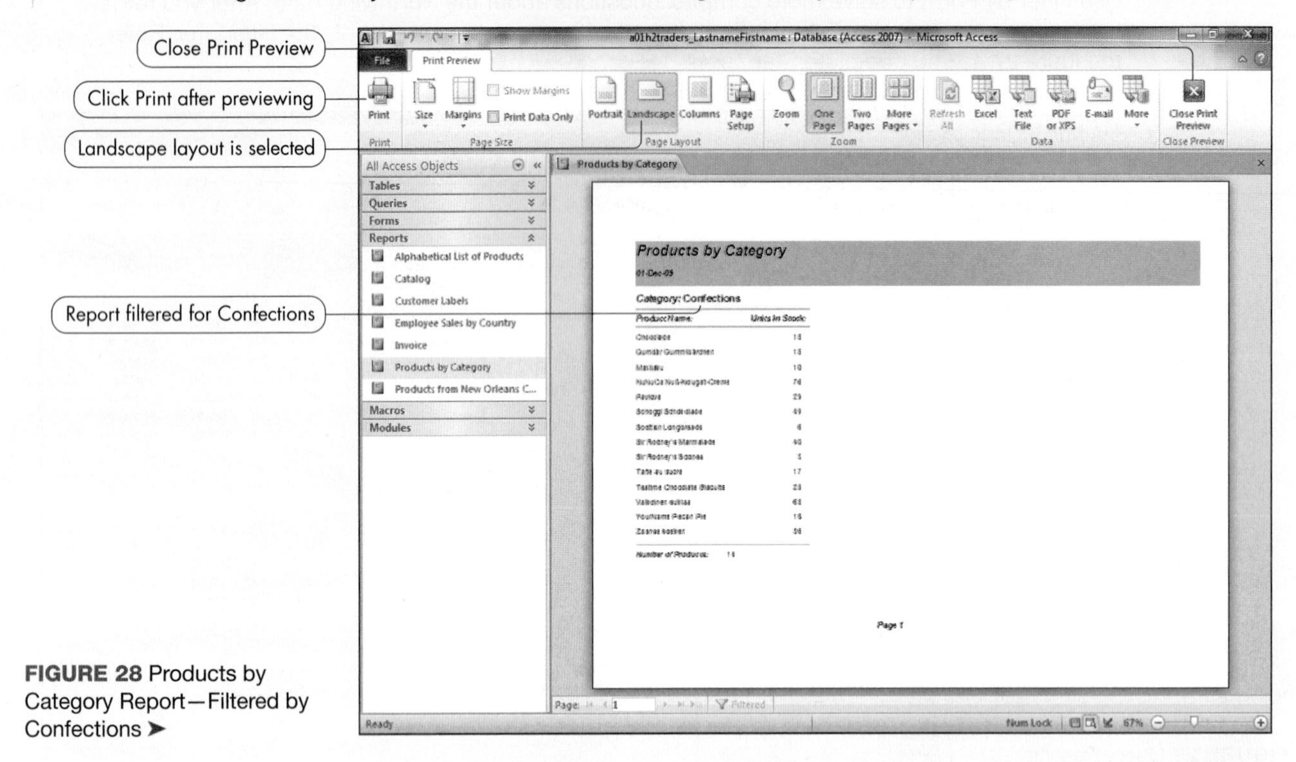

FIGURE 28 Products by Category Report—Filtered by Confections ➤

a. Click the **Queries group** in the Navigation Pane to collapse the listed queries, and then click the **Reports group** in the Navigation Pane to expand the list of available reports.

b. Open the Products by Category report located in the Reports group on the Navigation Pane. You may need to scroll down to locate it.

   The report should open in Print Preview with a gray title background highlighting the report title. The Print Preview displays the report exactly as it will print. This report was formatted to display in three columns.

> **TROUBLESHOOTING:** If you do not see the gray title background and three columns, you probably opened the wrong object. The database also contains a Product by Category query. It is the source for the Products by Category report. Make sure you open the report (shown with the green report icon) and not the query. Close the query and open the report.

c. Examine the Confections category products. You should see *Your Name Pecan Pie.*

   You created this product by entering data in a form in Hands-On Exercise 1. You later discovered that changes made to a form affect the related table. Now you see that other related objects also change when the source data changes.

d. Right-click the **Products by Category tab**, and then select **Report View** from the shortcut menu.

   The Report view displays the information a little differently. It no longer shows three columns. If you clicked the Print command while in Report view, the columns would print even though you do not see them. The Report view permits limited data interaction (for example, filtering).

e. Scroll down in the report until you see the title *Category: Confections.* Right-click the word *Confections* in the title. Select **Equals "Confections"** from the shortcut menu.

   The report now displays only *Confections.*

f. Right-click the **Products by Category tab**, and then select **Print Preview** from the shortcut menu.

   If you need to print a report, always view the report in Print Preview prior to printing.

g. Click **Close Print Preview** in the Close Preview group.

h. Save and close the report.

The next time the report opens in Report view, it will not be filtered. However, since the filter was saved, the filter can be reapplied by clicking Toggle Filter in the Sort & Filter group.

STEP 5 REMOVE A FILTER

You notice that Access keeps asking you to save your changes when you close a table or query. You say "Yes" each time since you do not want to lose your data. Now you need to remove the filters that you saved. Refer to Figure 29 as you complete Step 5.

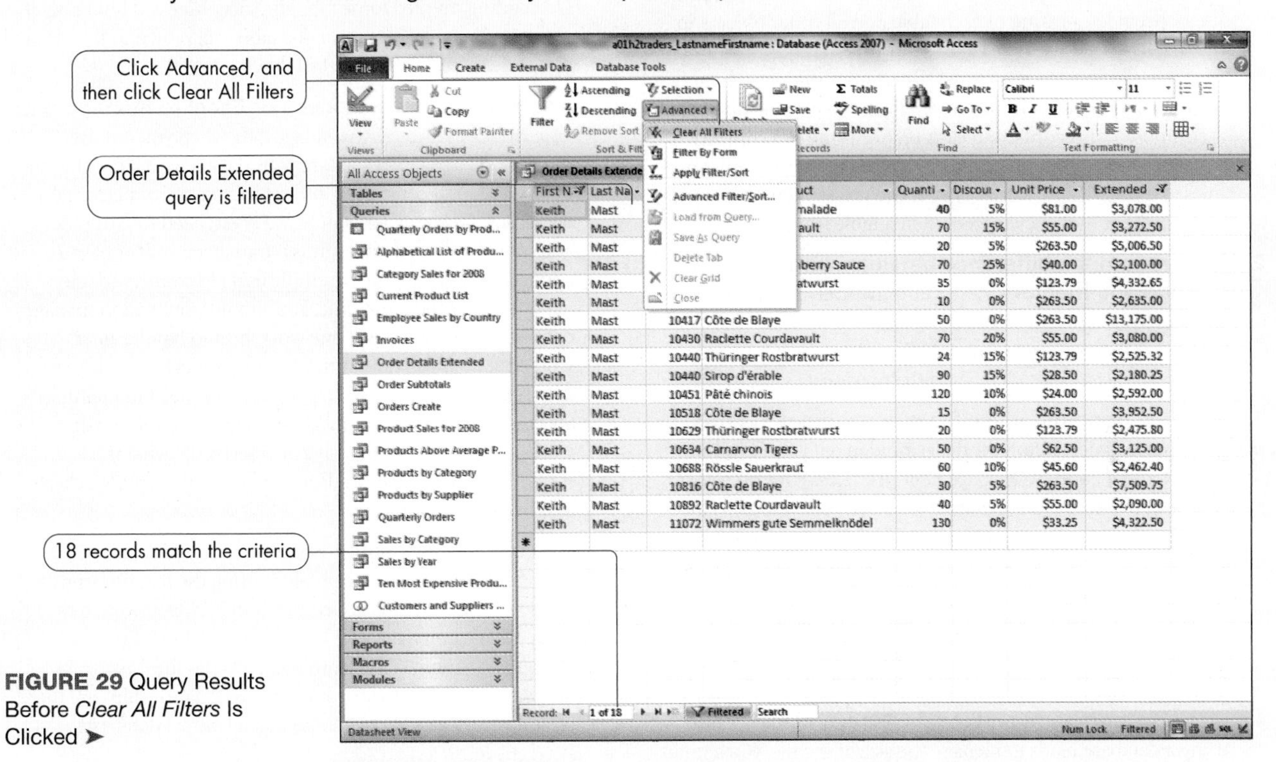

FIGURE 29 Query Results Before *Clear All Filters* Is Clicked ➤

a. Click the **Queries group** in the Navigation Pane to expand the list of available reports, then open the Order Details Extended query.

All 2,155 records should display in the query. You have unfiltered the data. However, the filter from the previous step still exists.

b. Click **Toggle Filter** in the Sort & Filter group.

You will see the same 18 filtered records that you created in Step 3.

c. Click **Advanced** in the Sort & Filter group, and then click **Clear All Filters.**

All 2,155 records are shown again.

d. Close the query. A dialog box opens asking if you want to save changes. Click **Yes**.

e. Open the Order Details Extended query.

f. Click **Advanced** in the Sort & Filter group.

g. Check to ensure the Clear All Filters option is dim, indicating there are no saved filters. Save and close the query.

h. Click the **File tab**, and then click **Compact & Repair Database**.

i. Click the **File tab**, and then click **Exit** (to exit Access).

j. Submit based on your instructor's directions.

CHAPTER OBJECTIVES REVIEW

After reading this chapter, you have accomplished the following objectives:

1. **Navigate among the objects in an Access database.** An Access database has six types of objects: tables, forms, queries, reports, macros, and modules. The Navigation Pane displays these objects and enables you to open an existing object or create new objects. You may arrange these by Object Type or by Tables and Related Views. The Tables and Related Views provides a listing of each table and all other objects in the database that use that table as a source. Thus, one query or report may appear several times, listed once under each table from which it derives information. Each table in the database is composed of records, and each record is in turn composed of fields. Every record in a given table has the same fields in the same order. The primary key is the field (or combination of fields) that makes every record in a table unique.

2. **Understand the difference between working in storage and memory.** Access automatically saves any changes in the current record as soon as you move to the next record or when you close the table. The Undo Current Record command reverses the changes to the previously saved record.

3. **Practice good database file management.** Because organizations depend on the data stored in databases, you need to implement good file management practices. For example, you need to develop an organized folder structure so you can easily save and retrieve your database files. You also need to develop a naming convention so it is easy to determine which file contains which data. As you learn new Access skills, it is recommended that you make a copy of the original database file and practice on the copy. This practice provides a recovery point in the event you make a fatal error.

4. **Back up, compact, and repair Access files.** Because using a database tends to increase the size of the file, you should always close any database objects and compact and repair the database prior to closing the file. Compact & Repair will reduce the size of the database by removing temporary objects and unclaimed space due to deleted objects. Adequate backup is essential when working with an Access database (or any other Office application). For increased security, a duplicate copy of the database can be created at the end of every session and stored externally (on a flash drive or an external hard drive).

5. **Create filters.** A filter is a set of criteria that is applied to a table to display a subset of the records in that table. Access lets you Filter by Selection or Filter by Form. The application of a filter does not remove the records from the table, but simply hides them temporarily from view.

6. **Sort table data on one or more fields.** The records in a table can be displayed in ascending or descending order by first selecting the appropriate column and clicking Ascending or Descending on the Home tab. The sort order will hold only if you save the table; otherwise the table will return to the original sort order when you close the table.

7. **Know when to use Access or Excel to manage data.** You should use Access to manage data when you require multiple related tables to store your data; have a large amount of data; need to connect to and retrieve data from external databases, such as Microsoft SQL Server; need to group, sort, and total data based on various parameters; and/or have an application that requires multiple users to connect to one data source at the same time. You should use Excel to manage data when you only need one worksheet to handle all of your data (i.e., you do not need multiple worksheets); have mostly numeric data—for example, if you need to maintain an expense statement; require subtotals and totals in your worksheet; want to primarily run a series of "what if" scenarios on your data; and/or need to create complex charts and/or graphs.

8. **Use the Relationships window.** Access enables you to create relationships between tables using the Relationships window. A *relationship* is a connection between two tables using a common field. The benefit of a relationship is to efficiently combine data from related tables for the purpose of creating queries, forms, and reports. Relationships are the reason why Access is referred to as a relational database.

9. **Understand relational power.** A relational database contains multiple tables and enables you to extract information from those tables in a single query. The related tables must be consistent with one another, a concept known as referential integrity. Once referential integrity is set, Access enforces data validation to protect the integrity of a database. No system, no matter how sophisticated, can produce valid output from invalid input. Changes made in one object can affect other related objects. Relationships are based on joining the primary key from one table to the foreign key of another table.

KEY TERMS

Access speed
Backup
Compact and Repair
Comparison operator
Criterion
Database
Datasheet view
Design view
Enforce referential integrity
Field
Filter
Filter by Form
Filter by Selection
Foreign key
Form
Join lines
Navigation Pane
Object
Primary key
Query
Record
Relational database management system
Relationship
Report
Sort
Sort Ascending
Sort Descending
Table

MULTIPLE CHOICE

1. Which sequence represents the hierarchy of terms, from smallest to largest?
   (a) Database, table, record, field
   (b) Field, record, table, database
   (c) Record, field, table, database
   (d) Field, record, database, table

2. You perform several edits in a table within an Access database. When should you execute the Save command?
   (a) Immediately after you add, edit, or delete a record
   (b) Each time you close a table or a query
   (c) Once at the end of a session
   (d) Records are saved automatically; the save command is not required.

3. You have opened an Access file. The left pane displays a table with forms, queries, and reports listed below a table name. Then another table and its objects display. You notice some of the object names are repeated under different tables. Why?
   (a) The Navigation Pane has been set to Object Type. The object names repeat because a query or report is frequently based on multiple tables.
   (b) The Navigation Pane has been set to Tables and Related Views. The object names repeat because a query or report is frequently based on multiple tables.
   (c) The Navigation Pane has been set to Most Recently Used View. The object names repeat because an object has been used frequently.
   (d) The database objects have been alphabetized.

4. Which of the following is not true of an Access database?
   (a) Every record in a table has the same fields as every other record.
   (b) Every table in a database contains the same number of records as every other table.
   (c) Text, Number, Autonumber, and Currency are valid data types.
   (d) Each table should contain a primary key; however, a primary key is not required.

5. Which of the following is true regarding the record selector box?
   (a) A pencil symbol indicates that the current record already has been saved.
   (b) An empty square indicates that the current record has not changed.
   (c) An asterisk indicates the first record in the table.
   (d) A gold border surrounds the active record.

6. You have finished an Access assignment and wish to turn it in to your instructor for evaluation. As you prepare to transfer the file, you discover that it has grown in size. It is now more than double the original size. You should:
   (a) Zip the database file prior to transmitting it to the instructor.
   (b) Turn it in; the size does not matter.
   (c) Compact and repair the database file prior to transmitting it to the instructor.
   (d) Delete extra tables or reports or fields to make the file smaller.

7. Which of the following will be accepted as valid during data entry?
   (a) Adding a record with a duplicate primary key
   (b) Entering text into a numeric field
   (c) Entering numbers into a text field
   (d) Omitting an entry in a required field

8. Which of the following conditions is available through Filter by Selection?
   (a) The AND condition
   (b) The OR condition
   (c) An Equals condition
   (d) A delete condition

9. You open an Access form and use it to update an address for customer Lee Fong. After closing the form, you later open a report that generates mailing labels. What will the address label for Lee Fong show?
   (a) The new address
   (b) The old address
   (c) The new address if you remembered to save the changes made to the form
   (d) The old address until you remember to update it in the report

10. You are looking at an Employees table in Datasheet view. You want the names sorted alphabetically by last name and then by first name—for example, Smith, Andrea is listed before Smith, William. To accomplish this, you must:
    (a) First sort ascending on first name and then on last name.
    (b) First sort descending on first name and then on last name.
    (c) First sort ascending on last name and then on first name.
    (d) First sort descending on last name and then on first name.

1 Member Rewards

The Prestige Hotel chain caters to upscale business travelers and provides state-of-the-art conference, meeting, and reception facilities. It prides itself on its international, four-star cuisine. Last year, it began a member rewards club to help the marketing department track the purchasing patterns of its most loyal customers. All of the hotel transactions are stored in the database. Your task is to update a customer record and identify the customers who had weddings in St. Paul. This exercise follows the same set of skills as used in Hands-On Exercise 1 in the chapter. Refer to Figure 30 as you complete this exercise.

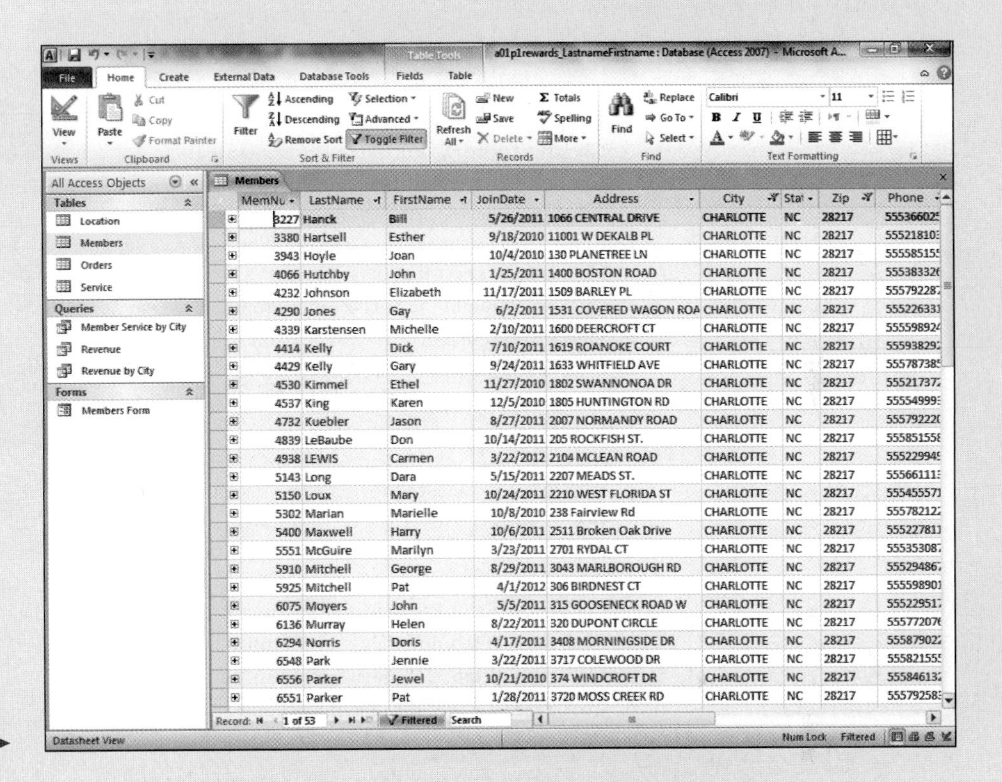

FIGURE 30 Member Service by City—Filtered and Sorted ➤

a. Open the *a01p1rewards* file, and then save the database as **a01p1rewards_LastnameFirstname**.
b. Open the Members Form, and then click **New (blank) record** on the bottom navigation bar. (It has a yellow asterisk.)
c. Enter the information in the following table in the form. Press **Tab** to move to the next field.

Field Name	Value
MemNumber	4852
LastName	your last name
FirstName	your first name
JoinDate	7/30/2010
Address	124 West Elm, Apt 12

(Continued)

Field Name	Value
City	your hometown
State	your state
Zip	your zip
Phone	9995551234
Email	your e-mail
OrderID	9325
ServiceDate	8/1/2012
ServiceID	3
NoInParty	2
Location	20

d. Click the **Close (X) button** to close the form.
e. Double-click the **Members table** in the Navigation Pane. Use **Find** to verify your name is in the table.
f. In the Members table, find a record that displays *Charlotte* as the value in the City field. Click **Charlotte** to select that data value.
g. Click **Selection** in the Sort & Filter group on the Home tab. Select **Equals "Charlotte"**.
h. Find a record that displays *28217* as the value in the Zip field. Click **Zip** to select that data value.
i. Click **Selection** in the Sort & Filter Group, and then select **Equals "28217"**.
j. Right-click on any phone number field with a missing phone number, and then click **Does not Equal Blank.**
k. Click any value in the FirstName field. Click **Ascending** in the Sort & Filter group on the Home tab. Click any value in the LastName field. Click **Ascending** in the Sort & Filter group on the Home tab.
l. Click the **File tab**, click **Print**, and then click **Print Preview** to preview the sorted and filtered query.
m. Click **Close Print Preview** in the Close Preview group. Close the query (do not save when asked).
n. Click the **File tab**, and then click **Compact and Repair Database**.
o. Click the **File tab**, click **Save & Publish**, and then double-click **Back Up Database**.
p. Click **Save** to accept the default backup file name with today's date.
q. Click the **File tab**, and then click **Exit** (to exit Access).
r. Submit based on your instructor's directions.

2 Custom Coffee

The Custom Coffee Company provides coffee, tea, and snacks to offices in Miami. Custom Coffee also provides and maintains the equipment for brewing the beverages. The firm has a reputation for providing outstanding customer service. To improve customer service even further, the owner recently purchased an Access database to keep track of customers, orders, and products. This database will replace the Excel spreadsheets currently maintained by the office manager. The Excel spreadsheets are out of date and they do not allow for data validation while data is being entered. The company hired a temp to verify and enter all the Excel data into the Access database. This exercise follows the same set of skills as used in Hands-On Exercises 2 and 3 in the chapter. Refer to Figure 31 as you complete this exercise.

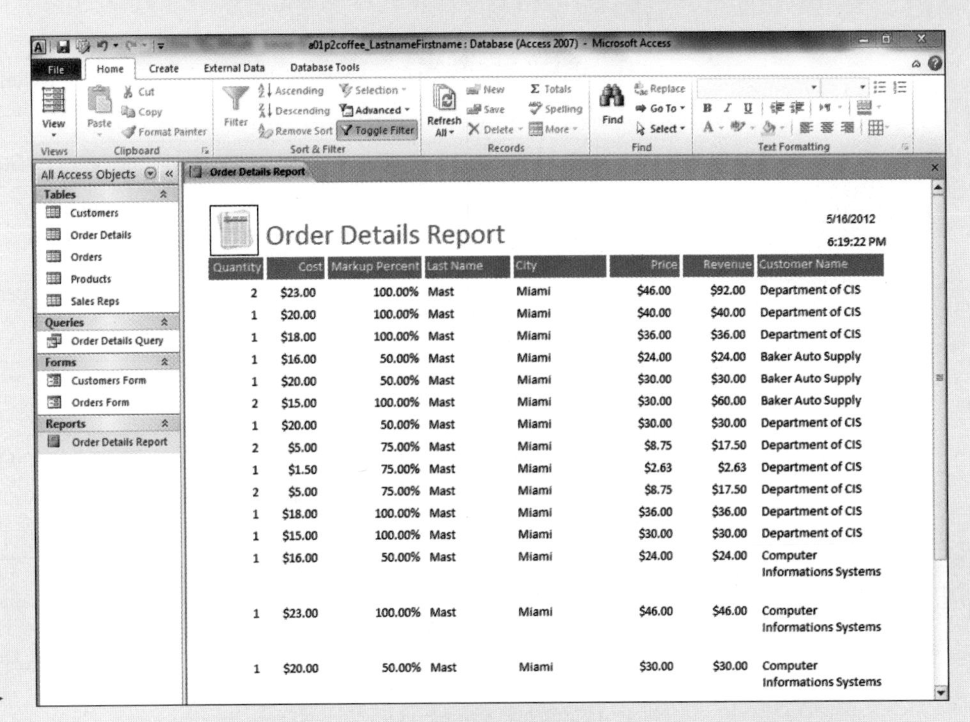

FIGURE 31 Order Details Report Filtered for *YourName* ➤

a. Open the *a01p2coffee* file, and then save the database as **a01p2coffee_LastnameFirstname**.
b. Click the **Database Tools tab**, and then click **Relationships** in the Relationships group. Review the table relationships. Take note of the join line between the Customers and Orders Tables.
c. Click **Close** in the Relationships group.
d. Double-click the **Sales Reps table** in the Navigation Pane to open it. Replace *YourName* with your name in both the LastName and FirstName fields. Close the table by clicking the **Close (X) button** on the right side of the Sales Reps window.
e. Double-click the **Customers Form form** to open it. Click **New (blank) record** in the navigation bar at the bottom of the window. Add a new record by typing the following information; press **Tab** after each field.

Customer Name:	***your name* Company**
Contact:	your name
Email:	***your name*@yahoo.com**
Address1:	**123 Main St**
Address2:	**Skip**
City:	**Miami**
State:	**FL**
Zip Code:	**33133**
Phone:	**(305) 555-1234**
Fax:	**Skip**
Service Start Date:	**1/17/2012**
Credit Rating:	**A**
Sales Rep ID:	**2**

Notice the pencil in the top-left margin of the form window. This symbol indicates the new record has not been saved to storage. Press **Tab**. The pencil symbol disappears, and the new customer is automatically saved to the table.

f. Close the Customers Form form.

g. Double-click the **Orders Form form** to open it. Click **New (blank) record** in the navigation bar at the bottom of the window. Add a new record by typing the following information:

Customer ID:	**15** (Access will convert it to *C0015*)
Payment Type:	**Cash** (select using the arrow)
Comments:	**Ship this order in 2 days**
Product ID:	**4** (Access will convert it to *P0004*)
Quantity:	**2**

h. Add a second product using the following information:

Product ID:	**6** (Access will convert it to *P0006*)
Quantity:	**1**

i. Close the form (save changes if asked.)

j. Double-click the **Order Details Report** to open it in Report view. Right-click your name in the Last Name field, and then select **Equals "Your Name"** from the shortcut menu. Right-click **Miami** in the City field, and then select **Equals "Miami"** from the shortcut menu.

k. Click the **File tab**, click **Print**, and then click **Print Preview.**

l. Click **Close Print Preview** in the Close Preview group. Close the report.

m. Click the **File tab**, click **Info**, and then click **Compact and Repair Database.**

n. Click the **File tab**, click **Save & Publish**, and then double-click **Back Up Database.** Use the default backup file name.

o. Click the **File tab**, and then click **Exit** (to exit Access).

p. Submit based on your instructor's directions.

MID-LEVEL EXERCISES

1 Real Estate

You are the senior partner in a large, independent real estate firm that specializes in home sales. Most of your time is spent supervising the agents who work for your firm. The firm has a database containing all of the information on the properties it has listed. You use the database to help evaluate the productivity of your team during weekly sales meetings you hold with each sales agent. Today, you are evaluating agent Angela Scott, who is responsible for the high-end properties at the firm. To prepare for your meeting, find all properties that are listed for over $1,000,000, and have four or more bedrooms. When you find these properties, sort the data by Subdivision then by list price in ascending order. Refer to Figure 32 as you complete this exercise.

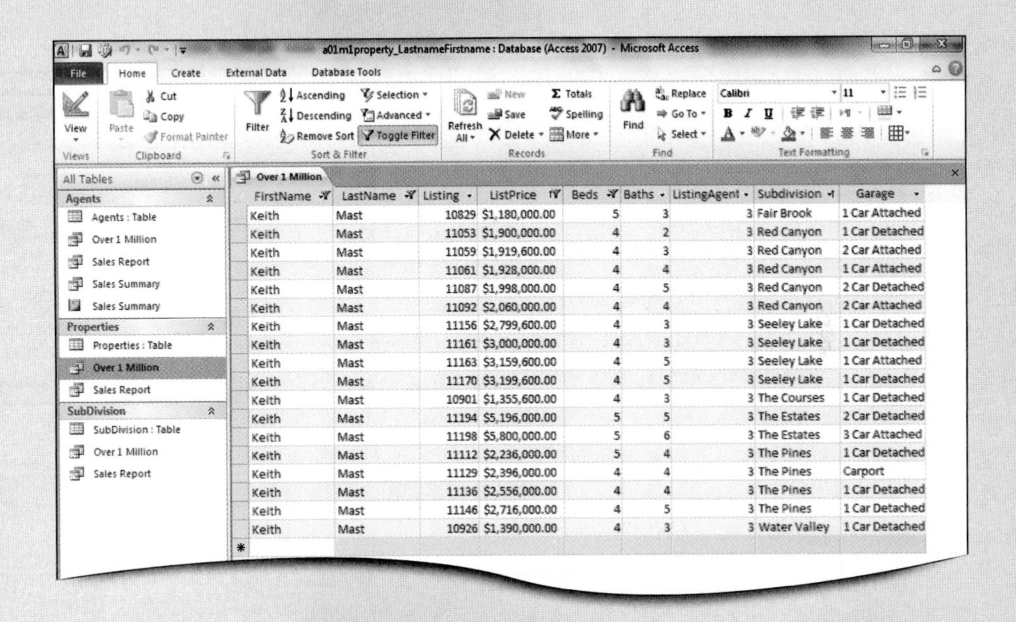

FirstName	LastName	Listing	ListPrice	Beds	Baths	ListingAgent	Subdivision	Garage
Keith	Mast	10829	$1,180,000.00	5	3	3	Fair Brook	1 Car Attached
Keith	Mast	11053	$1,900,000.00	4	2	3	Red Canyon	1 Car Detached
Keith	Mast	11059	$1,919,600.00	4	3	3	Red Canyon	2 Car Attached
Keith	Mast	11061	$1,928,000.00	4	4	3	Red Canyon	1 Car Attached
Keith	Mast	11087	$1,998,000.00	4	5	3	Red Canyon	2 Car Detached
Keith	Mast	11092	$2,060,000.00	4	4	3	Red Canyon	2 Car Attached
Keith	Mast	11156	$2,799,600.00	4	3	3	Seeley Lake	1 Car Detached
Keith	Mast	11161	$3,000,000.00	4	3	3	Seeley Lake	1 Car Detached
Keith	Mast	11163	$3,159,600.00	4	5	3	Seeley Lake	1 Car Attached
Keith	Mast	11170	$3,199,600.00	4	5	3	Seeley Lake	1 Car Detached
Keith	Mast	10901	$1,355,600.00	4	3	3	The Courses	1 Car Detached
Keith	Mast	11194	$5,196,000.00	5	5	3	The Estates	2 Car Detached
Keith	Mast	11198	$5,800,000.00	5	6	3	The Estates	3 Car Attached
Keith	Mast	11112	$2,236,000.00	5	4	3	The Pines	1 Car Detached
Keith	Mast	11129	$2,396,000.00	4	4	3	The Pines	Carport
Keith	Mast	11136	$2,556,000.00	4	4	3	The Pines	1 Car Detached
Keith	Mast	11146	$2,716,000.00	4	5	3	The Pines	1 Car Detached
Keith	Mast	10926	$1,390,000.00	4	3	3	Water Valley	1 Car Detached

FIGURE 32 Your Properties Listed for Over $1 Million ➤

a. Open the *a01m1property* file, and then save the database as **a01m1property_LastnameFirstname.**
b. Open the Agents table. Find and replace *YourName* with your name in the FirstName and LastName fields. Notice the pencil appears in the record selector box on the left while you type your name, then disappears once the record has been saved. Close the table.
c. Open the Over 1 Million query, and then create a filter by form on the data. Set the criteria to identify more than three bedrooms, a listing price over $1,000,000, and sales rep first and last names of your name.
d. Sort the filtered results by ascending **ListPrice** and by ascending **Subdivision.**
e. Save and close the query.
f. Compact and repair the database.
g. Back up the database. Use the default backup file name.
h. Exit Access.
i. Submit based on your instructor's directions.

2 National Conference

The Association of Higher Education will host its National Conference on your campus next year. To facilitate the conference, the information technology department has replaced last year's Excel spreadsheets with an Access database containing information on the rooms, speakers, and sessions. Your assignment is to create a room itinerary that will list all of the sessions, dates, and times for each room. The list will be posted on the door of each room for the duration of the conference. Refer to Figure 33 as you complete this exercise.

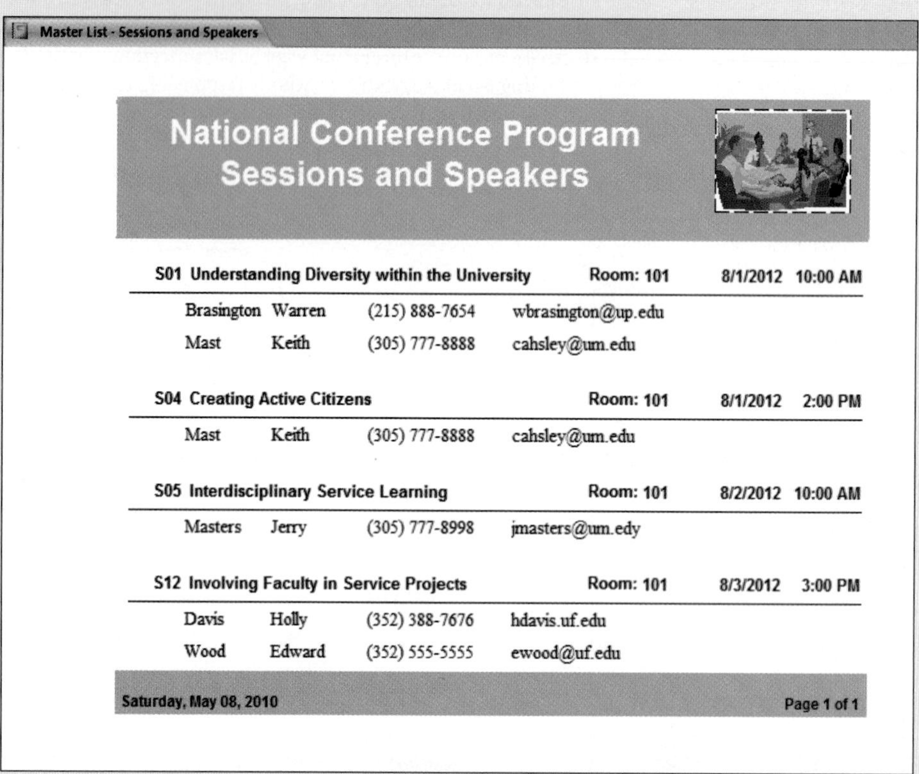

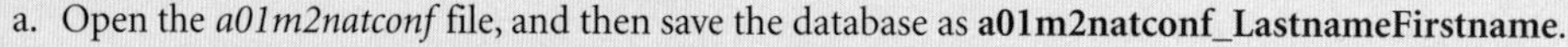

FIGURE 33 Sessions and Speakers Report—Room 101 ➤

a. Open the *a01m2natconf* file, and then save the database as **a01m2natconf_LastnameFirstname**.
b. Open the Relationships window.
c. Review the objects in the database to see if any of the existing objects will provide the room itinerary information described above.

DISCOVER 

d. Open the SessionSpeaker table. Scroll to the first blank record at the bottom of the table, and then enter a new record using SpeakerID: **99** and SessionID: **09**. (Note: speaker 99 does not exist.) How does Access respond? Press **Esc**. Close the SessionSpeaker table. In the Relationships window, right-click on the join line between the Speakers table and SessionSpeaker table, and then click **Delete**. Click **Yes**, and then close the Relationships window. Open the SessionSpeaker table, and then enter the same record again. How does Access respond this time? Close the SessionSpeaker table. Open the Speakers table. Find and replace *YourName* with your name. Close the Speakers table.
e. Open the Speaker - Session Query query, and then apply a filter to identify the sessions where you or Holly Davis are the speakers. Use **Filter by Form** and the **Or tab**.
f. Sort the filtered results in ascending order by the RoomID field.
g. Save and close the query.
h. Open the Master List – Sessions and Speakers report in Report view.
i. Apply a filter that limits the report to sessions in Room 101 only.
j. Click the **File tab**, click **Print**, and then click **Print Preview**.
k. Click **Close Print Preview** in the Close Preview group.
l. Close the report.
m. Compact and repair the database.
n. Back up the database. Use the default backup file name.
o. Exit Access (and save the relationships layout when asked).
p. Submit based on your instructor's directions.

CAPSTONE EXERCISE

Your boss expressed a concern about the accuracy of the inventory reports in the bookstore. He needs you to open the inventory database, make modifications to some records, and determine if the changes you make carry through to the other objects in the database. You will make changes to a form and then verify those changes in a table, a query, and a report. When you have verified that the changes update automatically, you will compact and repair the database and make a backup of it.

Database File Setup

You will open an original database file, and then save the database with a new name. Use the new database to replace an existing employee's name with your name, examine the table relationships, and then complete the remainder of this exercise.

a. Open the *a01c1books* file, and then save the database as **a01c1books_LastnameFirstname**.

b. Open the Maintain Authors form.

c. Navigate to Record 7, and then replace *YourName* with your name.

d. Add a new Title: **Technology in Action**. The ISBN is **0-13-148905-4**, the PubID is **PH**, the PublDate is **2006**, the Price is **$89.95** (just type 89.95, no $), and StockAmt is **95** units.

e. Move to any other record to save the new record. The pencil that appeared in the record selector box on the left while you were typing has now disappeared. Close the form.

f. Open the Maintain Authors form again, and then navigate to Record 7. The changes are there because Access works from storage, not memory. Close the form.

Sort a Query and Apply a Filter by Selection

You need to reorder a detail query so that the results are sorted alphabetically by the publisher name.

a. Open the Publishers, Books, and Authors query.

b. Click in any record in the PubName column, and then sort the field in ascending order.

c. Check to make sure that three books list you as the author.

d. Click your name in the Author's Last Name field, and then filter the records to show only your books.

e. Close the query and save the changes.

View a Report

You need to examine the *Publishers, Books, and Authors* report to determine if the changes you made in the Maintain Authors form appear in the report.

a. Open the Publishers, Books, and Authors report.

b. Check to make sure that the report shows three books listing you as the author.

c. Check the layout of the report in Print Preview.

d. Close the report.

Filter a Table

You need to examine the Books table to determine if the changes you made in the Maintain Authors form carried through to the related table. You also will filter the table to display books published after 2006 with fewer than 100 copies in inventory.

a. Open the Books table.

b. Create a filter that will identify all books published after 2006 with fewer than 100 items in stock.

c. Apply the filter.

d. Preview the filtered table.

e. Close the table and save the changes.

Compact and Repair a Database, Back Up a Database

Now that you are satisfied that any changes made to a form or query carry through to the table, you are ready to compact, repair, and back up your file.

a. Compact and repair your database.

b. Create a backup copy of your database, accept the default file name, and save it.

c. Exit Access.

d. Submit based on your instructor's directions.

Applying Filters, Printing, and File Management

GENERAL CASE 

The *a01b1bank* file contains data from a small bank. Open the *a01b1bank* file, and then save the database as **a01b1bank_LastnameFirstname**. Check the table relationships by opening the Relationships window, and then close the window. Use the skills from this chapter to perform several tasks. Open the Customer table, and sort the data in ascending order by LastName. Open the Branch table and make yourself the manager of the Western branch. Remove the Field1 field from the table design. Close the Branch table. Open the Branch Customers query and filter it to show only the accounts at the Campus branch with balances less than $2,000.00. Display the filtered query results in print preview. Close and save the query. Compact, repair, and back up your database, and then exit Access.

Filtering a Report

RESEARCH CASE 

Open the *a01b2nwind* file, and then save the database as **a01b2nwind_LastnameFirstname**. Open the Employees table and replace *YourName* with your first and last names. Before you can filter the Revenue report, you need to update the criterion in the underlying query to match the dates in the database. Right-click the Revenue query in the Navigation Pane, and then click Design View in the shortcut list. Scroll to the right until you see *Between #1/1/2007# And #3/31/2007#* in the OrderDate criteria row. Change the criterion to **Between #1/1/2012# And #3/31/2012#**. Save and close the query. Open the Revenue report. Use the tools that you have learned in this chapter to filter the report for only your sales of Confections. Close the report. Compact, repair, and back up your database, and then exit Access.

Coffee Revenue Queries

DISASTER RECOVERY 

A coworker called you into his office, explained that he was having difficulty with Access 2010, and asked you to look at his work. Open the *a01b3recover* file, and then save the database as **a01b3recover_LastnameFirstname**. Open the Relationships window, review the table relationships, and then close the window. Your coworker explains that the 2012 Product Introduction Report report is incorrect. It shows that Sazcick is the sales representative for Coulter Office Supplies and the Little, Joiner, & Jones customers, when in fact they are your customers. First, replace *YourName* in the Sales Reps table. Next, find the source of the error and correct it. Preview the corrected report. Compact, repair, and back up your database, and then exit Access.

ACCESS

RELATIONAL DATABASES AND QUERIES

Designing Databases and Extracting Data

CASE STUDY | Bank Auditor Uncovers Mishandled Funds

Watch the
Set-up
Video
for this
Case Study!

During a year-end review, a bank auditor uncovers mishandled funds at Commonwealth Federal Bank, in Wilmington, Delaware. In order to analyze the data in more detail, the auditor asks you to create an Access database so he can enter the compromised accounts, the associated customers, and the involved employees. Once the new database is created and all the data is entered, you will help the auditor answer questions by creating and running queries.

As you begin, you realize that some of the data is contained in Excel spreadsheets. After discussing this with the auditor, you decide importing this data directly into the new database would be best. Importing from Excel into Access is commonplace and should work well. Importing will also help avoid errors that are associated with data entry. Once the Excel data has been imported, you will use queries to determine which data does not belong in the database. Unaffected records will be deleted.

This chapter introduces the Bank database case study to present the basic principles of table and query design. You will use tables and forms to input data, and you will create queries and reports to extract information from the database in a useful and organized way. The value of that information depends entirely on the quality of the underlying data—the tables.

OBJECTIVES

AFTER YOU READ THIS CHAPTER, YOU WILL BE ABLE TO:

1. Design data
2. Create tables
3. Understand table relationships
4. Share data with Excel
5. Establish table relationships
6. Create a single-table query
7. Specify criteria for different data types
8. Copy and run a query
9. Use the Query Wizard
10. Create a multi-table query
11. Modify a multi-table query

Table Design, Properties, Views, and Wizards

Good database design begins with the tables. Tables provide the framework for all of the activities you perform in a database. If the framework is poorly designed, the rest of the database will be poorly designed as well. Whether you are experienced in designing tables or just learning how, the process should not be done haphazardly. You should follow a systematic approach when creating tables for a database. This process will take practice; however, over time you will begin to see the patterns and eventually see the similarities among all databases.

In this section, you will learn the principles of table design and the other essential guidelines used when creating tables. After developing and testing the table design on paper, you will implement that design in Access. The first step is to list all the tables you need for the database and then list all the fields in each table. When you create the tables in Access, you will refine them further by changing the properties of various fields. You will also be introduced to the concept of data validation. You want to make sure the data entered into the database is valid for the field and valid for the organization. Allowing invalid data into the tables will only cause problems later.

Designing Data

Most likely you have a bank account and you know that your bank or credit union maintains data about you. Your bank has your name, address, phone number, and Social Security number. It also knows what accounts you have (checking, savings, money market), if you have a credit card with that bank, and what its balance is. Additionally, your bank keeps information about its branches. If you think about the data your bank maintains, you could make a list of the categories of data needed to store that information. These categories for the bank—customers, accounts, branches—become the tables in the bank's database. Previously, we defined a table as a collection of records. In this chapter, we expand on the definition—a ***table*** is a storage location in a database that holds related information. A table consists of records, and each record is made up of a number of fields. A bank's customer list is an example of a table: It contains a record for each bank customer, and each customer's details are contained in fields such as first and last name, street, city, state, and zip code. Figure 1 shows a customer table and two other tables found in a sample bank database.

A **table** is a storage location in a database that holds related information. A table consists of records, and each record is made up of a number of fields.

During the design process, it will help if you consider the output required for the database. Looking at the output will help determine the tables and fields needed to produce that output. Think of the specific fields you need in each table; list the fields under the correct table and assign each field a data type (such as text, number, or date) as well as its size (length) or format. The order of the fields within the table and the specific field names are not significant. What is important is that the tables contain all necessary fields so that the system can produce the required information.

Customers Table
- CustomerID
- FirstName
- LastName
- Street
- City
- State
- Zip
- Phone

Accounts Table
- AccountID
- CustomerID
- BranchID
- OpenDate

Branch Table
- BranchID
- Manager
- Location
- StartDate

FIGURE 1 Tables and Fields in a Sample Bank Database ➤

Figure 1 shows the tables and fields needed in a sample bank database. After the tables have been identified, add the necessary fields using these six guidelines:

1. Include the necessary data.
2. Design for now and the future.
3. Store data in its smallest parts.
4. Add calculated fields to a table.
5. Design to accommodate date arithmetic.
6. Link tables using common fields.

Include the Necessary Data

...ask yourself what information will be expected from the database, and then determine the data required to produce that information.

A good way to determine what data is necessary in the tables is to create a rough draft of the reports you will need and then to design tables that contain the fields necessary to create those reports. In other words, ask yourself what information will be expected from the system, and then determine the data required to produce that information. Consider, for example, the tables and fields in Figure 1. Is there required information that could not be generated from those tables?

- You can determine which branch a customer uses.
- You cannot, however, generate the monthly bank statement. In order to generate a customer bank statement (showing all deposits and withdrawals for the month), you would need to add an additional table—the Account Activity table.
- You can determine who manages a particular branch and which accounts are located there.
- You can determine how long a customer has banked with the branch because the date he or she opened the account is stored in the Accounts table.

If you discover a missing field, you can insert a row anywhere in the appropriate table and add the missing field. The databases found in a real bank are more complex, with more tables and more fields; however, the concepts illustrated here apply to both our sample bank database and to real bank databases.

Design for Now and the Future

As the data requirements of an organization evolve over time, the information systems that hold the data must change as well. When designing a database, try to anticipate the future needs of the system, and then build in the flexibility to satisfy those demands. For example, when you add a text field, make sure that the number of characters allocated is sufficient to accommodate future expansion. On the other hand, if you include all the possible fields that anyone might ever need, you could drive up the cost of the database. Each additional field can increase the cost of the database, since it will require additional employee time to enter and maintain the data. The additional fields will also require more storage space, which you will need to calculate, especially when working with larger databases. Good database design must balance the data collection needs of the company with the cost associated with collection and storage.

Good database design must balance the data collection needs of the company with the cost associated with collection and storage.

Suppose you are designing a database for a college. You would need to store each student's name, address, and phone number. You will need to store multiple phone numbers for most students—a cell phone number, a work number, and an emergency number. As a database designer, you will need to design the tables to accommodate multiple entries for similar data.

Store Data in Its Smallest Parts

The table design in Figure 1 divides a customer's name into two fields (Firstname and Lastname) to reference each field individually. You might think it easier to use a single field consisting of both the first and last name, but that approach is too limiting. Consider a list of customers stored as a single field:

- Sue Grater
- Rick Grater
- Nancy Gallagher
- Harry Weigner
- Barb Shank
- Pete Shank

The first problem in this approach is the lack of flexibility: You could not easily create a salutation for a letter of the form *Dear Sue* or *Dear Ms. Gallagher* because the first and last names are not accessible individually.

A second difficulty is that the list of customers cannot be easily displayed in alphabetical order by last name because the last name begins in the middle of the field. The names could easily be alphabetized by first name because the first name is at the beginning of the field. However, the most common way to sort names is by the last name, which can be done more efficiently if the last name is stored as a separate field.

Think of how an address might be used. The city, state, and postal code should always be stored as separate fields. Any type of mass mailing requires you to sort on postal codes to take advantage of bulk mail. Other applications may require you to select records from a particular state or postal code, which can be done more efficiently if you store the data as separate fields. Often database users enter the postal code, and the database automatically retrieves the city and state information. You may need to direct a mailing only to a neighborhood or to a single street. The guideline is simple: Store data in its smallest parts.

Add Calculated Fields to a Table

A **calculated field** produces a value from an expression or function that references one or more existing fields.

A ***calculated field*** produces a value from an expression or function that references one or more existing fields. Access 2010 enables you to store calculated fields in a table using the calculated data type. An example of a calculated field can be found in the bank database. Suppose the bank pays its customers 1.0% interest on the principal each month. A calculated field, such as Monthly Interest, could store the expression Principal x .01. The interest amount would then appear on the customer's monthly bank statement.

Previous versions of Access did not have the option of adding a calculated field to a table. Calculated fields were not available because they do not adhere to conventional database design principles. Database design principles avoid storing data that can be derived from other data. The Monthly Interest field mentioned above can be derived from the product of Principal x .01; therefore, you would not need to store the Monthly Interest value.

The new calculated field* can be very useful in certain circumstances, like a Monthly Interest field. Storing calculated data in a table enables you to add the data easily to queries, forms, and reports without the trouble of an additional calculation. Storing calculated data in a table may increase the size of the database slightly, but the benefits may outweigh this drawback.

Design to Accommodate Date Arithmetic

Calculated fields are frequently created with numeric data, as the Monthly Interest field example above illustrates. You can also create calculated fields using date/time data. If you want to store the length of time a customer has been a customer, you would first create a field to hold the start date for each customer. Next, you would create a calculated field that contains an expression that subtracts the start date from today's date. The resulting calculation would store the number of days each customer has been a customer. Divide the results by 365 to convert days to years.

This same concept applies to bank accounts; a bank is likely to store the Open Date for each account in the Accounts table, as shown in Figure 1. Using this date, you can subtract the open date from today's date and calculate the number of days the account has been open. (Again, divide the results by 365 to convert to years.) If you open the Accounts table at least one day later, the results of the calculated field will be different.

A **constant** is an unchanging value, like a birth date.

Date arithmetic is the process of subtracting one date from another, or adding or subtracting a constant from a date.

A person's age is another example of a calculated field using date arithmetic—date of birth is subtracted from today's date and the results are divided by 365. It might seem easier to store a person's age rather than the birth date to avoid the calculation. But that would be a mistake because age changes over time and would need to be updated each time age changes. Storing the date of birth is much better since the data remains ***constant***. You can use ***date arithmetic*** to subtract one date from another to find out the number of days, months, or years that have lapsed between them. You can also add or subtract a constant from a date.

Link Tables Using Common Fields

As you create the tables and fields for the database, keep in mind that the tables will be joined in relationships using common fields. Draw a line between common fields to indicate the joins, as shown in Figure 2. These join lines will be created in Access when you learn to create table relationships later in the chapter. For now, you should name the common fields the same and make sure they have the same data type. For example, CustomerID in the Customers table will join to the CustomerID field in the Accounts table. CustomerID must have the same data type (in this case number/long integer) in both tables; otherwise, the join line will not be allowed.

Data redundancy is the unnecessary storing of duplicate data in two or more tables.

Avoid ***data redundancy***, which is the unnecessary storing of duplicate data in two or more tables. You should avoid duplicate information in multiple tables in a database, because errors may result. Suppose the customer address data was stored in both the

*If you add a calculated field to a table in Access 2010, you will not be able to open the table using Access 2007.

Customers and Accounts tables. If a customer moved to a new address, a possible outcome would be that the address would be updated in only one of the two tables. The result would be unreliable data. Depending on which table served as the source for the output, either the new or the old address might be given to the person requesting the information. Storing the address in only one table is more reliable.

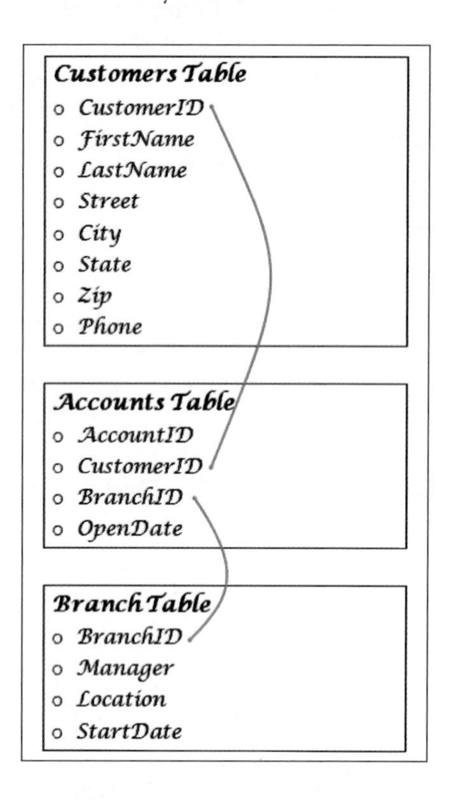

FIGURE 2 Create Relationships Using Common Fields ➤

Creating Tables

Before you can begin creating your tables, you must first create a new blank database and save it to a specific storage location. If you are creating tables in an existing database, you open the existing database and then create new tables or modify existing ones.

Access provides several ways to create a table. You can create a table by creating the fields in Design view (as shown in Figure 3) or by entering table data into a new row in Datasheet view, or you can import data from another database or application such as Excel. Regardless of how a table is first created, you can always modify it later to include a new field or to change an existing field.

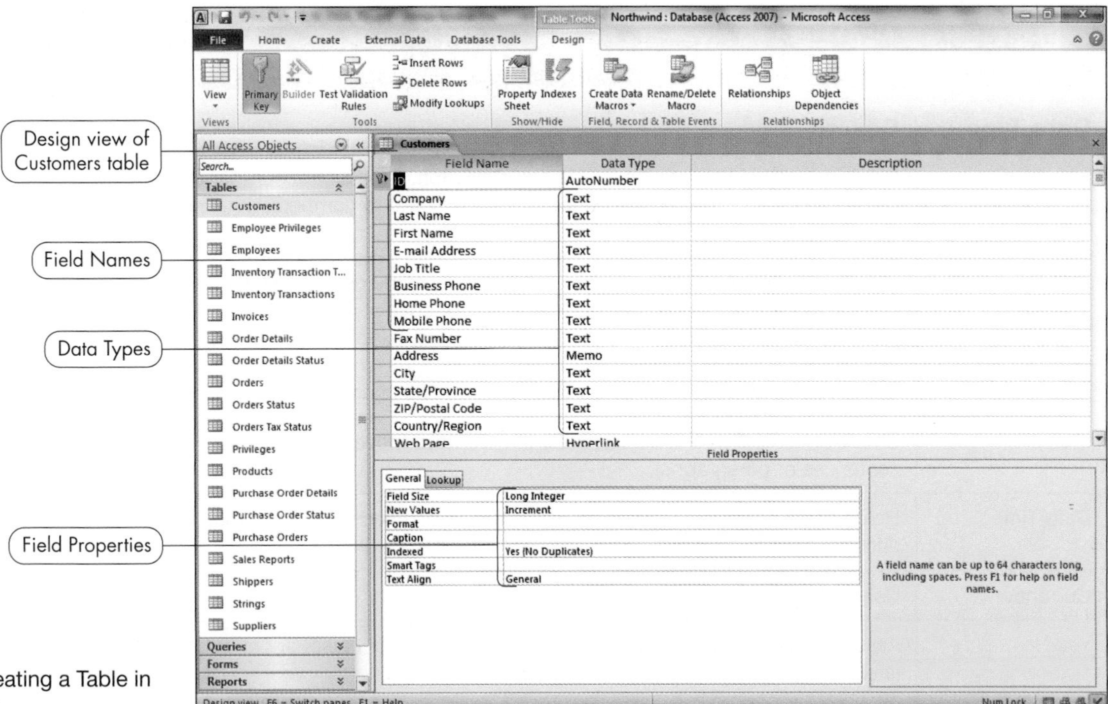

FIGURE 3 Creating a Table in Design View ➤

CamelCase notation uses no spaces in multi-word field names, but uses uppercase letters to distinguish the first letter of each new word.

The **data type** determines the type of data that can be entered and the operations that can be performed on that data.

Each field in a table has a field name to identify the data that it holds. The field name should be descriptive of the data and can be up to 64 characters in length, including letters, numbers, and spaces. Database developers use ***CamelCase notation*** for field names, object names, and filenames. Instead of spaces in multi-word field names, use uppercase letters to distinguish the first letter of each new word, for example, ProductCost or LastName. It is best to avoid spaces in field names, since spaces can cause problems when creating the other objects based on tables—such as queries, forms, and reports.

Every field also has a ***data type*** that determines the type of data that can be entered and the operations that can be performed on that data. Access recognizes 10 data types.

Establish a Primary Key

As you learned earlier, the primary key is the field (or combination of fields) that uniquely identifies each record in a table. Access does not require that each table have a primary key. However, good database design usually includes a primary key in each table. You should select unique and infrequently changing data for the primary key. For example, a complete address (street, city, state, and postal code) may be unique but would not make a good primary key because it is subject to change when someone moves.

You probably would not use a person's name as the primary key, because several people could have the same name. A customer's account number, on the other hand, is unique and is a frequent choice for the primary key, as in the Customers table in this chapter. The primary key can be easily identified in many tables; for example, a PartNumber in a parts table, the ISBN in the book database of a bookstore, or a Student ID that uniquely identifies a student. When no primary key occurs naturally, you can create a primary key field with the AutoNumber data type. The ***AutoNumber*** data type is a number that automatically increments each time a record is added.

The **AutoNumber** data type is a number that automatically increments each time a record is added.

REFERENCE Data Types and Uses

Data Type	Description	Example
Number	Contains a value that can be used in a calculation, such as the number of credits a course is worth. The contents are restricted to numbers, a decimal point, and a plus or minus sign.	Credits
Text	Stores alphanumeric data, such as a customer's name or address. It can contain alphabetic characters, numbers, and/or special characters (i.e., an apostrophe in O'Malley). Social Security Numbers, telephone numbers, and postal codes should be designated as text fields since they are not used in calculations. A text field can hold up to 255 characters.	Last name
Memo	Stores up to 65,536 characters; used to hold descriptive data (several sentences or paragraphs).	Notes or comments
Date/Time	Holds dates or times and enables the values to be used in date or time arithmetic.	10/31/2012
Currency	Used for fields that contain monetary values.	Account balance
Yes/No	Assumes one of two values, such as Yes or No, True or False, or On or Off (also known as a Boolean).	Dean's list
OLE	Contains an object created by another application. OLE objects include spreadsheets, pictures, sounds, or graphics.	One photo
AutoNumber	A special data type used to assign the next consecutive number each time you add a record. The value of an AutoNumber field is unique for each record in the file.	Customer ID
Hyperlink	Stores a Web address (URL) or the path to a folder or file. Hyperlink fields can be clicked to retrieve a Web page or to launch a file stored locally.	http://www.keithmast.com
Attachment	Used to store multiple images, spreadsheet files, Word documents, and other types of supported files.	An Excel workbook; a photo
Calculated	The results of an expression that references one or more existing fields.	[IntRate] + 0.25

In Figure 4, the book's ISBN is the natural primary key for the book table because no two book titles can have the same ISBN. This field uniquely identifies the records in the table. Figure 5 depicts the Speakers table, where no unique field can be identified from the data. When this happens, you can add the SpeakerID field with an AutoNumber data type. Access will automatically number each speaker record sequentially with a unique ID as each record is added.

ISBN provides a unique identifier

AuthorCode	Title	ISBN	PubID	PublDate	Price	StockAmt
15	Chasing the Dime	0-316-15391-5	LBC	2002	$51.75	400
13	Blackhills Farm	0-275-41199-7	KN	2002	$18.87	528
13	Blood and Gold	0-679-45449-7	KN	2001	$18.87	640
11	Reaching for Glory	0-684-80408-5	SS	2001	$24.00	480
14	From a Buick 8	0-743-21137-5	SS	2002	$16.80	368
15	City of Bones	0-316-15405-9	LBC	2002	$20.76	394
16	Follow the Stars Home	0-553-58102-3	BB	2000	$6.99	496
14	Hearts in Atlantis	0-684-85351-5	SS	1999	$28.00	528
12	Personality Injuries	0-742095692-X	FSG	1999	$27.00	403
15	Darkness More than Midnight	0-316-15407-5	LBC	2001	$20.76	432
13	Interview with the Vampire	0-394-49821-6	KN	1976	$19.57	371
16	True Blue	0-553-38398-0	BB	2002	$7.50	492

FIGURE 4 Books Table with a Natural Primary Key ➤

SpeakerID (AutoNumber data type) is the primary key

Next record will be assigned SpeakerID 17

SpeakerID	First Name	Last Name	Address	City	Sta	Zip Co	Phone Number	Email
1	YourName	YourName	10000 SW 59 Court	Miami	FL	33146	(305) 777-8888	cahsley@um.edu
2	Warren	Brasington	9470 SW 25 Street	Philadelphia	PA	19104	(215) 888-7654	wbrasington@up.edu
3	James	Shindell	14088 Malaga Avenue	Miami	FL	33146	(305) 773-4343	jshindell@um.edu
4	Edward	Wood	400 Roderigo Avenue	Gainesville	FL	32611	(352) 555-5555	ewood@uf.edu
5	Kristine	Park	9290 NW 59 Steet	Athens	GA	30602	(706) 777-1111	kpark@ug.edu
6	William	Williamson	108 Los Pinos Place	Tuscaloosa	AL	35487	(205) 888-4554	wwilliamson@ua.edu
7	Holly	Davis	8009 Riviera Drive	Gainesville	FL	32611	(352) 388-7676	hdavis.uf.edu
8	David	Tannen	50 Main Street	Philadelphia	PA	19104	(215) 777-2211	dtannen@up.edu
9	Jeffrey	Jacobsen	490 Bell Drive	Athens	GA	30602	(706) 388-9999	jjacobsen@ug.edu
10	Jerry	Masters	2000 Main Highway	Miami	FL	33146	(305) 777-8998	jmasters@um.edy
11	Kevin	Kline	2980 SW 89 Street	Gainesville	FL	32611	(352) 877-8900	kkline@uf.edu
12	Jessica	Withers	110 Center Highway	Athens	GA	30602	(706) 893-8872	jwithers@ug.edu
13	Betsy	Allman	2987 SW 14 Avenue	Philadelphia	PA	19104	(215) 558-7748	ballman@up.edu
14	Mary	Miller	1008 West Marine Road	Miami	FL	33146	(305) 877-4993	mmiller@um.edu
15	Nancy	Vance	1878 W. 6 Street	Gainesville	FL	32611	(352) 885-4330	nvance@uf.edu
16	George	Jensen	42-15 81 Street	Elmhurst	NY	11373	(718) 555-6666	gjensen@school.edu
(New)								

FIGURE 5 Speakers Table with an AutoNumber Primary Key ➤

Explore Foreign Key

A foreign key, as defined earlier, is a field in one table that is also the primary key of another table. The CustomerID is the primary key in the Customers table. It serves to uniquely identify each customer. It also appears as a foreign key in a related table. For example, the Accounts table contains the CustomerID field to establish which customer owns the account. A CustomerID can appear only once in the Customers table, but it may appear multiple times in the Accounts table (when viewed in Datasheet view) since one customer may own multiple accounts (checking, money market, home equity).

If you were asked to create an Access database for the speakers at a national conference, you would create a database with the tables Speakers and SessionSpeaker. You would add a primary key field to the Speakers table (SpeakerID) along with the speaker's First Name and Last Name; you would add two fields to the SessionSpeaker table (SpeakerID and SessionID). The SpeakerID in the SessionSpeaker table enables you to join the two tables in a relationship. The SpeakerID field in the SessionSpeaker table is an example of a foreign key. Figure 6 shows portions of the Speakers and SessionSpeaker tables.

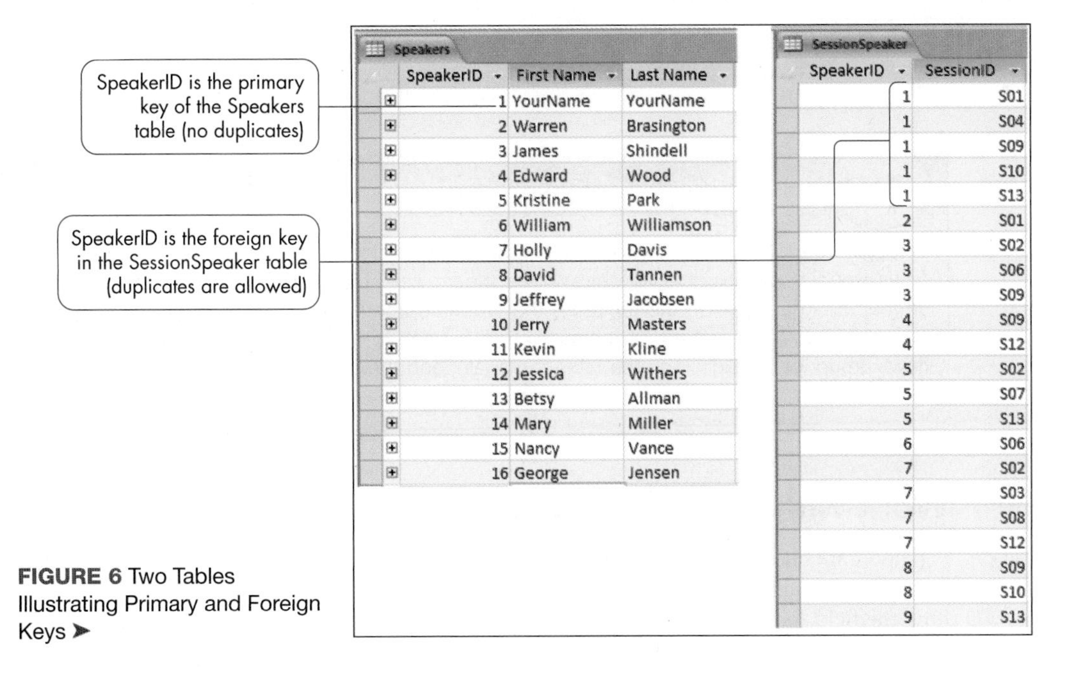
SpeakerID is the primary key of the Speakers table (no duplicates)
SpeakerID is the foreign key in the SessionSpeaker table (duplicates are allowed)
Speakers
SessionSpeaker

SpeakerID	First Name	Last Name
1	YourName	YourName
2	Warren	Brasington
3	James	Shindell
4	Edward	Wood
5	Kristine	Park
6	William	Williamson
7	Holly	Davis
8	David	Tannen
9	Jeffrey	Jacobsen
10	Jerry	Masters
11	Kevin	Kline
12	Jessica	Withers
13	Betsy	Allman
14	Mary	Miller
15	Nancy	Vance
16	George	Jensen

SpeakerID	SessionID
1	S01
1	S04
1	S09
1	S10
1	S13
2	S01
3	S02
3	S06
3	S09
4	S09
4	S12
5	S02
5	S07
5	S13
6	S06
7	S02
7	S03
7	S08
7	S12
8	S09
8	S10
9	S13

FIGURE 6 Two Tables Illustrating Primary and Foreign Keys ➤

Use Table Views

As defined earlier, users can work in Datasheet view to add, edit, and delete records. The Datasheet view of an Access table resembles an Excel spreadsheet and displays data in a grid format—rows represent records, and columns represent fields. Datasheet view indicates the current record using a gold border; you can select a record by clicking the record selector on the left side of each record, as shown in Figure 7. Use the new blank record (marked with an asterisk) at the end of the table to add a new record. Design view is used to create and modify the table structure by adding and editing fields and by setting the field properties.

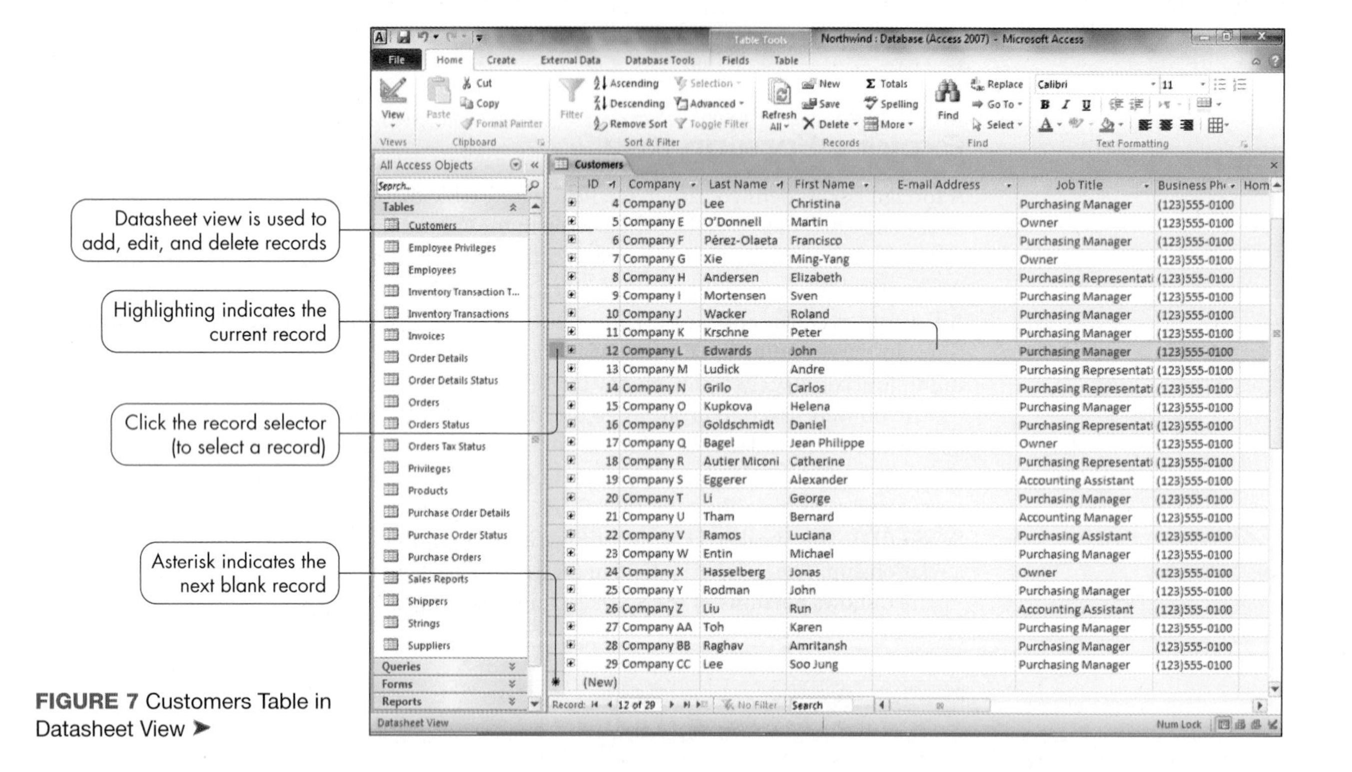
Datasheet view is used to add, edit, and delete records
Highlighting indicates the current record
Click the record selector (to select a record)
Asterisk indicates the next blank record
Northwind : Database (Access 2007) - Microsoft Access
All Access Objects
Customers

FIGURE 7 Customers Table in Datasheet View ➤

> **TIP** Toggle Between Datasheet and Design Views
>
> To toggle from Datasheet view to Design view, click the Home tab, and then click View in the Views group. If you click the view arrow by accident, select the view you want from the menu. Or you can right-click on the table tab that appears above the datasheet and then choose Design View from the shortcut menu. To toggle back to Datasheet view, click View in the Views group, or right-click on the table tab again, and then choose Datasheet View from the shortcut menu.

Work with Field Properties

A **field property** is a characteristic of a field that determines how the field looks and behaves.

A **text data type** can store either text or numerical characters.

A field's data type determines the type of data that can be entered and the operations that can be performed on that data. A ***field property*** is a characteristic of a field that determines how the field looks and behaves. (The reference table on the following page lists the field properties for a typical field.)

A field with a ***text data type*** can store either text or numerical characters. A text field can hold up to 255 characters; however, you can limit the characters by reducing the field size

A **number data type** can store only numerical data.

A **caption property** is used to create a more readable label that appears in the top row in Datasheet view and in forms and reports.

A **validation rule** prevents invalid data from being entered into the field.

property. For example, you would limit the State field to only two characters since all state abbreviations are two letters. A field with a ***number data type*** can store only numerical data. Set the Format field property to Integer to display the field contents as integers from –32768 to 32768. Set the Format field property to Long Integer for larger values.

You can use the ***caption property*** to create a more readable label that appears in the top row in Datasheet view and in forms and reports. For example, a field named ProductCostPerUnit could have the caption *Per Unit Product Cost.* The caption displays at the top of a table or query column in Datasheet view and when the field is used in a report or form. You must use the actual field name, ProductCostPerUnit, in any calculation.

Set the validation rule property to restrict data entry in a field to ensure the correct type of data is entered or that the data does not violate other enforced properties. The ***validation rule*** checks the data entered when the user exits the field. If the data entered violates the validation rule, an error message appears and prevents the invalid data from being entered into the field.

The field properties are set to default values according to the data type, but you can modify them if necessary. The property types are defined in the following Reference table.

In Hands-On Exercise 1, you will create a new database and enter data into a table. Then you will switch to the table's Design view to add additional fields and modify selected field properties of various fields within the table.

REFERENCE Access Table Property Types and Descriptions

Property Type	Description
Field Size	Determines the maximum characters of a text field or the format of a number field.
Format	Changes the way a field is displayed or printed, but does not affect the stored value.
Input Mask	Simplifies data entry by providing literal characters that are typed for every entry, such as hyphens in a Social Security Number or slashes in a date. It also imposes data validation by ensuring that data entered conforms to the mask.
Caption	This enables an alternate name to be displayed other than the field name; alternate names appear in datasheets, forms, and reports.
Default Value	This option automatically enters a predetermined value for a field each time a new record is added to the table. For example, if most of your customers live in Los Angeles, you might consider setting the default value for the City to Los Angeles to save data entry time.
Validation Rule	Requires the data entered to conform to the specified rule.
Validation Text	Specifies the error message that is displayed when the validation rule is violated.
Required	Indicates that a value for this field must be entered.
Allow Zero Length	Enables text or memo strings of zero length.
Indexed	Increases the efficiency of a search on the designated field.
Expression	Used for calculated fields only. Enter the expression you want Access to evaluate and store.
Result Type	Used for calculated fields only. Enter the format for the calculated field results.

HANDS-ON EXERCISES

1 Table Design, Properties, Views, and Wizards

Assisting the bank auditor at Commonwealth Federal Bank as he investigates the mishandled funds will be a great opportunity for you to showcase your Access skills. Be sure to check your work each step of the way since your work will come under substantial scrutiny. Do a good job with this Access project and more opportunities might come your way, along with a promotion.

Skills covered: Create a New Database • Create a Table by Entering Data • Change the Primary Key, Modify Field Properties, and Delete a Field • Modify Table Fields in Design View • Create a New Field in Design View • Switch Between the Table Design and the Table Datasheet Views

STEP 1 CREATE A NEW DATABASE

To start a new Access database project, you first need to create a new database. Use the Access interface to create a new file for the mishandled funds database. Refer to Figure 8 as you complete Step 1.

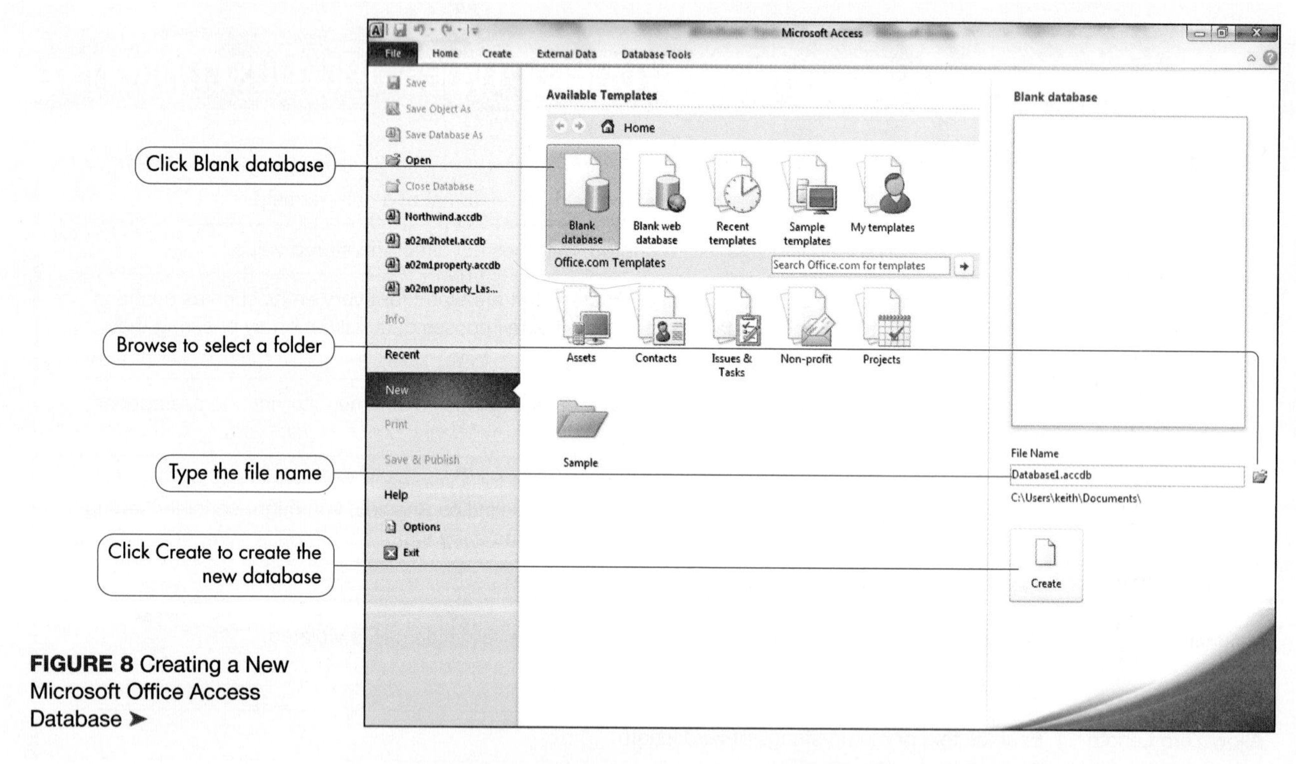

FIGURE 8 Creating a New Microsoft Office Access Database ➤

a. Start Microsoft Access.

You will see the Backstage view with New selected by default.

b. Click **Blank database** in the Available Templates section of the Backstage view.

c. Type **a02h1bank_LastnameFirstname** into the **File Name box.**

d. Click **Browse**—the yellow folder icon—to find the folder location designated by your instructor, and then click **OK.**

e. Click **Create** to create the new database.

Access will create the new database named *a02h1bank_LastnameFirstname*, and a new table will automatically appear in Datasheet view.

TROUBLESHOOTING: If you have a problem finding your file, use the Windows search tool to locate the file.

STEP 2 CREATE A TABLE BY ENTERING DATA

Create a new Branch table and enter the branch data as instructed. Only branches with suspicious data will be added. Refer to Figure 9 as you complete Step 2.

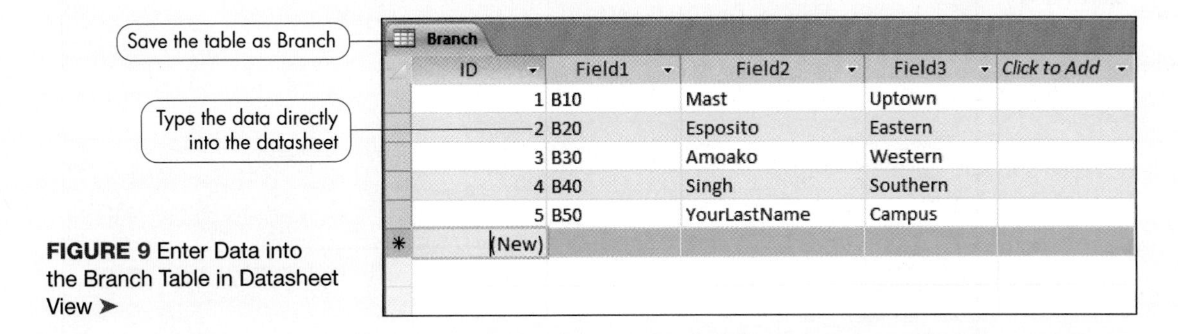

FIGURE 9 Enter Data into the Branch Table in Datasheet View ➤

a. Type **B10** in the second column, and then click **Click to Add**.

   The column heading becomes Field1 and Click to Add now appears as the third column.

b. Type **Mast** in the third column, press **Tab**, and then type **Uptown** in the fourth column.

   You can advance to the next field by pressing Tab or move to the previous field by pressing Shift+Tab.

c. Press **Tab** three times. Type **B20**, press **Tab**, type **Esposito**, press **Tab**, and then type **Eastern**.

d. Enter the additional data for the new table as shown in Figure 9. Replace *YourLastName* with your last name.

e. Click **Save** on the Quick Access Toolbar. Type **Branch** in the **Save As dialog box**, and then click **OK**.

   Entering data provides an easy way to create the table initially. You can now modify the table in Design view as described in the next several steps.

STEP 3 CHANGE THE PRIMARY KEY, MODIFY FIELD PROPERTIES, AND DELETE A FIELD

It is common to modify tables even after data has been entered; however, pay attention to the messages from Access after you make a design change. In this example, you will be modifying the Branch table field names to match the auditor's requirements. Refer to Figure 10 as you complete Step 3.

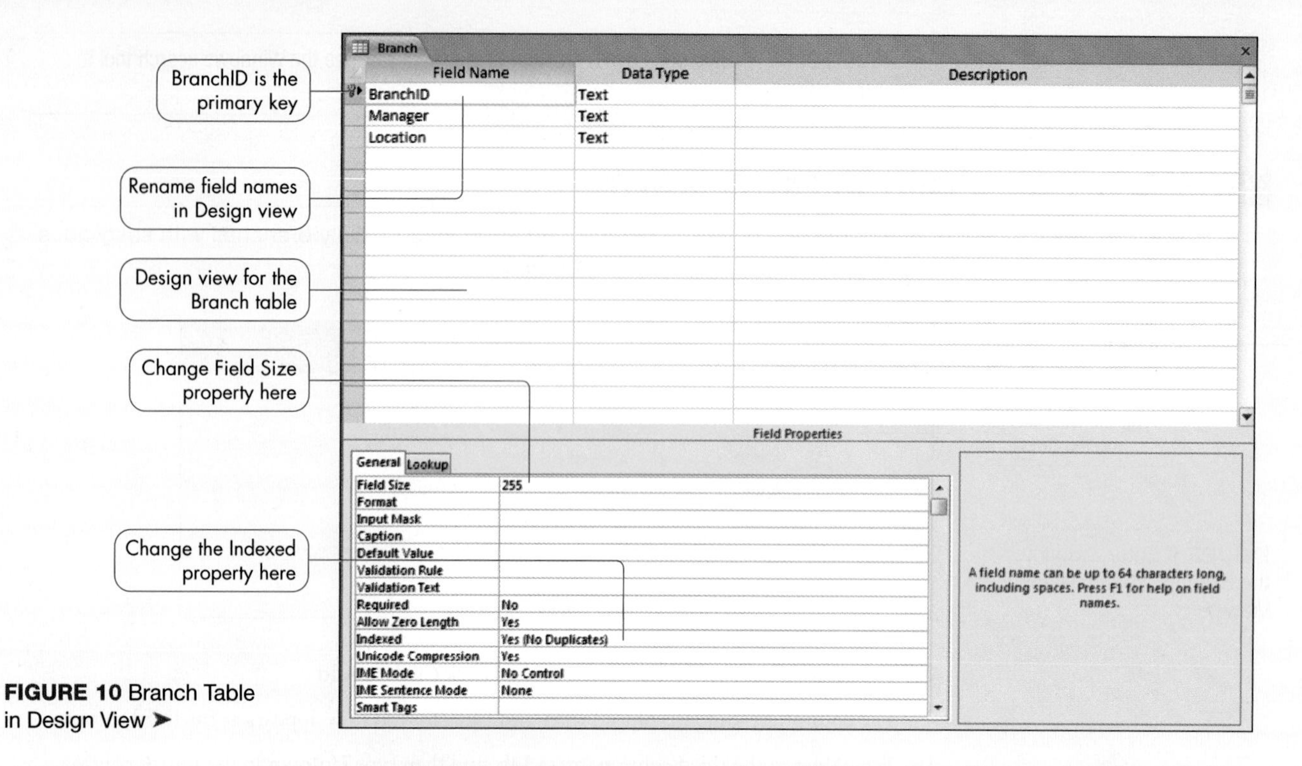

FIGURE 10 Branch Table in Design View ➤

a. Click **View** in the Views group to switch to the Design view of the Branch table.

   The fields are named ID, Field1, Field2, and Field3, because they are the default names given to the fields when you create the table in Datasheet view. These field names are not descriptive of the data, so you need to change Field1, Field2, and Field3 to BranchID, Manager, and Location, respectively. You will also delete the ID field.

b. Click the **ID field** to select it. Click **Delete Rows** in the Tools group. Click **Yes** to both warning messages.

   Access responds with a warning that you are about to permanently delete a field and a second warning that the field is the primary key. You delete the field since you will set a different field as the primary key.

c. Double-click the **Field1 field name** to select it, if necessary, and then type **BranchID**. Replace *Field2* with **Manager** and *Field3* with **Location**.

d. Click the **BranchID field.**

   The cell field name now has an orange border as shown in Figure 10.

e. Click **Primary Key** in the Tools group.

   You set BranchID as the primary key. The Indexed property in the *Field Properties* section at the bottom of the design window displays *Yes (No Duplicates)*.

f. Click **Save** to save the table.

You can right-click a row selector to display a shortcut menu to copy a field, set the primary key, and insert or delete rows. Use the shortcut menu to make these specific changes to the design of a table.

STEP 4 MODIFY TABLE FIELDS IN DESIGN VIEW

You need to modify the table design further to comply with the bank auditor's specifications. Be aware of messages from Access that indicate you may lose data. Refer to Figure 11 as you complete Step 4.

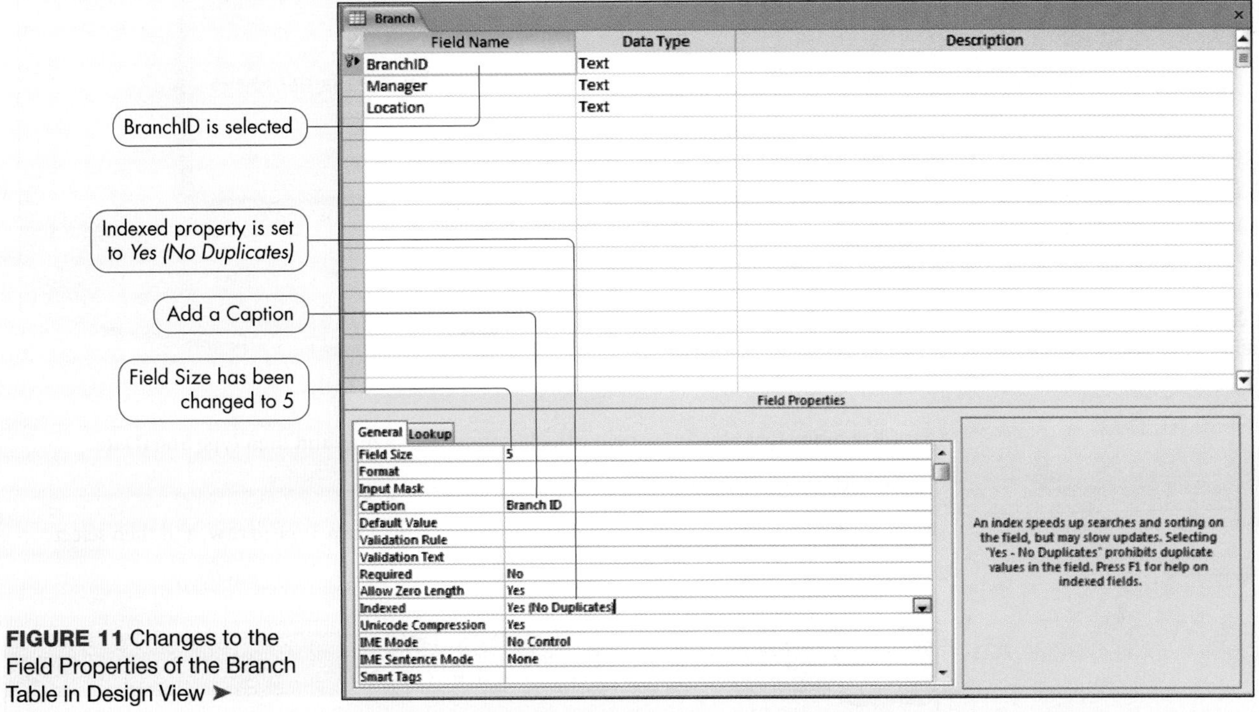

FIGURE 11 Changes to the Field Properties of the Branch Table in Design View ➤

a. Click the **BranchID field name** in the top section of the design window; modify the BranchID field properties in the bottom of the design window:

- Click in the **Field Size property**, and then change *255* to **5**.
- Click in the **Caption property**, and then type **Branch ID**. Make sure *Branch* and *ID* have a space between them.

  A caption provides a more descriptive field name. It will appear as the column heading in Datasheet view.
- Check the Indexed property; confirm it is *Yes (No Duplicates).*

b. Click the **Manager field name** at the top of the window; modify the following field properties:

- Change the **Field Size property** from *255* to **30.**
- Click in the **Caption property**, and then type **Manager's Name.**

c. Click the **Location field name,** and then modify the following field properties:

- Change the **Field Size property** from *255* to **30.**
- Click in the **Caption property**, and then type **Branch Location.**

STEP 5 CREATE A NEW FIELD IN DESIGN VIEW

You notify the auditor that a date field is missing in your new table. Modify the table and add the new field. The data can be entered at a later time. Refer to Figure 12 as you complete Step 5.

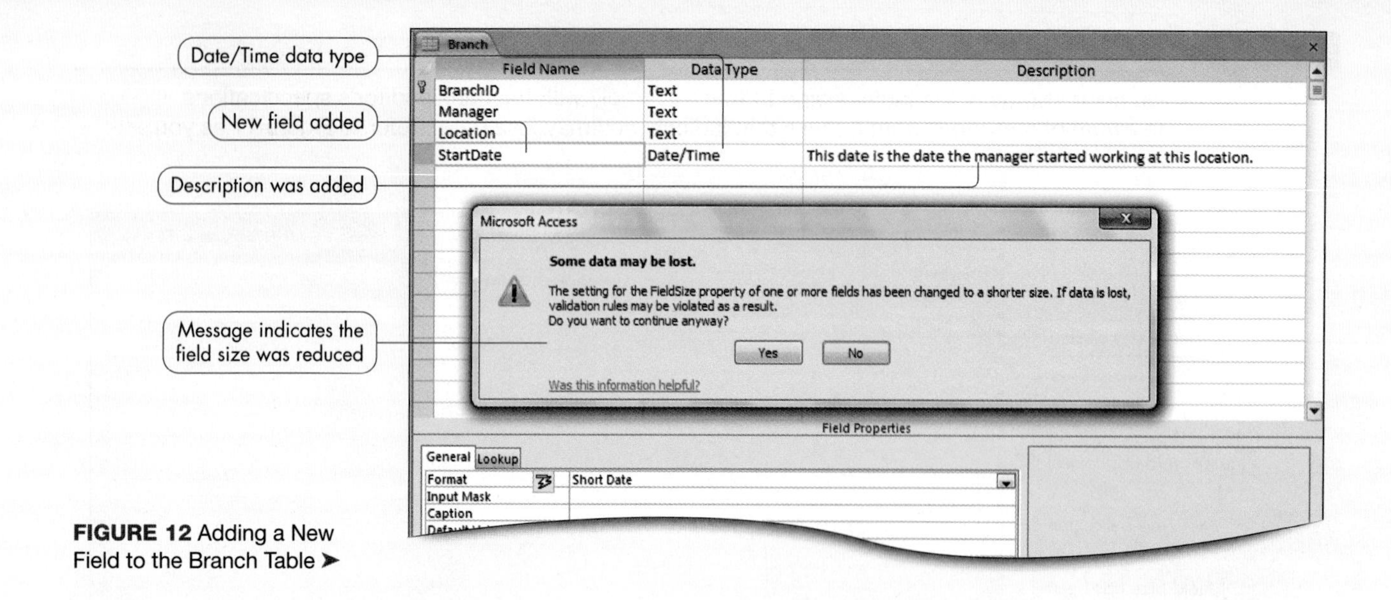

FIGURE 12 Adding a New Field to the Branch Table ➤

a. Click in the first blank row below the Location field name, and then type **StartDate**.

   You added a new field to the table.

b. Press **Tab** to move to the Data Type column. Click the **Data Type arrow**, and then select **Date/Time**.

> **TIP Keyboard Shortcut for Data Types**
>
> You also can type the first letter of the data type such as *d* for Date/Time, *t* for Text, or *n* for number. To use the keyboard shortcut, click on the field name, and then press Tab to advance to the Data Type column. Next, type the first letter of the data type.

c. Press **Tab** to move to the Description column, and then type **This is the date the manager started working at this location.**

d. Click in the **Format property**, click the arrow, and then select **Short Date** from the list of date formats.

e. Click in the **Caption property**, and then type **Manager's Start Date.**

f. Click **Save** on the Quick Access Toolbar to save the changes you made to the *a02h1bank_LastnameFirstname* database.

   A warning dialog box opens to indicate that "Some data may be lost" since the size of the BranchID, Manager, and Location field properties were shortened. It asks if you want to continue anyway. Always read the Access warnings! In this case, you can click Yes to continue. You changed the size of the BranchID field from 255 to 5 in Step 4a.

g. Click **Yes** in the warning box.

STEP 6 SWITCH BETWEEN THE TABLE DESIGN AND THE TABLE DATASHEET VIEWS

As you work with the auditor, you will need to modify tables in the bank database from time to time. To modify the table, you will need to switch between Design view and Datasheet view. Refer to Figure 13 as you complete Step 6.

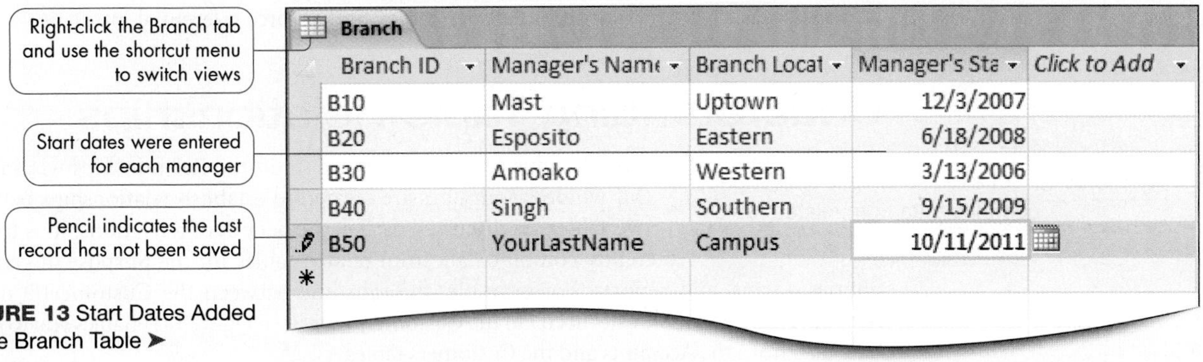

Right-click the Branch tab and use the shortcut menu to switch views

Start dates were entered for each manager

Pencil indicates the last record has not been saved

Branch

Branch ID	Manager's Name	Branch Locat	Manager's Sta	Click to Add
B10	Mast	Uptown	12/3/2007	
B20	Esposito	Eastern	6/18/2008	
B30	Amoako	Western	3/13/2006	
B40	Singh	Southern	9/15/2009	
B50	YourLastName	Campus	10/11/2011	
*				

FIGURE 13 Start Dates Added to the Branch Table ➤

a. Right-click the **Branch tab** shown in Figure 13, and then select **Datasheet View** from the shortcut menu. (To return to the Design view, right-click the tab again, and then select Design View.)

b. Click inside the **Manager's Start Date** in the first record, and then click the **Calendar**. Use the navigation arrows to find and select **December 3, 2007** from the calendar.

   You can also enter the dates by typing them directly into the StartDate field.

c. Type directly in each field the Start Date for the rest of the managers as shown in Figure 13.

d. Click the **Close button** at the top-right corner of the datasheet, below the Ribbon.

> **TROUBLESHOOTING:** If you accidentally click the Close button on top of the Ribbon, you will exit out of Access completely. To start again, launch Access, click the File tab, click Recent, and then select the first database from the recent documents list.

e. Double-click the **Branch table** in the Navigation Pane to open the table. Check the start dates.

   The start dates are still there even though you did not save your work in the previous step. Access saves the data to the hard drive as soon as you move off the current record (or close an object).

f. Click the **File tab**, click **Print**, and then click **Print Preview**.

   Occasionally, users will print an Access table. However, database developers usually create reports to print table data.

g. Click **Close Print Preview**. Close the Branch table.

h. Click the **File tab**, and then click **Compact & Repair Database** (the top button).

i. Click the **File tab**, click **Save & Publish**, and then double-click **Back Up Database** in the right column. Accept *a02h1bank_LastnameFirstname_date* as the file name, and then click **Save**.

   You created a backup of the database. The original database, *a02h1bank_LastnameFirstname*, remains open.

j. Keep the database onscreen if you plan to continue with Hands-On Exercise 2. If not, close the database and exit Access.

Multiple Table Databases

In Figure 1, the sample bank database contains three tables—Customers, Accounts, and Branch. You already created one table, the Branch table, in the previous section using the Datasheet view. The two remaining tables will be created using a different method—importing data from Excel. In this section, you will learn how to import data from Excel, modify tables, create indexes, create relationships between tables, and enforce referential integrity.

Understanding Table Relationships

The benefit of a relationship is to efficiently combine data from related tables.

Relationships between tables are set in the Relationships window. In this window, join lines are created to establish relationships between two tables. As discussed earlier, the benefit of a relationship is to efficiently combine data from related tables for the purpose of creating queries, forms, and reports. For example, the join line between the CustomerID in the Accounts table and the CustomerID in the Customers table (see Figure 14) enables you to combine data from the Accounts and the Customers tables.

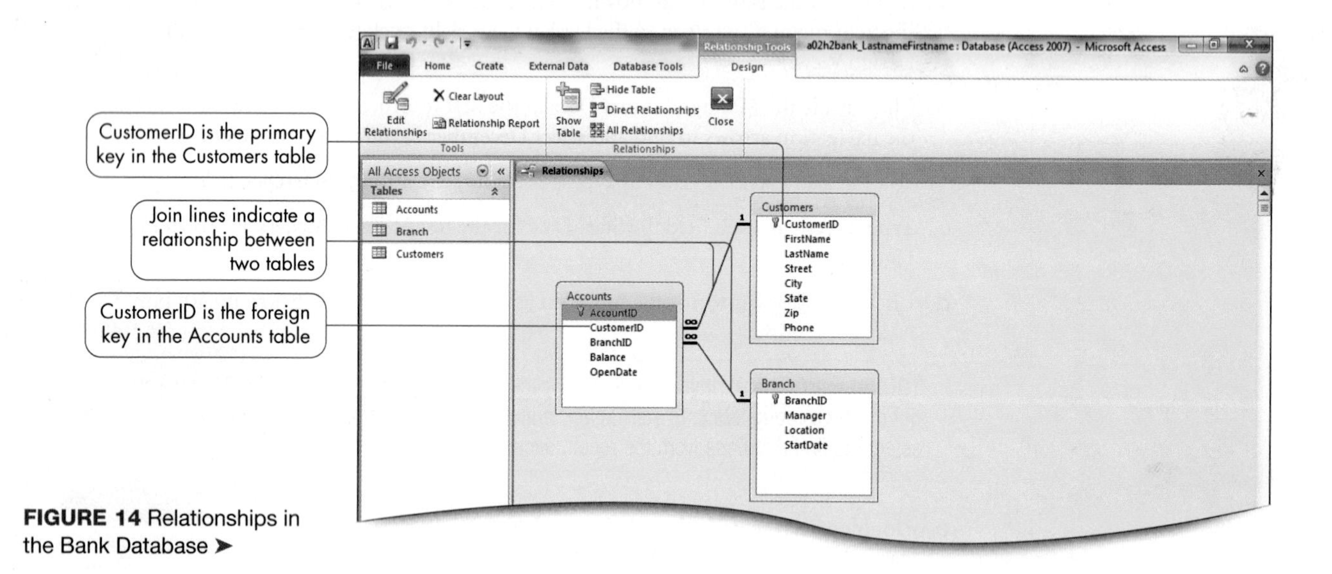

FIGURE 14 Relationships in the Bank Database ➤

The primary key of a table plays a significant role when setting relationships. You cannot join two tables unless a primary key has been set in the primary table. In our Bank database, the CustomerID has been set as the primary key in the Customers table. Therefore, a relationship can be set between the Customers table and the Accounts table. Similarly, the Branch table can be joined to the Accounts table since BranchID has been set as the primary key in the Branch table.

Relationships between tables will almost always be set using primary and foreign keys.

The other side of the relationship join line is most often the foreign key of the related table. A foreign key is a field in one table that is also the primary key of another table. In the previous example, CustomerID in the Accounts table is a foreign key; BranchID in the Accounts table is a foreign key. Relationships between tables will almost always be set using primary and foreign keys.

Establish Referential Integrity

When **referential integrity** is enforced, you cannot enter a foreign key value in a related table unless the primary key value exists in the primary table.

When you create a relationship in Access, the Edit Relationships dialog box appears, as shown in Figure 15. The first check box, Enforce Referential Integrity, should be checked in most cases. When ***referential integrity*** is enforced, you cannot enter a foreign key value in a related table unless the primary key value exists in the primary table. In the case of the Bank database, a customer's account information (which includes CustomerID) cannot be entered into the Accounts table unless the customer information is first entered into the Customers table. If you attempt to enter an account prior to entering the customer information, an error will appear, as shown in Figure 16. When referential integrity is enforced, you cannot delete a record in one table if it has related records in other tables.

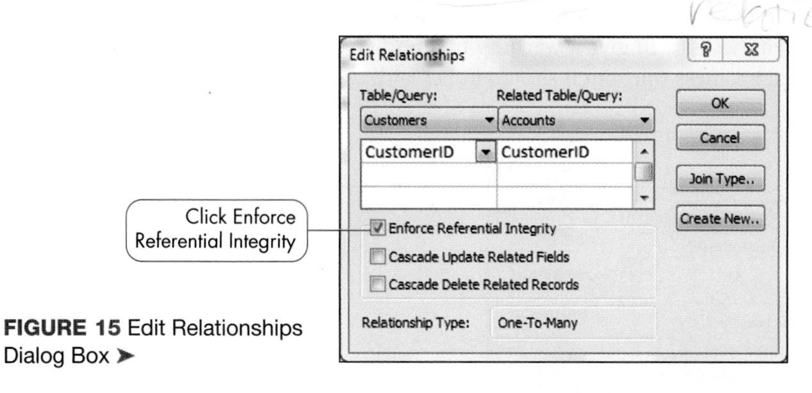

FIGURE 15 Edit Relationships Dialog Box ➤

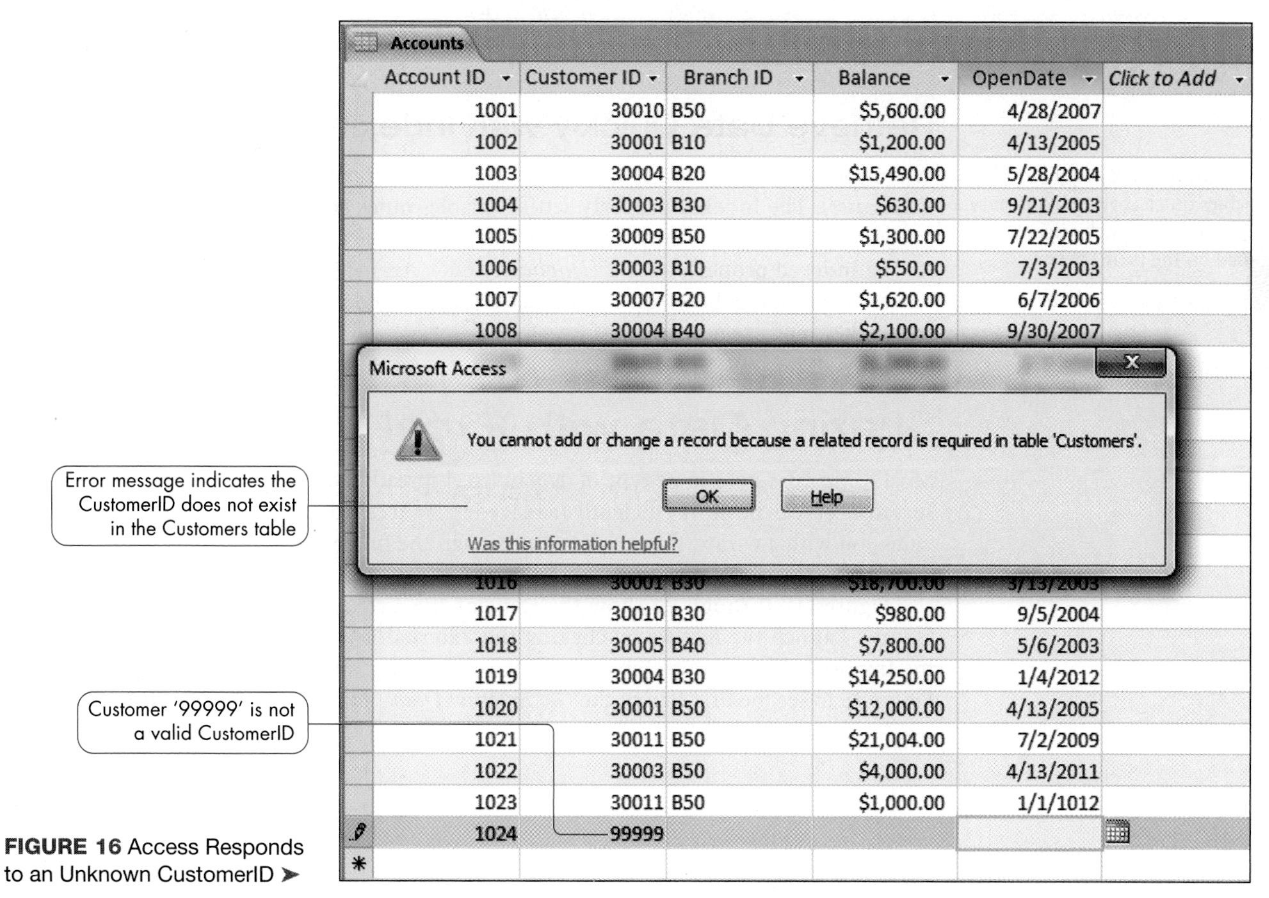

Account ID	Customer ID	Branch ID	Balance	OpenDate	Click to Add
1001	30010	B50	$5,600.00	4/28/2007	
1002	30001	B10	$1,200.00	4/13/2005	
1003	30004	B20	$15,490.00	5/28/2004	
1004	30003	B30	$630.00	9/21/2003	
1005	30009	B50	$1,300.00	7/22/2005	
1006	30003	B10	$550.00	7/3/2003	
1007	30007	B20	$1,620.00	6/7/2006	
1008	30004	B40	$2,100.00	9/30/2007	
1017	30010	B30	$980.00	9/5/2004	
1018	30005	B40	$7,800.00	5/6/2003	
1019	30004	B30	$14,250.00	1/4/2012	
1020	30001	B50	$12,000.00	4/13/2005	
1021	30011	B50	$21,004.00	7/2/2009	
1022	30003	B50	$4,000.00	4/13/2011	
1023	30011	B50	$1,000.00	1/1/1012	
1024	99999				

FIGURE 16 Access Responds to an Unknown CustomerID ➤

Set Cascade Options

Cascade Update Related Fields is an option that directs Access to automatically update all foreign key values in a related table when the primary key value is modified in a primary table.

Cascade Delete Related Records is an option that directs Access to automatically delete all records in related tables that match the primary key that is deleted from a primary table.

When you create a relationship in Access and click the Enforce Referential Integrity checkbox, Access gives you two additional options—Cascade Update Related Fields and Cascade Delete Related Records. Check the ***Cascade Update Related Fields*** option so that when the primary key is modified in a primary table, Access will automatically update all foreign key values in a related table (see Figure 17). If a CustomerID is updated for some reason, all the CustomerID references in the Accounts table will automatically be updated.

Check the ***Cascade Delete Related Records*** option so that when the primary key is deleted in a primary table, Access will automatically delete all records in related tables that reference the primary key (see Figure 17). If one branch of a bank closes and its record is deleted from the Branch table, any account that was not transferred to a different branch would be deleted. Access will give a warning first and enable you to avoid the action. This may be a desired business rule, but it should be set with caution.

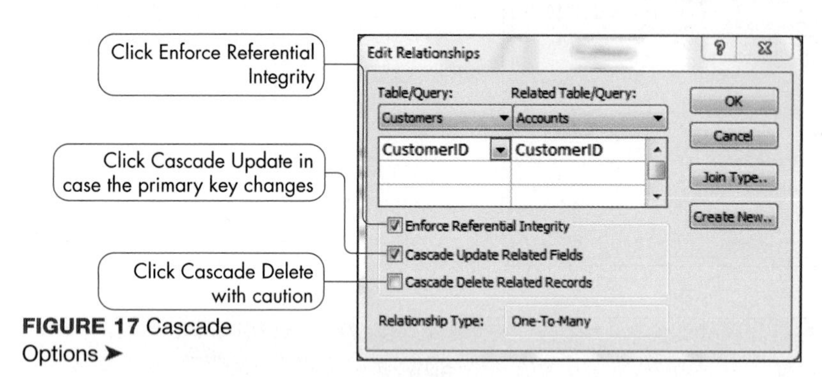

FIGURE 17 Cascade Options ➤

Retrieve Data Quickly with Indexing

The **indexed property** setting enables quick sorting in primary key order and quick retrieval based on the primary key.

When you set the primary key in Access, the ***indexed property*** is automatically set to *Yes (No Duplicates)*. The Indexed property setting enables quick sorting in primary key order and quick retrieval based on the primary key. For non-primary key fields, it may be beneficial to set the Indexed property to *Yes (Duplicates OK)*. Again, Access uses indexing to sort and retrieve data quickly based on the indexed field. As a general rule, indexed fields are usually foreign keys and are numeric.

Sharing Data with Excel

Most companies store some type of data in Excel spreadsheets. Often the data stored in those spreadsheets can be more efficiently managed in an Access database. Fortunately, Access provides you with a wizard that guides you through the process of importing data from Excel. Access can also export data to Excel easily.

Figures 18 through 24 show the steps of the *Get External Data - Excel Spreadsheet* feature. Launch the feature by clicking the External Data tab and then clicking Excel in the Import & Link Group. Table 1 describes the four groups on the External Data tab. See Figure 18 to see the first step of the *Get External Data - Excel Spreadsheet* feature.

TABLE 1 Options on the External Data Tab	
Group	**When Used**
Import & Link	To bring data into an Access database. The data sources include Excel, Access (other Access files), ODBC Database, Text File, XML File, and More.
Export	To send a portion of a database to other applications. You might use this to create a Mail Merge letter and envelopes in Word. You could create an Excel file for a coworker who is not using Access, or you could share your data over the Internet via a SharePoint List.
Collect Data	You could create an e-mail mail merge to send e-mails to your clients and then use Access to manage the clients' responses.
Web Linked Lists	Use these commands to interact with SharePoint lists on the Internet. If an Internet connection is unavailable, you can work offline and synchronize with SharePoint later.

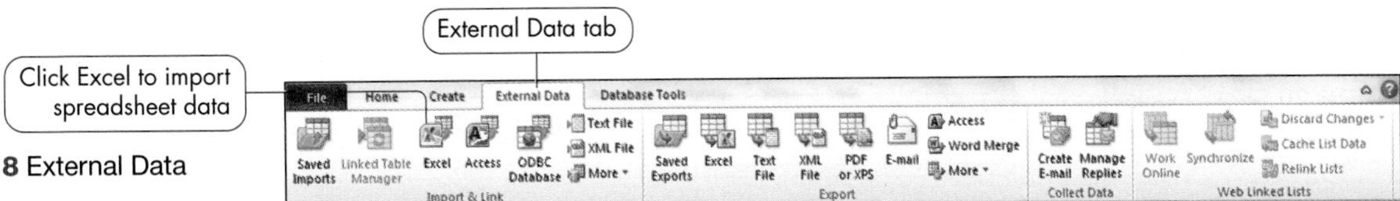

FIGURE 18 External Data Tab ➤

Figure 19 shows the *Get External Data - Excel Spreadsheet* dialog box. This step enables you to locate the Excel file you want to import by clicking Browse. It asks you to choose among three options for the incoming data: Place it in a new table, append the data to an existing table, or create a link to the Excel source.

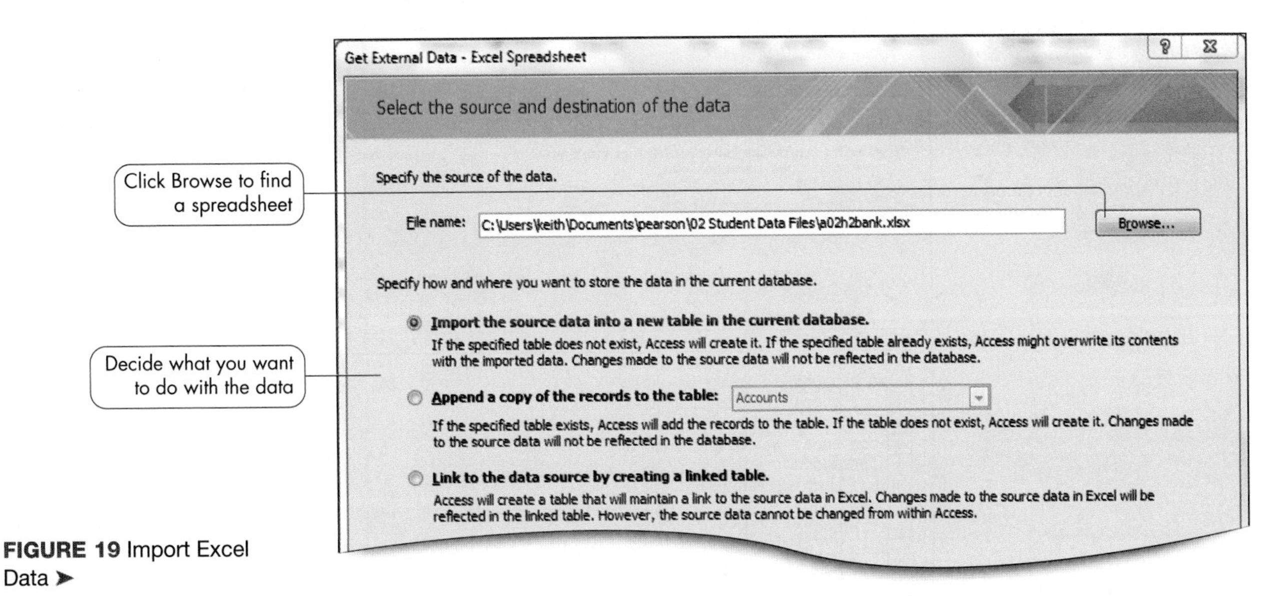

FIGURE 19 Import Excel Data ➤

After you select an Excel workbook and accept the default option, import the source data into a new table in the current database, and then click OK. The Import Spreadsheet Wizard dialog box launches and displays a list of the worksheets in the specified workbook. The Customers worksheet is selected; click the Accounts worksheet, which will be imported first (see Figure 20). The bottom of the Import Spreadsheet Wizard dialog box displays a preview of the data stored in the specified worksheet.

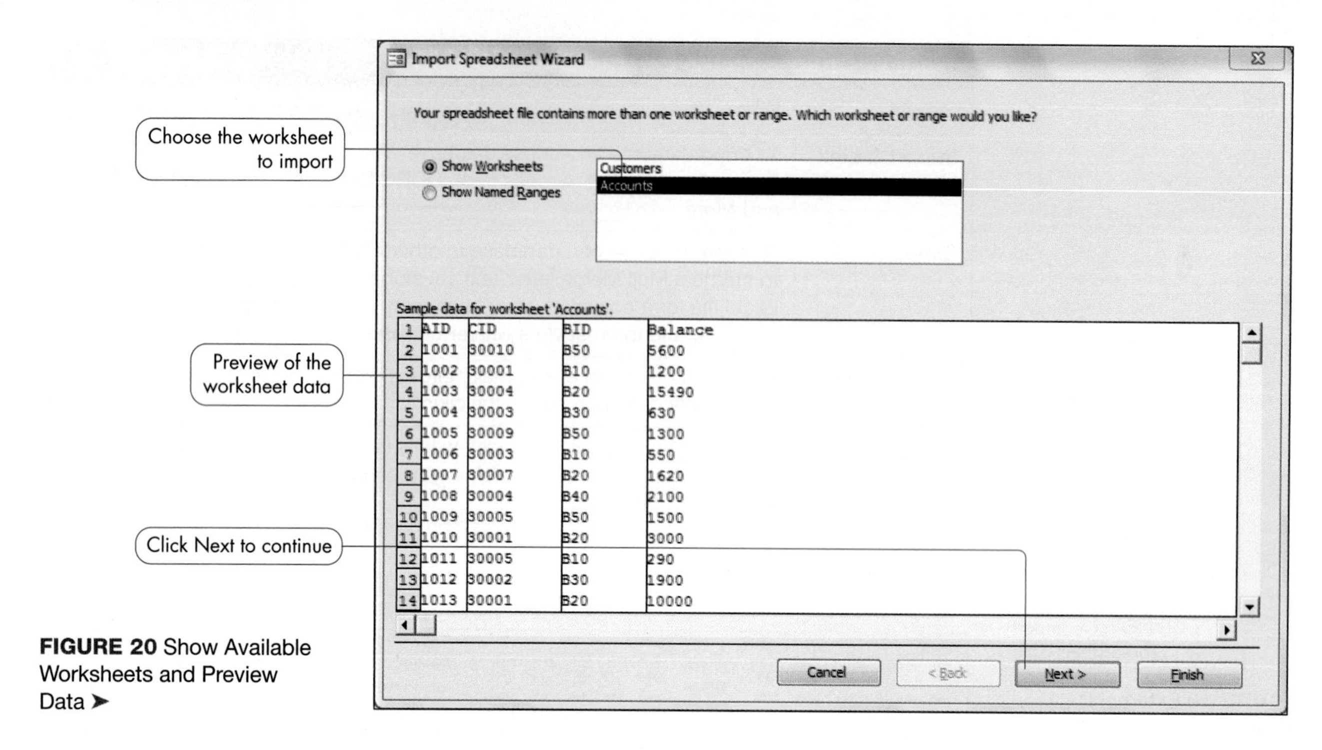

FIGURE 20 Show Available Worksheets and Preview Data ➤

Although a well-designed spreadsheet may include descriptive column headings, not all spreadsheets are ready to import. You may have to revise the spreadsheet before importing it. The second window of the Import Spreadsheet Wizard dialog box contains a check box that enables you to convert the first row of column headings to field names in Access (see Figure 21). If a column heading row exists in the spreadsheet, check the box. If no column headings exist, leave the check box unchecked, and the data will import using Field1, Field2, Field3, etc.

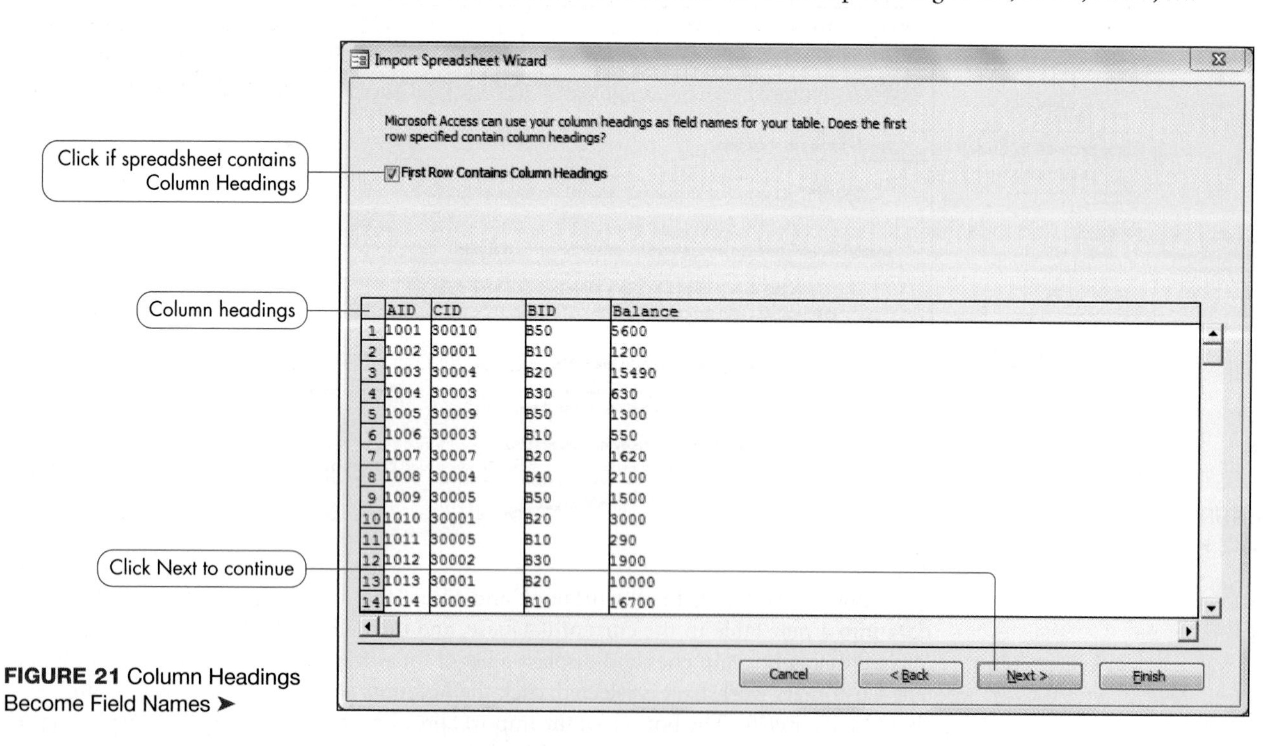

FIGURE 21 Column Headings Become Field Names ➤

The third window of the Import Spreadsheet Wizard dialog box enables you to specify field options (see Figure 22). The AID field is shown in this figure. Because it will become this table's primary key, you need to set the Indexed Property to *Yes (No Duplicates)*.

To modify the field options of the other fields, click the Field Name column heading, and then make the changes. Not all Access table properties are supported by the wizard. You will need to open the table in Design view after importing it to make additional field property changes.

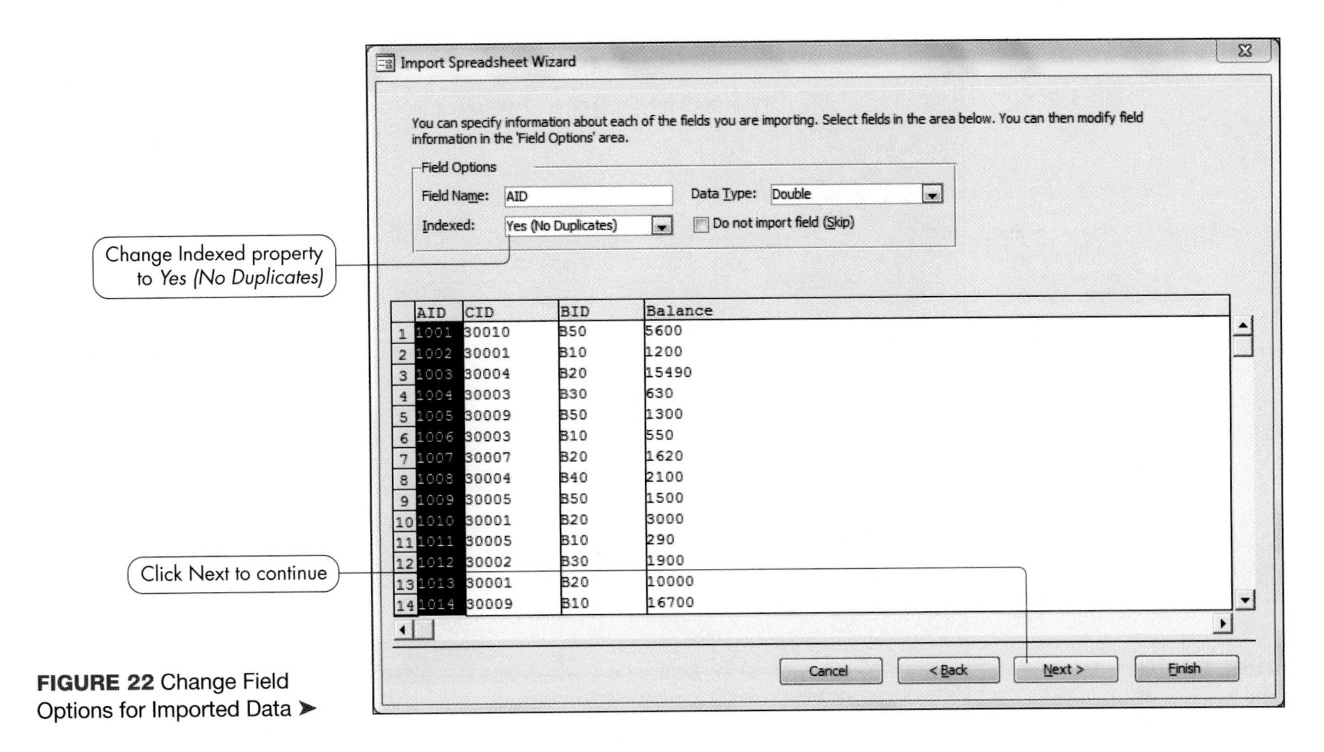

FIGURE 22 Change Field Options for Imported Data ➤

The fourth window of the Import Spreadsheet Wizard dialog box enables you to choose a primary key before the import takes place (see Figure 23). If the option *Let Access add primary key* is selected, Access will generate an AutoNumber field and designate it as the primary key. Otherwise, you can designate a field to be the primary key. In the import described in the figure, the Excel data has a unique identifier (AID) that will become the table's primary key.

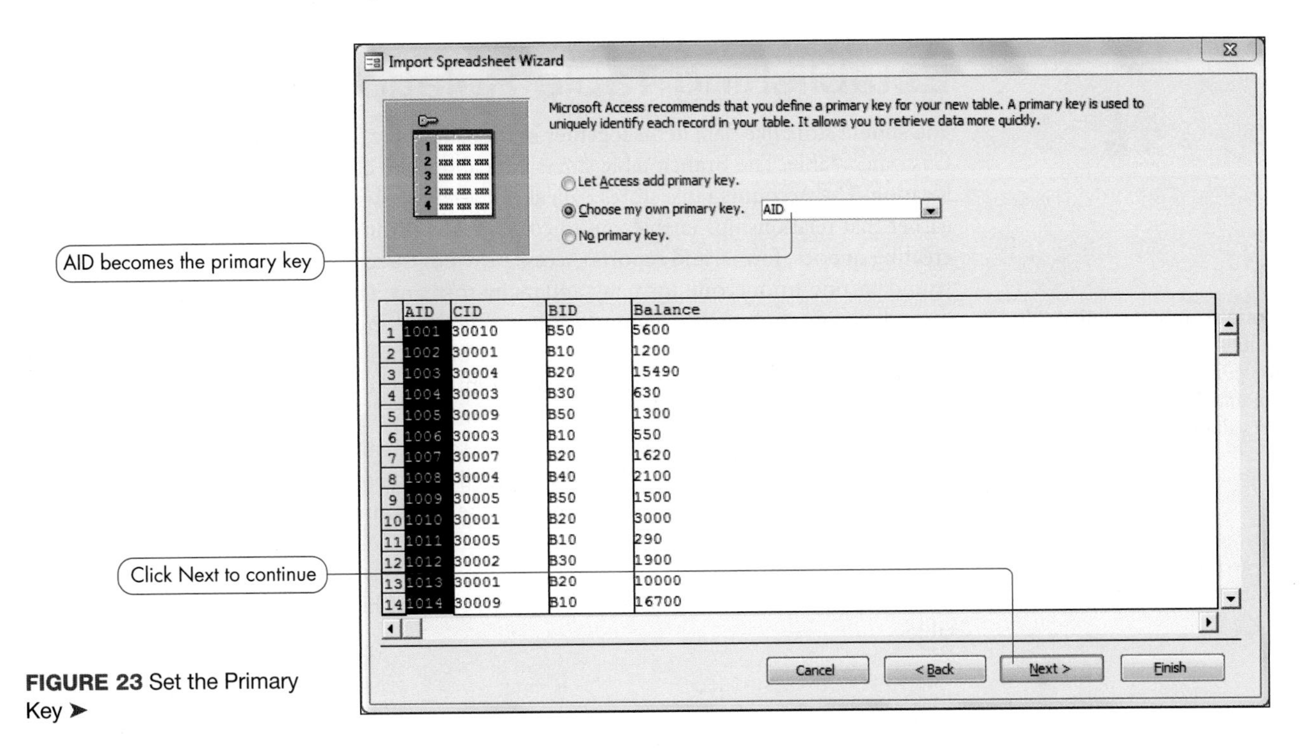

FIGURE 23 Set the Primary Key ➤

Use the final window of the Import Spreadsheet Wizard to name the Access table. If the worksheet in the Excel workbook was named, Access uses the worksheet name as the table name (see Figure 24).

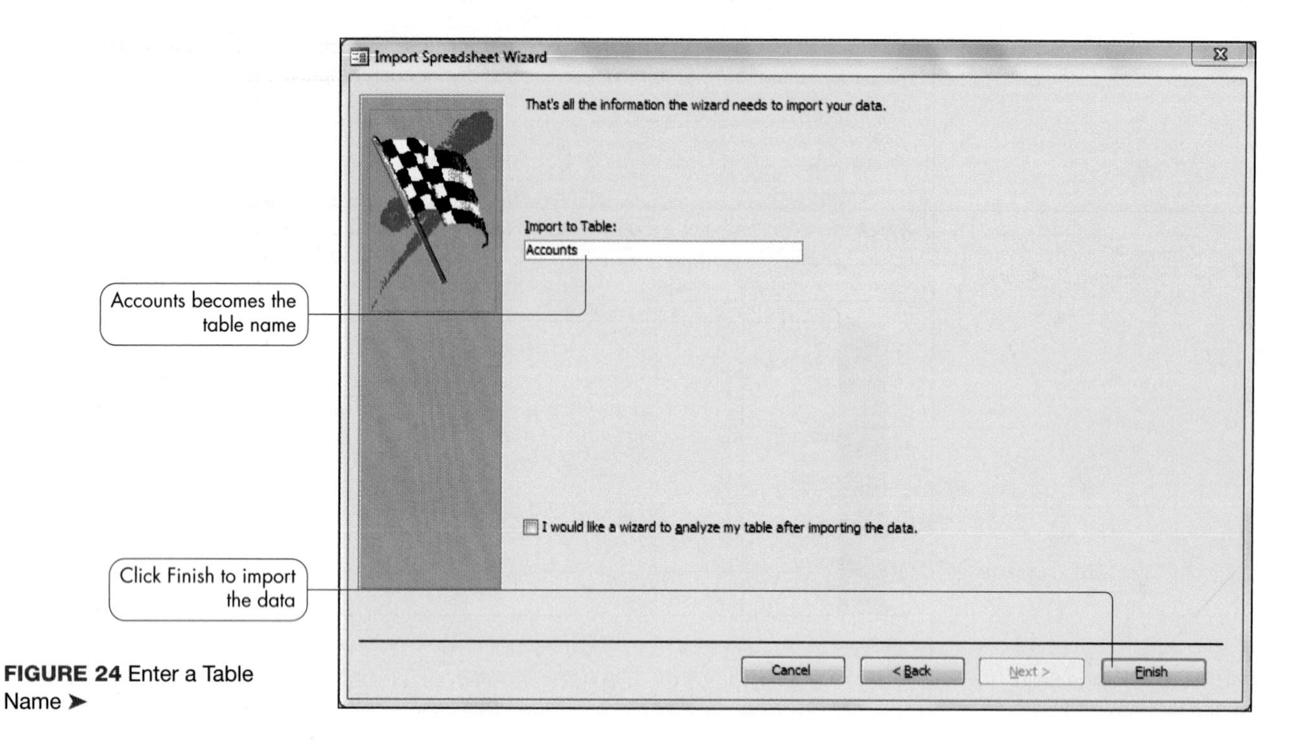

FIGURE 24 Enter a Table Name ➤

Finally, the Wizard will ask if you wish to save the import steps. If the same worksheet is imported from Excel to Access on a recurring basis, you could save the parameters and use them again. To save the import steps such as the indexing option and any new field names, click Saved Imports in the Import group. Saving the import steps will help you import the data the next time it is needed.

Establishing Table Relationships

A **one-to-many relationship** is established when the primary key value in the primary table can match many of the foreign key values in the related table.

You should store like data items together in the same table. The customer data is stored in the Customers table. The Branch table stores data about the bank's branches, management, and location. The Accounts table stores data about account ownership and balances. You learned earlier that relationships enable you to combine data from related tables for the purpose of creating queries, forms, and reports. Access provides three different relationships for joining your data: one-to-one, one-to-many, and many-to-many. The most common type by far is the one-to-many relationship. A ***one-to-many relationship*** is established when the primary key value in the primary table can match many of the foreign key values in the related table. For example, a bank customer will be entered into the Customers table once and only once. The primary key value, which is also the customer's CustomerID number, might be 1585. That same customer could set up a checking, savings, and money market account. With each account, the CustomerID (1585) is required and therefore will occur three times in the Accounts table. The value appears once in the Customers table and three times in the Accounts table. Therefore, the relationship between Customers and Accounts would be described as one-to-many.

Table 2 lists and describes all three types of relationships you can create between Access tables.

TABLE 2 Relationship Types	
Relationship Name	**Definition**
One-to-Many	This relationship is between a primary key in the first table and a foreign key in the second table. The first table must have only one occurrence of each value. For example, each customer must have a unique identification number in the Customers table, or each employee must have a unique EmployeeID in the Employee table. The foreign key field in the second table may have repeating values. For example, one customer may have many different account numbers, or one employee can perform many services.
One-to-One	Two different tables use the same primary key. Exactly one record exists in the second table for each record in the first table. Sometimes security reasons require a table to be split into two related tables. For example, anyone in the company can look in the Employee table and find the employee's office number, department assignment, or telephone extension. However, only a few people need to have access to the employee's salary, Social Security Number, performance review, or marital status. Both tables use the same unique identifier to identify each employee.
Many-to-Many	This is an artificially constructed relationship giving many matching records in each direction between tables. It requires construction of a third table called a junction table. For example, a database might have a table for employees and one for projects. Several employees might be assigned to one project, but one employee might also be assigned to many different projects. When Access connects to databases using Oracle or other software, you find this relationship type.

Establish a One-to-Many Relationship

Click the Database Tools tab, and then click Relationships in the Relationships group; the Relationships window opens (as shown in Figure 25). If this were an established database, this window would already contain tables and join lines indicating the relationships that were established in the database.

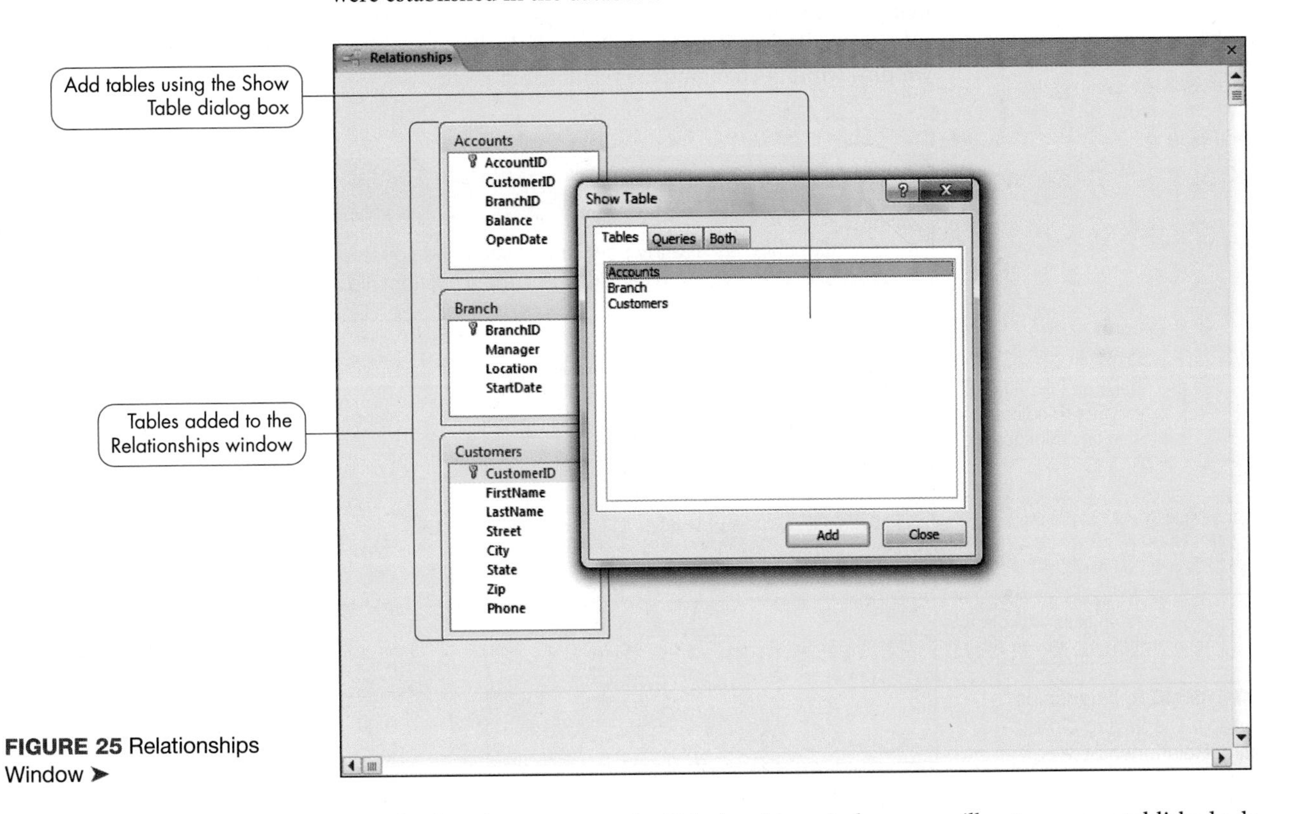

FIGURE 25 Relationships Window ➤

The first time you open the Relationships window, you will not see any established relationships; you must first use the Show Table dialog box to add the required tables to the Relationships window. Select the tables you want to use to set relationships, and then add them to the Relationships window by clicking Add (as shown in Figure 25).

TIP **Navigating Between the Relationships Window and a Table's Design**

When you right-click on a table's title bar in the Relationships window, the shortcut menu offers you a chance to open the table in Design view. This is a convenient feature because if you want to link **one** table to another table, the joined fields must have the same data type, and a table may contain a field with the wrong data type. This shortcut enables you to check the fields and revise them if necessary.

Where necessary, expand the table windows to display the complete list of field names shown in the table.

Establish the relationships by dragging the common field name from the primary table onto the common field name in the related table. (The common field name does not have to be an exact match, but the data type and field size must be the same.) When you release the mouse, the Edit Relationships dialog box opens (look back at Figure 15). Click Enforce Referential Integrity, and then click Create; Access checks the table data to ensure that the rules you are attempting to establish can be met. For example, in the bank database, if you attempt to enforce referential integrity between the Branch table and the Accounts table, Access will verify that one BranchID value exists in the Branch table for each BranchID value in the Accounts table. If one BranchID value (e.g., B80) in the Accounts table does not exist in the Branch table, Access cannot establish the relationship with referential integrity enforced. The data must be corrected prior to checking enforce referential integrity.

Figure 26 shows the Relationships window for the Bank database and all the relationships created using referential integrity. The join line between the CustomerID field in the Customers table and the CustomerID field in the Accounts table indicates that a one-to-many relationship has been set. You can rearrange the tables by dragging the tables by the title bar. You can switch the positions of the Branch and Accounts tables in the Relationships window without changing the relationship itself.

TIP **Editing a Relationship**

If the relationship has already been established and you need to edit it, right-click the join line. You can also right-click the join line to delete a relationship.

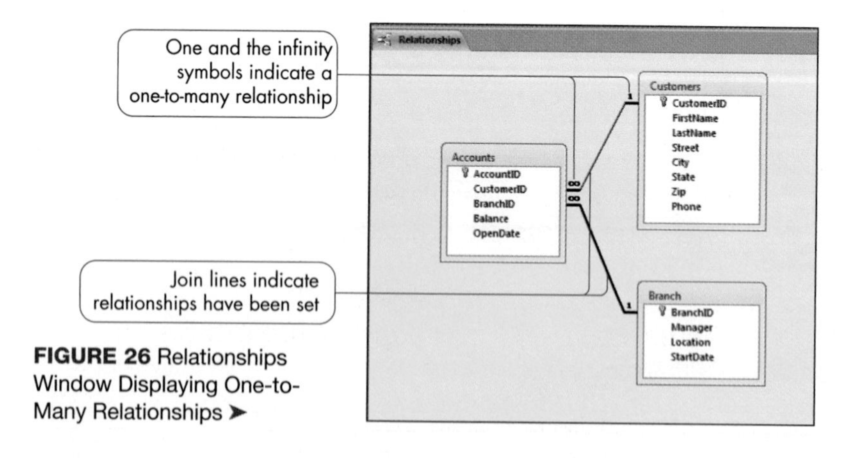

FIGURE 26 Relationships Window Displaying One-to-Many Relationships ➤

In the following Hands-On Exercise, you will create two additional tables by importing data from Excel spreadsheets into the Bank database. You will establish and modify field properties. Then you will connect the newly imported data to the Branch table by establishing relationships between the tables.

HANDS-ON EXERCISES

2 Multiple Table Databases

You created a new Bank database, and you created a new Branch table. Now you are ready to import Commonwealth Federal's customer and account data from Excel spreadsheets. Even though you believe the Excel data is formatted correctly, you decided to open the Excel spreadsheets before you import them into Access. Once you are satisfied the data is structured properly, you can begin the import process.

Skills covered: Import Excel Data into an Access Table • Import Additional Excel Data • Modify an Imported Table's Design • Add Data to an Imported Table • Establish Table Relationships • Test Referential Integrity

STEP 1 IMPORT EXCEL DATA INTO AN ACCESS TABLE

You and the auditor have discovered several of Commonwealth's Excel spreadsheets that contain customer data. These files need to be analyzed, so you decide to import the Excel data into Access. Refer to Figure 27 as well as Figures 19 through 24 as you complete Step 1.

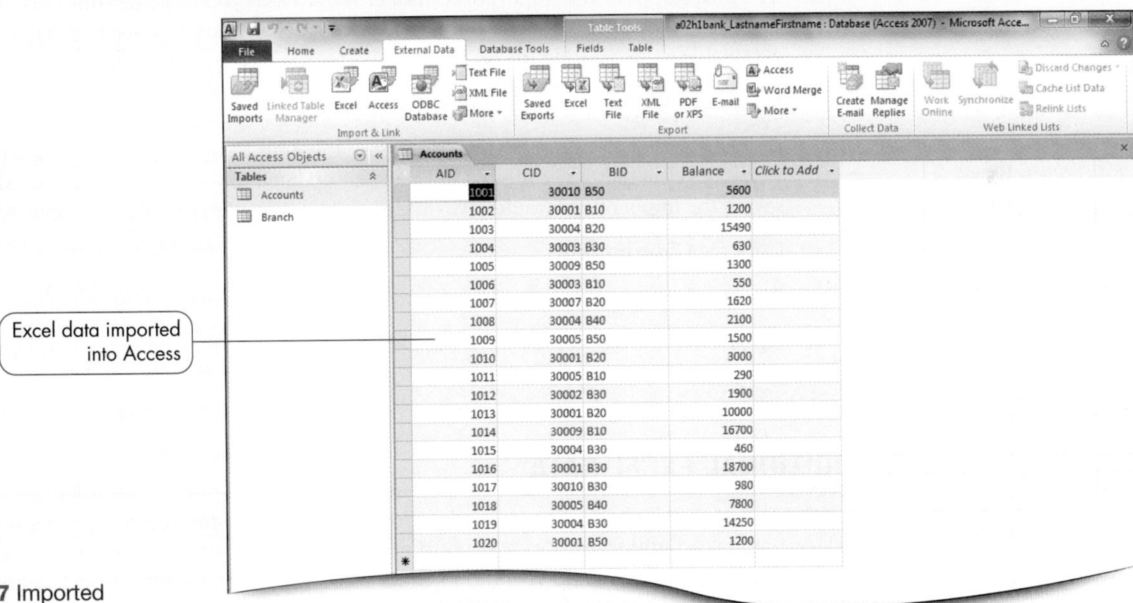

FIGURE 27 Imported Accounts Table ➤

a. Open *a02h1bank_LastnameFirstname* if you closed it at the end of Hands-On Exercise 1. Click the **File tab**, click **Save Database As**, and then type **a02h2bank_LastnameFirstname**, changing *h1* to *h2*. Click **Save**.

b. Click the Enable Content button below the Ribbon to indicate you trust the contents of the database.

> **TROUBLESHOOTING:** Throughout the remainder of this chapter and textbook, click the Enable Content button whenever you are working with student files.

c. Click the **External Data tab**, and click **Excel** in the Import & Link group to launch the *Get External Data - Excel Spreadsheet* feature. Select the **Import the source data into a new table in the current database option**, if necessary, as shown in Figure 19.

d. Click **Browse**, and then go to the student data folder. Select the *a02h2bank* workbook. Click **Open**, and then click **OK** to open the Import Spreadsheet Wizard.

The top of the first window shows all of the worksheets in the workbook. This particular workbook contains only two worksheets: Customers and Accounts. The Customers worksheet is active, and a list of the data contained in the Customers worksheet displays in the Wizard.

e. Click **Accounts** (see Figure 20), and then click **Next**.

f. Ensure that the *First Row Contains Column Headings* check box is checked to tell Access that column headings exist in the Excel file (see Figure 21).

   The field names, AID, CID, BID, and Balance, will import from Excel along with the data stored in the rows in the worksheet. The field names will be modified later in Access.

g. Click **Next**.

   The AID (AccountID) will become the primary key in this table. It needs to be a unique identifier, so we must change the properties to no duplicates.

h. Ensure that *AID* is displayed in the Field Name box in Field Options. Then click the **Indexed arrow**, and then select **Yes (No Duplicates)**, as shown in Figure 22. Click **Next**.

i. Click the **Choose my own primary key option** (see Figure 23). Make sure that the *AID* field is selected. Click **Next**.

   The final screen of the Import Spreadsheet Wizard asks you to name your table. The name of the Excel worksheet was Accounts, and Access defaults to the worksheet name. It is an acceptable name (see Figure 24).

j. Click **Finish** to accept the Accounts table name.

   A dialog box opens asking if you wish to save the steps of this import to use again. If this were sales data that was collected in Excel and updated to the database on a weekly basis, saving the import steps would save time. You do not need to save this example.

k. Click the **Close button**.

   The new table displays in the Navigation Pane and resides in the Bank database.

l. Open the imported Accounts table in Datasheet view, and then compare it to Figure 27. Close the table.

STEP 2 IMPORT ADDITIONAL EXCEL DATA

The first spreadsheet that you imported contained account information related to the mishandled funds. The auditor has asked you to import a second spreadsheet that contains customer account information. Follow the same process as you did in Step 1 as you answer each Import Wizard question. Refer to Figure 28 as well as Figures 19 through 24 as you complete Step 2.

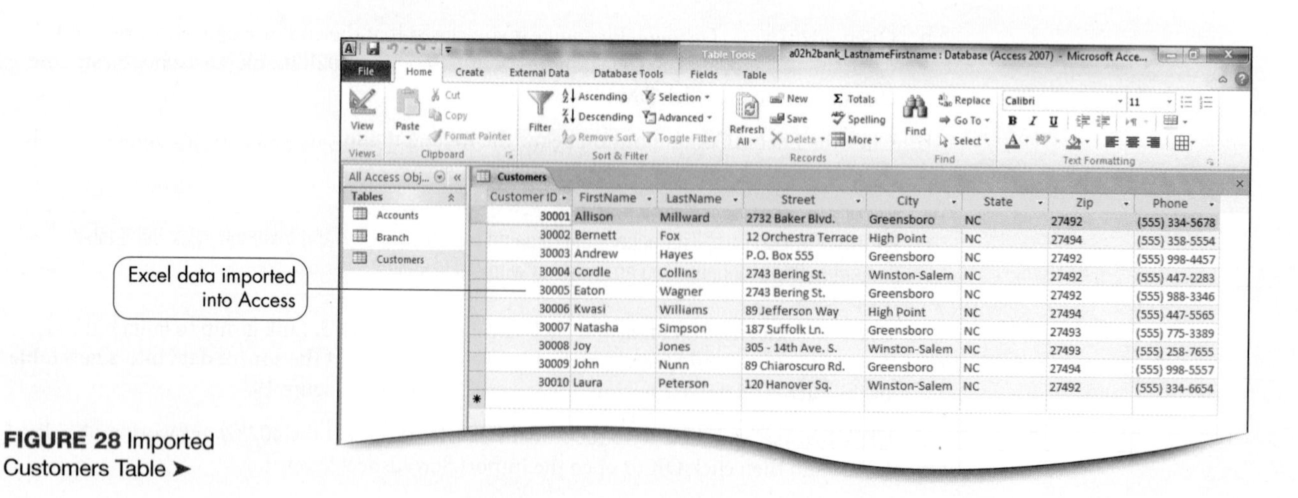

FIGURE 28 Imported Customers Table ➤

a. Click the **External Data tab**, and then click **Excel** in the Import & Link group to launch the *Get External Data - Excel Spreadsheet* feature. Select the **Import the source data into a new table in the current database option**, if necessary.

b. Click **Browse**, and then go to the student data folder. Select the *a02h2bank* workbook. Click **Open**, and then click **OK** to open the Import Spreadsheet Wizard.

   The Customers worksheet is active; you will import this worksheet.

c. Click **Next**.

d. Ensure that the *First Row Contains Column Headings* check box is checked to tell Access that column headings exist in the Excel file. Click **Next**.

   The CID will become the primary key in this table. It needs to be a unique identifier, so you change the properties to no duplicates.

e. Ensure that *CID* is displayed in the Field Name box in Field Options. Click the **Indexed arrow**, and then select **Yes (No Duplicates)**. Click **Next**.

f. Click the **Choose my own primary key option**. Make sure that the *CID* field is selected. Click **Next**.

   Access defaults to the table name Customers.

g. Click **Finish** to accept the Customers table name.

h. Click **Close** on the Save Import Steps dialog box.

   The Navigation Pane contains three tables: Accounts, Branch, and Customers.

i. Open the imported Customers table in Datasheet view, and then compare it to Figure 28. Close the table.

STEP 3 MODIFY AN IMPORTED TABLE'S DESIGN

The Excel worksheets became Access tables when you imported them into the Bank database. However, in order to answer all the auditor's questions (using queries), you need to modify the tables so that each field has the correct data type and field size. Refer to Figure 29 as you complete Step 3.

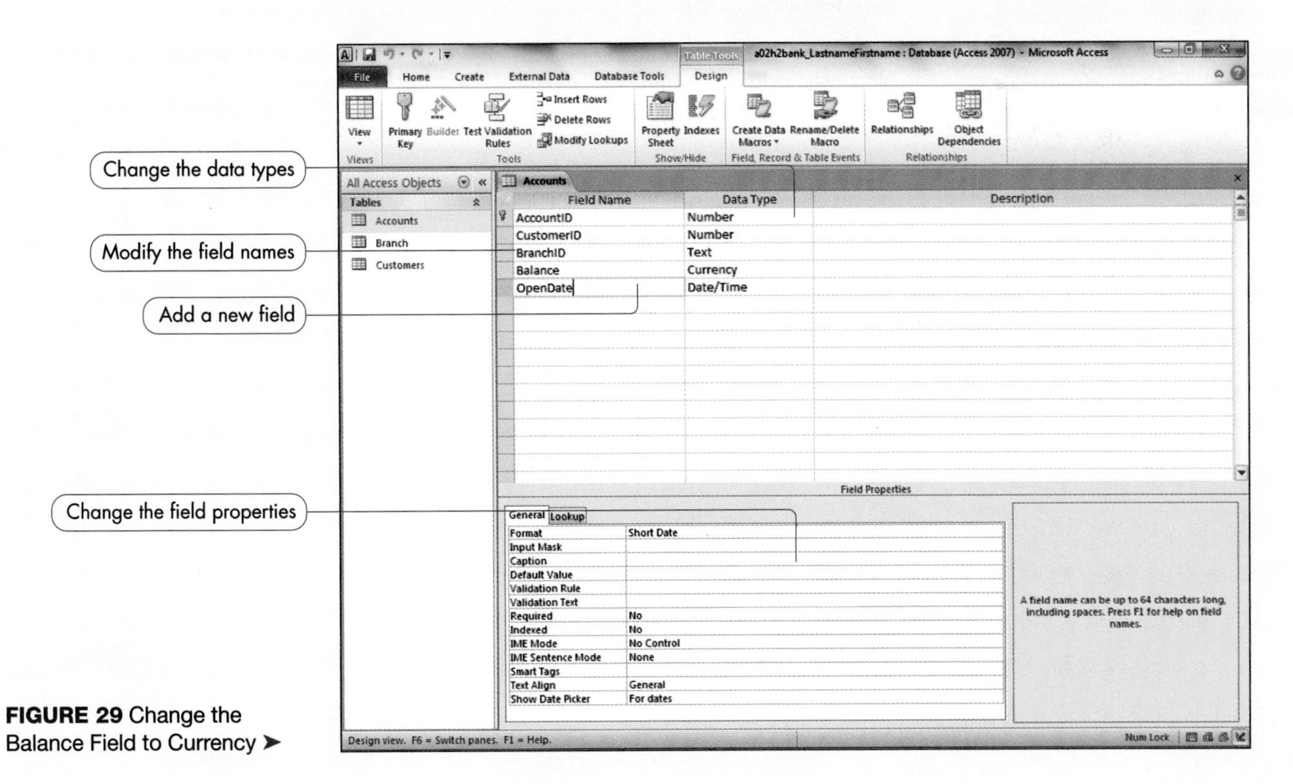

FIGURE 29 Change the Balance Field to Currency ➤

a. Double-click the **Accounts table** in the Navigation Pane to open it in Datasheet view.

b. Click **View** in the Views group on the Home tab to switch to Design view.

c. Change the AID field name to **AccountID**.

d. Change the Field Size property to **Long Integer** in the Field Properties at the bottom of the design window.

   Long Integer ensures that there will be enough numbers as the number of accounts grow over time. Importing data from Excel saves typing, but modifications will usually be required.

e. Type **Account ID** in the **Caption property box** for the AccountID field. The caption contains a space between *Account* and *ID*.

f. Change the CID field name to **CustomerID**.

g. Change the Field Size property to **Long Integer** in the Field Properties at the bottom of the design window.

   You can select the Field Size option using the arrow, or you can type the first letter of the option you want. For example, type *l* for Long Integer or *s* for Single. Make sure the current option is completely selected before you type the letter.

h. Type **Customer ID** in the **Caption property box** for the CustomerID field. The caption contains a space between *Customer* and *ID*.

i. Click the **BID field**. Change the BID field name to **BranchID**.

j. Type **5** in the **Field Size property box** in the Field Properties.

k. Type **Branch ID** in the **Caption property box** for the Branch ID field.

l. Change the Data Type of the Balance field from *Number* to **Currency**.

m. Type a new field name, **OpenDate**, under the Balance field name. Assign data type **Date/Time**, and then add the **Short Date format** in the Field Properties.

n. Click **View** in the Views group to switch to Datasheet View. Read the messages, and then click **Yes** twice.

   In this case, it is OK to click Yes because the size of three fields was shortened. The new OpenDate field will store the date that each account was opened.

o. Add the OpenDate values as shown below:

Account ID	OpenDate
1001	4/28/2007
1002	4/13/2005
1003	5/28/2004
1004	9/21/2003
1005	7/22/2005
1006	7/3/2003
1007	6/7/2006
1008	9/30/2007
1009	2/7/2006
1010	3/18/2010
1011	10/16/2012
1012	3/14/2007
1013	5/15/2009
1014	9/17/2007
1015	4/4/2003
1016	3/13/2003
1017	9/5/2004
1018	5/6/2003
1019	1/4/2012
1020	4/13/2005

p. Right-click the **Customers table** in the Navigation Pane, and then select **Design View** from the shortcut menu. Change the CID field name to **CustomerID**. Change the Field Size property of the CustomerID field to **Long Integer**, and then add a caption, **Customer ID**. Take note of the intentional space between *Customer* and *ID*.

   The Accounts table and the Customers table will be joined using the CustomerID field. Both fields must have the same data type.

q. Change the Field Size property to **20** for the FirstName, LastName, Street, and City fields. Change the Field Size for State to **2**.

r. Change the data type for Zip and Phone to **Text**. Change the Field size property to **15** for both fields. Remove the @ symbol from the Format property where it exists for all fields in the Customers table.

s. Click the **Phone field name**, and then click **Input Mask** in Field Properties. Click **Build** on the right side to launch the Input Mask Wizard. Click **Yes** to save the table, and then click **Yes** to the *some data may be lost* warning. Click **Finish** to apply the default phone number Input Mask.

   The phone number input mask will enable users to enter 6105551212 and Access to display (610) 555-1212.

t. Click **Save** to save the design changes to the Customers table. Read the Warning Box, and then click **Yes**.

STEP 4 ADD DATA TO AN IMPORTED TABLE

Now that you have created the Access tables, add data as directed by the auditor. You may also need to update and delete records if you and the auditor decide the information is no longer needed. Refer to Figure 30 as you complete Step 4.

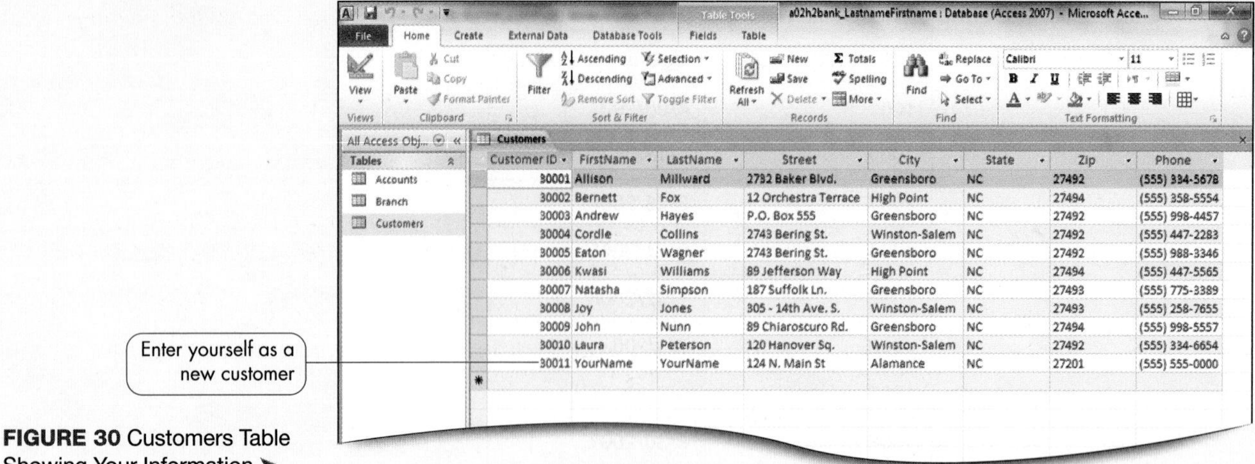

Customer ID	FirstName	LastName	Street	City	State	Zip	Phone
30001	Allison	Millward	2732 Baker Blvd.	Greensboro	NC	27492	(555) 334-5678
30002	Bernett	Fox	12 Orchestra Terrace	High Point	NC	27494	(555) 358-5554
30003	Andrew	Hayes	P.O. Box 555	Greensboro	NC	27492	(555) 998-4457
30004	Cordle	Collins	2743 Bering St.	Winston-Salem	NC	27492	(555) 447-2283
30005	Eaton	Wagner	2743 Bering St.	Greensboro	NC	27492	(555) 988-3346
30006	Kwasi	Williams	89 Jefferson Way	High Point	NC	27494	(555) 447-5565
30007	Natasha	Simpson	187 Suffolk Ln.	Greensboro	NC	27493	(555) 775-3389
30008	Joy	Jones	305 - 14th Ave. S.	Winston-Salem	NC	27493	(555) 258-7655
30009	John	Nunn	89 Chiaroscuro Rd.	Greensboro	NC	27494	(555) 998-5557
30010	Laura	Peterson	120 Hanover Sq.	Winston-Salem	NC	27492	(555) 334-6654
30011	YourName	YourName	124 N. Main St	Alamance	NC	27201	(555) 555-0000

FIGURE 30 Customers Table Showing Your Information ➤

a. Click **View** in the Views group to display the Customers table in Datasheet view.

   The asterisk at the bottom of the table data in the row selector area is the indicator of a place to enter a new record.

b. Click the **Customer ID field** in the record after *30010*. Type **30011**. Fill in the rest of the data using your information as the customer. You may use a fictitious address and phone number.

c. Close the Customers table. Click the **Accounts table tab** if necessary.

d. Locate the new row indicator—the * in the row selector—and click in the **Account ID column**. Type **1021**. Type **30011** as the **Customer ID** and **B50** as the **Branch ID**. Type **21004** for the Balance field value. Type **7/2/2009** for the OpenDate.

e. Close the Accounts table; keep the database open.

STEP 5 ESTABLISH TABLE RELATIONSHIPS

The tables for the bank investigation have been designed. Now, you will need to establish connections between the tables. Look at the primary and foreign keys as a guide. Refer to Figure 31 as you complete Step 5.

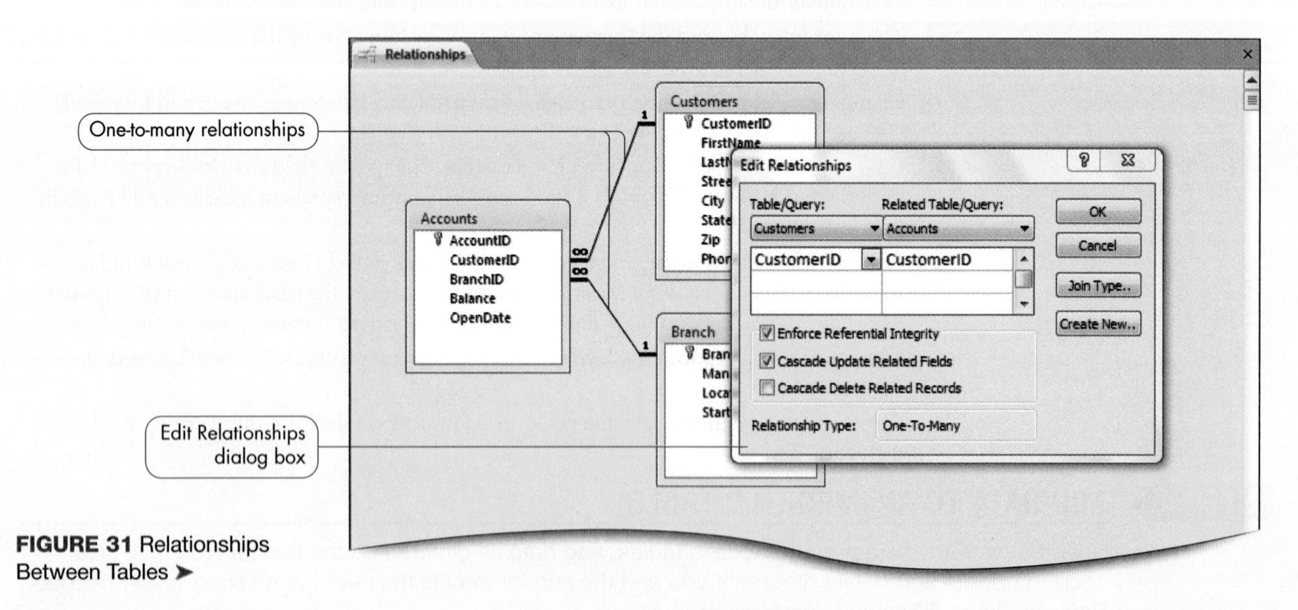

FIGURE 31 Relationships Between Tables ➤

a. Click the **Database Tools tab**, and then click **Relationships** in the Relationships group.

   The Relationships window opens and the Show Table dialog box appears.

> **TROUBLESHOOTING:** If the Show Table dialog box does not open, click Show Table in the Relationships group on the Relationships Tools Design tab.

b. Double-click each of the three tables displayed in the Show Table dialog box to add them to the Relationships window. (Alternatively, click a table, and then click Add.) Click **Close** in the Show Table dialog box.

> **TROUBLESHOOTING:** If you have a duplicate table, click the title bar of the duplicated table, and then press Delete.

c. Resize the Customers table box so all the fields are visible. Arrange the tables as shown in Figure 31.

d. Drag the **BranchID field** in the Branch table onto the BranchID field in the Accounts table. The Edit Relationships dialog box opens. Click the **Enforce Referential Integrity** and **Cascade Update Related Fields check boxes**. Click **Create.**

   A black line displays, joining the two tables. It has a 1 on the end near the Branch table and an infinity symbol on the end next to the Accounts table. You have established a one-to-many relationship between the Branch and Accounts tables.

e. Drag the **CustomerID field** in the Customers table onto the CustomerID field in the Accounts table. The Edit Relationships dialog box opens. Click the **Enforce Referential Integrity** and **Cascade Update Related Fields check boxes**. Click **Create.**

   You have established a one-to-many relationship between the Customers and Accounts tables. A customer will have only a single CustomerID number. The same customer may have many different accounts: Savings, Checking, CDs, etc.

> **TROUBLESHOOTING:** If you get an error message when you click Create, verify the data types of the joined fields are the same. To check the data types from the Relationships window, right-click the title bar of a table, and then select Table Design from the shortcut menu. Modify the data type and field size of the join fields if necessary.

f. Click **Save** on the Quick Access Toolbar to save the changes to the Relationships. Close the Relationships window.

STEP 6 TEST REFERENTIAL INTEGRITY

The design of the bank database must be 100% correct; otherwise, data entry may be compromised. Even though you are confident that the table relationships are correct, you decide to test them by entering some invalid data. If the relationships are working, the invalid data will be rejected by Access. Refer to Figure 32 as you complete Step 6.

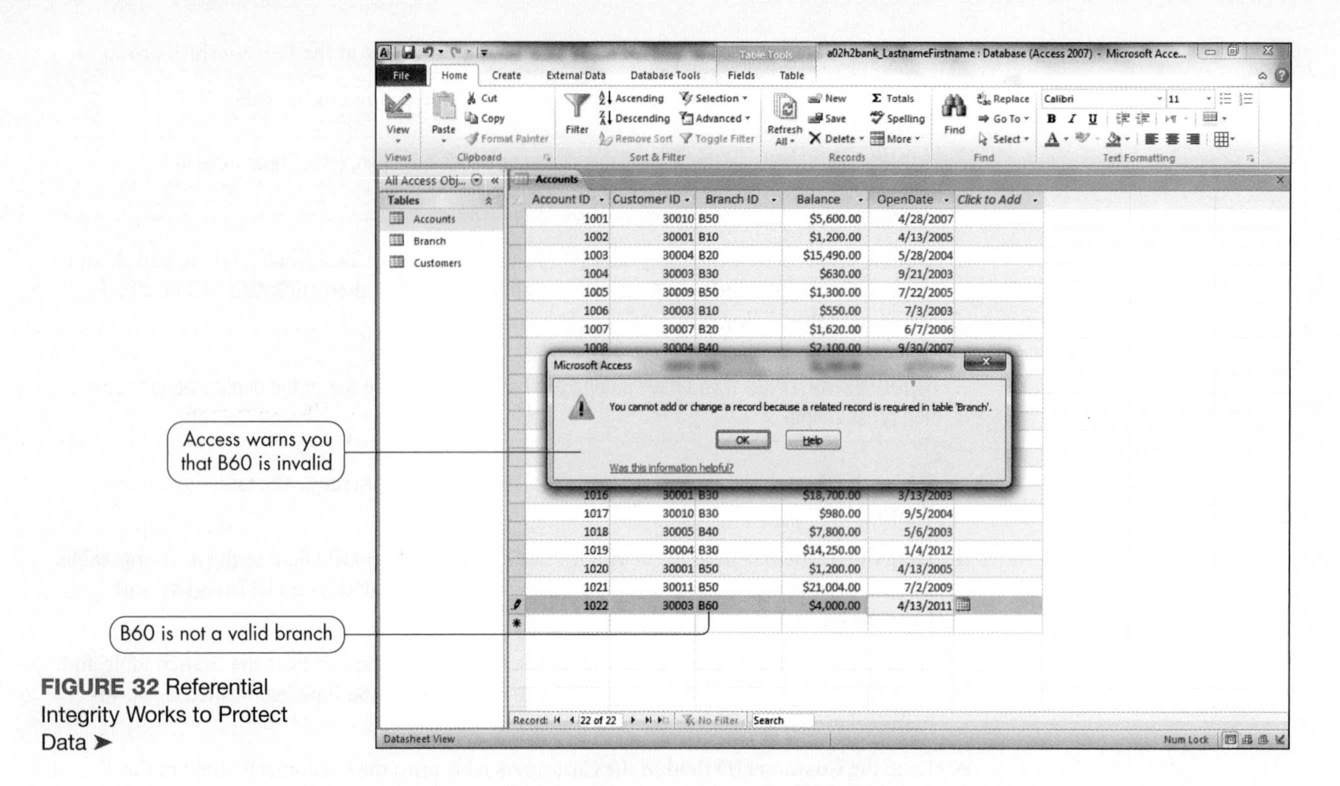

FIGURE 32 Referential Integrity Works to Protect Data ➤

a. Double-click the **Accounts table** to open it in Datasheet view.

b. Add a new record, pressing **Tab** after each field: Account ID: **1022**, Customer ID: **30003**, Branch ID: **B60**, Balance: **4000**, OpenDate: **4/13/2011**.

A warning message is telling you that a related record in the Branch table is required since the Accounts table and the Branch table are connected by a relationship with enforce referential integrity checked.

c. Click **OK**. Double-click the **Branch table** in the Navigation Pane, and then examine the data in the BranchID field. Notice the Branch table has no B60 record. Close the Branch table.

d. Replace *B60* with **B50** in the new Accounts record, and then press **Tab** three times. As soon as the focus moves to the next record, the pencil symbol disappears and your data is saved.

You successfully identified a BranchID that Access recognizes. Because referential integrity between the Accounts and Branch tables has been enforced, Access looks at each data entry item in a foreign key and matches it to a corresponding value in the table where it is the primary key. In Step 6b, you attempted to enter a nonexistent BranchID and were not allowed to make that error. In Step 6d, you entered a valid BranchID. Access examined the index for the BranchID in the Branch table and found a corresponding value for B50.

e. Close the Accounts table. Reopen the Accounts table; you will find that the record you just entered for 1022 has been saved. Close the table.

f. Close all open tables, if necessary.

g. Click the **File tab**, and then click **Compact & Repair Database**.

h. Click the **File tab**, click **Save & Publish**, and then double-click **Back Up Database**. Accept *a02h2bank_LastnameFirstname_date* as the file name, and then click **Save**.

You just created a backup of the database. The *a02h2bank_LastnameFirstname* database remains open.

i. Keep the database onscreen if you plan to continue with Hands-On Exercise 3. If not, close the database and exit Access.

Single-Table Queries

A **query** enables you to ask questions about the data stored in a database.

If you wanted to see which customers currently have an account with a balance over $5,000, you could find the answer by creating an Access query. A ***query*** enables you to ask questions about the data stored in a database. Since data is stored in tables in a database, you always begin a query by asking, "Which table holds the data I want?" For the question about account balances over $5,000, you would reference the Accounts table. In some cases, the data may be held in two or more tables. Multi-table queries will be covered later; for now, you will limit your study of queries to only one table.

If you want to invite customers in a certain zip code to the Grand Opening of a new branch, you could create a query based on the Customers table.

Query Design view enables you to create queries; the Design view is divided into two parts—the top portion displays the tables, and the bottom portion (known as the query design grid) displays the fields and the criteria.

You use the ***Query Design view*** to create queries; the Design view is divided into two parts—the top portion displays the tables, and the bottom portion (known as the query design grid) displays the fields and the criteria.

Using the Query Design view, you select only the fields you want arranged in the order that you want them. The design grid also enables you to sort the records based on one or more fields. You can also create calculated fields to display data based on expressions that use the fields in the underlying table. For example, you could calculate the monthly interest earned on each bank account.

In this section, you will use the Query Wizard and Query Design to create queries that display only data that you select.

Creating a Single-Table Query

The **Simple Query Wizard** provides dialog boxes to guide you through the query design process.

You can create a single-table query in two ways—by using the Simple Query Wizard or by using the Query Design tool in the Queries group. Like all of the Microsoft wizards, the ***Simple Query Wizard*** provides dialog boxes to guide you through the query design process. The wizard is helpful for users who are not experienced with Access or with queries. More advanced users will usually use the Query Design tool to create queries. This method provides the most flexibility when creating queries (but without the prompting of the wizard). You can add criteria to a query while in the Query Design view, as compared to the wizard where you cannot add criteria while the wizard is running. After the query is created, you can switch to Design view and add criteria manually.

After you design a query (using either method), you can display the results of the query by switching to Datasheet view. A query's datasheet looks and acts like a table's datasheet, except that it is usually a subset of the records found in the entire table. The subset only shows the records that match the criteria that were added in the query design. The subset will usually contain different sorting of the records than the sorting in the underlying table. Datasheet view allows you to enter a new record, modify an existing record, or delete a record. Any changes made in Datasheet view are reflected in the underlying table.

TIP Caution: Changes Made to Query Results Overwrite Table Data

Be aware that query results display the actual records that are stored in the underlying table(s). On the one hand, being able to correct an error immediately while it is displayed in query results is an advantage. You save time by not having to close the query, open the table, find the error, fix it, and run the query again. However, you should use caution when editing records in query results since you might not expect to change the table data.

Create a Single-Table Select Query

As stated above, more experienced users create queries using the Query Design tool. To begin click the Create tab, and then click Query Design in the Queries group. The Show Table dialog box appears automatically. Select the table that you need in your query, and then click Add to add the table to the top section of the query design, as shown in Figure 33. After the table has been added, close the Show Table dialog box and begin dragging the fields from the table to the query design grid. The grid holds the fields as well as the criteria (for filtering records) and the sorting options. Figure 34 shows the Design view of a sample query with four fields, with criteria set for one field, and sorting set on another field. After the query design is finished, click Run in the Results group to show the results in Datasheet view, as shown in Figure 35.

A **select query** displays only the records that match the criteria entered in Design view.

By default, when you create a query, you create a select query, which is the most common type of query. A ***select query*** displays only the records that match the criteria entered in Design view. A select query does not change the data. Other types of queries, known as action queries, can update, append, or delete records when they are run. Examples include Update Query, Append Query, and Make Table Query.

TIP Examine the Records

An experienced Access user always examines the records returned in the query results. Verify that the records in the query results match the criteria that you specified in Design view. As you add additional criteria, the number of records returned will usually decrease.

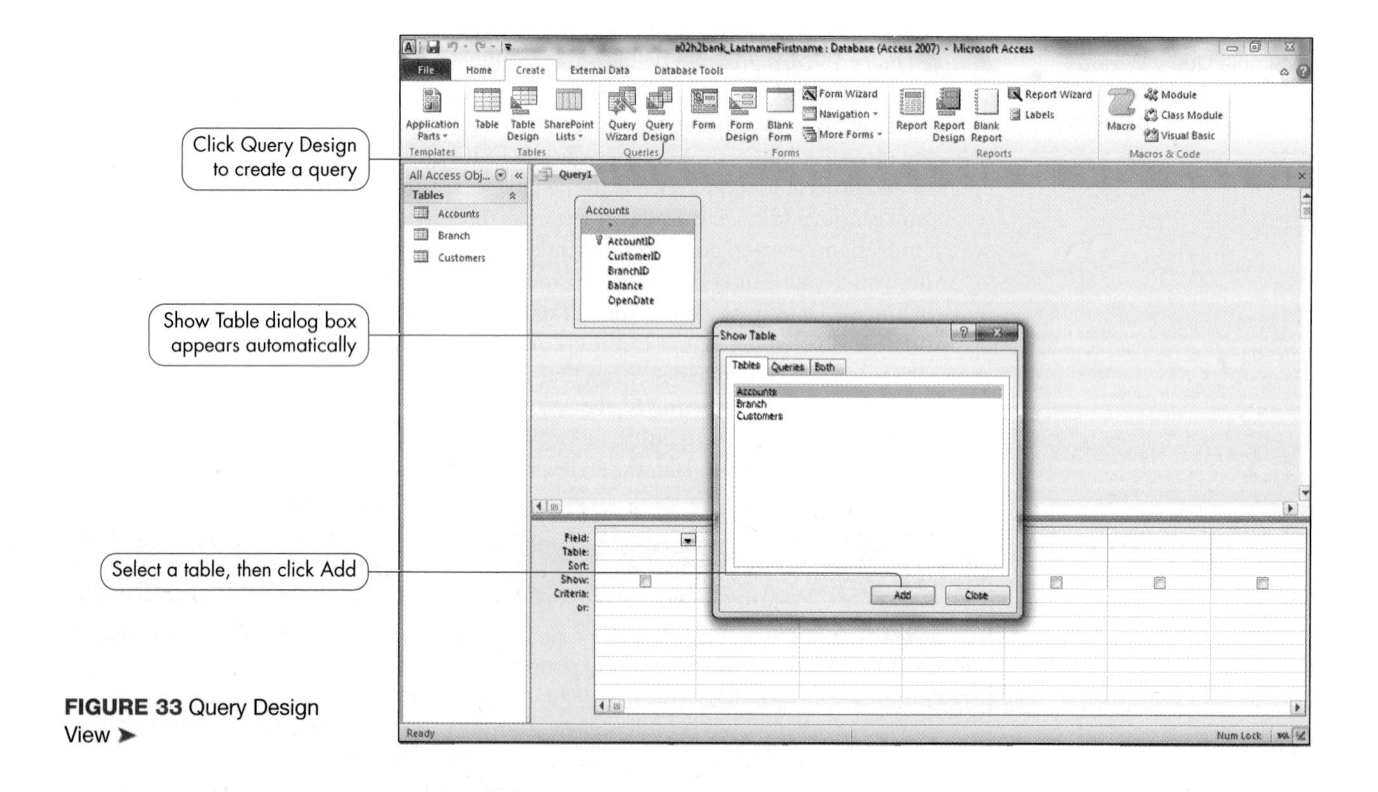

FIGURE 33 Query Design View ➤

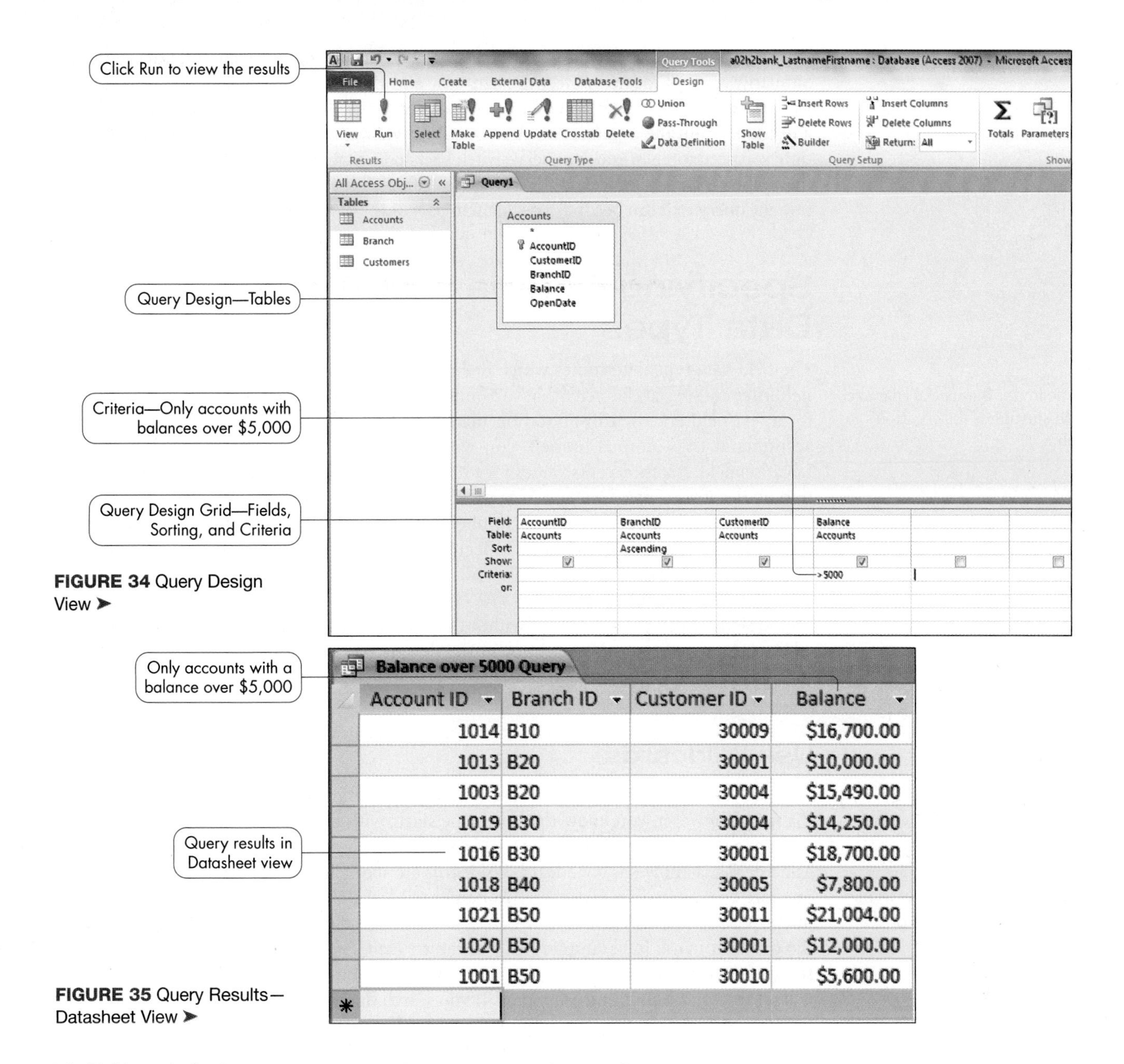

FIGURE 34 Query Design View ➤

FIGURE 35 Query Results—Datasheet View ➤

The **Field row** in the Query Design view displays the field name.

The **Table row** in the Query Design view displays the data source.

The **Sort row** in the Query Design view enables you to sort in ascending or descending order.

The **Show row** in the Query Design view controls whether the field will be displayed in the query results.

The **Criteria row** in the Query Design view determines which records will be selected.

Use Query Design View

The Query Design view consists of two parts. The top portion contains tables with their respective field names. If a query contains more than one table, the join lines between tables will be displayed as they were created in the Relationships window.

The bottom portion (known as the query design grid) contains columns and rows. Each field in the query has its own column and contains multiple rows. The rows permit you to control the query results.

- The ***Field row*** in the Query Design view displays the field name.
- The ***Table row*** in the Query Design view displays the data source.
- The ***Sort row*** in the Query Design view enables you to sort in ascending or descending order.
- The ***Show row*** in the Query Design view controls whether the field will be displayed in the query results.
- The ***Criteria row*** in the Query Design view is used to set the rules that determine which records will be selected, such as customers with accounts greater than $5,000.

When you developed the tables, you toggled between the Design view and Datasheet view. Similarly, you will toggle between Design view and Datasheet view when you create queries. Use Design view to specify the criteria; you can use the results to answer a question or to make a decision about the organization. Use Datasheet view to see the results of your query. Each time you need to fine-tune the query, switch back to Design view, make a change, and then test the results in Datasheet view. After you are satisfied with the query results, you may want to save the query so it can become a permanent part of the database and can be used later.

Specifying Criteria for Different Data Types

A **delimiter** is a special character that surrounds the criterion's value.

The field data type determines which delimiters are required for the criterion of a field. A ***delimiter*** is a special character that surrounds the criterion's value. You need to enter criteria for a text field enclosed in quotation marks. To find only the records of customers with accounts at the Campus branch, you would enter *Campus* as the criterion under the Location field. Access accepts values for text fields in the design grid with or without quotation marks; if you enter *Campus*, Access will add the quotes for you. You enter the criteria for a numeric field, currency, or AutoNumber as plain digits (no quotations). You can enter numeric criteria with or without a decimal point and with or without a minus sign. (Commas and dollar signs are not allowed.) When the criterion is in a date field, you enclose the criterion in pound signs, such as *#10/14/2012#*. Access accepts a date with or without the pound signs; if you enter 1/1/2012 without the pound signs, Access will add the pound signs when you move to another column in the design grid. The date value should be in the mm/dd/yyyy format. You enter criteria for a Yes/No field as *Yes* or *No*.

Use Wildcards

A **wildcard** is a special character that can represent one or more characters in the criterion of a query.

Suppose you want to search for the last name of a customer but you are not sure how to spell the name; however, you know that his name starts with the letters Sm. You can specify the criteria in the LastName field as Sm*, which would display all last names that begin with *Sm*. The asterisk is known as a wildcard. ***Wildcards*** are special characters that can represent one or more characters in a text value. You enter wildcard characters in the Criteria row of a query. A question mark is a wildcard that stands for a single character in the same position as the question mark; for example, *H?ll* will return *Hall*, *Hill*, and *Hull*. The asterisk wildcard stands for any number of characters in the same position as the asterisk; for example, S*nd will return *Sand*, *Stand*, and *StoryLand*. If you search the two-letter state code field using criterion Like *?C*, Access will return *DC*, *NC*, and *SC*. If you search the same field using criterion Like *C, Access will return *DC*, *NC*, and *SC*. If you search the same field using criterion Like C*, Access will return *CA*, *CO*, and *CT*.

Use Comparison Operators in Queries

A **comparison operator**, such as equal (=), not equal (<>), greater than (>), less than (<), greater than or equal to (>=), and less than or equal to (<=), can be used in the criteria of a query.

A ***comparison operator***, such as equal (=), not equal (<>), greater than (>), less than (<), greater than or equal to (>=), and less than or equal to (<=), can be used in the criteria of a query. Comparison operators enable you to limit the query results to only those records that meet the criteria. For example, if you only want to see accounts that have a balance greater than $5,000, you would type >5000 in the criteria row. Table 3 shows more comparison operator examples as well as other sample expressions.

TABLE 3 Sample Query Criteria

Expression	Example
>10	For a Price field, items with a price over $10.00.
<10	For a Price field, items with a price under $10.00.
>=10	For a Price field, items with a price of at least $10.00.
<=10	For a Price field, items with a price of $10.00 or less.
=10	For a Price field, items with a price of exactly $10.00.
<>10	For a Price field, items with a price not equal to $10.00.
#2/2/2012#	For a field with a Date/Time data type, such as a ShippedDate field, orders shipped on February 2, 2012.
"Harry"	For a Text field, find the name Harry.
Date()	For an OrderDate field, orders for today's date.
Between #1/1/2012# and #3/31/2012#	For a specified interval between a start and end date, including the start and end dates.

Work with Null and Zero-Length Strings

Null is the term Access uses to describe a blank field.

Sometimes finding what is missing is an important part of making a decision. For example, if you need to know which orders have been completed but not shipped, you would ask for the orders with a missing ShipDate. Are there missing phone numbers or addresses for some of your customers? Ask for customers with a missing PhoneNumber. The term that Access uses for a blank field is ***null***. Table 4 gives two illustrations of when to use the null criterion in a query.

TABLE 4 Establishing Null Criteria Expressions

Expression	Example
Is Null	For an Employee field in the Customers table when the customer has not been assigned a sales representative.
Is Not Null	For the ShipDate field; a value inserted indicates the order was shipped to the customer.

Understand Query Sort Order

The **query sort order** determines the order of records in the query's Datasheet view.

The ***query sort order*** determines the order of records in a query's Datasheet view. You can change the order of records by specifying the sort order in the Design view. The sort order is determined from left to right. The order of columns should be considered when first creating the query. For example, a query sorted by Lastname and then by Firstname must have those two fields in the correct order in the design grid. Change the order of the query fields in the design grid to change the sort order of the query results. To change the order of fields, select the column you want to move by clicking the column selector. Release the mouse, then click again and drag the selected field to its new location. To insert additional columns in the design grid, first select a column, and then click Insert Columns in the Query Setup group. The inserted column will insert to the left of the selected column.

Establish AND, OR, and NOT Criteria

Recall the earlier question, "Which customers currently have an account with a balance over $5,000?" This question was answered by creating a query with a single criterion, as shown in Figure 34. At times, questions are more specific and require queries with multiple criteria. For example, you may need to know "Which customers from the Eastern branch currently have an account with a balance over $5,000?" To answer this question, you need to specify

The **AND logical operator** returns only records that meet all criteria.

The **OR logical operator** returns records meeting any of the specified criteria.

The **NOT logical operator** returns all records except the specified criteria.

criteria in multiple fields. When the criteria are in the same row of the query design grid, Access interprets the instructions using the ***AND logical operator***. This means that the query results will display only records that match *all* criteria. When the criteria are positioned in different rows of the design grid, Access interprets the instructions using the ***OR logical operator***. The query results will display records that match any of the specified criteria. The ***NOT logical operator*** returns all records except the specified criteria. For example, "Not Eastern" would return all accounts except those opened at the Eastern branch.

Figure 36a shows a query with an AND logical operator. It will return all of the B20 branch accounts with balances over $5,000. (Both conditions must be met for the record to be included.) Figure 36b shows a query with an OR logical operator. It will return all of the B20 branch accounts regardless of balance plus all accounts at any branch with a balance over $5,000. (One condition must be met for a record to be included.) Figure 36c shows a query that uses the NOT logical operator. It will return all of the accounts—excluding the B20 branch—with a balance over $5,000. Figure 36d shows a query that combines AND and OR logical operators. The top row will return B20 branch accounts with a balance over $5,000, and the second row will return B30 branch accounts with a balance over $15,000.

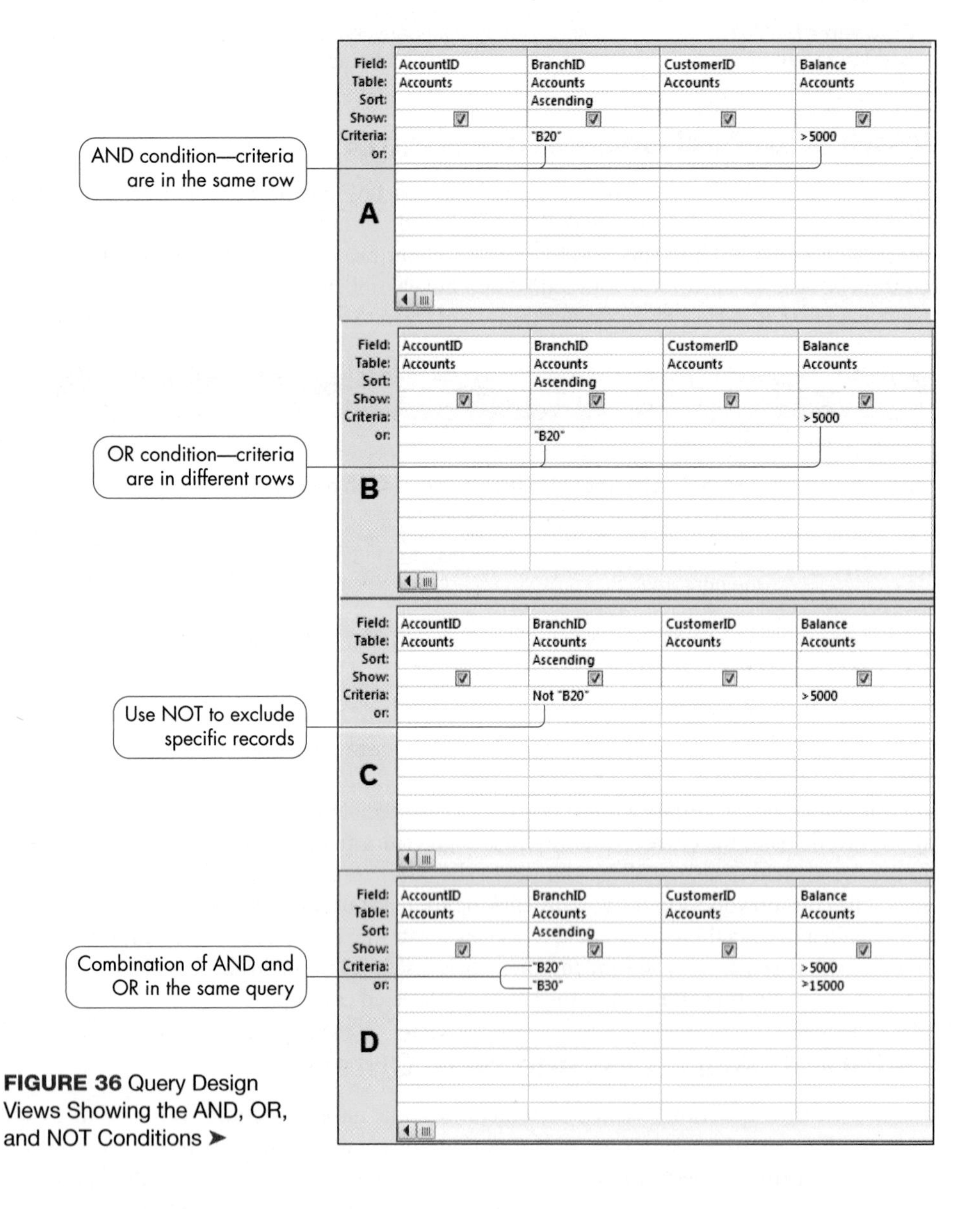

FIGURE 36 Query Design Views Showing the AND, OR, and NOT Conditions ➤

Copying and Running a Query

After you create a query, you may want to create a duplicate copy to use as the basis for creating a similar query. Duplicating a query saves time when you need the same tables and fields but with slightly different criteria.

Several ways exist to run a query. One method is to locate the query in the Navigation Pane, and then double-click it. A similar method is to select the query, and then press Enter. Another way is to click Run in the Results group, when you are in Design view.

Copy a Query

Sometimes you have a one-of-a-kind question about your data. You would create a query to answer this question and then delete the query. However, sometimes you need a series of queries where each query is similar to the first. For example, you need "Sales for This Month" in Houston, in Dallas, and in Chicago. In cases like this, you create a query for the first city and then save the query. Click Save As to save a copy of the query and name it for the second city. Change the criteria to match the second city. Repeat the process for the third city.

Run a Query

The **Run command** (the red exclamation point) is used to produce the query results.

After you create a query and save it, you can run it directly from the Design view. You run a query by clicking ***Run command*** (the red exclamation point) in the Results group. In the sample databases, the queries run quickly. For larger databases, query results may take several minutes to display. When you design queries in larger databases, include all necessary fields and tables, but do not include fields or tables that are not necessary to answer the question. You can also run a query from the Navigation Pane. Locate the query you want to run, and then double-click the query. The results will appear as a tab in the main window. (Note: This method is only recommended for select queries. This method is not recommended for action queries, which will be covered later.)

Using the Query Wizard

You may create a query directly in Design view or by using the Query Wizard. Even if you initiate the query with a wizard, you will need to learn how to modify it in Design view. Often, copying an existing query and making slight modifications to its design is much faster than starting at the beginning with the wizard. You also will need to know how to add additional tables and fields to an existing query when conditions change. To launch the Query Wizard, click the Create tab, and then click Query Wizard in the Queries group (see Figure 37).

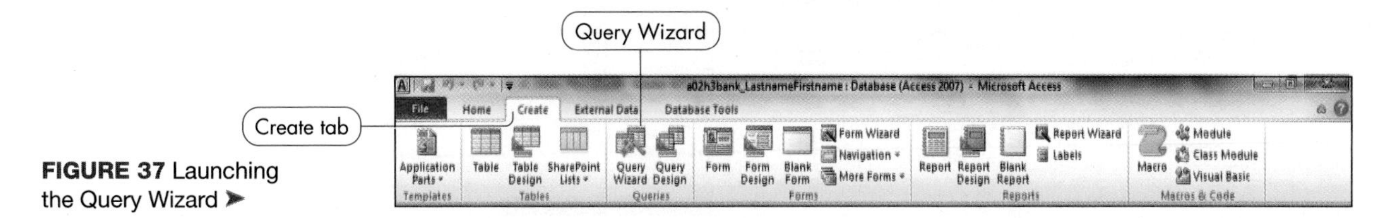

FIGURE 37 Launching the Query Wizard ➤

Select the Simple Query Wizard in the Query Wizard dialog box, as shown in Figure 38.

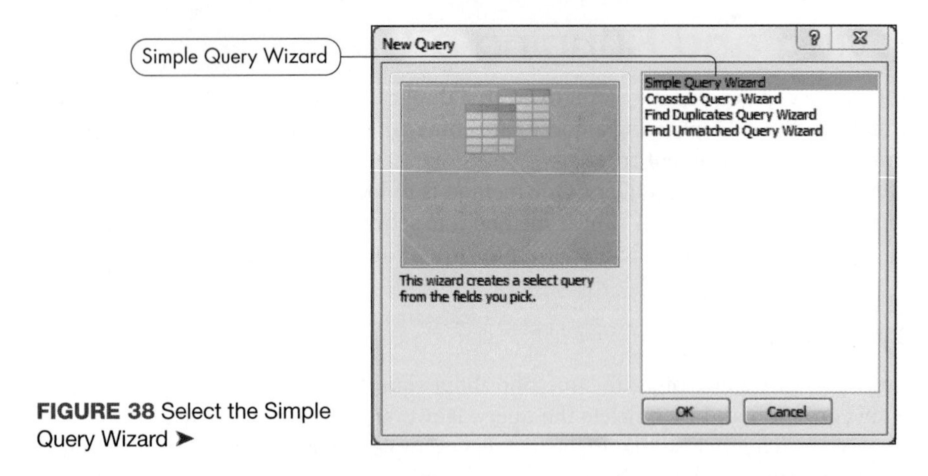

FIGURE 38 Select the Simple Query Wizard ➤

In the first step of the Simple Query Wizard dialog box, you specify the tables or queries and fields needed in your query. When you select a table from the Tables/Queries arrow, a list of the table's fields displays in the Available Fields list box. See Figures 39 and 40.

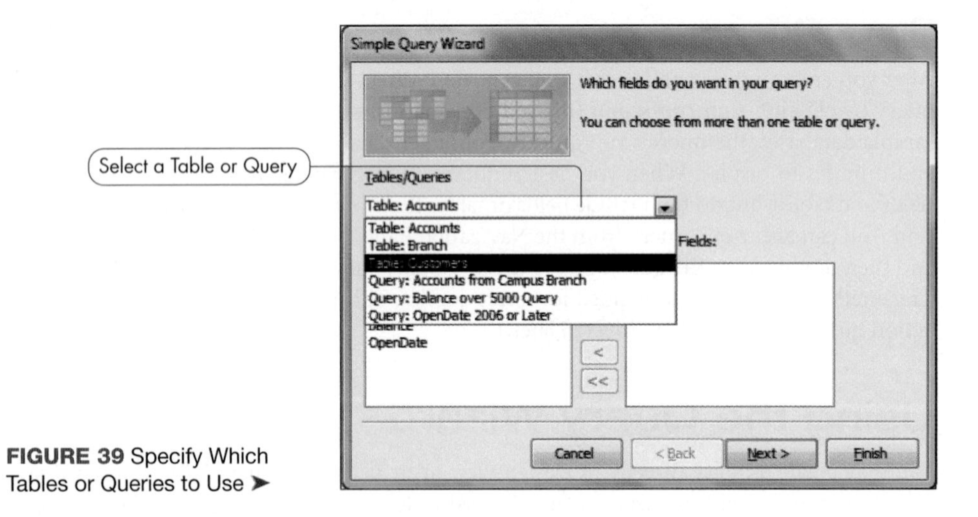

FIGURE 39 Specify Which Tables or Queries to Use ➤

Select the necessary fields, and then add them to the Selected Fields list box using the directional arrows shown in Figure 40.

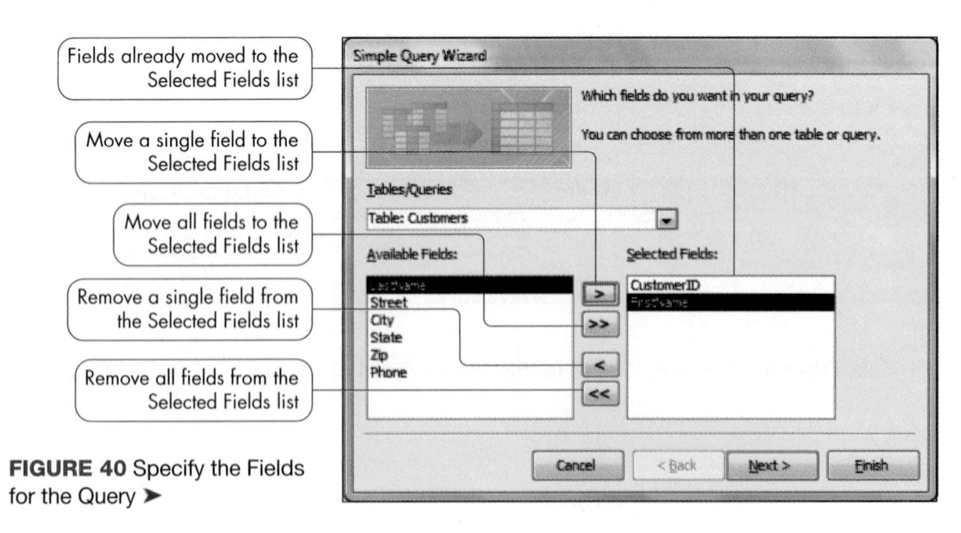

FIGURE 40 Specify the Fields for the Query ➤

In the next screen (shown in Figure 41), you choose between a detail and a summary query. The detail query shows every field of every record in the result. The summary query enables you to group data and view only summary records. For example, if you were interested in the total funds deposited at each of the bank branches, you would set the query to Summary, click Summary Options, and then click sum on the balance field. Access would then sum the balances of all accounts for each branch.

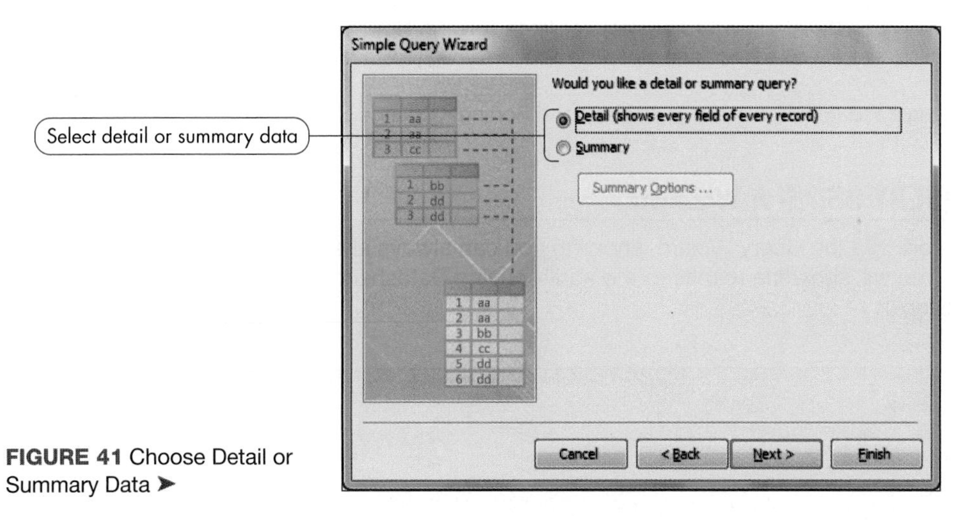

FIGURE 41 Choose Detail or Summary Data ➤

The final dialog box of the Simple Query Wizard asks for the name of the query. Assign a descriptive name to your queries so that you know what each does by looking at the query name. See Figure 42.

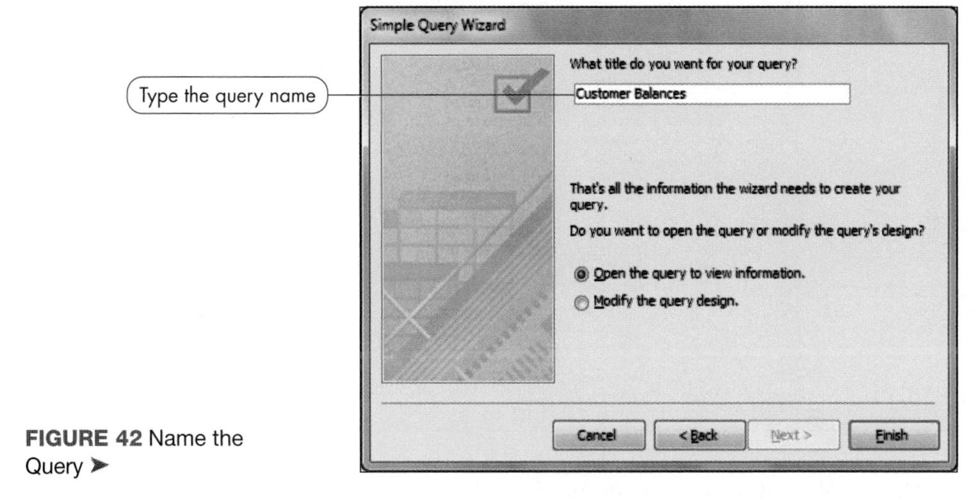

FIGURE 42 Name the Query ➤

The next Hands-On Exercise enables you to create and run queries in order to find answers to questions you have about your data. You will use the Query Wizard to create a basic query and then modify the query in Design view by adding an additional field and by adding query criteria.

HANDS-ON EXERCISES

3 Single-Table Queries

The tables and table relationships have been created, and some data has been entered. Now, you need to begin the process of analyzing the bank data for the auditor. You will do so using queries. You decide to begin with the Accounts table.

Skills covered: Create a Query Using a Wizard • Specify Query Criteria and Sorting • Change Query Data

STEP 1 CREATE A QUERY USING A WIZARD

You decide to start with the Query Wizard, knowing you can always alter the design of the query later in Design view. You will show the results to the auditor using Datasheet view. Refer to Figure 43 as you complete Step 1.

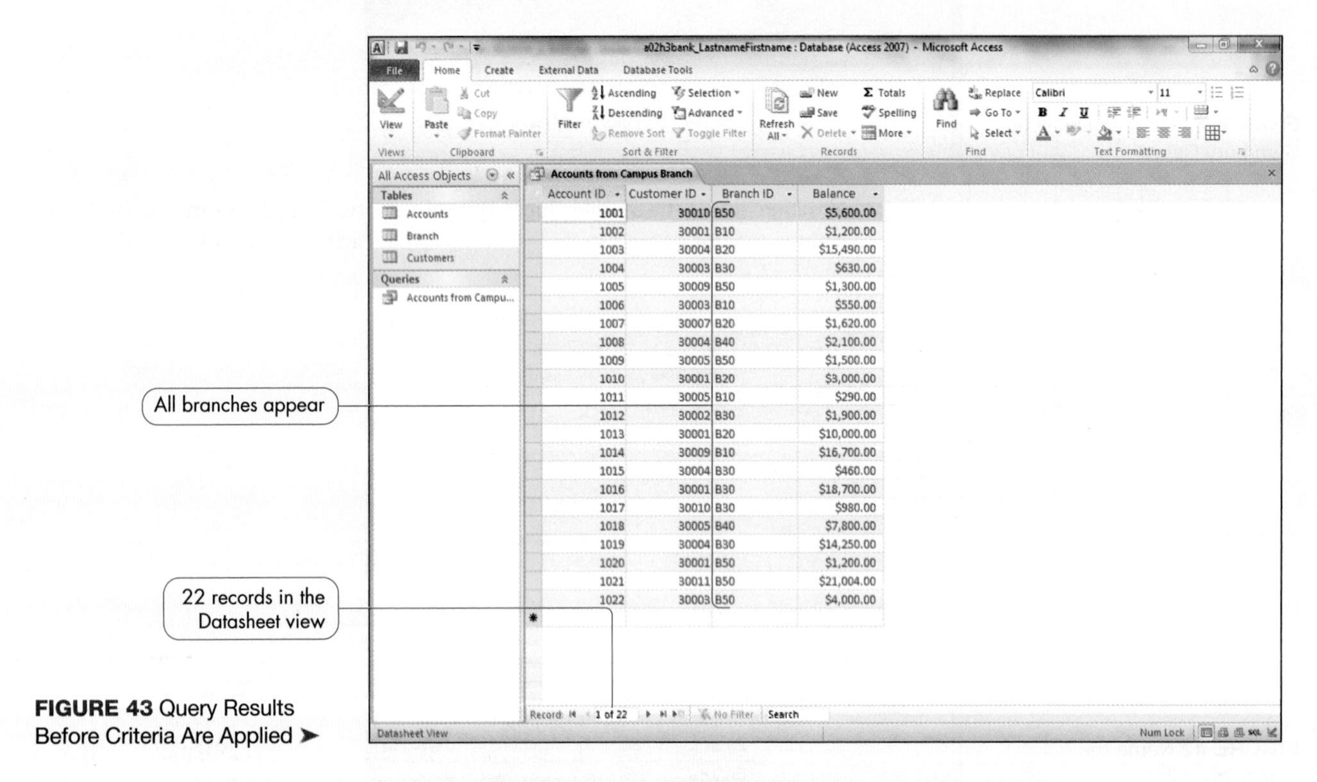

FIGURE 43 Query Results Before Criteria Are Applied ➤

a. Open *a02h2bank_LastnameFirstname* if you closed it at the end of Hands-On Exercise 2. Click the **File tab**, click **Save Database As**, and then type **a02h3bank_LastnameFirstname**, changing *h2* to *h3*. Click **Save**.

b. Click the **Create tab**, and then click **Query Wizard** in the Queries group to launch the New Query wizard.

   The New Query Wizard dialog box opens. Simple Query Wizard is selected by default.

c. Click **OK**.

d. Verify that **Table: Accounts** is selected.

e. Select **AccountID** from the **Available Fields list**, and then click >. Repeat the process with **CustomerID**, **BranchID**, and **Balance**. The four fields should now appear in the Selected Fields list box. Click **Next**.

f. Confirm **Detail** is selected, and then click **Next**.

g. Name the query **Accounts from Campus Branch**. Click **Finish**.

This query name describes the data in the query results. Your query should have four fields: AccountID, CustomerID, BranchID, and Balance.

STEP 2 SPECIFY QUERY CRITERIA AND SORTING

The auditor indicated that the problem seems to be confined to the Campus branch. You use this knowledge to revise the query accordingly. Refer to Figure 44 as you complete Step 2.

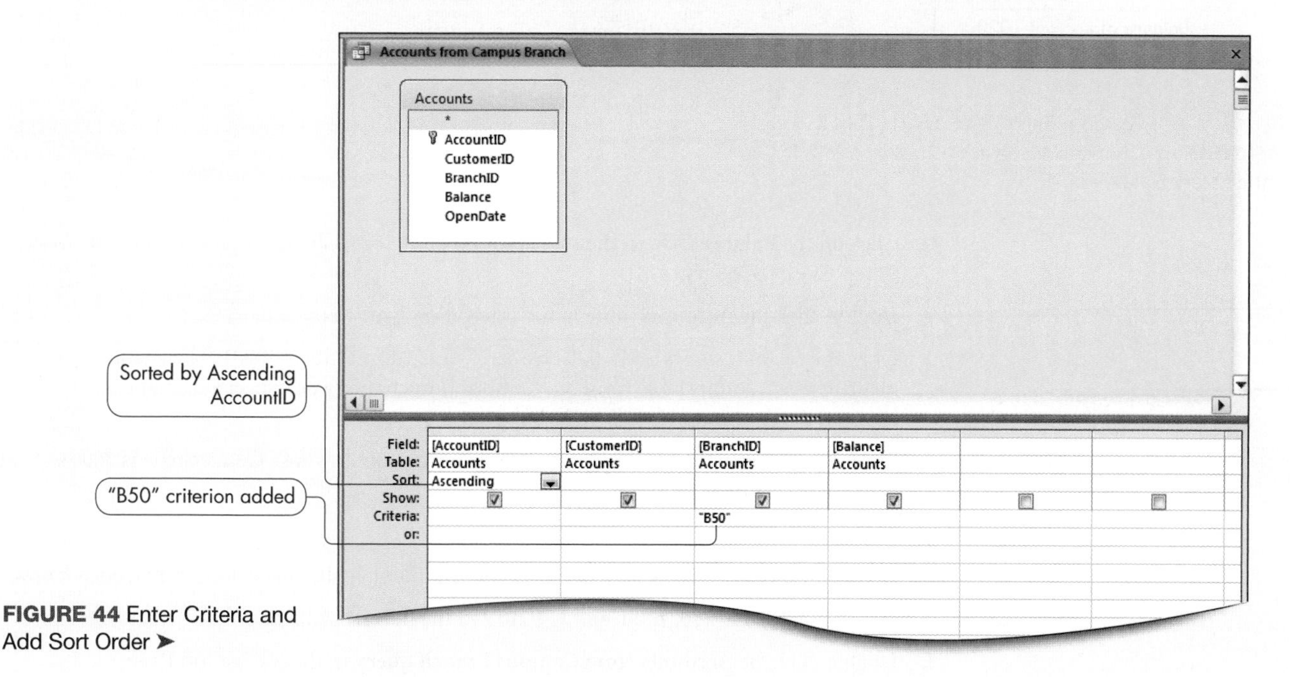

FIGURE 44 Enter Criteria and Add Sort Order ➤

a. Click the **Home tab**, and then click **View** in the Views group to views the Accounts from Campus Branch query in Design view.

You have created the Campus Branch Customers query to view only those accounts at the Campus branch. However, other branch's accounts also display. You need to limit the query results to only the records of interest.

b. Click in the **Criteria row** (fifth row) in the **BranchID column**, and then type **B50**.

B50 is the BranchID for the Campus branch. Access queries are not case sensitive; therefore, b50 and B50 will produce the same results. Access adds quotation marks around text criteria.

c. Click in the **Sort row** (third row) in the **AccountID column**, and then choose **Ascending** from the list.

d. Click **Run** in the Results group.

You should see six records, all from Branch B50, in the query results.

e. Save the query.

STEP 3 CHANGE QUERY DATA

When the query results are on the screen, the auditor notices that some of the data is incorrect, and one of the accounts is missing. From your experience with Access, you explain to the auditor that the data can be changed directly in a query rather than switching back to the table. Refer to Figure 45 as you complete Step 3.

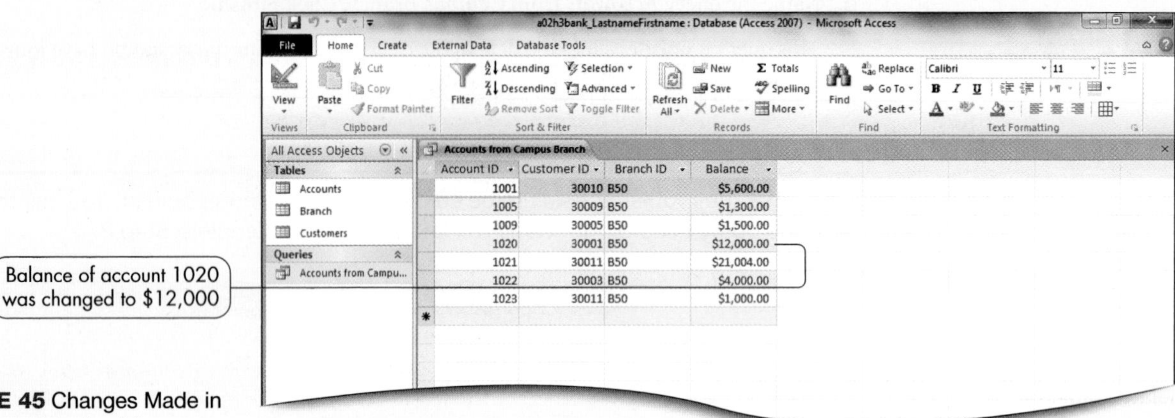

FIGURE 45 Changes Made in the Query Datasheet ➤

a. Click on the **Balance field** in the record for account *1020*. Change *$1,200* to **$12,000.** Press **Enter.** Close the query.

b. Double-click the **Accounts table** in the Navigation Pane to open it.

   Only one account shows a $12,000 balance. The Customer ID is 30001. The change you made in the Accounts table from the Campus Branch query datasheet automatically changed the data stored in the underlying table.

c. Open the Customers table. Find the name of the customer whose CustomerID is *30001*. Close the Customers table.

   Allison Millward's CustomerID number is 30001.

d. Add a new record to the Accounts table. The Accounts table should be open. If not, open it now.

e. Type **1023, 30011, B50, 1000,** and **1/4/2012** in the new record. Press **Tab.**

f. Double-click the **Accounts from Campus Branch query** in the Navigation Pane.

   Customer 30011 now shows two accounts: one with a balance of $21,004 and one with a balance of $1,000.

g. Close the Accounts from Campus Branch query. Close the Accounts table.

h. Click the **File tab,** and then click **Compact & Repair Database.**

i. Click the **File tab,** click **Save & Publish,** and then double-click **Back Up Database.** Accept *a02h3bank_date* as the file name, and then click **Save.**

   You just created a backup of the database. The *a02h3bank_LastnameFirstname* database remains open.

j. Keep the database onscreen if you plan to continue with Hands-On Exercise 4. If not, close the database and exit Access.

Multi-Table Queries

A **multi-table query** contains two or more tables. It enables you to take advantage of the relationships that have been set in your database.

The sample bank database contains three tables: Customers, Accounts, and Branch. You learned how to connect the tables through relationships in order to store data efficiently and enforce consistent data entry. ***Multi-table queries*** contain two or more tables. They enable you to take advantage of the relationships that have been set in your database. When you need to extract information from a database with a query, most times you will need multiple tables to provide the answers you need.

One table may contain the core information that you need. Another table may contain the related data that makes the query relevant to the users. For example, the Accounts table will list the balances of each account at the bank—the key financial information. However, the Accounts table does not list the contact information of the owner of the account. Therefore, the Customers table is needed to provide the additional information.

Creating a Multi-Table Query

Related tables are tables that are joined in a relationship using a common field.

Creating a multi-table query is similar to creating a single-table query; however, choosing the right tables and managing the table relationships will require some additional skills. First, you should only include related tables in a multi-table query. ***Related tables*** are tables that are joined in a relationship using a common field. As a rule, related tables should already be established when you create a multi-table query. Using Figure 46 as a guide, creating a query with the Accounts and Branch tables would be acceptable, as would using Accounts and Customers tables, or Accounts, Branch, and Customers tables. All three scenarios include related tables. Creating a query with the Branch and Customers tables would not be acceptable, since these tables are *not* directly related.

TIP Print the Relationship Report to Help Create a Multi-Table Query

When creating a multi-table query, you should only include related tables. As a guide, you can print the Relationship Report in the Tools group on the Relationship Tools Design tab when the Relationships window is open. This report will help you determine which tables are related in your database.

In the previous example, you answered the question "Which customers from the Campus branch have an account with a balance over $5,000?" Figure 35 displays the datasheet results of the query. To make this report more useful, we can add the Branch Location (in place of the BranchID) and the Customer LastName (in place of the CustomerID). To make these changes we would need to add the Branch table and the Customers table to the query design.

Add Additional Tables to a Query

As discussed earlier, you can modify a saved query using Design view for the query. If you wanted to change the Balance Over $5000 query, first open the query in Design view. To add additional tables to a query, open the Navigation Pane, and then drag tables directly into the top portion of the query design grid. For example, the Branch and Customers tables were added to the query as shown in Figure 46. The join lines between tables indicate that relationships were previously set in the Relationships window.

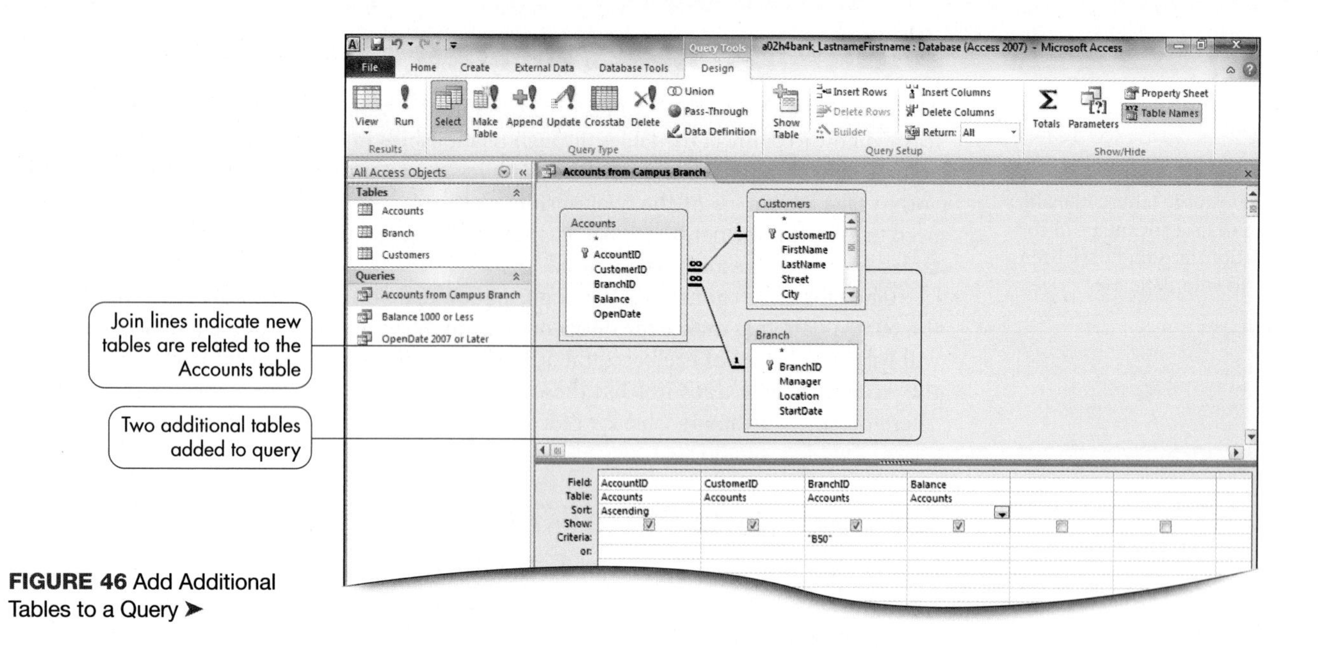

FIGURE 46 Add Additional Tables to a Query ➤

Get Answers Using a Multi-Table Query

You can get key information from your database using a multi-table query. For example, if you want to know how many orders each customer placed since the database was created, you would create a new query and add the Customers and Orders tables to the Query Design view. After you verify that the join lines are correct, add the CustomerID field from the Customers table and the OrderID field from the Order table to the query design grid. When you run the query, the results show duplicates in the CustomerID column because Customers place multiple orders.

To fix the duplicate CustomerID problem, return to the Query Design view, and then click Totals in the Show/Hide group. Both columns show the Group By option in the Total row. Change the total row of the OrderID field to Count, and then run the query again. This time the results show one row for each customer and the number of orders each customer placed since the database was created.

Modifying a Multi-Table Query

To modify multi-table queries, you use the same techniques you learned for single-table queries. Add tables using the Show Table dialog box; remove tables by clicking the unwanted table and then pressing Delete. Add fields by double-clicking the field you want; remove fields by clicking the column selector and then pressing Delete. Join lines between related tables should appear automatically in a query if the relationships were previously established, as shown in Figure 46.

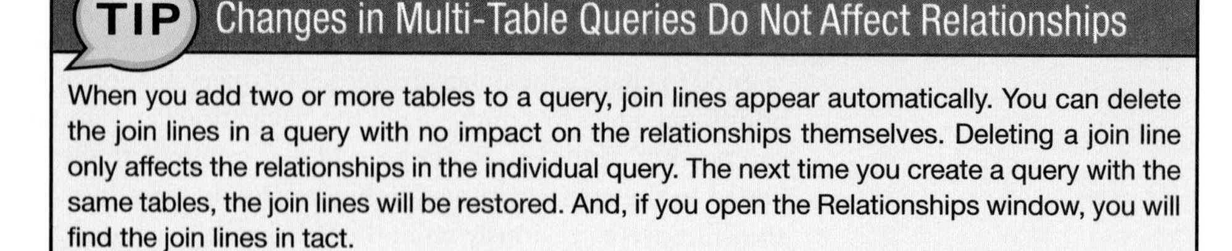

TIP Changes in Multi-Table Queries Do Not Affect Relationships

When you add two or more tables to a query, join lines appear automatically. You can delete the join lines in a query with no impact on the relationships themselves. Deleting a join line only affects the relationships in the individual query. The next time you create a query with the same tables, the join lines will be restored. And, if you open the Relationships window, you will find the join lines in tact.

Add and Delete Fields in a Multi-Table Query

In Figure 46, three tables, as well as the join lines between the tables, now appear in the top pane of the Query Design view. All the fields from each of the tables are available to be used in the query design grid. Figure 47 shows that Location (from the Branch table) and LastName (from the Customers table) have been added to the design, and BranchID and CustomerID have been deleted. The BranchID was deleted from the query; therefore, the 'B50' criterion was removed as well. 'Campus' was added to the Location field's criteria row in order to extract the same results. Because criteria values are not case sensitive, typing 'campus' is the same as typing 'Campus', and both will return the same results. Run the query to see that the datasheet is more useful now that the Location and LastName fields have been added. The results are shown in Figure 48.

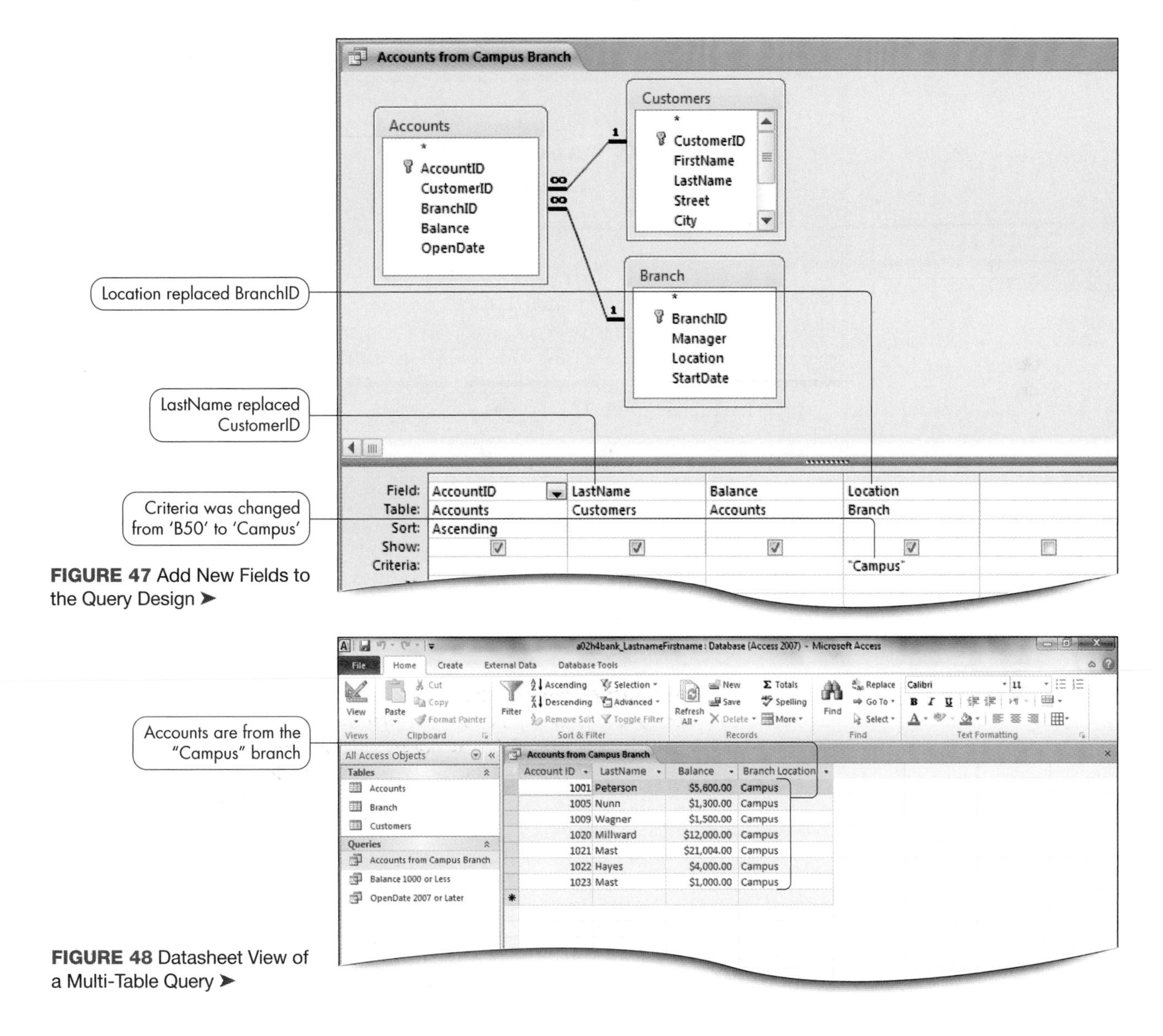

FIGURE 47 Add New Fields to the Query Design ➤

FIGURE 48 Datasheet View of a Multi-Table Query ➤

Fix a Common Problem in a Multi-Table Query

In Figure 49, two tables are added to the query design, but no join line connects them. The results of the query will be unpredictable and larger (i.e., more records) than expected. The Customers table contains 11 records, and the Branch table contains 5 records. Since Access does not know how to interpret the unrelated tables, the results will show 55 records—every possible combination of customer and branch (11 × 5). See Figure 50.

To fix this problem, you can create join lines using the existing tables if the tables facilitate this. Or you can add an additional table that will provide a join between all three tables. In the Branch query, you can add the Accounts table, which will facilitate a join between the two existing tables, Customers and Branch. As soon as the third table is added to the query design, the join lines appear automatically, as shown in Figure 47.

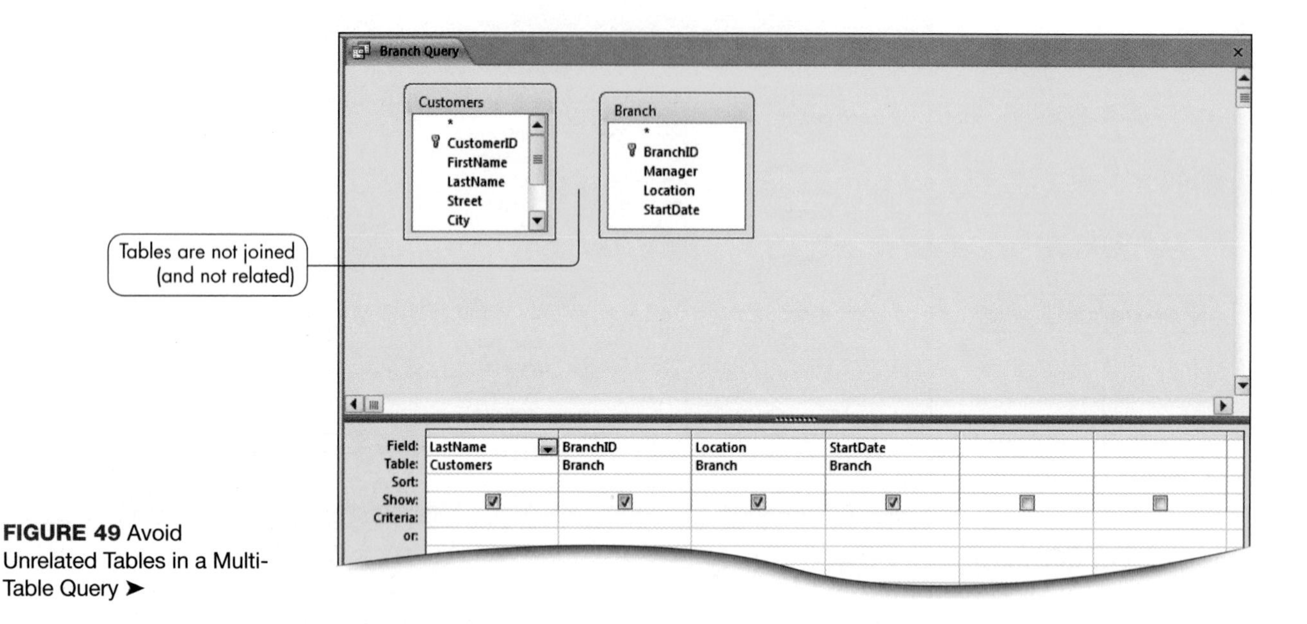

FIGURE 49 Avoid Unrelated Tables in a Multi-Table Query ➤

Access shows one record for every Branch for each Customer

Result shows 55 Records

Query1

LastName	Branch ID	Branch Location	Manager's Start Date
Millward	B10	Uptown	12/1/2007
Millward	B20	Eastern	6/17/2008
Millward	B30	Western	3/11/2006
Millward	B40	Southern	9/15/2009
Millward	B50	Campus	10/11/2011
Fox	B10	Uptown	12/1/2007
Fox	B20	Eastern	6/17/2008
Fox	B30	Western	3/11/2006
Fox	B40	Southern	9/15/2009
Fox	B50	Campus	10/11/2011
Hayes	B10	Uptown	12/1/2007
Hayes	B20	Eastern	6/17/2008
Hayes	B30	Western	3/11/2006
Hayes	B40	Southern	9/15/2009
Hayes	B50	Campus	10/11/2011
Collins	B10	Uptown	12/1/2007
Collins	B20	Eastern	6/17/2008
Collins	B30	Western	3/11/2006
Collins	B40	Southern	9/15/2009
Collins	B50	Campus	10/11/2011
Wagner	B10	Uptown	12/1/2007
Wagner	B20	Eastern	6/17/2008
Wagner	B30	Western	3/11/2006
Wagner	B40	Southern	9/15/2009
Wagner	B50	Campus	10/11/2011
Williams	B10	Uptown	12/1/2007
Williams	B20	Eastern	6/17/2008

Record: 1 of 55 No Filter Search

FIGURE 50 Query Result with Unrelated Tables ➤

Add a Join Line in a Multi-Table Query

Over time, your database will grow, and additional tables will be added. Occasionally, new tables are added to the database but not added to the Relationships window. When queries are created with the new tables, join lines will not be established. When this happens, you can create temporary join lines in the query design. These join lines will provide a temporary relationship between two tables and enable Access to interpret the query properly.

The process of creating a multi-table query works the same as creating a single-table query (covered previously in this chapter). In the Query Design view, you will add fields to the bottom portion (the query design grid), set the sorting, decide whether to show the fields, and add criteria as needed. You should take some precautions when working with multiple tables; these precautions will be discussed later.

HANDS-ON EXERCISES

myitlab
HOE4 Training

4 Multi-Table Queries

Based on the auditor's request, you will need to evaluate the data further. This requires creating queries that are based on multiple tables, rather than a single table. You decide to open an existing query, add additional tables, and then save the query with a new name.

Skills covered: Add Additional Tables to a Query • Create a Multi-Table Query • Modify a Multi-Table Query

STEP 1 ➤ ADD ADDITIONAL TABLES TO A QUERY

The previous query was based on the Accounts table, but now you need to add information to the query that is in the Branch table. You will need to add the Branch and Customers tables to the query. Refer to Figure 51 as you complete Step 1.

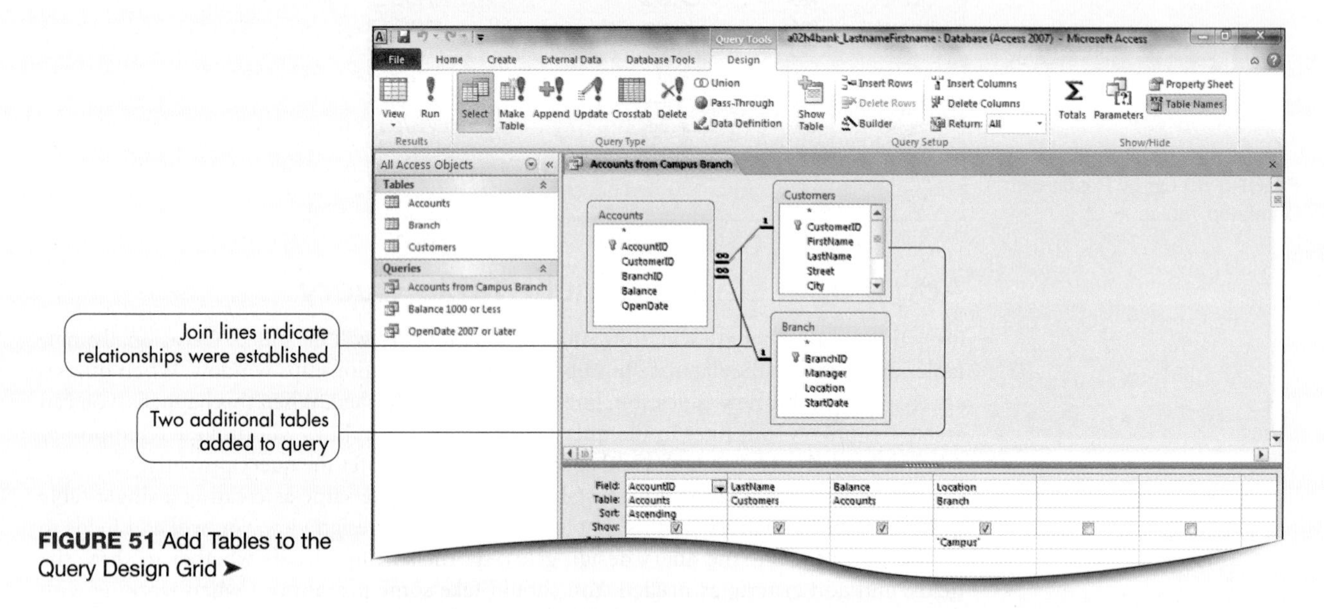
Join lines indicate relationships were established
Two additional tables added to query

FIGURE 51 Add Tables to the Query Design Grid ➤

a. Open *a02h3bank_LastnameFirstname* if you closed it at the end of Hands-On Exercise 3. Click the **File tab**, click **Save Database As**, and then type **a02h4bank_LastnameFirstname**, changing *h3* to *h4*. Click **Save**.

b. Right-click the **Accounts from Campus Branch query** in the Navigation Pane, and then select **Design View** from the shortcut menu.

c. Drag the **Branch table** from the Navigation Pane to the top pane of the query design grid next to the Accounts table.

   A join line connects the Branch table to the Accounts table. The query inherits the join lines from the relationships created in the Relationships window.

d. Drag the **Location field** from the Branch table to the first empty column in the design grid.

   The Location field should be positioned to the right of the Balance column.

e. Click the **Show check box** under the BranchID field to clear the check box and hide this field in the results.

   The BranchID field is no longer needed since the Location field provides the same information. Because you unchecked the BranchID show check box, the BranchID field will not appear the next time the query is opened.

f. Delete the **B50 criterion** in the BranchID field.

g. Type **Campus** as a criterion in the **Location field**, and then press **Enter**.

   Access adds quotation marks around *Campus* for you; quotes are required for text criteria. You are substituting the Location criterion (*Campus*) in place of the BranchID criterion (B50).

h. Remove Ascending from the AccountID sort row. Click in the **Sort row** of the Balance field. Click the arrow, and then select **Descending** from the list.

   The query will be sorted by descending balance order. The largest balance will be listed first, and the smallest will be last.

i. Click **Run** in the Results group.

   Only Campus accounts should appear in the datasheet. Next, you will add the Customer LastName and criteria, and then delete CustomerID from the query.

j. Click **View** in the Views group to return to the Design view.

k. Drag the **Customers table** from the Navigation Pane to the top section of the query design grid.

   The one-to-many relationship lines automatically connect the Customers table to the Accounts table (similar to step c above).

l. Drag the **LastName field** in the Customers table to the second column in the design grid.

   The LastName field should be positioned to the right of the AccountID field.

m. Click the column selector in the CustomerID field to select it. Press **Delete**.

   The CustomerID field is no longer needed in the results because we added the LastName field.

n. Click **Run** in the Results group.

o. Save and close the query.

STEP 2 CREATE A MULTI-TABLE QUERY

After discussing the query results with the auditor, you realize that another query is needed to show those customers with account balances of $1,000 or less. You create the query and view the results in Datasheet view. Refer to Figure 52 as you complete Step 2.

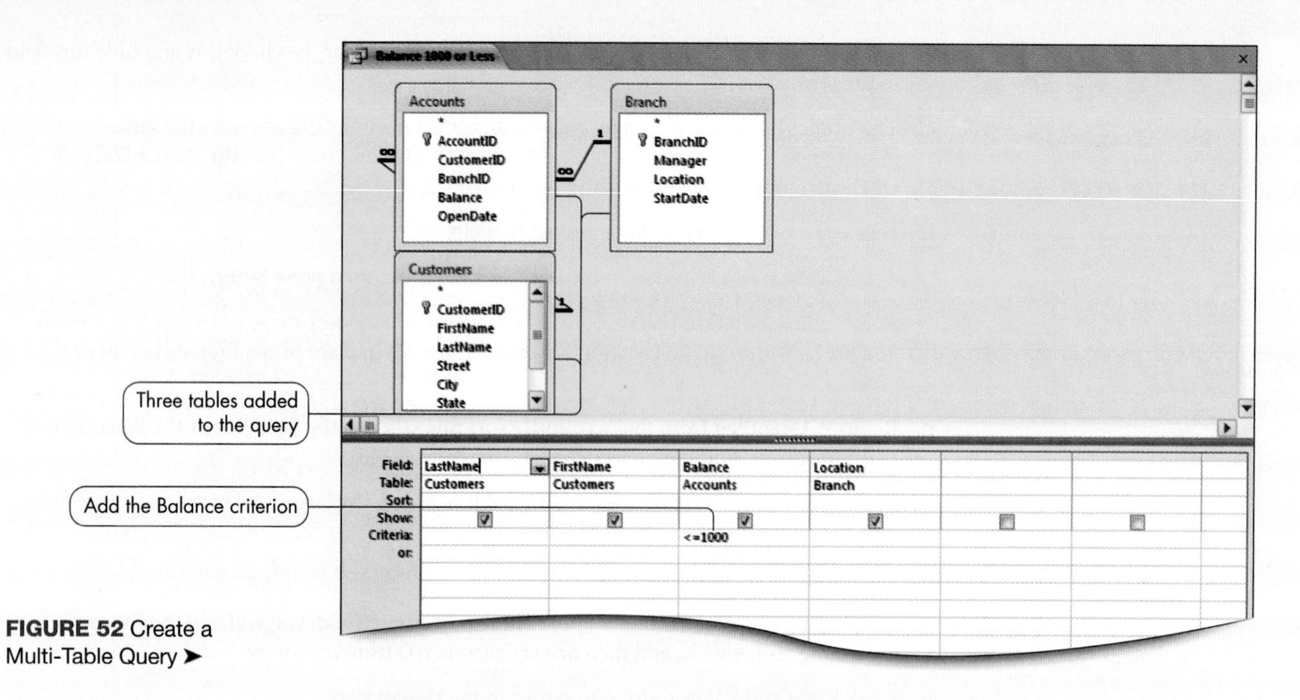

FIGURE 52 Create a Multi-Table Query ➤

a. Click the **Create tab**, and click **Query Design** in the Queries group.

b. Double-click each table name in the Show Table dialog box to add each one to the Query Design view. Click **Close** in the Show Table dialog box.

c. Double-click the following fields to add them to the design grid: **LastName, FirstName, Balance,** and **Location.**

d. Type **<=1000** in the **Criteria row** of the Balance column.

e. Click **Run** in the Results group to see the query results.
   Six records appear in the query results.

f. Click **Save** on the Quick Access Toolbar, and then type **Balance 1000 or Less** as the Query Name in the **Save As dialog box.** Click **OK.**

STEP 3 MODIFY A MULTI-TABLE QUERY

The auditor requests additional changes to the Balance 1000 or Less query you just created. You will modify the criteria to display the accounts that were opened after January 1, 2006, with balances of $2,000 or less. Refer to Figure 53 as you complete Step 3.

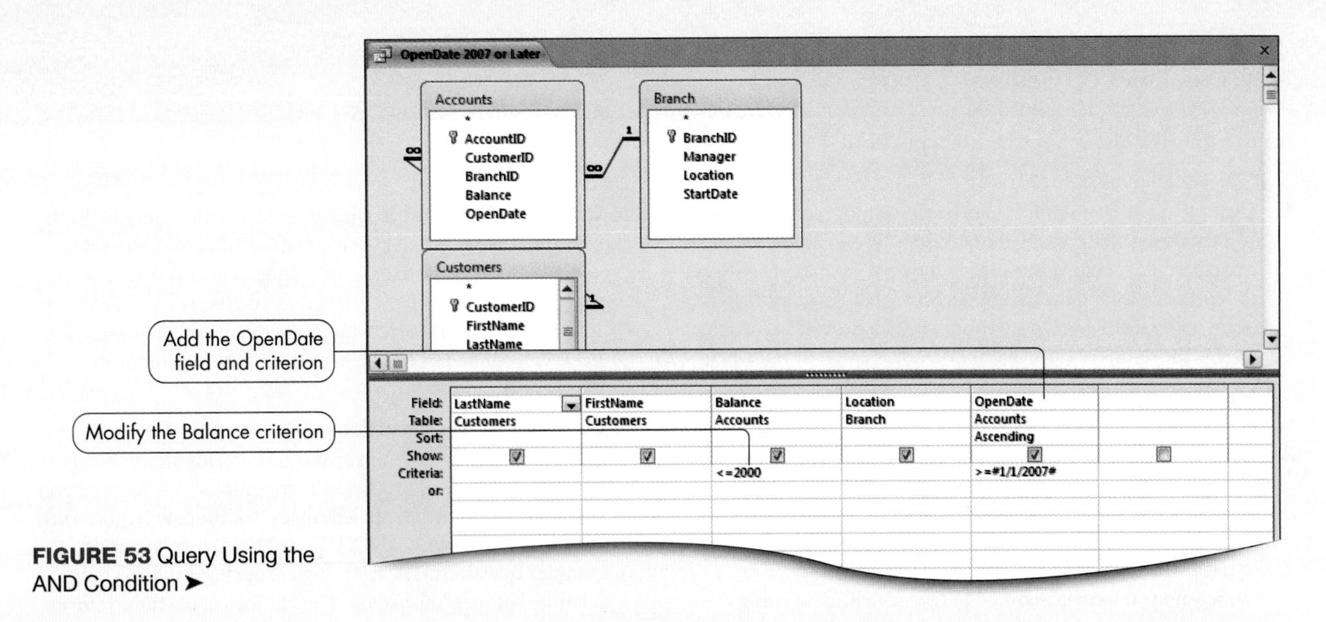

FIGURE 53 Query Using the AND Condition ➤

a. Click **View** in the Views group to switch the *Balance 1000 or Less* query to Design view.

b. Type **<=2000** in place of *<=1000* in the **Criteria row** of the Balance field.

c. Double-click the **OpenDate field** in the Accounts table in the top section of the Query Design view to add it to the first blank column in the design grid.

d. Type **>=1/1/2007** in the **Criteria row** of the OpenDate field to extract only accounts that have been opened since January 2007.

   After you type the expression and then move to a different column, Access will add the # symbols automatically.

e. Click **Run** in the Results group to display the results of the query.

   Three records appear in the query results.

f. Click the **File tab**, click **Save Object As**, and type **OpenDate 2007 or Later** as the query name. Click **OK.**

g. Click the **File tab** again to return to the database.

h. Click **View** in the Views group to return to the Design view of the query.

i. Click in the **Sort row** of the OpenDate field, and then select **Ascending.**

j. Click **Run** in the Results group to display the results of the query.

k. Save and Close the query.

l. Click the **File tab**, and then click **Compact & Repair Database.**

m. Click the **File tab**, click **Save & Publish**, and then double-click **Back Up Database.** Accept *a02h4bank_LastnameFirstname_date* as the file name, and then click **Save.**

   You just created a backup of the database. The *a02h4bank_LastnameFirstname* database remains open.

n. Click the **File tab**, and then click **Exit** (to exit Access).

o. Submit based on your instructor's directions.

CHAPTER OBJECTIVES REVIEW

After reading this chapter, you have accomplished the following objectives:

1. **Design data.** You should consider the output requirements of a database when creating the table structure. When developing a database, the designer must weigh the need for the data against the cost of collecting the data. You learned that design principles begin with identifying the tables of the database. You learned that storing the results of calculations in a table may assist you when creating queries, forms, and reports later. You also learned that data should be stored in its smallest parts.
2. **Create tables.** Access employs several ways to create a table. You can create a table by creating the fields in Design view or by entering table data into a new row in Datasheet view, or you can import data from another application such as Excel. You learned that each field needs a unique and descriptive name, and you were introduced to the CamelCase naming convention. Access accommodates many different types of data, including Text, Number, Date/Time, Yes/No, Memo, and others.
3. **Understand table relationships.** Relationships between tables are set in the Relationships window. In this window, join lines are created, and three options can be set: Enforce Referential Integrity, Cascade Update Related Fields, and Cascade Delete Related Records. When referential integrity is enforced, data cannot be entered into the related table unless it first exists in the primary table. Frequently, the primary key (unique identifier) from one table is entered as a foreign key in a related table. These two fields often become the basis of creating relationships between tables.
4. **Share data with Excel.** Microsoft Access can easily import and export data to (and from) Excel. You used the Import Wizard to import an Excel worksheet into an Access database table. The settings of the Import Wizard may be saved and reused when the import is cyclical.
5. **Establish table relationships.** You created relationship links between tables in the database and attempted to enter an invalid branch number in a related table. You discovered that the enforcement of referential integrity prevented you from creating an account in a nonexistent branch. The Cascade Update Related Fields option ensures that if the primary key is modified in one table, Access will automatically update all fields in related tables. Similarly, the Cascade Delete Related Records option ensures that if the primary key is deleted in one table, Access will automatically delete all records in related tables.
6. **Create a single-table query.** You created a query to display only those records that match certain criteria. You learned to add additional fields to an existing query, to add criteria, and to change the sort order of the query results. The primary sort field needs to be in the left-most position, with additional sort fields determined by their left-to-right positions in the query design grid.
7. **Specify criteria for different data types.** Different data types require different syntax. Date fields are enclosed in pound signs (#) and text fields in quotations ("). Numeric and currency fields require no delimiters. Additionally, you learned that logical operators, AND, OR, and NOT, help to answer complex questions. The AND logical operator returns only records that meet all criteria. The OR logical operator returns records meeting any of the specified criteria. The NOT logical operator returns all records except the specified criteria.
8. **Copy and run a query.** After specifying tables, fields, and conditions for one query, you can copy the query, rename it, and then modify the fields and criteria in the second query. Copying queries saves time since you do not have to select tables and fields again for queries that have a similar structure. To run a query during the design process, click Run in the Results group. To run a saved query, double-click the query name in the Navigation Pane.
9. **Use the Query Wizard.** An alternative way to create a select query is to use the Query Wizard. The wizard enables you to select tables and fields from lists. The last step of the wizard prompts you to save the query.
10. **Create a multi-table query.** Creating a multi-table query is similar to creating a single-table query; however, choosing the right tables and managing the table relationships requires some additional skills. You should only include related tables in a multi-table query. To add additional tables to a query, open the Navigation Pane, and then drag tables directly into the top section of the Query Design view.
11. **Modify a multi-table query.** To modify multi-table queries, you use the same techniques you used for single-table queries. Join lines between related tables should appear automatically in a query if the relationships were previously established. If join lines do not appear, the results will not be correct when you run the query. You can add temporary join lines from inside the query or set the Relationships permanently in the Relationships window.

KEY TERMS

AND logical operator
AutoNumber
Calculated field
CamelCase notation
Caption property
Cascade Delete Related Records
Cascade Update Related Fields
Comparison operator
Constant
Criteria row
Data redundancy
Data type
Date arithmetic
Delimiter
Field property
Field row
Indexed property
Multi-table query
NOT logical operator
Null
Number data type
One-to-many relationship
OR logical operator
Query
Query Design view
Query sort order
Referential integrity
Related tables
Run command
Select query
Show row
Simple Query Wizard
Sort row
Table
Table row
Text data type
Validation rule
Wildcard

MULTIPLE CHOICE

1. When entering, deleting, or editing table data:
   (a) The table must be in Design view.
   (b) The table must be in Datasheet view.
   (c) The table may be in either Datasheet or Design view.
   (d) Data may be entered only in a form.

2. Which of the following is true for the Query Wizard?
   (a) You can only select tables as the source.
   (b) No criteria can be added.
   (c) Fields from multiple tables are not allowed.
   (d) You do not need a summary.

3. Which of the following was not a suggested guideline for designing a table?
   (a) Include all necessary data.
   (b) Store data in its smallest parts.
   (c) Avoid calculated fields.
   (d) Link tables using common fields.

4. A query's specifications providing instructions about which records to include must be entered:
   (a) On the Show row of the query design grid.
   (b) On the Sort row of the query design grid.
   (c) On the Criteria row of the query design grid.
   (d) On the Table row of the query design grid.

5. An illustration of a one-to-many relationship would be:
   (a) A person changes his/her primary address.
   (b) A customer may have multiple orders.
   (c) A branch location has an internal BranchID code.
   (d) A balance field is totaled for all accounts for each person.

6. When adding criteria to the query design view:
   (a) The value you enter must be delimited by quotes (")(").
   (b) The value you enter must be delimited by pound signs (#).
   (c) The value you enter must be delimited by nothing ().
   (d) Access will add the correct delimiters for you ("),("), (#), or ().

7. Which of the following is true with respect to an individual's hire date and years of service?
   (a) Hire date should be a calculated field; years of service should be a stored field.
   (b) Hire date should be a stored field; years of service should be a calculated field.
   (c) Both should be stored fields.
   (d) Both should be calculated fields.

8. When importing data into Access, which of the following statements is true?
   (a) The Import Wizard only works for Excel files.
   (b) The wizard can be found on the Create tab.
   (c) You can assign a primary key while you are importing Excel data.
   (d) The wizard will import the data in one step after you select the file.

9. The main reason to enforce referential integrity in Access is to:
   (a) Limit the number of records in a table.
   (b) Keep invalid data from being entered into a table.
   (c) Make it possible to delete records.
   (d) Keep your database safe from unauthorized users.

10. It is more efficient to make a copy of an existing query, rather than create a new query, when which of the following is true?
    (a) The existing query contains only one table.
    (b) The existing query and the new query use the same tables and fields.
    (c) The existing query and the new query have the exact same criteria.
    (d) The original query is no longer being used.

PRACTICE EXERCISES

1 Tom & Erin's Bookstore

Tom and Erin Mullaney own and operate a bookstore in Philadelphia, Pennsylvania. Erin asked you to help her create an Access database because of your experience in this class. You believe that you can help her by creating a database and then importing the Excel spreadsheets they use to store the publishers and the books that they sell. You determine that a third table—for authors—is also required. Your task is to design and populate the three tables, set the table relationships, and enforce referential integrity. If you have problems, reread the detailed directions presented in the chapter. This exercise follows the same set of skills as used in Hands-On Exercises 1 and 2 in the chapter. Refer to Figure 54 as you complete this exercise.

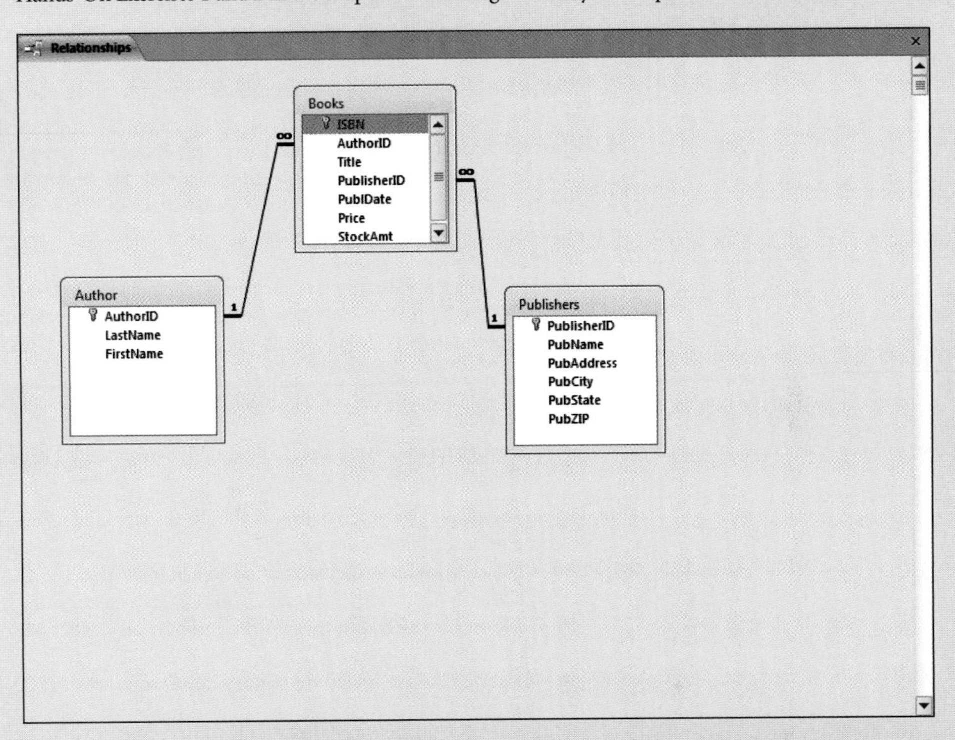

FIGURE 54 Access Relationships Window ➤

a. Start Access, and then click **Blank Database** in the Available Templates section of the Backstage view. Click **Browse** to choose a folder location to store the database, type **a02p1books_LastnameFirstname** as the file name, click **OK**, and then click **Create** to create the new database.

b. Type **11** in the **Click to Add column**, and then click **Click to Add**. The field name becomes *Field1*, and *Click to Add* now appears as the third column. Type **Wayne** and press **Tab**. The process repeats for the fourth column; type **John** and then press **Tab** twice.

c. The cursor returns to the first column where *(New)* is selected. Press **Tab**. Type the rest of the data using the following table. This data will become the records of the Author table.

ID	Field1	Field2	Field3
1	11	Wayne	John
(New)	12	Allen	Keith
	13	Scott	Michael
	14	Carl	Richard
	15	Keen	Clara
	16	Swartz	Millie
	17	Allen	John

d. Click **Save** on the Quick Access Toolbar. Type **Author** in the **Save As dialog box**, and then click **OK**.
e. Click **View** in the Views group to switch to the Design view of the Author table.
f. Select **Field1**—in the second row—in the top portion of the table design, and then type **AuthorID** to rename the field. In the *Field Properties* section in the lower portion of the table design, type **Author ID** in the **Caption property box**, and then verify that *Long Integer* appears for the Field Size property.
g. Select **Field2**, and then type **LastName** to rename the field. In the *Field Properties* section in the bottom portion of the table design, type **Author's Last Name** in the **Caption property box** and **20** as the field size.
h. Select **Field3**, and then type **FirstName** to rename the field. In the *Field Properties* section in the bottom portion of the table design, type **Author's First Name** as the caption, and then type **15** as the field size.
i. Click the **ID field row selector** (which shows the primary key) to select the row, and then click **Delete Rows** in the Tools group. Click **Yes** twice to confirm both messages.
j. Click the **AuthorID row selector**, and then click **Primary Key** in the Tools group to reset the primary key.
k. Click **Save** on the Quick Access Toolbar to save the design changes. Click **Yes** to the *Some data may be lost* message. Close the table.
l. Click the **External Data tab**, and then click **Excel** in the Import & Link group to launch the *Get External Data - Excel Spreadsheet* feature. Verify the *Import the source data into a new table in the current database* option is selected, click **Browse**, and then go to the student data folder. Select the *a02p1books* workbook, click **Open**, and then click **OK**. This workbook contains two worksheets. Follow these steps:
    - Select the **Publishers worksheet**, and then click **Next**.
    - Click the **First Row Contains Column Headings check box**, and then click **Next**.
    - Select the **PubID field**, click the **Indexed arrow**, select **Yes (No Duplicates)**, and then click **Next**.
    - Click the **Choose my own primary key arrow**, select **PubID**, if necessary, and then click **Next**.
    - Accept the name *Publishers* for the table name, click **Finish**, and then click the **Close button** without saving the import steps.
m. Repeat the Import Wizard to import the Books worksheet from the *a02p1books* workbook into the Access database. Follow these steps:
    - Select the **Books worksheet**, and then click **Next**.
    - Ensure the *First Row Contains Column Headings* check box is checked, and then click **Next**.
    - Click on the **ISBN column**, set the Indexed property box to **Yes (No Duplicates)**, and then click **Next**.
    - Click the **Choose my own primary key arrow**, select **ISBN** as the primary key field, and then click **Next**.
    - Accept the name *Books* as the table name. Click **Finish**, and then click the **Close button** without saving the import steps.
n. Right-click the **Books table** in the Navigation Pane, and then select **Design View**. Make the following changes:
    - Change the PubID field name to **PublisherID**.
    - Change the Caption property to **Publisher ID.**
    - Change the PublisherID Field Size property to **2**.
    - Click the **ISBN field** at the top, and then change the Field Size property to **13**.
    - Click the **Price field**, and then change the Price field Data Type to **Currency**.
    - Change the AuthorCode field name to **AuthorID**.
    - Change the AuthorID Field Size property to **Long Integer**.
    - Click the **ISBN field row selector** (which shows the primary key) to select the row, then release, press, and hold the mouse. Drag the row up to the first position.
    - Click **Save** on the Quick Access Toolbar to save the design changes to the Books table. Click **Yes** to the *Some data may be lost* warning.
    - Close the table.
o. Right-click the **Publishers table** in the Navigation Pane, and then select **Design View**. Make the following changes:
    - Change the PubID field name to **PublisherID**.
    - Change the PublisherID Field Size property to **2**.
    - Change the Caption property to **Publisher's ID**.
    - Change the Field Size property to **50** for the PubName and PubAddress fields.

- Change the Pub Address field name to **PubAddress** (remove the space).
- Change the PubCity Field Size property to **30**.
- Change the PubState Field Size property to **2**.
- Change the Pub ZIP field name to **PubZIP** (remove the space).
- Click **Save** on the Quick Access Toolbar to save the design changes to the Publishers table. Click **Yes** to the *Some data may be lost* warning. Close all open tables.

p. Click the **Database Tools tab**, and then click **Relationships** in the Relationships group. Click **Show Table** if necessary. Follow these steps:
- Double-click each table name in the Show Table dialog box to add it to the Relationships window, and then close the Show Table dialog box.
- Drag the **AuthorID field** from the Author table onto the AuthorID field in the Books table.
- Click the **Enforce Referential Integrity** and **Cascade Update Related Fields check boxes** in the Edit Relationships dialog box. Click **Create** to create a one-to-many relationship between the Author and Books tables.
- Drag the **PublisherID field** from the Publishers table onto the PublisherID field in the Books table.
- Click the **Enforce Referential Integrity** and **Cascade Update Related Fields check boxes** in the Edit Relationships dialog box. Click **Create** to create a one-to-many relationship between the Publishers and Books tables.
- Click **Save** on the Quick Access Toolbar to save the changes to the Relationships window.
- Click **Relationship Report** in the Tools group on the Design tab.
- Close the report; do not save it. Close the Relationships window.

q. Click the **File tab**, and then click **Compact & Repair Database**.

r. Click the **File tab**, click **Save & Publish**, and then double-click **Back Up Database**.

s. Click **Save** to accept the default backup file name with today's date.

t. Click the **File tab**, and then click **Exit** (to exit Access).

u. Submit based on your instructor's directions.

2 Davis Insurance Company

The Davis Insurance Company offers a full range of insurance services in four locations: Miami, Boston, Chicago, and Philadelphia. They store all of the firm's employee data in an Excel spreadsheet. This file contains employee name and address, job performance, salary, and title. The firm is converting from Excel to Access. A database file containing two of the tables already exists; your job is to import the employee data from Excel for the third table. Once imported, you will need to modify field properties and set new relationships. The owner of the company, Paul Davis, is concerned that some of the Philadelphia and Boston salaries may be below the guidelines published by the national office. He asks that you investigate the salaries of the two offices and create a separate query for each city. If you have problems, reread the detailed directions presented in the chapter. This exercise follows the same set of skills as used in Hands-On Exercises 2 and 3 in the chapter. Refer to Figure 55 as you complete this exercise.

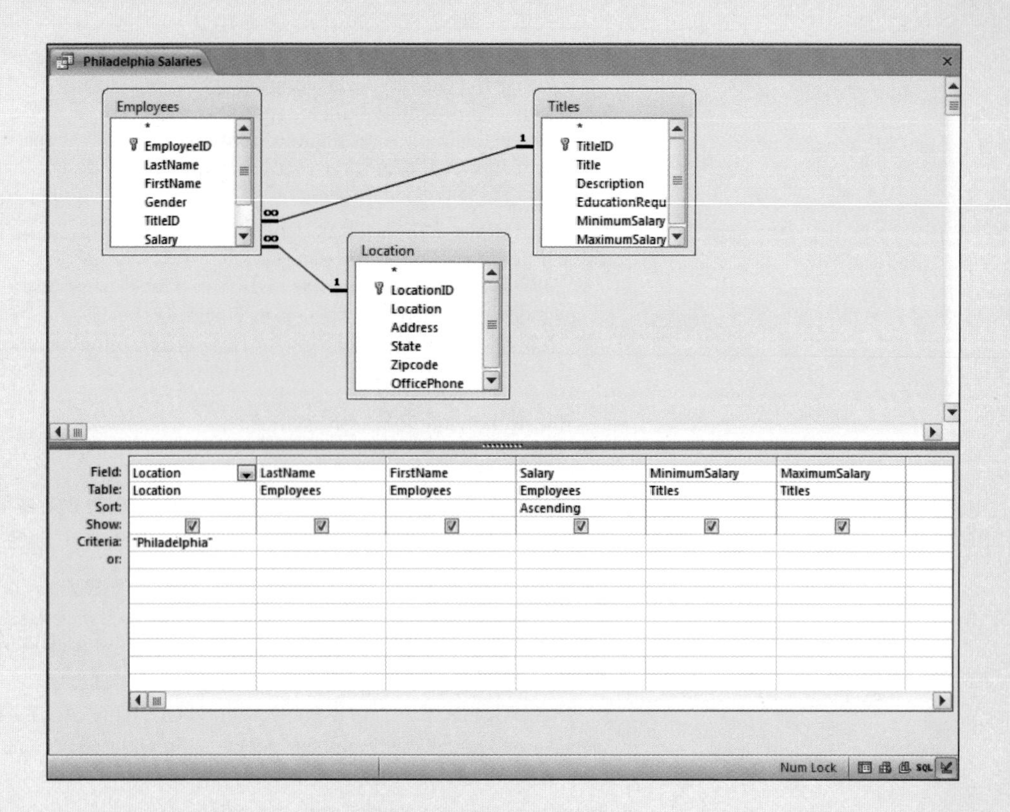

FIGURE 55 Philadelphia Salaries Query ➤

a. Open *a02p2insurance*. Click the **File tab**, click **Save Database As**, and then type **a02p2insurance_LastnameFirstname**. Click **Save**. In the Navigation Pane, double-click to open the **Location** and **Titles tables**, and then look at the contents to become familiar with the field names and the type of information stored in each table. Note the number of Position titles. Close the tables.

b. Click the **External Data tab**, click **Excel** in the Import & Link group, and then follow these steps:
   - Click **Browse**, and then locate the *a02p2employees* workbook. Select it, click **Open**, and then click **OK**.
   - Select the **Employees worksheet**, and then click **Next**.
   - Click the **First Row Contains Column Headings check box**, and then click **Next**.
   - Click the **Indexed arrow** for the EmployeeID field, select **Yes (No Duplicates)**, and then click **Next**.
   - Click **Choose my own primary key arrow**, select the **EmployeeID** as the primary key, and click **Next**.
   - Accept the name *Employees* for the table name, click **Finish**, and then click **Close** without saving the import steps.

c. Double-click the **Employees table** in the Navigation Pane, click the **Home tab**, and then click **View** in the Views group to switch to the Design view of the Employees table. Make the following changes:
   - Click the **LocationID field**, and then change the Field Size property to **3**.
   - Change the Caption property to **Location ID**.
   - Click the **TitleID field**, and then change the Field Size property to **3**.
   - Change the Caption property to **Title ID**.
   - Change the Salary data type to **Currency**, select **General Number** in the Format property in field properties, and then press **Delete**.
   - Save the design changes. Click **Yes** to the *Some data may be lost* warning.

d. Click **View** in the Views group to view the Employees table in Datasheet view, and then examine the data. Click any record in the Title ID, and then click **Ascending** in the Sort & Filter group on the Home tab. Multiple employees are associated with the T01, T02, T03, and T04 titles.

e. Double-click the **Titles table** in the Navigation Pane to open it in Datasheet view. Notice the T04 title is not in the list.

f. Add a new record in the first blank record at the bottom of the Titles table. Using the following data:
   - Type **T04** in the **TitleID field.**
   - Type **Senior Account Rep** in the **Title field.**
   - Type **A marketing position requiring a technical background and at least three years of experience** in the **Description field.**
   - Type **Four year degree** in the **Education Requirements field.**
   - Type **45000** in the **Minimum Salary field.**
   - Type **75000** in the **Maximum Salary field.**

g. Close all tables. Click **No** if you are asked to save the table.

h. Click the **Database Tools tab**, and then click **Relationships** in the Relationships group. Click **Show Table** if necessary. Follow these steps:
   - Double-click each table name in the Show Table dialog box to add them to the Relationships window, and then close the Show Table dialog box.
   - Drag the **LocationID field** in the Location table onto the LocationID field in the Employees table.
   - Click the **Enforce Referential Integrity** and **Cascade Update Related Fields check boxes** in the Edit Relationships dialog box. Click **Create** to create a one-to-many relationship between the Location and Employees tables.
   - Drag the **TitleID field** in the Titles table onto the TitleID field in the Employees table.
   - Click the **Enforce Referential Integrity** and **Cascade Update Related Fields check boxes** in the Edit Relationships dialog box. Click **Create** to create a one-to-many relationship between the Titles and Employees tables.
   - Click **Save** on the Quick Access Toolbar to save the changes to the Relationships window.
   - Close the Relationships window.

i. Click the **Create tab**, and then click the **Query Wizard** in the Queries group. Follow these steps:
   - Select **Simple Query Wizard**, and then click **OK**.
   - Select **Table: Location** in the Tables/Queries box.
   - Double-click **Location** in the **Available Fields list** to move it to the Selected Fields list.
   - Select **Table: Employees** in the **Tables/Queries list.**
   - Double-click **LastName**, **FirstName**, and **Salary**.
   - Select **Table: Titles** in the **Tables/Queries list.**
   - Double-click **MinimumSalary** and **MaximumSalary**. Click **Next.**
   - Select the **Detail (shows every field of every record) option**, and then click **Next.**
   - Type **Philadelphia Salaries** as the query title, and then click **Finish.**

j. Click the **Home tab**, and then click **View** to switch to the Design view of the Philadelphia Salaries Query. In the **Criteria row** of the Location field, type **Philadelphia**. Click in the **Sort row** in the Salary field, and then select **Ascending**. Click **Run** in the Results group on the Design tab. Visually inspect the data to see if any of the Philadelphia employees have a salary less than the minimum or greater than the maximum when compared to the published salary range. These salaries will need to be updated later. Save and close the query.

k. Right-click on the **Philadelphia Salaries query** in the Navigation Pane, and then select **Copy**. Right-click a blank area in the Navigation Pane, and then select **Paste**. In the Paste As dialog box, type **Boston Salaries** for the query name. Click **OK**.

l. Right-click on the **Boston Salaries query** in the Navigation Pane, and then click **Design View**. In the Criteria row of the Location field, replace *Philadelphia* with **Boston**. Click **Run** in the Results group on the Design tab. Visually inspect the data to see if any of the Boston employees have a salary less than the minimum or greater than the maximum when compared to the published salary range. Save and close the query.

m. Click the **File tab**, and then click **Compact & Repair Database**.

n. Click the **File tab**, click **Save & Publish**, and then double-click **Back Up Database.**

o. Click **Save** to accept the default backup file name with today's date.

p. Click the **File tab**, and then click **Exit** (to exit Access).

q. Submit based on your instructor's directions.

MID-LEVEL EXERCISES

1 Real Estate Firm

You are an intern in a large, independent real estate firm that specializes in home sales. A database contains all of the information on the properties marketed by your firm. Most real estate transactions involve two agents—one representing the seller (the listing agent) and the other the buyer (the selling agent). The firm owner has asked that you examine the records of recent listings (real estate is listed when the home owner signs a contract with an agent that offers the property for sale) and sort them by subdivision and the listing agent's name. The results need to include only the sold properties and be sorted by subdivision and the listing agent's last name. Refer to Figure 56 as you complete this exercise.

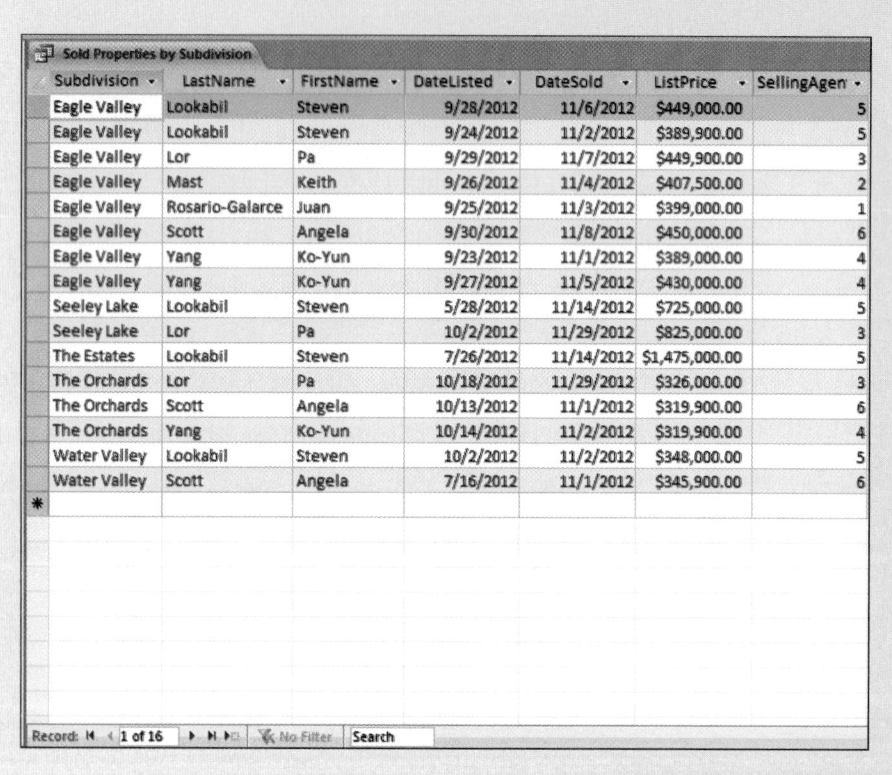

Sold Properties by Subdivision

Subdivision	LastName	FirstName	DateListed	DateSold	ListPrice	SellingAgen
Eagle Valley	Lookabil	Steven	9/28/2012	11/6/2012	$449,000.00	5
Eagle Valley	Lookabil	Steven	9/24/2012	11/2/2012	$389,900.00	5
Eagle Valley	Lor	Pa	9/29/2012	11/7/2012	$449,900.00	3
Eagle Valley	Mast	Keith	9/26/2012	11/4/2012	$407,500.00	2
Eagle Valley	Rosario-Galarce	Juan	9/25/2012	11/3/2012	$399,000.00	1
Eagle Valley	Scott	Angela	9/30/2012	11/8/2012	$450,000.00	6
Eagle Valley	Yang	Ko-Yun	9/23/2012	11/1/2012	$389,000.00	4
Eagle Valley	Yang	Ko-Yun	9/27/2012	11/5/2012	$430,000.00	4
Seeley Lake	Lookabil	Steven	5/28/2012	11/14/2012	$725,000.00	5
Seeley Lake	Lor	Pa	10/2/2012	11/29/2012	$825,000.00	3
The Estates	Lookabil	Steven	7/26/2012	11/14/2012	$1,475,000.00	5
The Orchards	Lor	Pa	10/18/2012	11/29/2012	$326,000.00	3
The Orchards	Scott	Angela	10/13/2012	11/1/2012	$319,900.00	6
The Orchards	Yang	Ko-Yun	10/14/2012	11/2/2012	$319,900.00	4
Water Valley	Lookabil	Steven	10/2/2012	11/2/2012	$348,000.00	5
Water Valley	Scott	Angela	7/16/2012	11/1/2012	$345,900.00	6

Record: 1 of 16 No Filter Search

FIGURE 56 Sold Properties by Subdivision Query Results ➤

a. Open *a02m1property*. Click the **File tab**, click **Save Database As**, and then type **a02m1property_LastnameFirstname**. Click **Save**. Open the Agents table. Find and replace Kia Hart's name with your name. Close the Agents table.

b. Open the SubDivision table in Design view, and then add the field **AssociationFee** with data type **Currency** to indicate the monthly fee for each subdivision. Save the table, switch to Datasheet view, and then enter in the AssociationFee field **95** for each subdivision without a pool and **125** for subdivisions with a pool. Close the table.

c. Open the Query Wizard, and then create a detail query using the Agents and Properties tables. Add the following fields: **LastName, FirstName, DateListed, DateSold, ListPrice, SellingAgent,** and **SubdivisionID**. Name the query **Sold Properties by Subdivision**. Run the query, and then examine the number of records.

d. In Design view, enter the appropriate criteria to exclude all of the records that contain properties from the Red Canyon Subdivision (SubdivisionID #7). Run the query, and then examine the number of records. It should be a smaller number than in step c.

e. Add the SubDivision table to the query design, and then drag the **Subdivision field** to the first column in the query design grid. Modify the SubdivisionID field so that the field does not show in the query results. Run the query, and then examine the results. The number of records should be the same as in step d; the first column will be different.

f. Sort the records by ascending Subdivision first, then by ascending LastName.

g. Add criteria that will limit the results to the properties sold after October 31, 2012. Run the query.
h. Save and close the query.
i. Compact and repair the database.
j. Make a backup copy of the database.
k. Close Access.
l. Submit based on your instructor's directions.

2 The Prestige Hotel

The Prestige Hotel chain caters to upscale business travelers and provides state-of-the-art conference, meeting, and reception facilities. It prides itself on its international, four-star cuisine. Last year, it began a member reward club to help the marketing department track the purchasing patterns of its most loyal customers. All of the hotel transactions are stored in the database. Your task is to help the managers of the Prestige Hotel in Denver and Chicago identify their customers who stayed in a room last year and who had three persons in their party. Refer to Figure 57 as you complete this exercise.

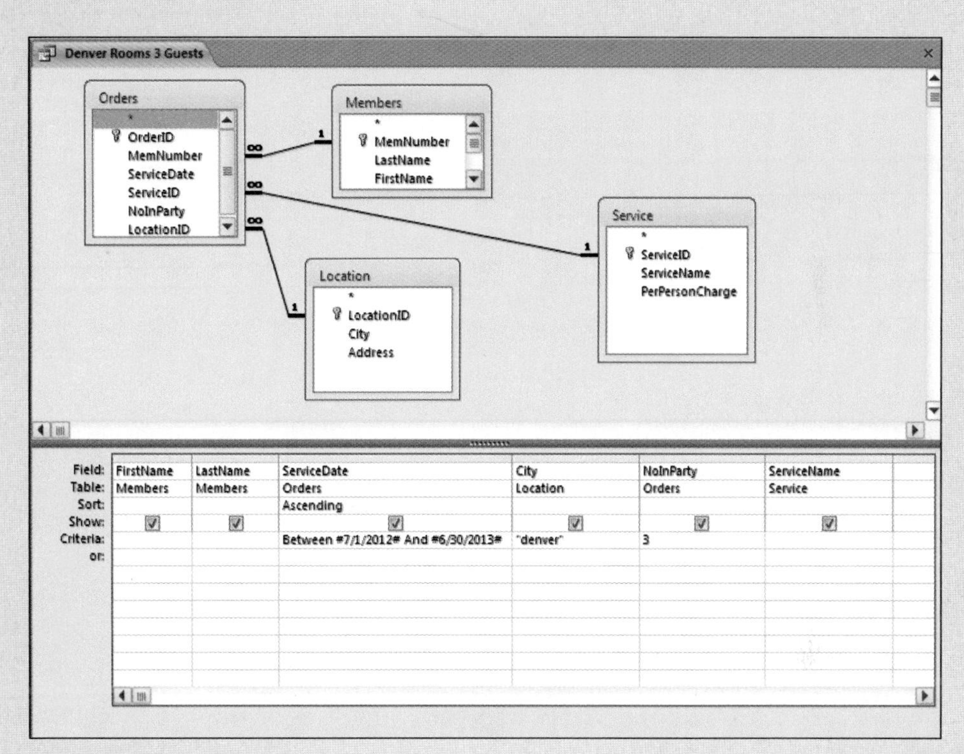

FIGURE 57 Denver Rooms 3 Guests Query ➤

a. Open *a02m2hotel*. Click the **File tab**. click **Save Database As**, and then type **a02m2hotel_LastnameFirstname**. Click **Save**. Review the data contained in the three tables. Specifically, look for the tables and fields containing the information you need: dates of stays in Denver suites, the members' names, and the numbers in the parties.
b. Import the Location data from the Excel file *a02m2location* into your database as a new table. Set the LocationID Indexed property to **Yes (No Duplicates)**, and then set the data type to **Long Integer**. Select the **LocationID field** as the primary key. Name the table **Location**.
c. Open the Relationships window, and then create a relationship between the Location table and the Orders table using the LocationID field. Enforce referential integrity, and then select **Cascade Update Related Fields**. Set the other two relationships as shown in Figure 57. Save and close the Relationships window.
d. Open the Members table, and then find Bryan Gray's name. Replace his name with your own first and last name. Now find Nicole Lee's name, and then replace it with your name.

e. Create a query with fields ServiceDate, City, NoInParty, ServiceName, FirstName, and LastName. Set the criteria to limit the output to **denver**. Use the Between command to only show services from **7/1/2012** to **6/30/2013**. Set the Number in Party criterion to **3**. Sort the results in ascending order by the Service Date.
f. Run the query, and then examine the number of records in the status bar at the bottom of the query. It should display *154*. If your number of records is different, examine the criteria.
g. Change the order of the query fields so that they display as FirstName, LastName, ServiceDate, City, NoInParty, and ServiceName. Compare your results to Figure 57.
h. Save the query as **Denver Rooms 3 Guests**. Close the query, and then copy it and rename the new query **Chicago Rooms 3 Guests**. One of your colleagues in Chicago asked for your help in analyzing the guest data.
i. Open the Chicago Rooms 3 Guests query in Design view, and then change the criterion for denver to **chicago**. Run and save the changes.

DISCOVER 

j. Combine the two previous queries into a third query named **Denver and Chicago Rooms 3 Guests**. Use the criteria from the two individual queries to create a combination AND – OR condition. The records in the combined query should equal the sum of the records in the two individual queries.
k. Compact, repair, and back up the database file. Close the database.
l. Submit based on your instructor's directions.

CAPSTONE EXERCISE

The Morris Arboretum in Chestnut Hill, Pennsylvania, tracks its donors in Excel. They also use Excel to store a list of plants in stock. As donors contribute funds to the Arboretum, they can elect to receive a plant gift from the Arboretum. These plants are both rare plants and hard-to-find old favorites, and they are part of the annual appeal and membership drive to benefit the Arboretum's programs. The organization has grown, and the files are too large and inefficient to handle in Excel. Your task will be to begin the conversion of the files from Excel to Access.

Create a New Database

You need to examine the data in the Excel worksheets to determine which fields will become the primary keys in each table and which fields will become the foreign keys. Primary and foreign keys are used to form the relationships between tables.

a. Locate the Excel workbook named *a02c1donors* and open it.

b. Locate the Excel workbook named *a02c1plants* and open it.

c. Examine the data in each worksheet and identify the column that will become the primary key in an Access table. Identify the foreign keys in each table.

d. Launch Access and create a new, blank database named **a02c1arbor_LastnameFirstname**.

Create a New Table

Use the new blank table created automatically by Access to hold the donations as they are received from the donors. Switch to Design view, and then save the table as **Donations**. Add the remaining field names in Design view. Note: The data for this table will be added later in this exercise.

a. Change *ID* to **DonationID** with an **AutoNumber Data Type**.

b. Add **DonorID** (a foreign key) as **Number (Long Integer) Data Type**.

c. Add **PlantID** (a foreign key) as **Number (Long Integer) Data Type**.

d. Enter two additional fields with an appropriate data type and field properties. Hint: You need the date of donation and the amount of donation.

e. Verify the primary key is *DonationID*.

f. Save the table. Close the table.

Import Data from Excel

You need to use the Import Spreadsheet Data Wizard twice to import a worksheet from each Excel workbook into Access. You need to select the worksheets, specify the primary keys, set the indexing option, and name the newly imported tables (see Figures 19 through 24).

a. Click the **Import Excel data command.**

b. Locate and select the *a02c1donors* workbook.

c. Set the DonorID field Indexed option to **Yes (No Duplicates)**.

d. Select **DonorID** as the primary key when prompted.

e. Accept the table name *Donors.*

f. Import the *a02c1plants* file, set the ID field as the primary key, and then change the indexing option to **Yes (No Duplicates)**.

g. Select the **ID** as the primary key when prompted.

h. Accept the table name *Plants.*

i. Open each table in Datasheet view to examine the data.

j. Change the ID field name in the Plants table to **PlantID**.

Create Relationships

You need to create the relationships between the tables using the Relationships window. Identify the primary key fields in each table and connect them with their foreign key counterparts in related tables. Enforce referential integrity, and check the Cascade Update Related Fields option.

a. Open the Donors table, and then change the Field Size property for DonorID to **Long Integer** so it matches the Field Size property of DonorID in the Donations table.

b. Open the Plants table, and then change the Field Size property for PlantID to **Long Integer** so it matches the Field Size property for PlantID in the Donations table.

c. Close the open tables, and then open the Relationships window.

d. Add the three tables to the Relationships window using the Show Table dialog box. Close the Show Tables dialog box.

e. Drag the **DonorID field** in the Donors table onto the DonorID field in the Donations table. Enforce referential integrity, and then check the **Cascade Update Related Fields option**. Drag the **PlantID field** from the Plants table onto the PlantID field of the Donations table. Enforce referential integrity, and then check the **Cascade Update Related Fields option.**

f. Close the Relationships window and save your changes.

Add Sample Data to the Donations Table

You need to add sample data to the Donations table. Add 20 records using the following guidelines:

a. Use any donor from the Donors table.

b. Enter the date of donation using dates from last month, this month, and next month.

c. Use any amount of donation.

d. Use any plant from the Plants table.

Use the Query Wizard

Use the Query Wizard to create a query of all donations greater than $100 in the Donations table. Use the following guidelines:

a. Include the DonorID and AmountOfDonation fields.

b. Name the query **Donations Over 100**.

c. Add criteria to include only donations of more than $100.

d. Sort by descending AmountOfDonation.

Create a Query in Design View

You need to create a query that identifies the people who have made a donation in the current month. The query should list the donor's full name, phone number, the amount of the donation, the date of the donation, and name of the plant they want. Sort the query by date of donation, then by donor last name and first name. This list will be given to the Arboretum staff so they can notify the donors that a plant is ready for pick up.

a. Click the **Create tab**, and then click **Query Design** in the Queries group.

b. Add the tables and fields necessary to produce the query as stated previously. Name the query **Plant Pickup List**.

c. Run and print the query from Datasheet view.

d. Compact, repair, and back up the file. Close the database.

e. Submit based on your instructor's directions.

Employee Performance Review

GENERAL CASE 

The *a02b1perform* file contains employee performance data for a large insurance agency. Open *a02b1perform*. Click the **File tab**, click **Save Database As**, and then type **a02b1perform_LastnameFirstname.** Click **Save**. Use the skills from this chapter to perform several tasks. Replace *yourname* in the Employees table with your name. The firm's employee policy states that an employee needs to maintain a performance rating of good or excellent to maintain employment. If an employee receives an average or poor performance rating, he or she receives a letter reminding him or her of this policy along with suggestions of how to improve. You are the manager of the Atlanta office. You need to identify the employees who need a letter of reprimand. You will prepare a query so that someone else can generate a form letter to the employees. You need to include fields in the query that contain the employees' first and last names, their position title, and their salary. You do not need to write the letter, only assemble the data that will later be merged into the letter. The query results need to be alphabetized by the employees' last names. As you work, consider the order that the fields will need to be used in the letter and order the query fields accordingly. Close the database. Check with your instructor and submit based on your instructor's directions.

Database Administrator Position

RESEARCH CASE 

You arrive at Secure Systems, Inc., for a database administrator position interview. After meeting the Human Resources coordinator, you are given a test to demonstrate your skills in Access. You are asked to create a database from scratch to keep track of all the candidates for the positions currently open at Secure Systems. Use these requirements:

a. Name the database **a02b2admin_LastnameFirstname.**
b. Create three tables: Candidates, JobOpenings, and Interviews.
c. Include a field to rank each candidate on a scale of 1 to 5 (5 is highest).
d. Set the table relationships.
e. Add 10 candidates—yourself and 9 other students in your class.
f. Add the Database Administrator job and four other sample jobs.
g. Add eight sample Interviews—four for the Database Administrator position and four others.
h. Create a query that lists all the Database Administrator interviews with a ranking of 4 or 5.
i. Add the last name and first name of the candidate to the query design. Sort by last name and first name. Run the query.
j. Close the database. Submit based on your instructor's directions.

May Beverage Sales

DISASTER RECOVERY 

A coworker called you into his office, explained that he was having difficulty with Access 2010, and asked you to look at his work. Open *a02b3traders*. Click the **File tab**, click **Save Database As**, and then type **a02b3traders_LastnameFirstname.** Click **Save.** It contains two queries, *May 2012 Orders of Beverages and Confections* and *2012 Beverage Sales by Ship Country*. The May 2012 Orders of Beverages and Confections query is supposed to have only information from May 2012. You find other dates included in the results. Change the criteria of ShippedDate to exclude the other dates. The 2012 Beverage Sales by Ship Country query returns no results. Check the criteria in all fields. Once the criteria are fixed, the records need to be ordered by ShipCountry. After you find and correct the error(s), close the database. Submit based on your instructor's directions.

ACCESS

CUSTOMIZE, ANALYZE, AND SUMMARIZE QUERY DATA

Creating and Using Queries to Make Decisions

CASE STUDY | Housing Slump Means Opportunity for College Students

Watch the
Set-up
Video
for this
Case Study!

Two students from Montgomery County Community College decided they would take advantage of the declining housing market. After taking several business courses at MCCC and a weekend seminar in real estate investing, Jeff Bryan and Bill Ryder were ready to test their skills in the marketplace. Jeff and Bill had a simple strategy—buy distressed properties at a significant discount, then resell the properties for a profit one year later when the market rebounds.

As they drove through the surrounding neighborhoods, if they noticed a For Sale sign in the yard, they would call the listing agent and ask for the key information such as the asking price, the number of bedrooms, square feet, and days on the market. Since they were just starting out, they decided to target houses that were priced at $100,000 or below and only houses that were on the market at least six months.

For the first two months, they gathered lots of information and began to get a feel for the houses and prices in the area. Some neighborhoods were definitely more distressed than others! But they still had not made any offers. The two MCCC investors realized they needed a more scientific approach to finding an investment property. Based on a tip from the real estate seminar, they decide to gather free lists of homes for sale and use that information to prequalify houses that meet their criteria. They have asked you to help them import the lists into Access. Once the data is in Access, Jeff, Bill, and you will be able to easily identify the qualifying properties.

This new database approach should help them become more successful and hopefully help them acquire their first investment property. And who knows, you might even become one of the partners.

OBJECTIVES AFTER YOU READ THIS CHAPTER, YOU WILL BE ABLE TO:

1. Understand the order of operations
2. Create a calculated field in a query
3. Create expressions with the Expression Builder
4. Use built-in functions in Access
5. Perform date arithmetic
6. Add aggregate functions to datasheets and queries

Calculations, Expressions, and Functions

Previously, you learned that Access now allows calculated fields to be added to tables. In previous versions of Access, you could not add calculated fields to tables; you could only add calculated fields to queries, forms, and reports. In Access 2010, many situations exist where you will still need to add arithmetic calculations—using expressions and functions—to queries, forms, and reports.

In Access 2010, many situations exist where you will still need to add arithmetic calculations ... to queries, forms, and reports.

For example, many Access developers prefer to create calculated fields in queries. Queries with calculated fields can then become the data source (or record source) for forms and reports. Calculated fields on a form cannot be edited the same way fields from a table can be edited. Calculated fields can only be displayed on a form. For example, if you store information about credit cards in a table, you would enter the bank (Chase), the credit card type (Visa), and the interest rate (9%). You would not enter the current amount due. That amount would be calculated and displayed on the form. You will recognize this restriction later when you create a form containing calculated fields.

In this section, you will learn about the order of operations and how to create a calculated field in a query.

Understanding the Order of Operations

The **order of operations** determines the sequence by which operations are calculated in an expression.

The ***order of operations*** determines the sequence by which operations are calculated in an expression. Evaluate expressions in parentheses first, then exponents, then multiplication and division, and, finally, addition and subtraction. Operations of equal value will be calculated from left to right. Table 1 shows some examples of the order of operations. You must have a solid understanding of these rules in order to create calculated fields in Access. Access, like Excel, uses the following symbols:

- Parentheses ( )
- Exponentiation ^
- Multiplication *
- Division /
- Addition +
- Subtraction –

TABLE 1 Examples of Order of Operations

Expression	Order to Perform Calculations	Output
=2+3*3	Multiply first, and then add.	11
=(2+3)*3	Add the values inside the parentheses first, and then multiply.	15
=2+2^3	Evaluate the exponent first, 2^3=2*2*2 or 8. Then add.	10
=(2+2)^3	Add the parenthetical values first (2+2=4), and then raise the result to the 3rd power. 4^3=4*4*4.	64
=10/2+3	Divide first, and then add.	8
=10/(2+3)	Add first to simplify the parenthetical expression, and then divide.	2
=10*2–3*2	Multiply first, and then subtract.	14

Creating a Calculated Field in a Query

When creating a query, in addition to using fields from tables, you may also need to create a calculation based on the fields from one or more tables. For example, a table might contain the times when employees clock in and out of work. You could create a calculated field to calculate how many hours each employee worked by subtracting the ClockIn field from the ClockOut field. You create calculated fields in the Design view of a query. A formula used to calculate new fields from the values in existing fields is known as an ***expression***. An expression can consist of a number of different elements to produce the desired output. The elements used in an expression may include the following:

An **expression** is a formula used to calculate new fields from the values in existing fields.

- Identifiers (the names of fields, controls, or properties)
- Arithmetic operators (e.g., * , / , + , or –)
- Functions (built-in functions like Date() or IIf())
- ***Constants*** (numbers such as 30 or .5)

A **constant** refers to a value that does not change.

You can use calculations to create a new value based on an existing field, verify data entered, set grouping levels in reports, or to help set query criteria.

Build Expressions with Correct Syntax

Expressions are entered in the first row of the query design grid. You must follow the correct ***syntax***—the set of rules that Access follows when evaluating expressions. You can create expressions to perform calculations using field names, constants, and functions. If you use a field name, such as Balance, in an expression, you must spell the field name correctly or Access will display an error. You should assign descriptive field names to the calculated fields. Access ignores spaces in calculations. An example of an expression with correct syntax is:

Syntax is the set of rules that Access follows when evaluating expressions.

```
MonthlyInterest: [Balance] * .035 / 12
```

In the above expression, if you omit the brackets [ ] around Balance, Access will add them for you. The arithmetic operators, the * symbol (multiply) and the / symbol (divide), first multiply the operands, [Balance] and .035, and then divide the result by 12. In calculated fields, the operands are usually a constant, a field name, or another calculated field. Figure 1 shows the NewBalance field which adds the [Balance] and the calculated field [MonthlyInterest]. This calculation will show the total amount owed.

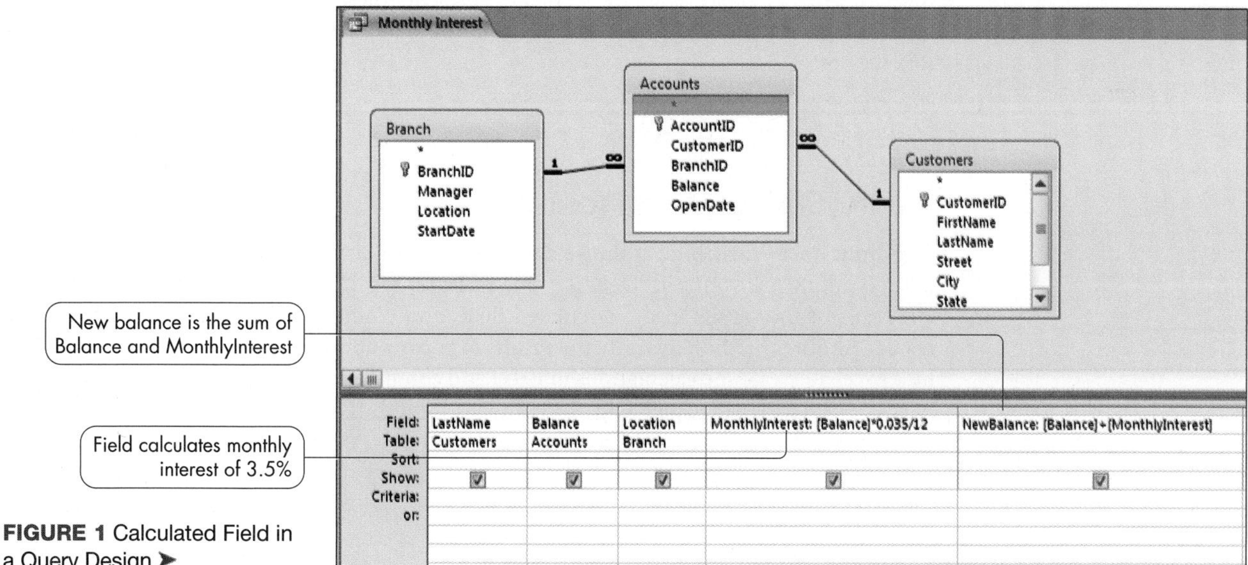

FIGURE 1 Calculated Field in a Query Design ➤

The query contains a second calculated field named NewBalance. Its value is derived from the sum of the original balance plus the monthly interest amount. The query results, as shown in Figure 2, display a decimal number in the Interest column. The NewBalance column appears to be rounded to two decimal places since the output is in currency format. However, when you click in the NewBalance field, Access displays the extra digits that are stored behind the scenes.

Monthly Interest

LastName	Balance	Branch Locat	MonthlyInterest	NewBalance
Peterson	$5,600.00	Campus	16.3333333333333	$5,616.3333
Millward	$1,200.00	Uptown	3.5	$1,203.50
Collins	$15,490.00	Eastern	45.1791666666667	$15,535.18
Hayes	$630.00	Western	1.8375	$631.84
Nunn	$1,300.00	Campus	3.79166666666667	$1,303.79
Hayes	$550.00	Uptown	1.60416666666667	$551.60
Simpson	$1,620.00	Eastern	4.725	$1,624.73
Collins	$2,100.00	Southern	6.125	$2,106.13
Wagner	$1,500.00	Campus	4.375	$1,504.38
Millward	$3,000.00	Eastern	8.75	$3,008.75
Wagner	$290.00	Uptown	0.845833333333333	$290.85
Fox	$1,900.00	Western	5.54166666666667	$1,905.54
Millward	$10,000.00	Eastern	29.1666666666667	$10,029.17
Nunn	$16,700.00	Uptown	48.7083333333333	$16,748.71
Collins	$460.00	Western	1.34166666666667	$461.34
Millward	$18,700.00	Western	54.5416666666667	$18,754.54
Peterson	$980.00	Western	2.85833333333333	$982.86
Wagner	$7,800.00	Southern	22.75	$7,822.75
Collins	$14,250.00	Western	41.5625	$14,291.56
Millward	$12,000.00	Campus	35	$12,035.00
YourName	$21,004.00	Campus	61.2616666666667	$21,065.26
Hayes	$4,000.00	Campus	11.6666666666667	$4,011.67
YourName	$1,000.00	Campus	2.91666666666667	$1,002.92
*				

Record: 1 of 23 No Filter Search

NewBalance appears to be rounded to two digits (currency format)

MonthlyInterest field shows a decimal number with many digits

Click in the NewBalance field to reveal a decimal number with four digits

FIGURE 2 Results of Calculated Fields in a Query ➤

Another example of when to use a calculated field is calculating a price increase for a product or service. Suppose you need to calculate a 10% price increase on certain products you sell. You could name the calculated field NewPrice and use the expression (current price) + (current price × 10%). The first segment represents the current price and the second segment adds an additional 10%. The expression would be entered into the query design grid as follows:

```
NewPrice: [CurrentPrice] + [CurrentPrice] * .10
```

Verify Calculated Results

After your query runs, look at the field values in the Datasheet view and also look at the calculated values. Ask yourself, "Does the data make sense?" Use a calculator to manually calculate some of the results in the calculated fields and compare the answers to the datasheet results. Another method to verify the results is to copy and paste all or part of the datasheet into Excel. Recreate the calculations in Excel and compare the answers to the query results in Access. The Access calculated field, the calculator, and the Excel calculations should all return identical results.

After verifying the calculated results, save the query for the next time you need to perform the same calculations.

TIP Resolve Rounding Problems

In Figure 2, the Balance field contains numbers in currency format; the MonthlyInterest field contains decimal numbers with many digits. When you add the two numbers, the sum—shown in the NewBalance field—appears to be in currency format. However, if you click the NewBalance field, the actual number is a decimal with four digits. Decimal numbers can cause rounding problems when you total the column. To resolve this problem, the MonthlyInterest field must be rounded to two decimal places prior to totaling the column.

Save a Query Containing Calculated Fields

As you already know, saving a query only saves the design of the query; saving does not save the data displayed in Datasheet view. While viewing the results of a query in Datasheet view, you can edit the data (and consequently update the data in the underlying table) providing the query is updatable. Calculated fields are the exception to this rule—calculated fields cannot be updated in Datasheet view. However, when the components of a calculated field are updated, the calculated field value will update automatically.

You can use a calculated field as input for other calculated fields. For example, calculate a 10% discount on an item (Calculation #1) and then calculate the sales tax on the discount price (Calculation #2).

In the first Hands-On Exercise, you will create calculated expressions, practice verification techniques, and recover from a common error.

Avoid Spaces in Calculated Field Names

Although you can use spaces in calculated field names, it is a good habit to not use spaces. For example, use NewPrice: [Price]*1.1 rather than New Price: [Price]*1.1. If you avoid spaces in calculated field names, it will be easier to reference these fields in other queries, related forms, and related reports.

HANDS-ON EXERCISES

1 Calculations, Expressions, and Functions

Using the data from the homes for sale lists that Jeff and Bill acquired, you are able to help them target properties that meet their criteria. As you examine the data, you discover other ways to analyze the properties. You create several queries and present your results to the two investors for their comments.

Skills covered: Create and Save a Query • Create a Calculated Field and Run the Query • Verify the Calculated Results • Recover from a Common Error

STEP 1 CREATE AND SAVE A QUERY

You begin your analysis by creating a query using the Properties and Agents tables. The Properties table contains all the properties the investors will evaluate; the Agents table contains a list of real estate agents who represent the properties' sellers. In this exercise, add the fields you need and only show properties that have not been sold. Refer to Figure 3 as you complete Step 1.

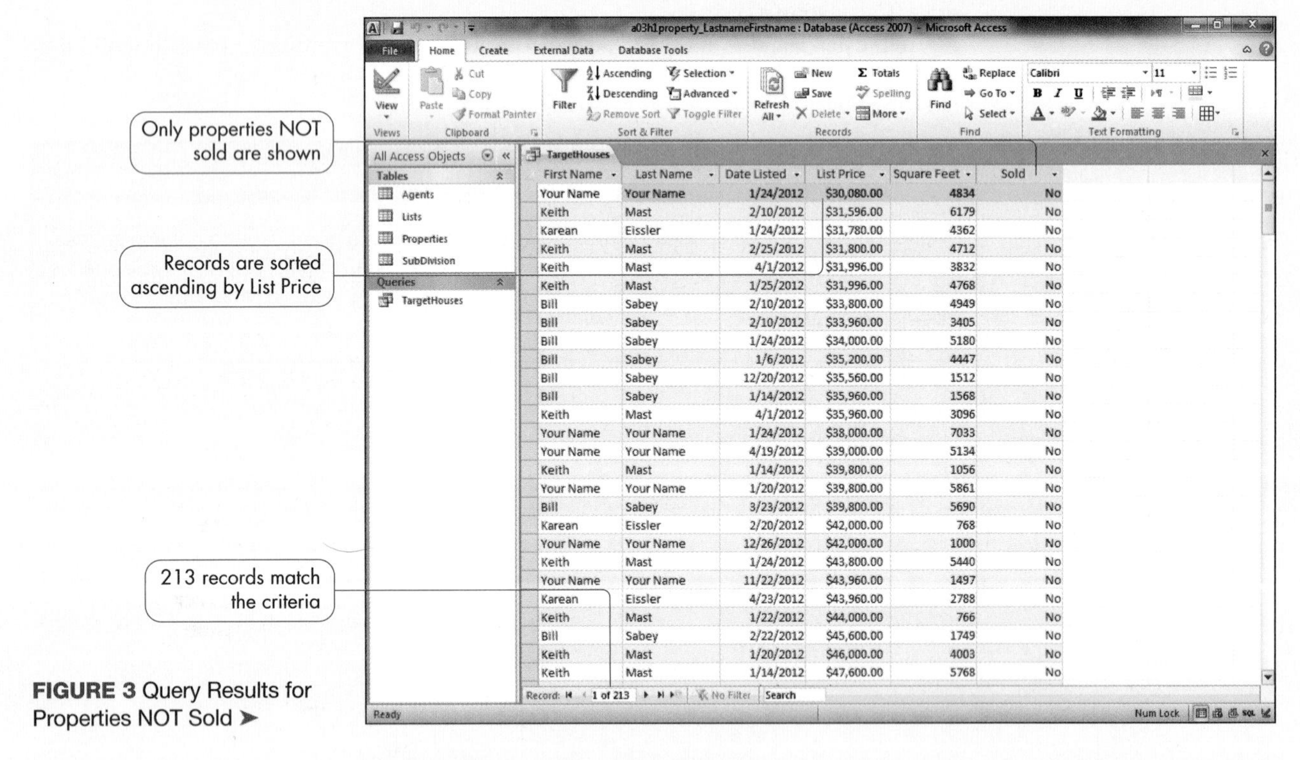

FIGURE 3 Query Results for Properties NOT Sold ➤

a. Open *a03h1property*. Click the **File tab**, click **Save Database As**, and then type **a03h1property_LastnameFirstname**. Click **Save**.

> **TROUBLESHOOTING:** Throughout the remainder of this chapter and textbook, click Enable Content whenever you are working with student files.

> **TROUBLESHOOTING:** If you make any major mistakes while completing this Hands-On Exercise, you can delete the *a03h1property_LastnameFirstname* file, repeat step a above, and then start over.

b. Open the Agents table, and then replace *Angela Scott* with your name. Close the table.

c. Click the **Create tab**, and then click **Query Design** in the Queries group to start a new query.

   The Show Table dialog box opens so you can specify the table(s) and/or queries to include in the query design.

d. Select the **Agents table**, and then click **Add**. Select the **Properties table**, and then click **Add**. Close the Show Table dialog box.

e. Double-click the **FirstName** and **LastName fields** in the Agents table to add them to the design grid.

f. Double-click the **DateListed, ListPrice, SqFeet,** and **Sold fields** in the Properties table to add them to the query design grid.

g. Click **Run** in the Results group to display the results in Datasheet view.

   You should see 303 properties in the results.

h. Click **View** in the Views group to switch to Design view. Type **No** in the **Criteria row** of the Sold field.

i. Select **Ascending** from the Sort row of the ListPrice field.

j. Click **Run** to see the results.

   You only want to see properties that were not sold. There should now be only 213 properties in the datasheet. Compare your results to those shown in Figure 3.

k. Save the query as **TargetHouses.**

STEP 2 CREATE A CALCULATED FIELD AND RUN THE QUERY

You need to create a calculated field to evaluate the relative value of all unsold properties on the market. To do this, you create a calculated field to analyze the sale price compared to the square footage of each property. Refer to Figure 4 as you complete Step 2.

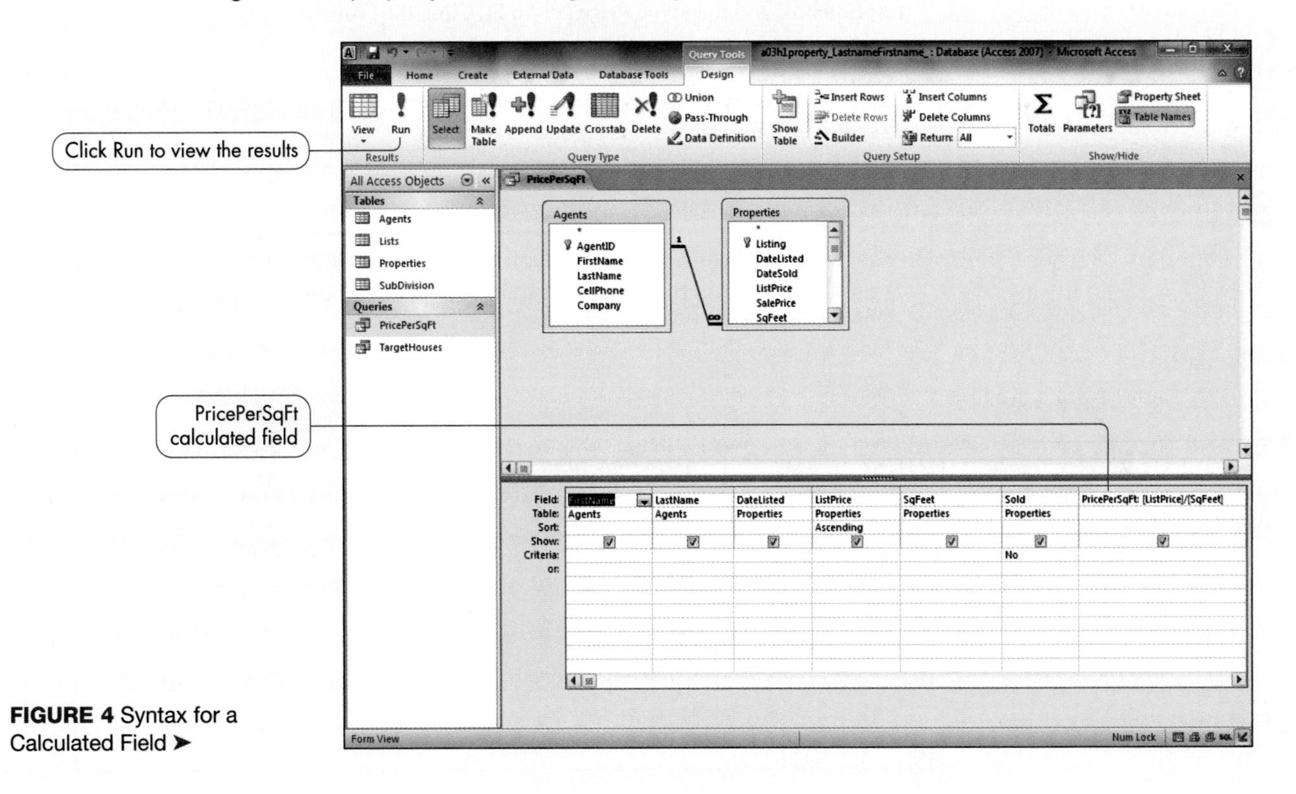

FIGURE 4 Syntax for a Calculated Field ➤

a. Click **View** in the Views group to switch to Design view.

> **TROUBLESHOOTING:** If you accidentally click the View arrow, Access displays a list of options. Select the Design View option.

The TargetHouses query is based on two tables. The top portion of Query Design view displays the two tables, Agents and Properties, and the bottom portion (query design grid) displays the fields currently in the query.

b. Click the **File tab**, and then select **Save Object As**. Type **PricePerSqFt** in the **Save As dialog box**, and then click **OK**.

You made a copy of the TargetHouses query so you can add a calculated field to the new query but still preserve the original query.

c. Click the **File tab** to return to the query.

d. Scroll to the right until you see the first blank column in the query design grid.

e. Click in the top row of the first blank column, type **PricePerSqFt: ListPrice/SqFeet**, and then press **Enter**. Widen the PricePerSqFt column in order to see the entire expression.

Access inserts square brackets around the fields for you. The new field divides the values in the ListPrice field by the values in the SqFeet field. The : after *PricePerSqFt* is required.

f. Click **Run** in the Results group to view the results.

The new calculated field, PricePerSqFt, is displayed. Widen the PricePerSqFt column, if necessary, to see all the values.

g. Click **View** to switch back to Design view. Use Figure 4 to check your syntax. Click in the **PricePerSqFt calculated field cell**, and then click **Property Sheet** in the Show/Hide group.

The Property Sheet controls how the results of the calculated field will display in Datasheet view when you run the query.

h. Click the **Format property arrow**, and then select **Currency** from the list. Click in the **Caption box**, and then type **Price Per Sq Ft**. Close the Property Sheet.

i. Click **Run** to view your changes.

The calculated field values are formatted with Currency, and the column heading displays *Price Per Sq Ft* instead of *PricePerSqFt*.

STEP 3 VERIFY THE CALCULATED RESULTS

Because you are in charge of the Access Database, you decide to verify your data prior to showing it to the investors. You use two methods to check your calculations: estimation and checking your results using Excel. Refer to Figure 5 as you complete Step 3.

Verified results in Excel

Calculated results from Access

First 10 rows of the Access query

	A	B	C	D	E	F	G	H	I
1	First Name	Last Name	Date Listed	List Price	Square Feet	Sold	Price Per Sq Ft		
2	Your Name	Your Name	1/24/2012	$30,080.00	4834	FALSE	$6.22	$6.22	
3	Keith	Mast	2/10/2012	$31,596.00	6179	FALSE	$5.11	$5.11	
4	Karean	Eissler	1/24/2012	$31,780.00	4362	FALSE	$7.29	$7.29	
5	Keith	Mast	2/25/2012	$31,800.00	4712	FALSE	$6.75	$6.75	
6	Keith	Mast	4/1/2012	$31,996.00	3832	FALSE	$8.35	$8.35	
7	Keith	Mast	1/25/2012	$31,996.00	4768	FALSE	$6.71	$6.71	
8	Bill	Sabey	2/10/2012	$33,800.00	4949	FALSE	$6.83	$6.83	
9	Bill	Sabey	2/10/2012	$33,960.00	3405	FALSE	$9.97	$9.97	
10	Bill	Sabey	1/24/2012	$34,000.00	5180	FALSE	$6.56	$6.56	
11	Bill	Sabey	1/6/2012	$35,200.00	4447	FALSE	$7.92	$7.92	
12									
13									
14									

FIGURE 5 Verify Calculated Results in Excel ➤

a. Examine the Price Per Sq Ft column in the current query.

One of the ways to verify the accuracy of the calculated data is to ask yourself if the numbers make sense.

b. Locate the eighth record with *Bill Sabey* as the listing agent, an asking price of *$33,960*, and square footage of *3405*. Ask yourself if the calculated value of *$9.97* makes sense.

The sale price is $33,960 and the square footage is 3405. You can verify the calculated field easily by rounding the two numbers (to 34,000 and 3400) and then dividing the values in your head (34,000 div by 3400 = 10) to verify that the calculated value, $9.97 per sq ft, makes sense.

c. Launch Excel, and then switch to Access. Click the first row selector, and then drag through the first 10 records (the tenth record has a list price of *$35,200*). Click **Copy** in the Clipboard group on the **Home tab**.

You will also verify the calculation in the first 10 records by pasting the results in Excel.

d. Switch to Excel, and then click **cell A1** of the blank workbook. Click **Paste** in the Clipboard group on the Home tab.

The field captions appear in the first row, and the 10 records appear in the next 10 rows. The fields are located in columns A–G. The calculated field results are pasted in column G as values rather than as a formula.

TROUBLESHOOTING: If you see pound signs (#####) in an Excel column, use the vertical lines between columns to increase the width.

e. Type **=D2/E2** in **cell H2**, and then press **Enter**. Copy the formula from **cell H2** and paste it into **cells H3 to H11**.

The formula divides the list price by the square feet. Compare the results in columns G and H. The numbers should be the same. If the values differ, look at both the Excel and Access formulas. Determine which is correct, and then find and fix the error in the incorrect formula.

f. Close Excel without saving the workbook. Return to the Access database, and then click **Save** on the Quick Access Toolbar to save the design modifications made to the PricePerSqFt query.

TIP Use Zoom (Shift+F2) to View Long Expressions

To see the entire calculated field expression, click the field in Query Design view, and then press Shift+F2. A new window will appear to enable you to easily see and edit the entire contents of the cell. Access refers to this window as the Zoom dialog box, as shown in Figure 6.

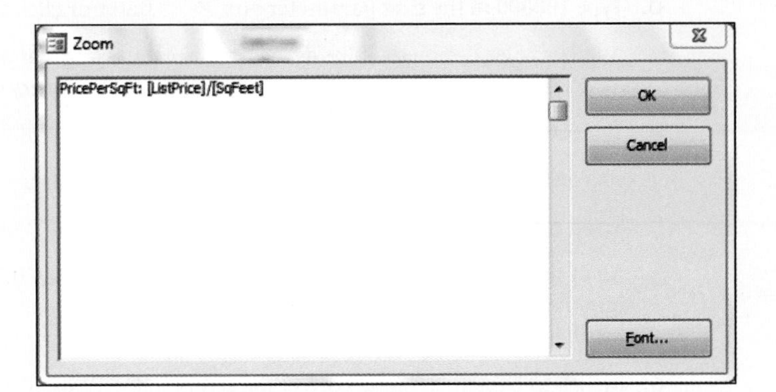

FIGURE 6 Use Zoom to See the Entire Calculated Field ➤

STEP 4 RECOVER FROM A COMMON ERROR

A few errors pop up as you test the new calculated fields. You check the spelling of the field names in the calculated field since that is a common mistake. Refer to Figure 7 as you complete Step 4.

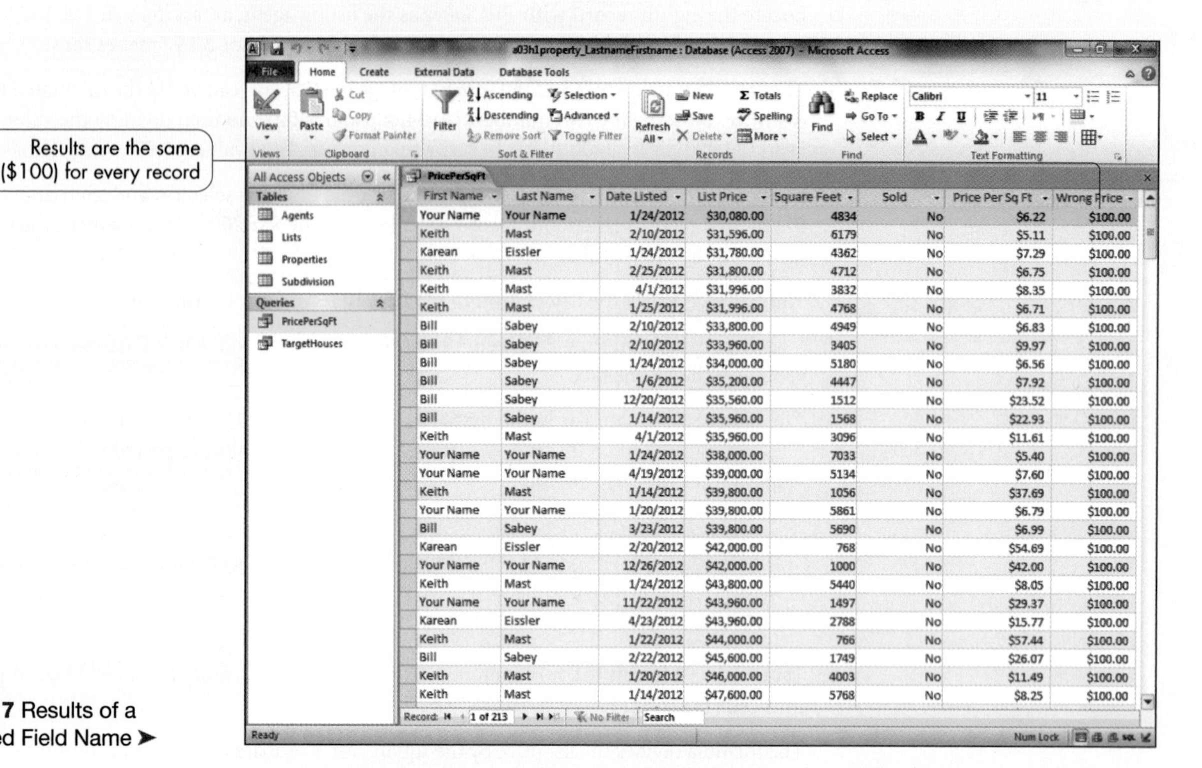
Results are the same ($100) for every record

FIGURE 7 Results of a Misspelled Field Name ➤

a. Click **View** in the Views group to switch to Design view. Scroll to the first blank column, and then click in the top row.

b. Type **WrongPricePerSqFt: xListPrice/xSqFeet**, and then press **Enter**. Widen the column to see the entire expression.

   Be sure that you added the extra *x's* to the field names. You are intentionally misspelling the field names to see how Access will respond. Access inserts square brackets around the fields for you.

c. Click **Run** in the Results group.

   You should see the Enter Parameter Value dialog box. The dialog box indicates that Access does not recognize xListPrice in the tables defined for this query in the first record. When Access does not recognize a field name, it will ask you to supply a value.

d. Type **100000** in the **first parameter box**. Press **Enter** or click **OK**.

   Another Enter Parameter Value dialog box displays, asking that you supply a value for xSqFeet. Again, this error occurs because the tables defined for this query do not contain an xSqFeet field.

e. Type **1000** in the **second parameter box**, and then press **Enter**.

   The query has the necessary information to run and returns the results in Datasheet view.

f. Scroll right and examine the results of the calculation for *WrongPricePerSqFt*.

   All of the records show 100 because you entered the values 100000 and 1000, respectively, into the parameter boxes. The two values are treated as constants and give the same results for all the records.

g. Return to Design view and correct the errors in the WrongPricePerSqFt field by changing the formula to **WrongPricePerSqFt: [ListPrice]/[SqFeet]**.

   Press Shift+F2 to view the calculated field and remove the *x* from the two field names.

h. Click in the **WrongPricePerSqFt calculated field**, click **Property Sheet**, and then change the Format property to **Currency**. Add the caption **Wrong Price Per Sq Ft**. Close the Property Sheet.

i. Run and save the query.

   The calculated values in the last two columns should be the same.

j. Close the query.

k. Click the **File tab**, and then click **Compact & Repair Database**.

l. Click the **File tab**, click **Save & Publish**, and then double-click **Back Up Database**. Accept *a03h1property_LastnameFirstname_date* as the file name, and then click **Save**.

   You just created a backup of the database you used to complete the first Hands-On Exercise. The *a03h1property_LastnameFirstname* database remains open.

m. Keep the database onscreen if you plan to continue with Hands-On Exercise 2. If not, close the database and exit Access.

TIP Learning from Your Mistakes

Following step-by-step instructions is a good way to begin learning about Access. If you want to become proficient, however, you must learn how to recover from errors. As you work through the rest of the Hands-On Exercises in this book, follow the instructions as presented and save your work along the way. Then go back a few steps and make an intentional error just to see how Access responds. Read the error messages (if any) and learn from your mistakes.

Expression Builder, Functions, and Date Arithmetic

The **Expression Builder** is a tool to help you create more complicated expressions.

In the last Hands-On Exercise, you calculated the price per square foot for real estate properties. That simple calculation helped you to evaluate all the properties on the investment list. You were able to type the expression manually.

When you encounter more complex expressions, you can use the ***Expression Builder*** tool to help you create more complicated expressions. When you create an expression in the field cell, you must increase the column width to see the entire expression. The Expression Builder's size enables you to easily see complex formulas and functions in their entirety.

In this section, you will learn how to create expressions using the Expression Builder. You also will learn how to use built-in functions. Finally, you will perform date arithmetic using the Expression Builder.

Creating Expressions with the Expression Builder

Launch the Expression Builder while in the query design grid to assist you with creating a calculated field (or other expression). The Expression Builder helps you create expressions by supplying you with the fields, operators, and functions you need to create them. When you use the expression builder to help you create expressions, you can eliminate spelling errors in field names. Another advantage is with functions; functions require specific arguments in a specific order. When you insert a function using the Expression Builder, the builder gives you placeholders that tell you where each argument belongs.

Launch the Expression Builder while in the query design grid to assist you with creating a calculated field.

After you create an expression in the Expression Builder, click OK to close the Expression Builder window. The expression is then entered into the current cell in the query design grid. From the query design, click Run in the Results group to view the results (in Datasheet view). If the results are incorrect, return to Design view and click the cell that contains the calculated field. Next, launch the Expression Builder again and make any corrections to the expression.

You can also use the Expression Builder when working with controls in forms and reports. For example, if you need a calculated field in a form, you can launch the Expression Builder by clicking Build on the right side of the control source box in the Property Sheet. You can also use the Expression Builder to select a built-in function—for example, to calculate a payment on a loan. It will take some practice to master the Expression Builder; however, the effort will be well worth it as you learn to create more complication expressions.

Launch the Expression Builder

To launch the Expression Builder, open a query in Design view and verify the Design tab is selected on the Ribbon. Click Builder in the Query Setup group and the Expression Builder launches, as shown in Figure 8. (You can also launch the Expression Builder by right-clicking the cell where you want the expression and selecting Build from the shortcut menu.) The top section of the Expression Builder dialog box contains a rectangular area (known as the *expression box*) where you create an expression. You can type your expression in the box manually, or you can use the Expression Elements, Expression Categories, and Expression Values in the bottom portion of the Expression Builder. Double-click an item in the *Expression Categories* or *Expression Values* section and it will automatically be added to the expression box.

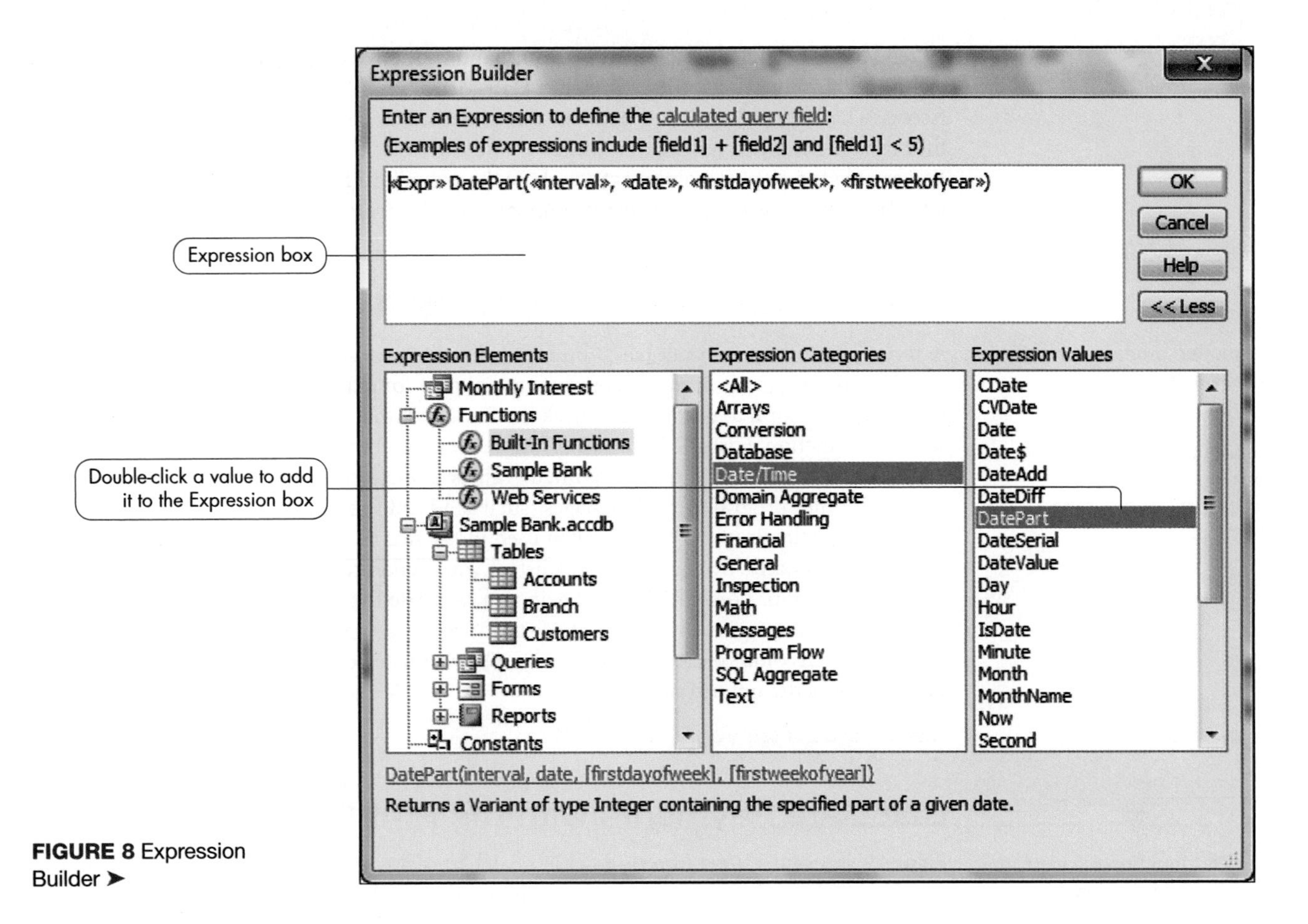

FIGURE 8 Expression Builder ➤

Create an Expression

The left column of the Expression Builder dialog box contains Expression Elements, which include the built-in functions, the tables and other objects from the current database, and common expressions. Select an item in this column; the middle column will show the list of options. For example, click a table in the left column and the fields from that table will appear in the middle column.

The middle column displays the Expression Categories based on the item selected in the Expression Elements box. For example, when the Built-in Functions item is selected in the Expression Elements box, the available built-in function categories are displayed in the Expression Categories box, such as the Date/Time category.

The right column displays the Expression Values, if any, for the categories that you selected in the Expression Categories box. For example, if you click Built-In Functions in the Expression Elements box, and then click Date/Time in the Expression Categories box, the Expression Values box lists all of the built-in functions in the Date/Time category, including DatePart.

You can create an expression by manually typing text in the expression box or by double-clicking the elements from the bottom section in the Expression Builder dialog box. For example, to create a calculated field using the fields in the tables, type the calculated field name, and then type a colon. Next, click the desired table listed in the *Expression Elements* section, and then double-click the field you want. Click the Operators item in the *Expression Elements* section, and then choose an operator (such as + or *) from the *Expression Categories* section (or just type the operator). The Expression Builder is flexible and will enable you to find what you need while still enabling you to modify the expression manually.

Calculated fields are relatively simple to create and most Access developers can create them without the Expression Builder. The main reason to use the builder for a calculated field is to eliminate spelling errors in field names. Using functions in Access almost always requires the Expression Builder since the syntax of functions can be difficult to remember.

When you double-click the Functions command in the Expression Elements box, and then click Built-In Functions, the Expression Categories box lists all the available functions in Access. The Expression Values box lists the functions in each of the categories. When you find the function you need, double-click it and the function appears in the expression box. You can see the <<placeholder text>> where the arguments belong; replace each placeholder text with the argument values, either numbers or fields from a table.

Using Built-In Functions in Access

A **function** produces a result based on inputs known as arguments.

An **argument** is a variable or constant that is needed to produce the output for a function.

A ***function*** produces a result based on inputs known as arguments. An ***argument*** is a variable or constant that is needed to produce the output for a function. Once you identify what you need a function to do, you can check the Built-in Functions in the Expression Builder to see if the function exists. If it does, add the function to the expression box and replace the <<placeholder text>> with the argument values. Functions work the same in Access and Excel and other programming languages (such as Visual Basic).

Consider the Property database you used in the first Hands-On Exercise. If you wanted to group each home by the year it was listed, you could create a year listed field using the DatePart function. This function will help you calculate the year listed using the DateListed field as one of the arguments. The DatePart function requires one other argument—the date interval, which could be day, month, or year. The year listed calculated field would be entered into the query design grid as follows:

```
YearListed: DatePart("yyyy", [DateListed])
```

Calculate Payments with the Pmt Function

The **Pmt function** calculates the monthly loan payment given the interest rate (monthly), term of the loan (in months), and the original value of the loan (the principal).

Figure 9 shows the ***Pmt function***, which calculates the monthly loan payment given the interest rate (monthly), term of the loan (in months), and the original value of the loan (the principal). To use this function, you need to supply the five arguments as field names from underlying tables or as constants.

The first argument is the interest rate per period. Interest rates are usually stated as annual rates, so you will need to convert them to monthly rates by dividing by 12. The second argument is the number of periods. Because loan terms are usually stated in years, you will need to convert the period to months by multiplying by 12. The next argument is the present value—or principal—of the loan. It tells you how much each customer has borrowed. The last two arguments, future value and type (both optional), are usually 0 or blank. The future value shows the amount the borrower will owe after the last payment has been made. The type argument tells Access whether the payment is made at the beginning or the end of the period.

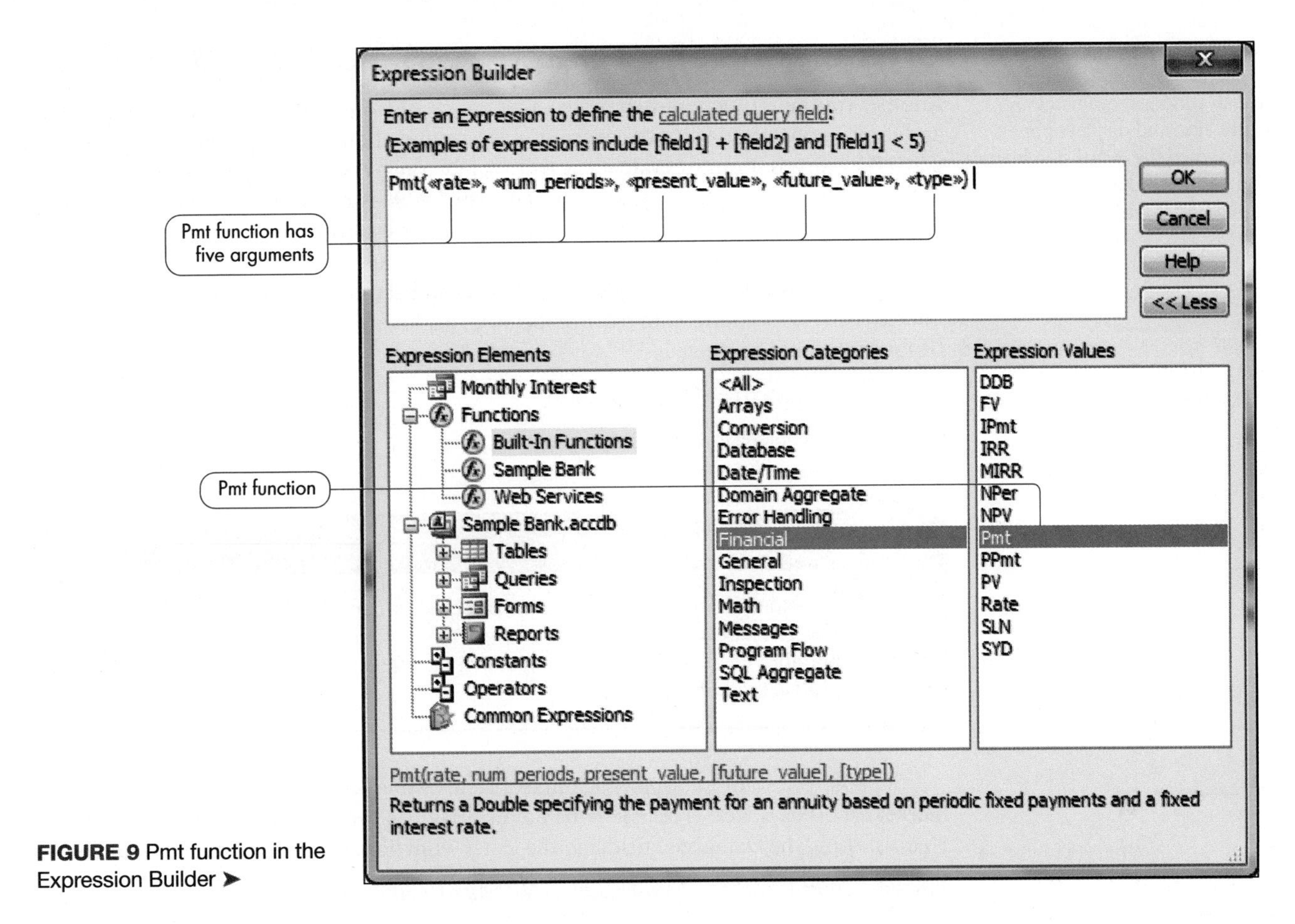

FIGURE 9 Pmt function in the Expression Builder ➤

The following example shows how to use the Pmt function to calculate the monthly payment on a $12,500 loan, at a 6.0% interest rate, with a four-year payback term. Table 2 describes the arguments for the Pmt function in more detail.

Function: Pmt(*rate, num_periods, present value, future value, type*)

Example: Pmt(0.06/12, 4*12, 12500)

TABLE 2 Arguments of the Pmt Function

Part	Description
()	Items inside the parentheses are arguments for the function. The arguments are separated by commas. Some arguments are optional; some arguments have a default value; in the Pmt function, the first three arguments are required and the last two are optional.
rate	Required. Expression or value specifying interest rate per period, usually monthly. A mortgage with an annual percentage rate of **6.0%** with monthly payments would have a rate entered as **0.06/12**. *The interest rate must match the period.*
num_periods	Required. Expression or integer value specifying total number of payment periods in the loan. For example, monthly payments on a four-year car loan give a total of 4 * 12 (or 48) payment periods.
present_value	Required. Expression or value specifying the present value of the money you borrow. If you borrow $12,500 for a car, the value would be 12500.
future_value	Optional. Expression or value specifying the future value after you've made the final payment. Most consumer loans have a future value of $0 after the final payment. However, if you want to save $50,000 over 18 years for your child's education, then 50000 is the future value. Zero is assumed if left blank.
type	Optional. Value (0 or 1) identifying when payments are due. Use 0 if payments are due at the end of the payment period (the default), or 1 if payments are due at the beginning of the period. Zero is assumed if left blank.

Create Conditional Output with the IIf Function

The **IIf function** evaluates an expression and displays one value when the expression is true and another value when the expression is false.

Another common function used in Access is the ***IIf function***, which evaluates an expression and displays one value when the expression is true and another value when the expression is false. The expression must evaluate as true or false only. For example, *balance >= 10000* or *City = "Sarasota"* are valid expressions. DateListed + *90* is not a valid expression for the IIf function since this expression will yield a date. Access evaluates the expression, determines whether it is true or false, then displays one value if the expression is true and another value if the expression is false. For example, if accounts with balances of $10,000 or more earn 3.5% interest, whereas accounts with balances below $10,000 earn only 1.5% interest, the following IIf function could be created:

Example: IIf (Balance>=10000, .035, .015)

Function: IIf (expression, truepart, falsepart)

Using Comparison Operators

To create an expression with a *greater than or equal to* comparison operator, type the two operators >=. To create an expression with a *less than or equal to* comparison operator, type the two operators <=. Both of these comparison operators require two operators and they must be typed in the correct order.

Suppose you want to display the phrase "New Listing" when a property has been on the market for 30 days, and "For Sale" when a property has been on the market for more than 30 days. Using the DateListed field and the Date() function, the calculated field would be:

PropertyStatus: IIf (Date() – [DateListed] <=30, "New Listing", "For Sale")

The expression Date() – [DateListed]<=30 evaluates each property and determines if the number of days on market is less than or equal to 30. When the expression is true, the function displays "New Listing." When the expression is false, the function displays "For Sale."

The IIf function can also evaluate text values. For example, to classify a list of customers based on whether they are in or out of the state of California, you could create the IIf function:

IIf([State]="CA", "CA", "Out of State")

TIP Use a Nested IIf

Experienced Access users sometimes need to create nested IIf functions. This happens when two conditions are not sufficient to evaluate an expression. For example, in the earlier example where a property was classified based on days on market, the function PropertyStatus: IIf(Date() – [DateListed]<=30,"New Listing","For Sale") was used. If a third status were needed for properties that were on the market for six months, the nested PropertyStatus: IIf(Date() – [DateListed]<=30,"New Listing", IIf(Date() – [DateListed]>=180,"Stagnant","For Sale")) would be used.

When you finish the expression, click OK to close the Expression Builder dialog box. If you are working in a query, nothing will happen until you run the query. Your newly calculated field displays in the Datasheet view of the query. If you are working in a form, switch to Form view to see the results of your expression. And if you are working in a report, click Print Preview to see the results.

REFERENCE Use the Expression Builder to Create a Calculated Field

1. Open the query in Design view.
2. Click in the top row of the first blank column.
3. Verify the Design tab is displayed.
4. Click Builder in the Query Setup group to launch the Expression Builder (or right-click in the blank column and select Build from the list).
5. Type the name of the calculated field followed by a colon (:).
6. If the expression requires a field from a table, select a table from the Expression Elements box, and then double-click field names as needed to add them to the expression.
7. Type an arithmetic operator (such as + or *), or click Operators in the Expression Elements box, and then double-click a symbol in the Expression Values box.
8. If the expression requires a function, double-click the Functions folder, click Built-In Functions to see the function categories displayed in the Expression Categories box, and then select the function category. From the Expression Values box, double-click the specific function needed, and then fill in the correct arguments.
9. Click OK to exit the Builder box and place the expression in the field cell.
10. Run the query.
11. Examine and verify the output.
12. Return to the Design view.
13. Modify the new expression if necessary.
14. Run the query.
15. Save the query.

Performing Date Arithmetic

Working with dates in Access can be challenging, especially when performing date arithmetic. This can be even more problematic if your output will contain multiple formats for the United States, Europe, and Asia. Each has their own method of formatting dates. Fortunately, Access has some built-in functions to help work with dates and date arithmetic.

Date formatting affects the date's display without changing the actual underlying value in the table.

Date formatting affects the date's display without changing the actual underlying value in the table. All dates and times in Access are stored as the number of days that have elapsed since December 31, 1899. For example, January 1, 1900, is stored as 1, indicating one day after December 31, 1899. If the time were 9:00 PM on November 20, 2010, no matter how the date or time is formatted, Access stores it as 40502.875. The 40502 represents the number of days elapsed since December 31, 1899, and the .875 reflects the fraction of the 24-hour day that has passed at 9:00 PM. Because dates are stored by Access as sequential numbers, you can calculate the total numbers of hours worked in a week if you record the starting and ending times for each day. Using ***date arithmetic*** you can create expressions to calculate lapsed time, such as a person's age based on birth date or the number of days past due an invoice is based on the invoice date.

All dates and times in Access are stored as the number of days that have elapsed since December 31, 1899.

Using **date arithmetic** you can create expressions to calculate lapsed time.

Identify Partial Dates with the DatePart Function

Using a date function, you can isolate a portion of the date that is of interest to you. If your company increases the number of weeks of annual vacation from two weeks to three weeks after an employee has worked for five or more years, then the only part of the date of interest is the time lapsed in years. Access has a function, the ***DatePart function***, to facilitate this. Table 3 shows the DatePart function parameters.

The **DatePart function** enables you to isolate a specific part of a date, such as the year.

Example: DatePart("yyyy", [Employees]![HireDate])

Function: DatePart(interval, date), firstdayofweek, firstweekofyear

Useful date functions are:

- Date—Inserts the current date into an expression.
- DatePart—Evaluates a date and returns only the portion of the date that is designated.
- DateDiff—Measures the amount of time elapsed between two dates. This is most often today's date as determined by the date function and a date stored in a field. For example, you might calculate the number of days a payment is past due by comparing today's date with the payment DueDate.

TABLE 3 Using the DatePart Function

Function Portion	Explanation
DatePart	An Access function that examines a date and returns a portion of the date.
«interval»	The first argument, the interval, describes the portion of the date that you wish to return. Use "yyyy" for years, "m" for month, or "d" for day.
«date»	The second argument, the date, tells Access where to find the Date/Time information. In this case, it is stored in the Employee table in a field named HireDate.
«firstdayofweek»	Optional. A constant that specifies the first day of the week. If not specified, Sunday is assumed.
«firstweekofyear»	Optional. A constant that specifies the first week of the year. If not specified, the first week is assumed to be the week in which January 1 occurs.

After you practice using the DatePart function, the syntax for all date functions will become easier to understand. In the next Hands-On Exercise, you will copy and paste a query, use the Expression builder, and use functions.

2 Expression Builder, Functions, and Date Arithmetic

As you learn more about Access, you find it easier to answer Jeff and Bill's questions about the properties using queries. When they ask you to calculate the price per bedroom and the price per room for each property, you use the Expression Builder to make the task easier. You also add two additional fields that calculate the days on market and the estimated commission for each property.

Skills covered: Copy and Paste a Query Using a New Name • Use the Expression Builder to Modify a Field • Use the Expression Builder to Add a Field • Use Functions • Work with Date Arithmetic and Add Criteria

STEP 1 COPY AND PASTE A QUERY USING A NEW NAME

You create a copy of the PricePerSqFt query from the previous Hands-On Exercise and paste it using a new name. You will add a few more calculated fields to the new query. Refer to Figure 10 as you complete Step 1.

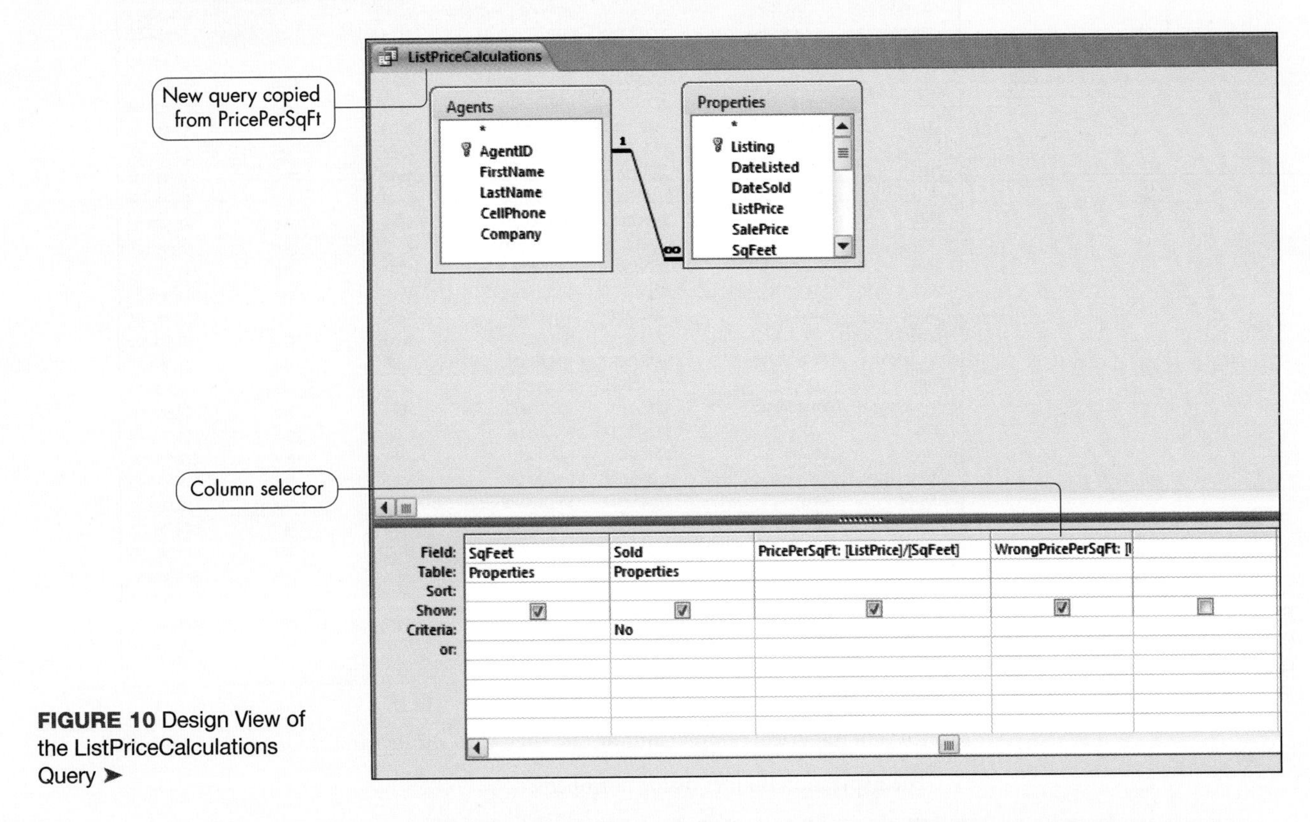

FIGURE 10 Design View of the ListPriceCalculations Query ➤

a. Open *a03h1property_LastnameFirstname* if you closed it at the end of Hands-On Exercise 1. Click the **File tab**, click **Save Database As**, and then type **a03h2property_LastnameFirstname**, changing *h1* to *h2*. Click **Save**.

b. Select the **PricePerSqFt query**, and then click **Copy** in the Clipboard group to copy the query.

c. Click **Paste**, and then type **ListPriceCalculations** as the query name. Click **OK**.

The new query is displayed in the Navigation Pane. The name of the query indicates that it contains calculations based on each property's list price.

d. Right-click **ListPriceCalculations**, and then choose **Design View** from the shortcut menu.

e. Delete the WrongPricePerSqFt field by clicking the column selector at the top of the column (as shown in Figure 10), and then pressing **Delete**.

The WrongPricePerSqFt field is not needed for this query.

f. Click **Run** to see the query results.

g. Click **View** to return to Design view. Save the query.

STEP 2 USE THE EXPRESSION BUILDER TO MODIFY A FIELD

You need another calculation to help Jeff and Bill determine which houses to purchase. You will use the Expression Builder to modify an existing field. Refer to Figure 11 as you complete Step 2.

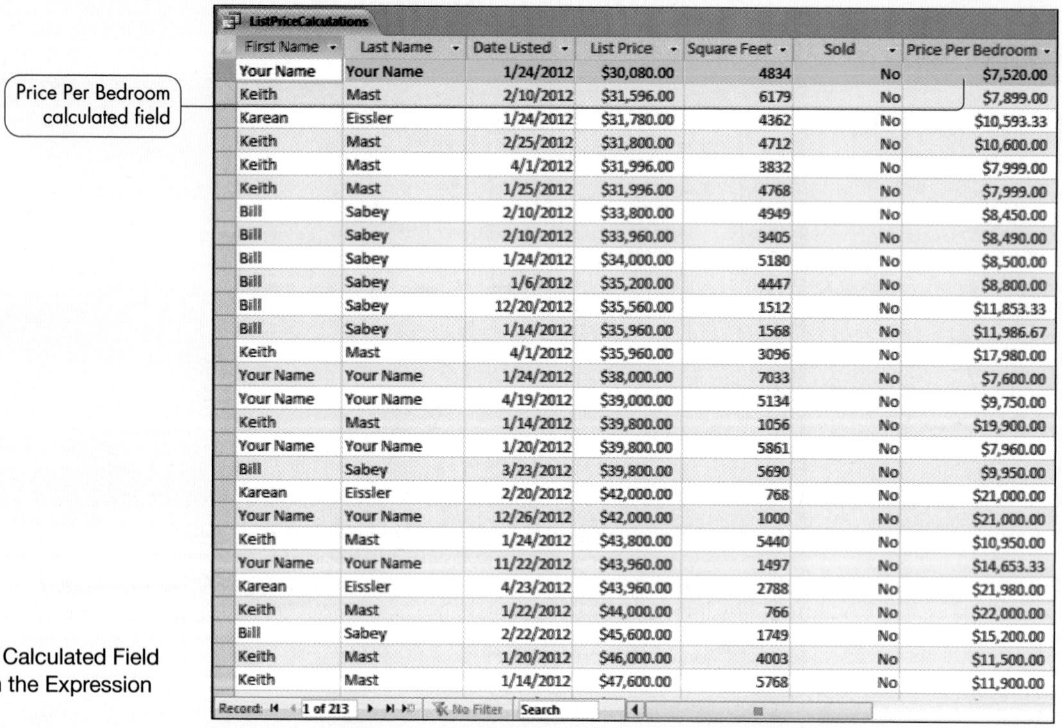

ListPriceCalculations

First Name	Last Name	Date Listed	List Price	Square Feet	Sold	Price Per Bedroom
Your Name	Your Name	1/24/2012	$30,080.00	4834	No	$7,520.00
Keith	Mast	2/10/2012	$31,596.00	6179	No	$7,899.00
Karean	Eissler	1/24/2012	$31,780.00	4362	No	$10,593.33
Keith	Mast	2/25/2012	$31,800.00	4712	No	$10,600.00
Keith	Mast	4/1/2012	$31,996.00	3832	No	$7,999.00
Keith	Mast	1/25/2012	$31,996.00	4768	No	$7,999.00
Bill	Sabey	2/10/2012	$33,800.00	4949	No	$8,450.00
Bill	Sabey	2/10/2012	$33,960.00	3405	No	$8,490.00
Bill	Sabey	1/24/2012	$34,000.00	5180	No	$8,500.00
Bill	Sabey	1/6/2012	$35,200.00	4447	No	$8,800.00
Bill	Sabey	12/20/2012	$35,560.00	1512	No	$11,853.33
Bill	Sabey	1/14/2012	$35,960.00	1568	No	$11,986.67
Keith	Mast	4/1/2012	$35,960.00	3096	No	$17,980.00
Your Name	Your Name	1/24/2012	$38,000.00	7033	No	$7,600.00
Your Name	Your Name	4/19/2012	$39,000.00	5134	No	$9,750.00
Keith	Mast	1/14/2012	$39,800.00	1056	No	$19,900.00
Your Name	Your Name	1/20/2012	$39,800.00	5861	No	$7,960.00
Bill	Sabey	3/23/2012	$39,800.00	5690	No	$9,950.00
Karean	Eissler	2/20/2012	$42,000.00	768	No	$21,000.00
Your Name	Your Name	12/26/2012	$42,000.00	1000	No	$21,000.00
Keith	Mast	1/24/2012	$43,800.00	5440	No	$10,950.00
Your Name	Your Name	11/22/2012	$43,960.00	1497	No	$14,653.33
Karean	Eissler	4/23/2012	$43,960.00	2788	No	$21,980.00
Keith	Mast	1/22/2012	$44,000.00	766	No	$22,000.00
Bill	Sabey	2/22/2012	$45,600.00	1749	No	$15,200.00
Keith	Mast	1/20/2012	$46,000.00	4003	No	$11,500.00
Keith	Mast	1/14/2012	$47,600.00	5768	No	$11,900.00

Record: 1 of 213 No Filter Search

Price Per Bedroom calculated field

FIGURE 11 Calculated Field Created with the Expression Builder ➤

a. Click in the **PricePerSqFt column**, and then click **Builder** in the Query Setup group.

The Expression Builder dialog box opens.

b. Change the PricePerSqFt field name to **PricePerBR**.

c. Double-click the **[SqFeet] field** in the expression, and then press **Delete**.

d. Under Expression Elements, click the **plus sign** (+) next to the *a03h2property_LastnameFirstname* database in the Expression Elements box to expand the list. Click the (+) next to *Tables*, and then click the **Properties table**.

The fields from the Properties table are now listed in the middle column (Expression Categories).

e. Double-click the **Beds field** to add it to the expression box.

The expression now reads *PricePerBR: [ListPrice]/[Properties]![Beds].*

f. Select the **[Properties]! prefix** in front of *Beds*, and then press **Delete**.

   The expression now reads *PricePerBR: [ListPrice]/[Beds].*

g. Click **OK**, and then click **Run** to view the query results.

h. Click **View** to switch to Design view, and then click the **PricePerBR field**. Click **Property Sheet** in the Show/Hide group, change the Format property to **Currency**, and then type **Price Per Bedroom** in the **Caption box**. Close the Property Sheet. Run the query and examine the changes.

i. Click **View** in the Views group to switch back to Design view. Save the query.

TIP Switching Between Object Views

You can switch between object views quickly by clicking View or you can click the View arrow and select the desired view from the list. Another way to switch between views is to right-click the object tab, and then select the view from the shortcut menu. See Figure 12.

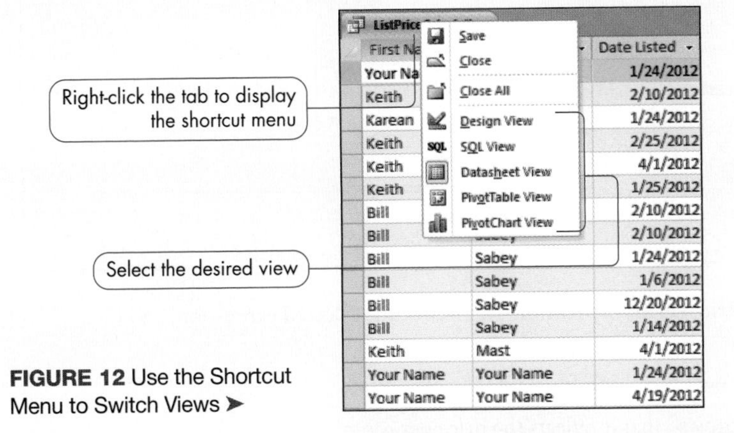

FIGURE 12 Use the Shortcut Menu to Switch Views ➤

TIP Expression Builder and Property Sheet

You can launch the Expression Builder by either clicking Builder in the Query Setup group on the Design tab or by right-clicking in the top row of the query design grid and selecting Build. Similarly, you can display the Property Sheet by clicking Property Sheet in the Show/Hide group on the Design tab or by right-clicking the top row of the query design grid and selecting Properties from the shortcut menu.

STEP 3 USE THE EXPRESSION BUILDER TO ADD A FIELD

The MCCC investors ask you for another calculation—the list price per room. For this calculation, you will assume that each property has a kitchen, a living room, a dining room, and the listed bedrooms and bathrooms. Refer to Figure 13 as you complete Step 3.

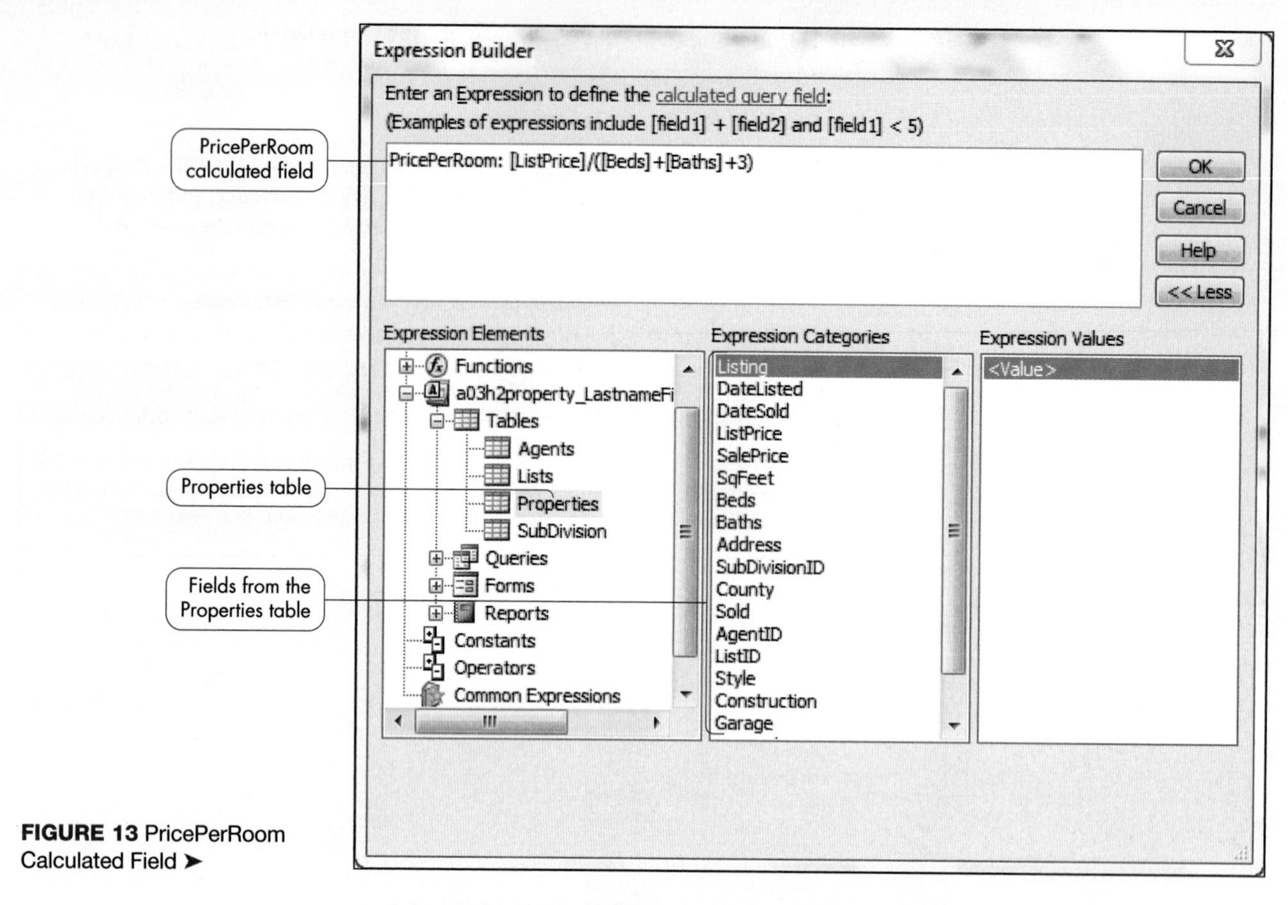

FIGURE 13 PricePerRoom Calculated Field ➤

a. Select the entire **PricePerBR expression**, right-click the selected expression, and then select **Copy**.

b. Right-click in the next blank column, and then click **Paste**.

   You will edit the copy so that it reflects the price per room.

c. Click the new field, and then click **Builder** in the Query Setup group.

d. Add **parentheses** around the [Beds] portion of the formula. Type a **plus sign** (+) after *[Beds]*, inside the parentheses.

   The expression box should read *PricePerBR: [ListPrice]/([Beds]+).*

e. Click the **plus sign** (+) next to the *a03h2property_LastnameFirstname* database in the Expression Elements box to expand the list. Click the **plus sign** (+) next to *Tables*, and then click the **Properties table**.

   The fields from the Properties table are now listed in the Expression Categories box.

f. Double-click the **Baths field** to add it to the expression box.

   The expression now reads *PricePerBR: [ListPrice]/([Beds]+[Properties]![Baths]).*

g. Type another plus sign after *[Baths]*, and then type **3**.

   The expression now reads *PricePerBR: [ListPrice]/([Beds]+[Properties]![Baths]+3).*

h. Delete the [Properties]! portion of the expression.

i. Change the PricePerBR field name to **PricePerRoom**.

   The expression now reads *PricePerRoom: [ListPrice]/([Beds]+[Baths]+3).*

j. Click **OK** to close the Expression Builder. Run the query. Widen the PricePerRoom column in order to see all the values.

k. Switch to **Design view**, click the **PricePerRoom field**, and then click **Property Sheet**.

l. Change the Format property to **Currency**, and then type **Price Per Room** in the **Caption box.** Close the Property Sheet.

m. Run the query and examine the query results.

n. Save the query, and then close the query.

STEP 4 USE FUNCTIONS

Jeff and Bill feel like they are close to making an offer on a house. They would like to calculate the estimated mortgage payment for each house. You create this calculation using the Pmt function. Refer to Figures 14 and 15 as you complete Step 4.

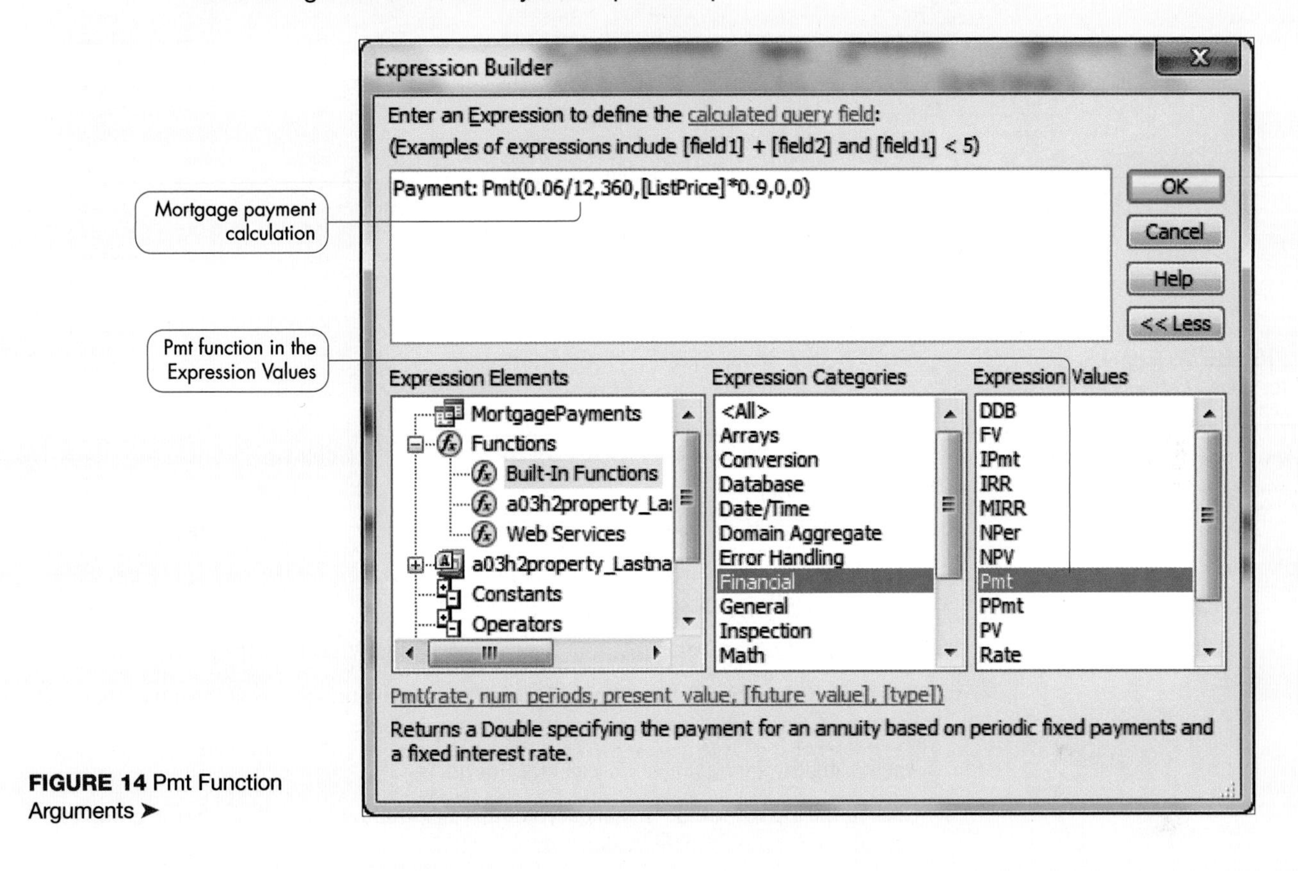

FIGURE 14 Pmt Function Arguments ➤

MortgagePayments

First Name	Last Name	Date Listed	List Price	Square Feet	Sold	Price Per Sq Ft	Payment
Your Name	Your Name	1/24/2012	$30,080.00	4834	No	$6.22	$162.31
Keith	Mast	2/10/2012	$31,596.00	6179	No	$5.11	$170.49
Karean	Eissler	1/24/2012	$31,780.00	4362	No	$7.29	$171.48
Keith	Mast	2/25/2012	$31,800.00	4712	No	$6.75	$171.59
Keith	Mast	4/1/2012	$31,996.00	3832	No	$8.35	$172.65
Keith	Mast	1/25/2012	$31,996.00	4768	No	$6.71	$172.65
Bill	Sabey	2/10/2012	$33,800.00	4949	No	$6.83	$182.38
Bill	Sabey	2/10/2012	$33,960.00	3405	No	$9.97	$183.25
Bill	Sabey	1/24/2012	$34,000.00	5180	No	$6.56	$183.46
Bill	Sabey	1/6/2012	$35,200.00	4447	No	$7.92	$189.94
Bill	Sabey	12/20/2012	$35,560.00	1512	No	$23.52	$191.88
Keith	Mast	4/1/2012	$35,960.00	3096	No	$11.61	$194.04
Bill	Sabey	1/14/2012	$35,960.00	1568	No	$22.93	$194.04
Your Name	Your Name	1/24/2012	$38,000.00	7033	No	$5.40	$205.05
Your Name	Your Name	4/19/2012	$39,000.00	5134	No	$7.60	$210.44
Keith	Mast	1/14/2012	$39,800.00	1056	No	$37.69	$214.76
Bill	Sabey	3/23/2012	$39,800.00	5690	No	$6.99	$214.76
Your Name	Your Name	1/20/2012	$39,800.00	5861	No	$6.79	$214.76
Your Name	Your Name	12/26/2012	$42,000.00	1000	No	$42.00	$226.63
Karean	Eissler	2/20/2012	$42,000.00	768	No	$54.69	$226.63
Keith	Mast	1/24/2012	$43,800.00	5440	No	$8.05	$236.34
Your Name	Your Name	11/22/2012	$43,960.00	1497	No	$29.37	$237.21
Karean	Eissler	4/23/2012	$43,960.00	2788	No	$15.77	$237.21
Keith	Mast	1/22/2012	$44,000.00	766	No	$57.44	$237.42
Bill	Sabey	2/22/2012	$45,600.00	1749	No	$26.07	$246.06
Keith	Mast	1/20/2012	$46,000.00	4003	No	$11.49	$248.21
Keith	Mast	1/14/2012	$47,600.00	5768	No	$8.25	$256.85

Record: 1 of 84 No Filter Search

Mortgage payment calculation

FIGURE 15 Payment Amounts for Each Property ➤

a. Select the **PricePerSqFt query**, and then click **Copy** in the Clipboard group to copy the query.

b. Click **Paste**, and then type **MortgagePayments** as the query name. Click **OK**.

The new query is displayed in the Navigation Pane. The name of the query indicates that it contains calculations based on each property's list price.

c. Right-click **MortgagePayments**, and then choose **Design View** from the shortcut menu.

d. Delete the WrongPricePerSqFeet field by clicking the column selector at the top of the column (as shown in Figure 10), and then pressing **Delete**.

The WrongPricePerSqFt is not needed for this query.

e. Click in the top row of the first blank column. Click **Builder** in the Query Setup group to open the Expression Builder dialog box.

You will use the Pmt function to calculate an estimated house payment for each of the sold properties. You make the following assumptions: 90% of the sale price will be financed, a 30-year term, monthly payments, and a fixed 6.0% annual interest rate.

f. Double-click **Functions** in the Expression Elements box, and then click **Built-In Functions**.

g. Click the **Financial category** in the Expression Categories box.

h. Double-click the **Pmt function** in the Expression Values box. The expression box displays:

Pmt(«rate», «num_periods», «present_value», «future_value», «type»)

i. Type **Payment:** to the left of the Pmt function. The expression box now displays:

Payment: Pmt(«rate», «num_periods», «present_value», «future_value», «type»)

TROUBLESHOOTING: If you forget to add the calculated field name to the left of the expression, Access will add *Expr1* to the front of your expression for you. You can edit the Expr1 name later, after the Expression Builder is closed.

j. Click each argument to select it, and then substitute the appropriate information. Make sure there is a comma between each argument.

Argument	Replacement Value
<<rate>>	0.06/12
<<num_periods>>	360
<<present_value>>	[ListPrice] * 0.9 *(this represents 90% of the list price)*
<<future_value>>	0
<<due>>	0

k. Examine Figure 14 to make sure that you have entered the correct arguments. Click **OK**. Run the query.

The Payment column shows *########*. Widen the column and notice the payment amounts are negative numbers. You will edit the formula to change the negative payment values to positive.

l. Right-click the **MortgagePayments tab**, and then choose **Design View** from the shortcut menu. Right-click the **Payment field**, and then select **Build**. Add a **minus sign** (–) to the left of *[ListPrice]*.

The expression now reads *Payment: Pmt(0.06/12,360,–[ListPrice]*0.9,0,0)*.

m. Click **OK**. Open the **Property Sheet** for *Payment*, and then change the format to **Currency**. Close the Property Sheet.

The calculated field values should now appear as positive values formatted as currency, as shown in Figure 15.

n. Run and save the query.

STEP 5 WORK WITH DATE ARITHMETIC AND ADD CRITERIA

You need to limit the query results to only houses on the market at least six months. The investors also want you to add the commission fee to the query since they are getting ready to make a purchase and this information will help them figure out their commission cost. Refer to Figure 16 as you complete Step 5.

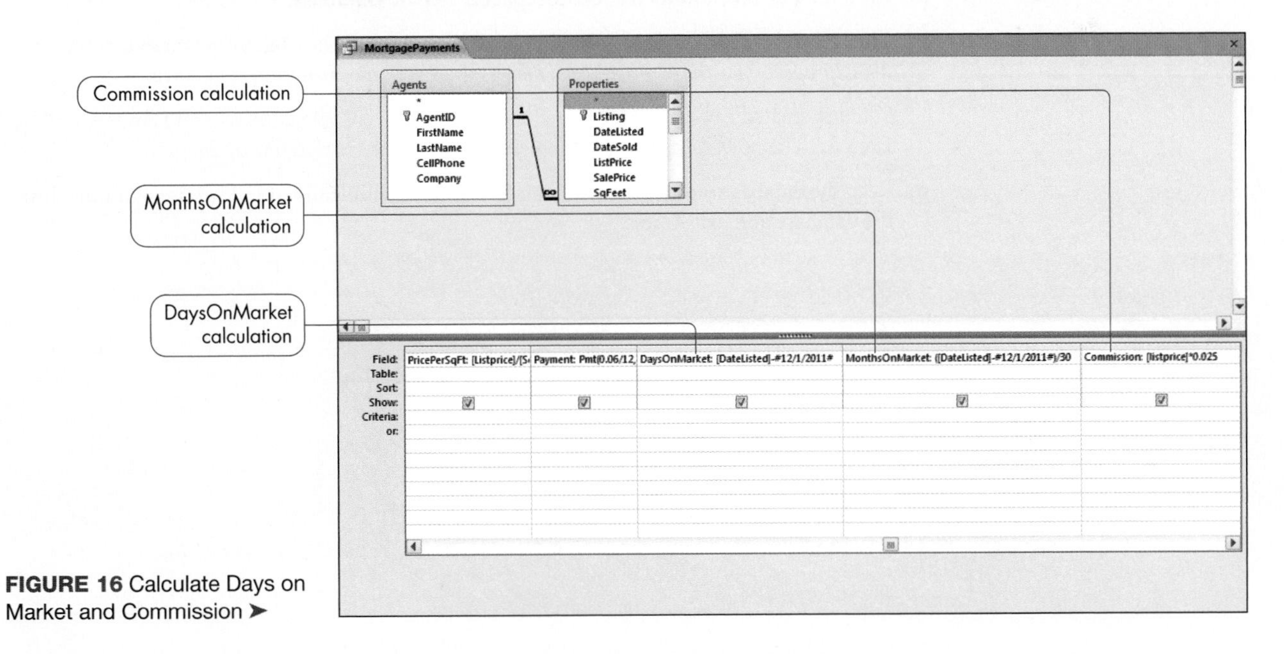

FIGURE 16 Calculate Days on Market and Commission ➤

a. Click **View** to return to the Design view of the MortgagePayments query. Click in the top row of the first blank column. Press **Shift+F2** to open the Zoom dialog box.

You need to enter an expression to calculate the number of days that each property has been on the market.

b. Type **DaysOnMarket: [DateListed] – #12/1/2011#.**

This will display the number of days a house has been on the market since 12/1/2011.

c. Click **OK** to close the Zoom dialog box. Open the **Property Sheet,** and then add the Caption to **Days on Market**. Close the Property sheet.

d. Type <=**100000** in the **Criteria row** of the **ListPrice column**. Run the query. Save the query.

This expression will limit the query results to only houses with a list price of $100,000 or less. There should be 84 records.

e. Click **View** to switch to Design view. Click in the top row of the first blank column. Press **Shift+F2** to open the Zoom dialog box.

f. Type the formula **MonthsOnMarket: ([DateListed] – #12/1/2011#) / 30.**

The formula for MonthsOnMarket requires placing parentheses around *[DateListed] – #12/1/2011#* and then dividing the result by 30. This is an example of how to control the order of operations.

g. Click **OK** to close the Zoom dialog box. Open the Property Sheet, and then change the Format to **Fixed**, and the Caption to **Months on Market**. Close the Property Sheet dialog box. Run the query. Save the query.

h. Switch to Design view. Click in the top row of the first blank column to create another calculated field. Open the Zoom dialog box, and then type the formula **Commission: ListPrice * .025**. Click **OK** to close the Zoom dialog box.

The Commission field displays the projected commission for each house. The agent earns 2.5% of the sale price.

i. Right-click the **Commission field**, and then select **Properties**. Change the format to **Currency**, and then close the Property Sheet.

j. Run the query, examine the results, and then save the query. Close the query.

The values in the Commission field now display in Currency format.

k. Click the **File tab**, and then click **Compact & Repair Database**.

l. Click the **File tab**, click **Save & Publish**, and then double-click **Back Up Database**. Accept *a03h2property_LastnameFirstname_date* as the file name, and then click **Save**.

You just created a backup of the database you used to complete the second Hands-On Exercise. The *a03h2property_LastnameFirstname* database remains open.

m. Keep the database onscreen if you plan to continue with Hands-On Exercise 3. If not, close the database and exit Access.

Aggregate Functions

An **aggregate function** performs calculations on an entire column of data and returns a single value.

Aggregate functions perform calculations on an entire column of data and return a single value. Aggregate functions—such as Sum, Average, and Minimum—are used when you need to evaluate a group of record values rather than the individual records in a table or query.

Aggregate functions—such as Sum, Average, and Minimum—are used when you need to evaluate a group of record values rather than the individual records in a table or query.

Access refers to aggregate functions as Totals. In the Datasheet view of a query or table, click Totals in the Records group on the Home tab to add a Total row to the bottom of the datasheet. Each column can have its own aggregate function. Numeric fields are eligible for all of the functions, whereas text fields are only eligible for the count function.

When you create a query in Design view, click Totals in the Show/Hide group to change it to a totals query. The Total row now appears and you can select from the list of aggregate functions (e.g., Sum, Avg, Min).

The Datasheet view of a query or table displays individual records; users can edit these records, enter a new record, or delete a record in Datasheet view. However, when you work within a totals query in Datasheet view, no updates are allowed. A user cannot add, update, or delete records that have been totaled.

A car dealer's monthly inventory report is a good example of a report that might contain aggregate information. The cars would be grouped by model, and then by options package and color. At the end of the report, a summary page would list the count of cars in each model for quick reference by the sales reps. In the property database, aggregate information could be grouped by county or by subdivision. For example, the average home price per county could be presented in a query or a report. This would give prospective buyers a good idea of home prices in their target counties. Almost every company or organization that uses a database will require some type of aggregate data.

Almost every company or organization that uses a database will require some type of aggregate data.

A list of common aggregate functions is shown in Table 4.

TABLE 4 Aggregate Functions

Function	Description	Use with Data Type(s)
Average	Calculates the average value for a column. The function ignores null values.	Number, Currency, Date/Time
Count	Counts the number of items in a column. The function ignores null values.	All data types except a column of multivalued lists.
Maximum	Returns the item with the highest value. For text data, the highest value is 'Z.' The function ignores null values.	Number, Currency, Date/Time, Text
Minimum	Returns the item with the lowest value. For text data, the lowest value is 'a.' The function ignores null values.	Number, Currency, Date/Time, Text
Standard Deviation	Measures how widely values are dispersed from an average value.	Number, Currency
Sum	Adds the items in a column. Works only on numeric and currency data.	Number, Currency
Variance	Measures the statistical variance of all values in the column.	Number

In this section, you will learn how to create and work with aggregate functions. Specifically, you will learn how to use the Total row and create a totals query.

Adding Aggregate Functions to Datasheets and Queries

Aggregate functions are most commonly used in tables, queries, and reports. Occasionally, aggregate functions are also added to the form footer section of forms. Aggregate data helps users evaluate the values in a single record as compared to the average of all the records.

If you are considering buying a property in Bucks county for $150,000 and the average price of a property in Bucks county is $450,000, you know you are getting a good deal (or buying a bad property).

A **Total row** displays as the last row in the Datasheet view of a table or query and provides a number of aggregate functions.

Access provides two methods of adding aggregate functions to a query—a ***Total row*** displayed as the last row in the Datasheet view of a table or query and a totals query created in query Design view.

The first method enables you to add a Total row to the Datasheet view. This method is quick and easy and has the advantage of showing the total information while still showing the individual records. Adding a Total row to a query or table can be accomplished by most users (even those who are not familiar with designing a query).

The second method requires you to add a Total row in the Query Design view. This method has the advantage of enabling you to group your data by categories. For example, you can use the Count function to show the number of houses sold in each county in each subdivision. You could also use the Average function to show the average sale price for houses sold in each subdivision.

Once the totals data are assembled, you can use them to make decisions. Who is the leading salesperson? Which subdivisions are selling the most houses? This method requires the user to understand how to alter the design of a query.

Access also permits aggregates in reports. The Report Wizard gives users a choice to show all detail records or summary-only statistics. Select summary only to see aggregate data. You will learn to use both methods of creating aggregate data.

Add a Total Row in a Query or Table

Figure 17 shows the Total row added to the Datasheet view of a query. Using the balance column as illustrated, you can choose any of the aggregate functions that apply to numeric fields. To begin, click Totals in the Records group on the Home tab. The Total row is added at the bottom of the datasheet, below the new record row of the query or table. In the Total row, you can select one of the aggregate functions by clicking in the cell and then clicking the arrow. The list of aggregate functions includes Sum, Average, Count, and others.

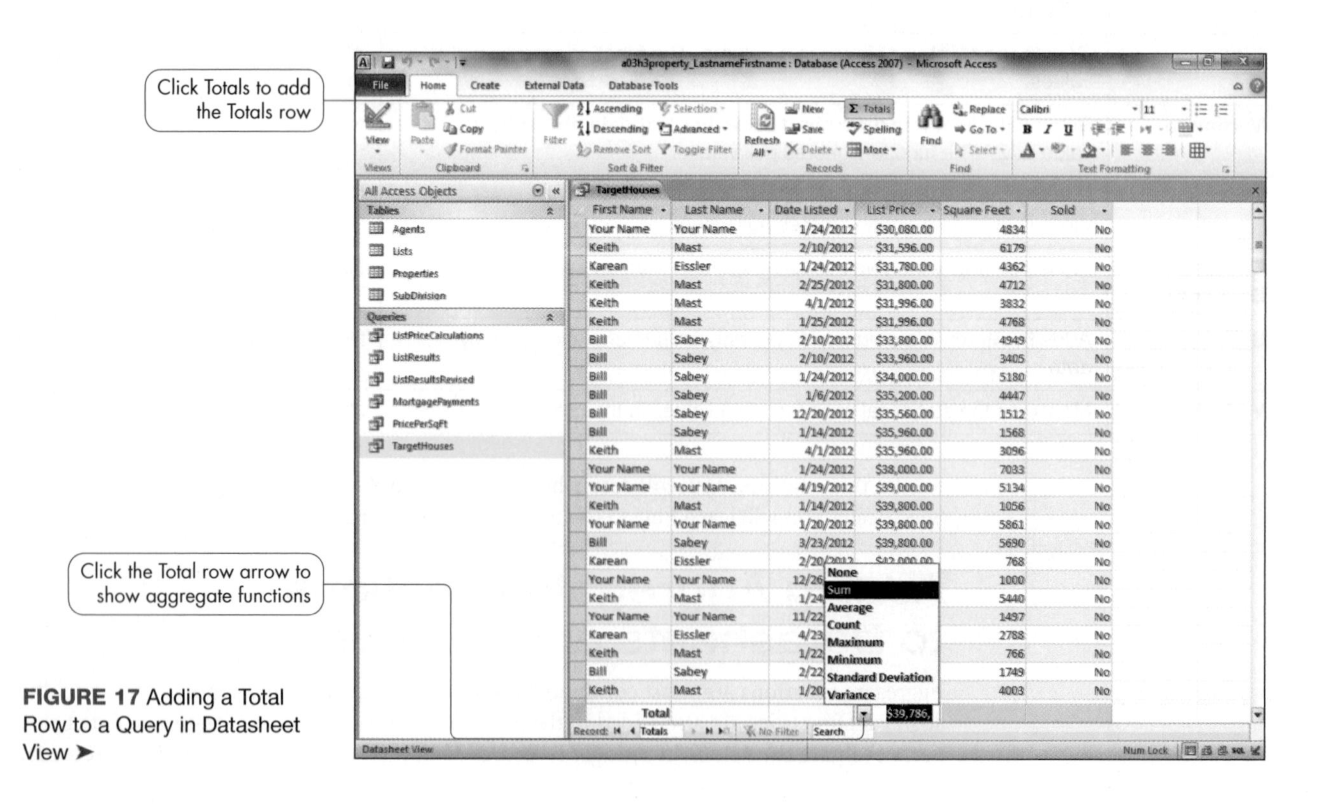

FIGURE 17 Adding a Total Row to a Query in Datasheet View ➤

Create a Totals Query

A **totals query** contains an additional row in the design grid and is used to display only aggregate data when the query is run.

A ***totals query*** contains an additional row in the query design grid and is used to display only aggregate data when the query is run. This is in contrast to using the Total row in a datasheet which shows both the detail records and the summary (as described in the previous section). The first column of a totals query will usually be a grouping field; the Total row will contain the Group function. The second and subsequent columns will usually contain the Count, Sum, or Avg function. Problems can arise when too many columns are included in a totals query; a typical totals query contains only two to five columns. Figure 18 shows the Design view of a totals query with three columns.

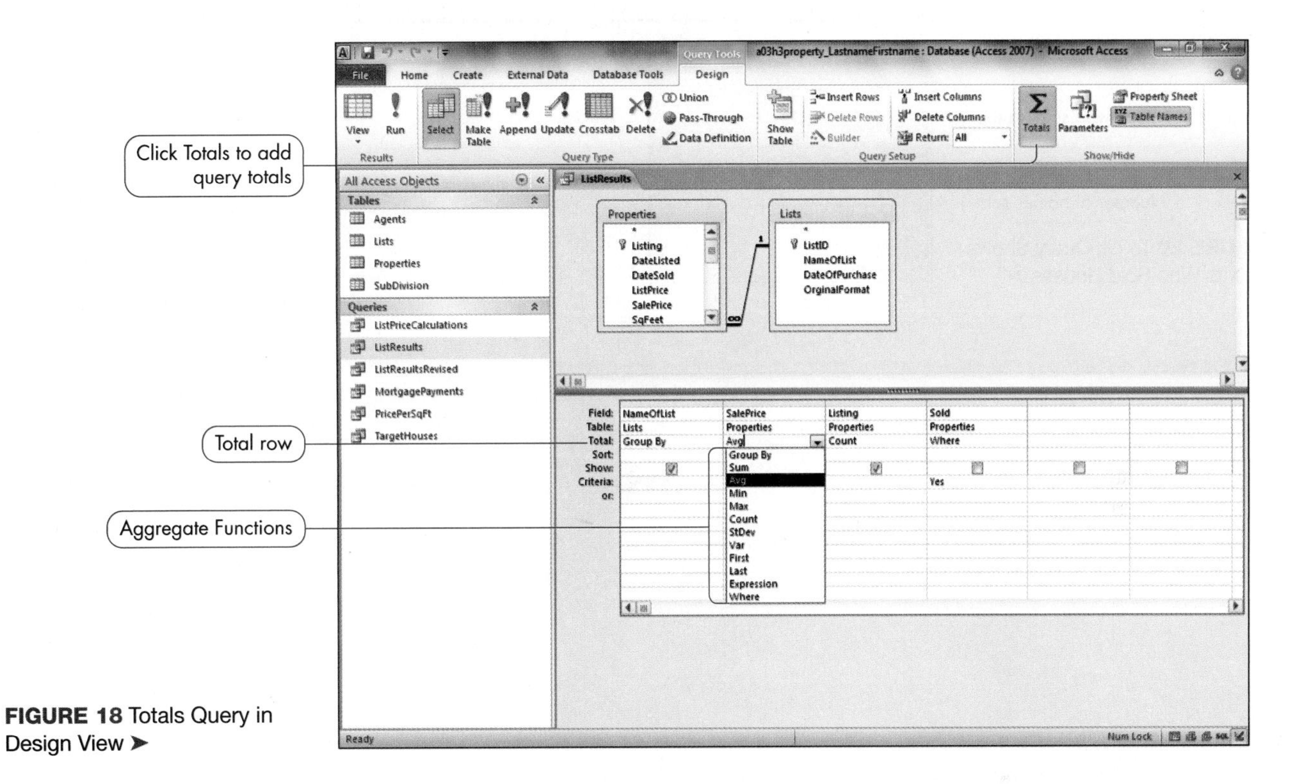

FIGURE 18 Totals Query in Design View ➤

Figure 18 groups the properties by county and then shows the count of houses and the average price in each county. You could add the Subdivision field to the second column of this query—to create a group within a group. The data will now be grouped by county and then by subdivision within each county. In order to show the subdivision field, you must add the Subdivision table to the query design. Figure 19 shows the results of the Housing Info by County by Subdivision totals query.

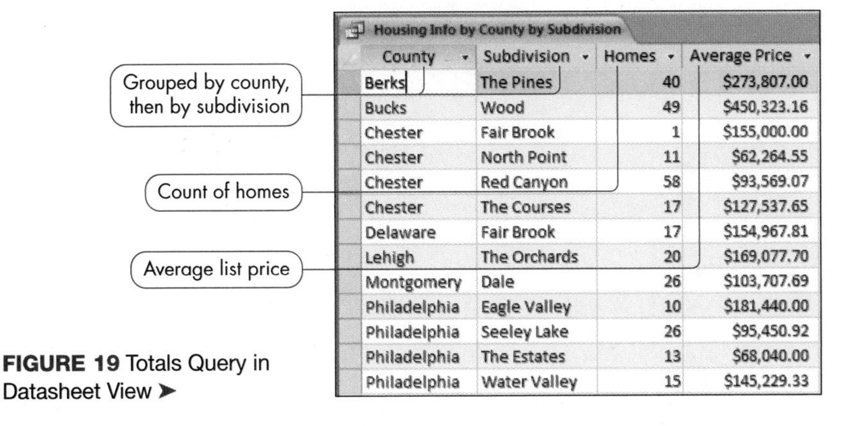

Housing Info by County by Subdivision

County	Subdivision	Homes	Average Price
Berks	The Pines	40	$273,807.00
Bucks	Wood	49	$450,323.16
Chester	Fair Brook	1	$155,000.00
Chester	North Point	11	$62,264.55
Chester	Red Canyon	58	$93,569.07
Chester	The Courses	17	$127,537.65
Delaware	Fair Brook	17	$154,967.81
Lehigh	The Orchards	20	$169,077.70
Montgomery	Dale	26	$103,707.69
Philadelphia	Eagle Valley	10	$181,440.00
Philadelphia	Seeley Lake	26	$95,450.92
Philadelphia	The Estates	13	$68,040.00
Philadelphia	Water Valley	15	$145,229.33

FIGURE 19 Totals Query in Datasheet View ➤

A Totals Query Helps Evaluate a Database

If you were asked to evaluate a database that contains home sales information, you could quickly determine which agents sold houses by creating a totals query with two tables and three fields. From the Properties and Agents tables, you would add the LastName field, the Listing field, and the Sold field. Click Totals in the Show/Hide group. Accept Group By in column one; change column two to Count, and change column three to Where. Add Yes to the Criteria row of column three. The results of this query would show which agents sold homes, as shown in Figure 20.

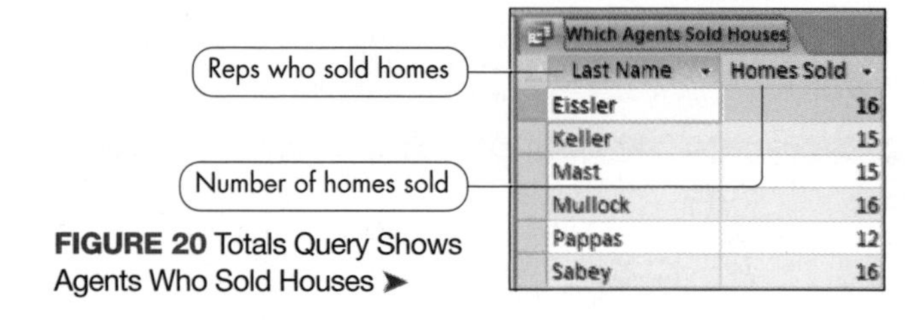

Which Agents Sold Houses

Last Name	Homes Sold
Eissler	16
Keller	15
Mast	15
Mullock	16
Pappas	12
Sabey	16

FIGURE 20 Totals Query Shows Agents Who Sold Houses ➤

HANDS-ON EXERCISES

3 Aggregate Functions

The investors decide it would be helpful to analyze the property lists they purchased. Some of the lists do not have homes that match their target criteria. The investors will either need to purchase new lists or alter their criteria. You create several totals queries to evaluate the property lists.

Skills covered: Add a Total Row to Datasheet View • Create a Totals Query Based on a Select Query • Add a Calculated Field to a Totals Query

STEP 1 ADD A TOTAL ROW TO DATASHEET VIEW

You begin your property list analysis by creating a Total row in the Datasheet view of the MortgagePayments query. This will give you a variety of aggregate information for each column. Refer to Figure 21 as you complete Step 1.

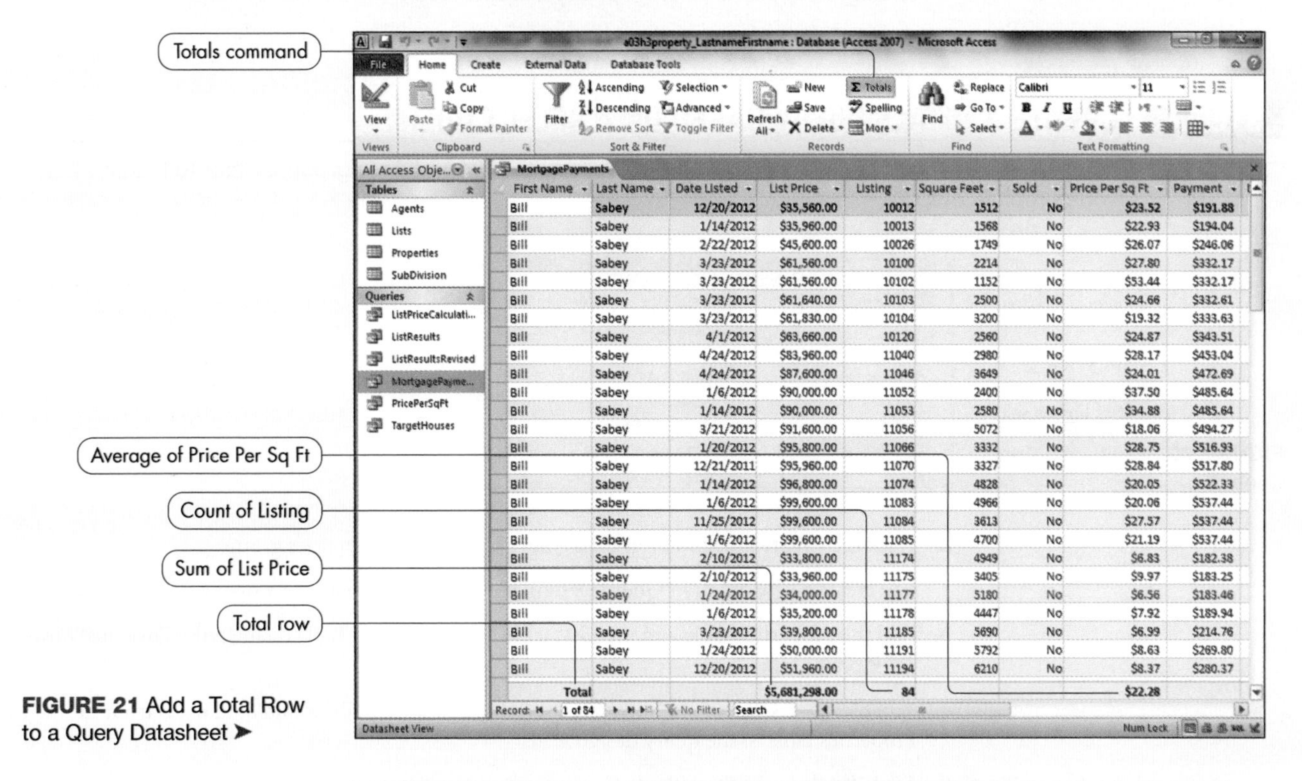

FIGURE 21 Add a Total Row to a Query Datasheet ➤

a. Open *a03h2property_LastnameFirstname* if you closed it at the end of Hands-On Exercise 2. Click the **File tab**, click **Save Database As**, and then type **a03h3property_LastnameFirstname**, changing *h2* to *h3*. Click **Save**.

b. Right-click the **MortgagePayments query** in the Navigation Pane, and then select **Design View** from the shortcut menu. Drag the **Listing field** from the Properties table to the fifth column.

   The Listing field is now in the fifth column and the other columns shift to the right.

c. Click **View** to switch to Datasheet view. Click **Totals** in the Records group on the Home tab to show the Total row.

   The Total row is now displayed as the last row of the query results. Click Totals again to hide the Total row, then one more time to show it.

d. Click in the cell that intersects the Total row and the List Price column.

e. Click the arrow, and then select **Sum** to display the total of all the properties that have not sold. Widen the List Price column if you can't see the entire total value.

   The total list price of all properties is $5,681,298.00.

f. Click the arrow in the Total row in the Listing column, and then select **Count** from the list.

   The count of properties in this datasheet is 84.

g. Click in the Total row in the Price Per Sq Ft column. Click the arrow, and then select **Average** to display the average price per square foot.

h. Save and close the query.

STEP 2 CREATE A TOTALS QUERY BASED ON A SELECT QUERY

You create a totals query to help Jeff and Bill evaluate the properties in groups. Refer to Figure 22 as you complete Step 2.

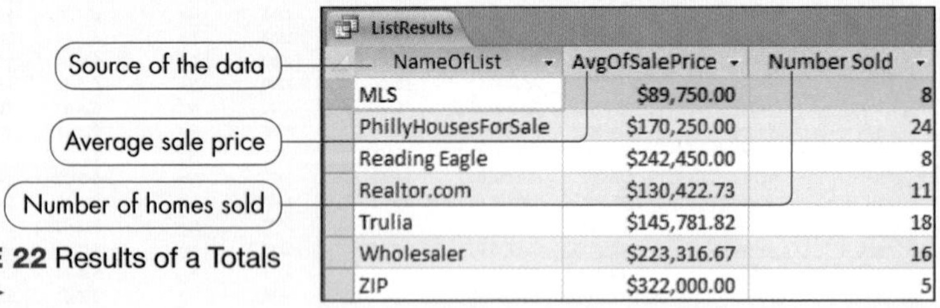

ListResults

NameOfList	AvgOfSalePrice	Number Sold
MLS	$89,750.00	8
PhillyHousesForSale	$170,250.00	24
Reading Eagle	$242,450.00	8
Realtor.com	$130,422.73	11
Trulia	$145,781.82	18
Wholesaler	$223,316.67	16
ZIP	$322,000.00	5

Source of the data

Average sale price

Number of homes sold

FIGURE 22 Results of a Totals Query ➤

a. Click the **Create tab**, and then click **Query Design** in the Queries group.

   You create a new query in Query Design; the Show Table dialog box opens.

b. Add the Properties table and the Lists table from the Show Table dialog box. Close the Show Table dialog box.

c. Add the NameOfList field from the Lists table and the SalePrice and Sold fields from the Properties table to the query design grid.

d. Click **Totals** in the Show/Hide Group to show the Total row.

e. Change the Total row to **Avg** in the SalePrice column.

f. Change the Total row to **Where** in the Sold column. Type **Yes** in the **Criteria row**.

   This criterion will limit the results to sold houses only.

g. Click in the **SalePrice field**, and then click **Property Sheet** in the Show/Hide group. Change the SalePrice format to **Currency**. Close the Property Sheet. Run the query.

   The query results indicate that the MLS list is the only source that is under the investor's target of $100,000 or less. They decide to continue using Realtor.com and Trulia even though the average price is over $100,000. The other sources will no longer be used.

h. Click **View** to switch to Design View. Add the Listing field from the Properties table to the fourth column in the design grid. Change the Total row for *Listing* to **Count**. Run the query.

   The query results now show the number of properties sold in each source, in addition to the average sale price. This will help determine which sources have been more effective.

i. Click **View** to return to the Design view of the query. Change the caption of the Listing column to **Number Sold.** Run the query, and then widen the columns as shown in Figure 22.

j. Save the query as **ListResults**. Keep the query open for the next step.

STEP 3 ADD A CALCULATED FIELD TO A TOTALS QUERY

The totals query helped group the houses into categories. However, the groups contain all the properties, even the ones that do not match the investor's criteria. You need to create a new query with the investor's criteria included. Refer to Figure 23 as you complete Step 3.

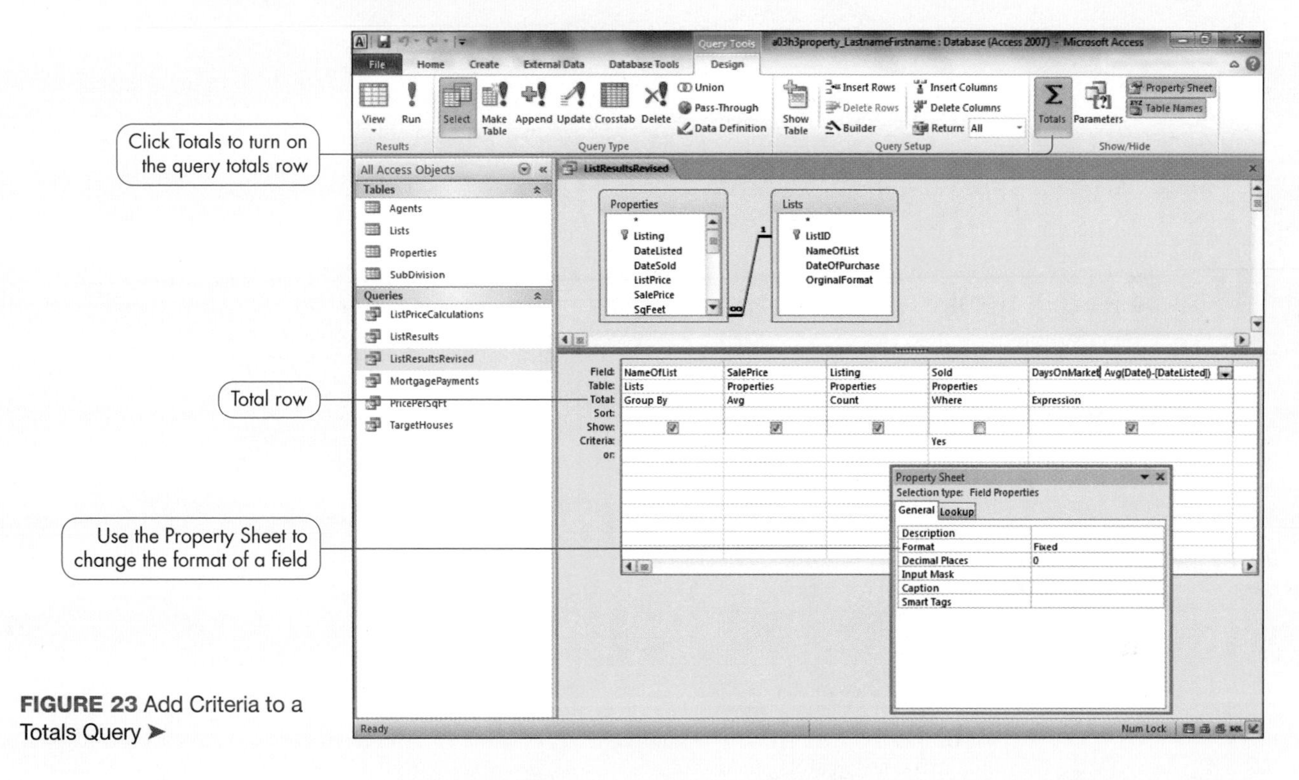

FIGURE 23 Add Criteria to a Totals Query ➤

a. Click the **File tab**, and then click **Save Object As**. Save the query as **ListResultsRevised.** Click the **File tab** to return to the query.

b. Click **Totals** in the Records group, and then add **Sum** to the Number Sold column.

   The total number of houses sold is 90.

c. Click **View** in the Views group to switch to Design view. In the first blank column, type **DaysOnMarket: [DateListed] – #12/1/2011#** to create a new calculated field. Change the Total row to **Avg.**

d. Right-click the **DaysOnMarket field**, and then select **Properties** from the shortcut menu. Change the Format property to **Fixed.** Close the Property Sheet.

e. Run the ListResultsRevised query, and then examine the DaysOnMarket.

f. Save and close the query.

g. Click the **File tab**, and then click **Compact & Repair Database**.

h. Click the **File tab**, click **Save & Publish**, and then double-click **Back Up Database**. Accept *a03h3property_LastnameFirstname_date* as the file name, and then click **Save**.

   You just created a backup of the database you used to complete the third Hands-On Exercise. The *a03h3property_LastnameFirstname* database remains open.

i. Click the **File tab**, and then click **Exit** (to exit Access).

j. Submit based on your instructor's directions.

CHAPTER OBJECTIVES REVIEW

After reading this chapter, you have accomplished the following objectives:

1. **Understand the order of operations.** The order of operations determines the sequence by which operations are calculated in an expression. Evaluate expressions in parentheses first, then exponents, then multiplication and division, and, finally, addition and subtraction. Operations of equal value will be calculated from left to right. A solid understanding of these rules will enable you to easily create calculated fields in Access.
2. **Create a calculated field in a query.** When creating a query, you may need to create a calculation based on the fields from one or more tables. Add a calculated field in the Design view of a query to the first blank column or by inserting a blank column where needed. A formula used to calculate new fields from the values in existing fields is known as an *expression*. An expression can consist of a number of fields, operators (such as * , / , + , or –), functions (such as IIf), and constants (numbers). When creating a calculated field, you must follow proper syntax—the set of rules that Access follows when evaluating an expression.
3. **Create expressions with the Expression Builder.** Launch the Expression Builder while in the query design grid to assist you with creating a calculated field (or other expression). The Expression Builder helps you create expressions by supplying you with the fields, operators, and functions you need to create them. When you use the Expression Builder to help you create expressions, you can eliminate spelling errors in field names. Another advantage is with functions; functions require specific arguments in a specific order. When you insert a function using the Expression Builder, the builder gives you placeholders that tell you where each argument belongs.
4. **Use built-in functions in Access.** A function produces a result based on variable inputs known as *arguments*. Once you identify what you need a function to do, you can open the Built-In Functions folder in the Expression Builder to see if the function exists. If it does, add the function to the expression box and supply the required arguments. Functions work the same in Access and Excel.
5. **Perform date arithmetic.** All dates and times in Access are stored as the number of days that have elapsed since December 31, 1899. Working with dates in Access can be challenging, especially when performing date arithmetic. Fortunately, Access has some built-in functions to help work with dates and date arithmetic. Sample functions include DateDiff (), DateAdd(), Date(), and Now(). These functions help perform arithmetic on date fields.
6. **Add aggregate functions to datasheets and queries.** Aggregate functions perform calculations on an entire column of data and return a single value. Aggregate functions—such as Sum, Average, and Minimum—are used when you need to evaluate a group of records rather than the individual records in a table or query. Access refers to aggregate functions as Totals. In the Datasheet view of a query or table, click Totals to add a Total row to the bottom of the datasheet. When you create a query in Design view, click Totals to show the Total row.

KEY TERMS

Aggregate function
Argument
Constant
Date arithmetic
Date formatting
DatePart function
Expression
Expression Builder
Function
IIf function
Order of operations
Pmt function
Syntax
Total row
Totals query

MULTIPLE CHOICE

1. Which of the following correctly identifies the rules for the order of operations?
   (a) Exponentiation, parentheses, addition, subtraction, multiplication, division
   (b) Parentheses, exponentiation, addition, subtraction, multiplication, division
   (c) Parentheses, exponentiation, multiplication, division, addition, subtraction
   (d) Addition, subtraction, multiplication, division, exponentiation, parentheses

2. What is the result of the following expression?
   (3 * 5) + 7 – 2 – 6 * 2
   (a) 12
   (b) 7
   (c) 28
   (d) 8

3. The Builder command that opens the Expression Builder is found in the:
   (a) Manage group on the Databases Tools tab.
   (b) Query Setup group on the Design tab.
   (c) Database Management group on the Design tab.
   (d) Design group on the Query Setup tab.

4. Which function enables you to insert today's date into an expression?
   (a) Date()
   (b) DatePart()
   (c) Now()
   (d) DateDiff()

5. You correctly calculated a value for the OrderAmount using an expression. Now you need to use the newly calculated value in another expression calculating sales tax. The most efficient method is to:
   (a) Run and save the query to make OrderAmount available as input to subsequent expressions.
   (b) Create a new query based on the query containing the calculated Order amount, and then calculate the sales tax in the new query.
   (c) Close the Access file, saving the changes when asked; reopen the file and reopen the query; calculate the sales tax.
   (d) Create a backup of the database, open the backup and the query, then calculate the sales tax.

6. If state law requires that a restaurant's wait staff be at least 21 to serve alcohol and you have a database that stores each employee's birth date in the Employee table, which of the following is the proper syntax to identify the employees' year of birth?
   (a) Age:DatePart("yyyy",[Employee]![BirthDate])
   (b) Age=DatePart("yyyy",[Employee]![BirthDate])
   (c) Age:DatePart("yyyy",[BirthDate]![Employee])
   (d) Age=DatePart("yyyy",[BirthDate]![Employee])

7. Which statement about a totals query is true?
   (a) A totals query is created in Datasheet view.
   (b) A totals query may contain several grouping fields but only one aggregate field.
   (c) A totals query is limited to only two fields, one grouping field, and one aggregate field.
   (d) A totals query may contain several grouping fields and several aggregate fields.

8. After creating a calculated field, you run the query and a parameter dialog box appears on your screen. How do you respond to the Parameter dialog box?
   (a) Click OK to make the parameter box go away.
   (b) Read the field name specified in the parameter box, and then look for a possible typing error in the calculated expression.
   (c) Type numbers in the parameter box, and then click OK.
   (d) Close the query without saving changes. Re-open it and try running the query again.

9. An updatable query contains student names. You run the query and while in Datasheet view, you notice a spelling error on one of the student's names. You correct the error in Datasheet view. Which statement is true?
   (a) The name is correctly spelled in this query but will be misspelled in the table and all other queries based on the table.
   (b) The name is correctly spelled in the table and in all queries based on the table.
   (c) The name is correctly spelled in this query and any other queries, but will remain misspelled in the table.
   (d) You cannot edit data in a query.

10. Which of the following is not true about the Total row in the query design grid?
    (a) The Total row enables you to apply aggregate functions to the fields.
    (b) The Total row can apply to fields stored in different tables.
    (c) The Total row is located between the Table and Sort rows.
    (d) The Total row can only be applied to numeric fields.

PRACTICE EXERCISES

1 Comfort Insurance

The Comfort Insurance Agency is a mid-sized company with offices located across the country. Each employee receives a performance review annually. The review determines employee eligibility for salary increases and the annual performance bonus. The employee data are stored in an Access database, which is used by the human resources department to monitor and maintain employee records. Your task is to calculate the salary increase for each employee; you will also calculate each employee's performance bonus for employees who have been employed at least one year. This exercise follows the same set of skills as used in Hands-On Exercises 1 and 2 in the chapter. Refer to Figure 24 as you complete this exercise.

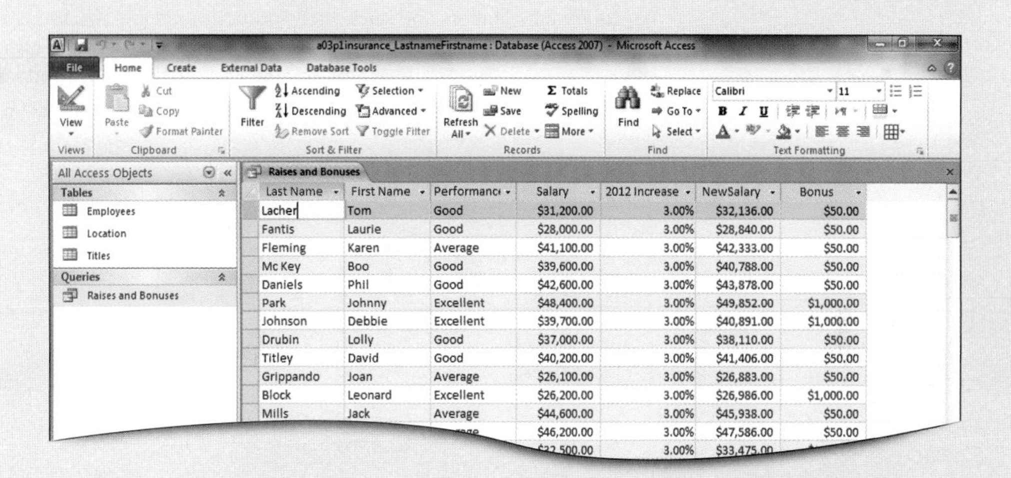

FIGURE 24 Raises and Bonuses ➤

a. Open *a03p1insurance*. Click the **File tab**, click **Save Database As**, and then type **a03p1insurance_LastnameFirstname**. Click **Save**.

b. Click the **Database Tools tab**, and then click **Relationships** in the Relationships group. Examine the table structure, relationships, and fields. Once you are familiar with the database, close the Relationships window.

c. Click the **Create tab**, and then click **Query Design** in the Queries group to start a new query. The Show Table dialog box opens. Add the Employees and Titles tables. Close the Show Table dialog box.

d. Add the **LastName**, **FirstName**, **Performance**, and **Salary fields** to the query. From the Titles table, add the **2012Increase field** to the query.

e. Click the top row of the first blank column in the query design grid, and then type **NewSalary:[Salary]*[2012Increase]+[Salary]** to create a calculated field.

f. Click **Run** in the Results group to run the query. (If you receive the Enter Parameter Value dialog box, check your expression carefully for spelling errors.) Look at the output in the Datasheet view. Verify that your answers are correct. Notice that the fourth column heading displays *2012 Increase*. This is the caption for the 2012Increase field in the Titles table that was carried over to the query. When a caption exists for a field in the table Design view, the caption also displays in the Query Datasheet view instead of the field name in the query.

g. Click **View** in the Views group to switch back to Design view. Open the Property Sheet, click in the **NewSalary calculated field**, and then change the format to **Currency**. Type **New Salary** in the **Caption box**. Close the Property Sheet.

h. Save the query as **Raises and Bonuses.**

i. Click the top row of the first blank column, and then click **Builder** in the Query Setup group. In the Expression Elements box, double-click the folder for **Functions**. Select the **Built-In Functions folder**. Scroll down the Expression Values box to locate the IIf function. Double-click **IIf** to insert the function.

j. Click <<**expression**>>, and then replace it with **Performance = "Excellent"**. Click <<**truepart**>>, and then replace it with **1000**. Click <<**falsepart**>>, and then replace it with **50**.

k. Type **Bonus:** to the left of *IIf*, as the calculated field name. Click **OK**.

l. Change the format of the Bonus field to **Currency** in the Property Sheet.

m. Run the query. Save and close the query.

n. Click the **File tab**, and then click **Compact and Repair Database**.

o. Click the **File tab**, click **Save & Publish**, and then double-click **Back Up Database**. Click **Save** to accept the default backup file name.

p. Click the **File tab**, and then click **Exit** (to exit Access).

q. Submit based on your instructor's directions.

2 Northwind Traders

Northwind Traders maintains a database to store all of its product and inventory information, customer information, and sales information. You are the marketing manager of Northwind Traders and use this database to monitor sales trends. You need to determine the revenue from each order filled in the last year, and to summarize the revenue figures by product category. This exercise follows the same set of skills as used in Hands-On Exercises 2 and 3 in the chapter. Refer to Figure 25 as you complete this exercise.

Revenue by Category

Category Name	Total Revenue	Average Discount
Beverages	$25,109.20	5.74%
Condiments	$11,148.23	6.96%
Confections	$18,018.21	4.00%
Dairy Products	$24,288.60	6.62%
Grains/Cereals	$9,539.75	3.46%
Meat/Poultry	$11,474.25	5.63%
Produce	$10,637.46	2.69%
Seafood	$11,302.55	5.74%

FIGURE 25 Revenue by Category ➤

a. Open *a03p2traders*. Click the **File tab**, click **Save Database As**, and then type **a03p2traders_LastnameFirstname**. Click **Save**.

b. Click the **Database Tools tab**, and then click **Relationships** in the Relationships group. Examine the tables, fields, and relationships. After you are familiar with the database, close the Relationships window.

c. Click the **Create tab**, and then click **Query Design** in the Queries group to start a new query. The Show Table dialog box opens.

d. Add the Orders, Order Details, Products, and Categories tables. Close the Show Table dialog box.

e. Add the following fields to the query design grid:
   - OrderDate from the Orders table
   - Quantity and Discount from the Order Details table
   - UnitPrice and ProductCost from the Products table
   - CategoryName from the Categories table

f. Save the query as **Revenue**.

g. Type **>=1/1/2012 and <=3/31/2012** into the **Criteria row** of the OrderDate column (to limit the results to orders placed in the first Qtr of 2012).

h. Click the top row of the first blank column, and then click **Builder** in the Query Setup group. Type **Revenue:UnitPrice * (1-Discount) * Quantity**. Click **OK**.

i. Click **Property Sheet** in the Show/Hide group, and then change the format of the Revenue field to **Currency**. Close the Property Sheet dialog box.

j. Click **Run** to run the query. Use a calculator to check several records to verify the revenue calculation is correct. Save the query, and then close it.

k. Click the **Create tab**, and then click **Query Design** in the Queries group. Click the **Queries tab** in the Show Table dialog box. Double-click the **Revenue query** to add it to the design grid. Click **Close** in the Show Table dialog box.

l. Double-click the **CategoryName**, **Revenue**, and **Discount fields** in the Revenue query to add them to the design grid. Run the query.

m. Switch to Design View, and then click **Totals** in the Show/Hide group on the Design tab. The Total row will display. Change the Revenue Total row to **Sum**, and then change the Discount Total row to **Avg**.

n. Click **Property Sheet** in the Show/Hide group. Change the Revenue format to **Currency** and the Discount format to **Percent**.

o. Run the query. Verify the results. Notice that the second and third column headings are *SumOfRevenue* and *AvgOfDiscount*, respectively, to indicate the functions used on those fields. Save the query as **Revenue by Category**.

p. Click **View** in the Views group to switch to Design view. Change the Revenue field caption to **Total Revenue** and the Discount field caption to **Average Discount**. Save the query, and then run the query to see the captions. Close the query.

q. Click the **File tab**, and then click **Compact & Repair Database**.

r. Click the **File tab**, click **Save & Publish**, and then double-click **Back Up Database**. Use the default backup file name.

s. Click the **File tab**, and then click **Exit** (to exit Access).

t. Submit based on your instructor's directions.

MID-LEVEL EXERCISES

1 The National Bank

You are the manager of the loan department of the National Bank. You need to monitor the total indebtedness of each customer to help them manage their debt load. Several customers may have multiple loans—a mortgage, a car loan, and a home equity loan. Your task is to use the Pmt function to calculate the loan payments for each loan and then to summarize the loans by customer. Refer to Figure 26 as you complete this exercise.

Payment Summary

Last Name	Total Payment
Collins	$3,318.36
Fox	$7,274.63
Greene	$3,798.04
Hayes	$717.03
Jones	$4,403.31
Peterson	$956.21
Simpson	$1,122.13
Wagner	$2,529.52
Williams	$3,462.30
Your name	$4,152.81
Total	$31,734.32

FIGURE 26 Payment Summary ➤

a. Open *a03m1bank*. Click the **File tab**, click **Save Database As**, and then type **a03m1bank_LastnameFirstname**. Click **Save.**

b. Open the Customers table. Replace *Megan Royes* with your name. Close the table.

c. Create a query that will calculate the payments for each loan. Add the following fields: LastName, Amount, InterestRate, Term, and Type from the Customers and Loans tables. Save the query as **Loan Payments.**

d. Create a calculated field for the loan payment of each loan. Remember to divide the annual interest rate by 12 and multiply the loan's term by 12. Include a **minus sign** (–) in front of the loan amount in the expression so the result returns a positive value.

e. Run the query. In the Datasheet view, add a Total row. Use it to calculate the average interest rate and the sum for the payment. Save and close the query.

f. Create a totals query based on the Loan Payments query. Add the LastName and Payment fields to the design grid. Group by the LastName field, and then sum the Payment field.

g. Format the Payment field as **Currency**, and then add the caption **Total Payment**.

h. Run the query. Add a Total row to the Datasheet view that will sum the Total Payments. Save this query as **Payment Summary**.

i. Compact the database. Back up the database. Exit Access.

j. Submit based on your instructor's directions.

2 Investment Properties

You are in charge of LGS Investment's database, which contains all of the information on the properties your firm has listed and sold. Your task is to determine the length of time each property was on the market before it sold. You also need to calculate the sales commission from each property sold. Two agents will receive commission on each transaction: the listing agent and the selling agent. You also need to summarize the sales data by employee and calculate the average number of days each employee's sales were on the market prior to selling and the total commission earned by the employees. Refer to Figure 27 as you complete this exercise.

Subdivision	Avg Days On Mkt	Sale Price	Listing Comm	Sell Comm
The Orchards	22.8	$1,288,000.00	$45,080.00	$32,200.00
Fair Brook	24.8	$1,053,900.00	$36,886.50	$26,347.50
Eagle Valley	39.0	$4,012,000.00	$140,420.00	$100,300.00
Wood	47.9	$1,428,650.00	$50,002.75	$35,716.25
Red Canyon	52.0	$3,790,000.00	$132,650.00	$94,750.00
Total		$11,572,550.00	$405,039.25	$289,313.75

FIGURE 27 Sales Summary ➤

a. Open *a03m2homes*. Click the **File tab**, click **Save Database As**, and then type **a03m2homes_LastnameFirstname**. Click **Save**.

b. Open the Agents table, and then replace *David Royes* with your name. Close the table.

c. Create a new query, add the necessary tables, and then add the following fields: LastName, DateListed, DateSold, SalePrice, SellingAgent, ListingAgent, and Subdivision. Type **Is Not Null** into the criterion row of the DateSold field. Save the query as **Sales Report**. Format the SalePrice field as **Currency**.

d. Using the Expression Builder, create the DaysOnMarket calculated field by subtracting DateListed from DateSold. This will calculate the number of days each sold property was on the market when it sold. Add an appropriate caption.

e. Calculate the commissions for the selling and listing agents using two calculated fields. The listing commission rate is **3.5%** and the selling commission rate is **2.5%**. Name the newly created fields **ListComm** and **SellComm**. These fields contain similar expressions. They need to be named differently so that the proper agent—the listing agent or the selling agent—gets paid. Add captions and format the fields as **Currency**.

f. Save the query after you verify that your calculations are correct. In Datasheet view, add the Total row. Calculate the Average number of days on the market and the sum for the SalePrice and the two commission fields. Save and close the query.

g. Create a totals query based on the Sales Report query. Group by LastName, and then show the average of the DaysOnMarket. Show the sum of SalePrice, ListComm, and SellComm. Format the fields as **Currency**, and then add appropriate captions. Run the query. Adjust column widths.

h. Add a Total row to the Datasheet view that will sum the sale price and commission fields. Save the query as **Sales Summary**.

i. Format the average of the Days on Market fields as fixed, one decimal place. (Note: if you do not see the Decimal Places property in the Property Sheet, switch to Datasheet view, then switch back to Design view.) Format the remaining numeric fields as **Currency**. Run the query.

DISCOVER 

j. Modify the query so the grouping is based on Subdivision, not LastName. Sort the query results so the fewest Days on Market is first and the most Days on Market is last. Limit the results to the top five rows.

k. Compact the database. Back up the database. Exit Access.

l. Submit based on your instructor's directions.

CAPSTONE EXERCISE

Northwind Traders, an international gourmet food distributor, is concerned about shipping delays over the last six months. Review the orders over the past six months and identify any order that was not shipped within 30 days. Each customer that falls within that time frame will be called to inquire about any problems the delay may have caused. In addition, an order summary and an order summary by country will be created.

Database File Setup

Open the food database, use Save As to make a copy of the database, and then use the new database to complete this capstone exercise. You will replace an existing employee's name with your name.

a. Locate and open *a03c1food.*

b. Click the **File tab**, click **Save Database As**, and then type **a03c1food_LastnameFirstname**.

c. Click **Save**.

d. Open the Employees table.

e. Replace *Rachael Eliza* with your name. Close the table.

DaysToShip Query

You need to create a query to calculate the number of days between the date an order was placed and the date the order was shipped for each order. As you create the query, run the query at several intervals so you can verify that the data looks correct. The result of your work will be a list of orders that took more than three weeks to ship. The salespeople will be calling each customer to see if there was any problem with their order.

a. Create a query using Query Design. Include the fields CompanyName, ContactName, ContactTitle, Phone, OrderID, LastName, OrderDate, and ShippedDate. Use the Relationships window to determine which tables you need before you begin.

b. Run the query, and then examine the records. Save the query as **Shipping Efficiency**.

c. Add a calculated field named **DaysToShip** to calculate the number of days taken to fill each order. (*Hint*: The expression will include the OrderDate and the ShippedDate; the results will not contain negative numbers.)

d. Run the query, and then examine the results. Does the data in the DaysToShip field look accurate? Save the query.

e. Add criteria to limit the query results to include any order that took more than 30 days to ship.

f. Add the ProductID and Quantity fields to the Shipping Efficiency query. Sort the query by ascending OrderID. When the sales reps contact these customers, these two fields will provide useful information about the orders.

g. Switch to Datasheet view to view the final results. This list will be distributed to the sales reps so they can contact the customers. In Design view, add the **Sales Rep caption** to the LastName field.

h. Save and close the query.

Order Summary Query

You need to create an Order Summary that will show the total amount of each order in one column and the total discount amount in another column. This query will require four tables: Orders, Order Details, Products, and Customers. Query to determine if employees are following the employee discount policy. You will group the data by employee name, count the orders, show the total dollars, and show the total discount amount. You will then determine which employees are following the company guidelines.

a. Create a query using Query Design and add the four tables above plus the Products table. Add the fields OrderID and OrderDate. Click **Totals** in the Show/Hide Group; the Total row for both fields should be Group By.

b. In the third column, add a calculated field: **ExtendedAmount: Quantity*UnitPrice**. Format the calculated field as Currency. This calculation will calculate the total amount for each order. Change the Total row to **Sum**.

c. In the fourth column, add a calculated field: **DiscountAmount: Quantity*UnitPrice*Discount**. Format the calculated field as **Currency**. This will calculate the total discount for each order. Change the Total row to **Sum**.

d. Run the query. Save the query as **Order Summary**. Return to Design view.

e. Enter the expression **Between 1/1/2012 And 12/31/2012** in the criteria of OrderDate. Change the Total row to **Where**. This expression will display only orders that were created in 2012.

f. Run the query and view the results. Save the query.

g. Add the **Total Dollars caption** to the ExtendedAmount field and add the **Discount Amt caption** to the DiscountAmount field.

h. Run the query. Save and close the query.

Order Summary by Country Query

You need to create one additional query based on the Order Summary query you created in the previous step. This new query will enable you to analyze the orders by country.

a. Select the **Order Summary query**, and then use **Save Object As** to create a new query named **Order Summary by Country**.

b. In Design view of the new query, replace the OrderID field with the Country field.

c. Run the query, and then examine the summary records; there should be 21 countries listed.

d. In Design view, change the sort order so that the country with the highest Total Dollars is first, and the country with the lowest Total Dollars is last.

e. Run the query and verify the results.

f. Save and close the query, and then close the database and exit Access.

g. Submit based on your instructor's directions.

Vacation Time for Bank Employees

GENERAL CASE 

The *a03b1vacation* file contains data from a local bank. Open *a03b1vacation*. Click the File tab, click Save Database As, and then type **a03b1vacation_LastnameFirstname**. Click Save. Replace *Your Name* in the Customers table and the Branch table with your name. Use the skills from this chapter to perform several tasks. The bank's employee handbook states that a manager can take two weeks of vacation each year for the first three years of service, and three weeks of vacation after three years of employment. The Branch table stores the start date of each manager.

Create a query to determine how many years each manager has worked for the bank.

- Add a new field to calculate the number of weeks of vacation each manager is eligible to take.
- Use a nested IIf function to change the weeks of vacation to zero for any employee with a start date later than today.
- Change the format of each field to the appropriate type, and then add appropriate captions for the calculated fields.
- Save the query as **Vacation**.

Create another query to summarize each customer's account balances.

- List the customer's last name, first name, and a total of all account balances.
- Format the query results, and then add appropriate captions.
- Add the grand total of all accounts to the Datasheet view.
- Save the query as **Customer Balances**.

Close the query, and then close the database. Submit based on your instructor's directions.

Combining Name Fields

RESEARCH CASE 

This chapter introduced you to expressions. Use a search engine to search for information using the phrase *Combine text values by using an expression*. Open *a03b2combine*. Click the File tab, click Save Database As, and then type **a03b2combine_LastnameFirstname**. Click Save. Using the information from the Internet, create an expression to combine the last and first name fields into one field that displays "last name, first name." (Make sure you include a comma and a space after the last name.) You will use the Customers table in your query with LastName and FirstName. Once you successfully combine the fields in the query, alphabetize the list by last name, first name. Save the query as **Combined Names**. Close the query, and then close the database. Submit your work based on your instructor's directions.

Coffee Revenue Queries

DISASTER RECOVERY 

A co-worker called you into his office, explained that he was having difficulty with Access 2010, and then asked you to look at his work. Open *a03b3coffee*. Click the File tab, click Save Database As, and then type **a03b3coffee_LastnameFirstname**. Click Save. Replace *Your Name* in the Sales Reps table with your name. It contains two queries: Revenue and Revenue by City. The Revenue query calculates ProductRetailPrice (Cost + Cost * MarkupPercent) and NetRevenue ((ProductRetailPrice – Cost) * Quantity). You manually calculate the first row and discover both the ProductRetailPrice and NetRevenue fields are incorrect. Diagnose the error(s) in the two fields and correct them. After correcting the Revenue query, correct the Revenue by City query. Run both queries, and then add appropriate captions. Save and close both queries. Close the database and exit Access. Submit based on your instructor's directions.

ACCESS

CREATING AND USING PROFESSIONAL FORMS AND REPORTS

Moving Beyond Tables and Queries

Watch the
Set-up Video
for this Case Study!

CASE STUDY | Coffee Shop Starts New Business

For over 10 years, the Santiago Coffee Shop was an ordinary coffee shop selling retail coffee, tea, and pastries to its loyal customers in Bucks County. Then, in 2005, owner Alex Santiago decided to use his knowledge of the coffee industry to sell coffee products to businesses in his area. This new venture grew quickly and soon became 25% of his annual revenue. Realizing that this new business would need more of his time each day, he decided to create an Access database to help track his customer, product, and order information.

With the help of a student from Bucks County Community College, he created tables for customers, products, sales reps, and orders. He is currently using these tables as his primary method of entering and retrieving information.

Alex wants to have one of his employees, Tonya, manage the database. But he does not want her to work in the tables; he wants her to work with forms. Alex heard that forms have an advantage over tables because they can be designed to show one record at a time—this will reduce data entry errors. Alex would also like to create several reports for his own benefit so he can stay on top of the business by reviewing the reports each week.

You have been hired to help Alex create the new forms and reports that he needs for his business. He will describe the forms and reports to you in detail and also provide written instructions. You will be expected to work independently to create the forms and reports. Remember to identify the data source for each new form and report.

OBJECTIVES

AFTER YOU READ THIS CHAPTER, YOU WILL BE ABLE TO:

1. Create forms using the form tools
2. Modify a form
3. Sort records in a form
4. Identify form sections
5. Revise forms using form views
6. Identify control types in forms
7. Create reports using report tools
8. Modify a report
9. Sort records in a report
10. Identify report sections
11. Revise reports using report views
12. Identify control types in reports

From Access Chapter 4 of *Exploring Microsoft Office 2010 Volume 1*, First Edition, Robert T. Grauer, Mary Anne Poatsy, Keith Mulbery, Michelle Hulett, Cynthia Krebs, Keith Mast.

Form Basics

A **form** is a database object that is used to add data into or edit data in a table.

A ***form*** is a database object that is used to add data into or edit data in a table. Most Access database applications use forms rather than tables for data entry and for looking up information. Three main reasons exist for using forms rather than tables for adding, updating, and deleting data. They are:

You are less likely to edit the wrong record by mistake.
You can create a form that shows data from more than one table simultaneously.
You can create Access forms to match paper forms.

You are less likely to edit the wrong record by mistake ... You can create a form that shows data from more than one table simultaneously ... You can create Access forms to match paper forms.

If you are adding data using a table with many columns, you could jump to the wrong record in the middle of a record accidentally. For example, you could enter the data for one record correctly for the first 10 fields but then jump to the row above and overwrite existing data for the remaining field values unintentionally. In this case, two records have incorrect or incomplete data. A form will not allow this type of error since most forms restrict entry to one record at a time.

Many forms require two tables as their record source. For example, you may want to view a customer's details (name, address, e-mail, phone, etc.) as well as all of the orders he or she has placed. This would require using data from both the Customers and the Orders tables in one form. Similarly, you may want to view the header information for an order while also viewing the detail line items for the order. This would require data from both the Orders and Order Details tables. Both of these examples enable a user to view two record sources at the same time and make changes—additions, edits, or deletions—to one or both sources of data.

Finally, when paper forms are used to collect information, it is a good idea to design the electronic forms to match the paper forms. This will make data entry more efficient and reliable. Access forms can be designed to emulate the paper documents already in use in an organization. This facilitates the simultaneous use of both paper forms and electronic data. Databases do not necessarily eliminate paper forms; they supplement and coexist with them.

In this section, you will learn the basics of form design. You will discover multiple methods to create and modify Access forms. And you will learn how to create calculated controls.

Creating Forms Using the Form Tools

Access provides a variety of options for creating forms. One size does not fit all—some developers may prefer a stacked layout form, whereas others prefer the multiple items form. The multiple items form can be styled to match a company's standards, whereas the datasheet form is simple and requires very little maintenance. And let's not forget the users; they will have their opinions about the type of forms they want to use.

Access provides 16 different tools for creating forms. The Forms group, located on the Create tab, contains four of the most common form tools (Form, Form Design, Blank Form, and Form Wizard), a list of Navigation forms, and a list of More Forms, as shown in Figure 1. Navigation forms provides a list of six templates to create a user interface for a database; the More Forms command lists six additional form tools (Multiple Items, Datasheet, Split Form, and more). Select a table or query, click one of the tools, and Access will create an automatic form using the selected table or query. The most common of these tools, the ***Form tool***, is used to create data entry forms for customers, employees, products, and other primary tables. A primary table has a single field as its primary key and represents the "one" side of a one-to-many relationship. Once the form is created, as shown in Figure 2, you can customize the form using the Layout or Design views. After the form is created, it should be tested by both the database designer and the end users.

The **Form tool** is used to create data entry forms for customers, employees, products, and other primary tables.

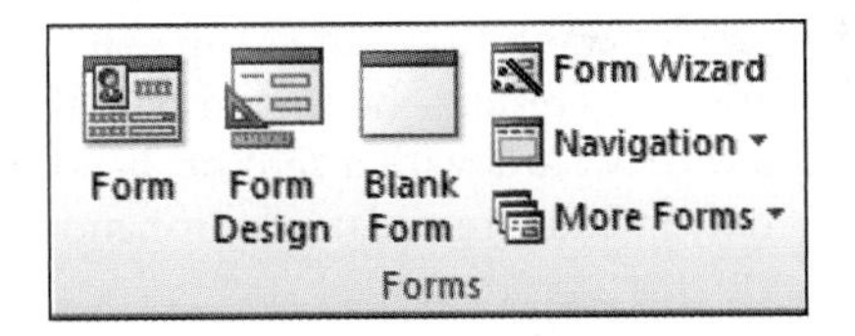

FIGURE 1 Forms Group ➤

A complete list of all the Form tools available in Access is found in the Form Tools Reference at the end of this section. Many of the tools will be covered in this chapter. Some will not be covered since they are not commonly used or because they are beyond the scope of this chapter (e.g., Form Design, Blank Form, Navigation forms, and Modal Dialog form). Use Microsoft Access Help to find more information about Form tools not covered in this chapter.

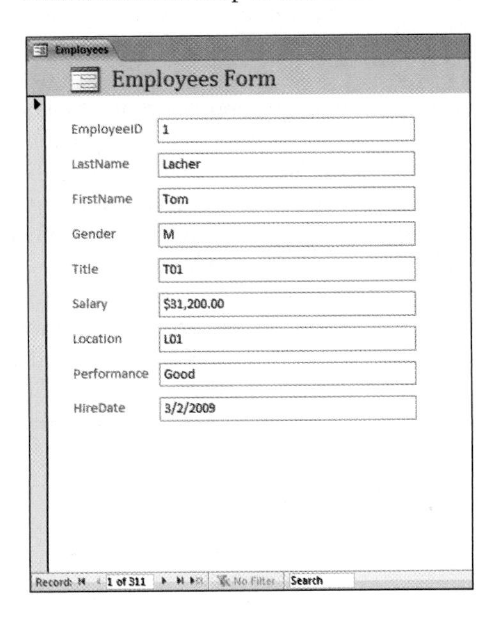

FIGURE 2 Employees Form Created with the Form Tool ➤

Ideally, a form should simplify data entry. Creating a form is a collaborative process between the form designer and the form users. This process continues throughout the life of the form, because the data needs of an organization may change. Forms designed long ago to collect information for a new customer account may not have an e-mail field; the form would have to be modified to include an e-mail field. The form designer needs to strike a balance between collecting the information users need to do their jobs and cluttering the form with extraneous fields. The users of the data know what they need and usually offer good feedback about which fields should be on a form. By listening to their suggestions, your forms will function more effectively, the users' work will be easier, and your data will contain fewer data entry errors.

Ideally, a form should simplify data entry.

Identify a Record Source

A **record source** is the table or query that supplies the records for a form or report.

Before you create a form, you must identify the record source. A ***record source*** is the table or query that supplies the records for a form or report. Use a table if you want to include all the records from a single table. Use a query if you need to filter the records in a table, or if you need to combine records from two or more related tables.

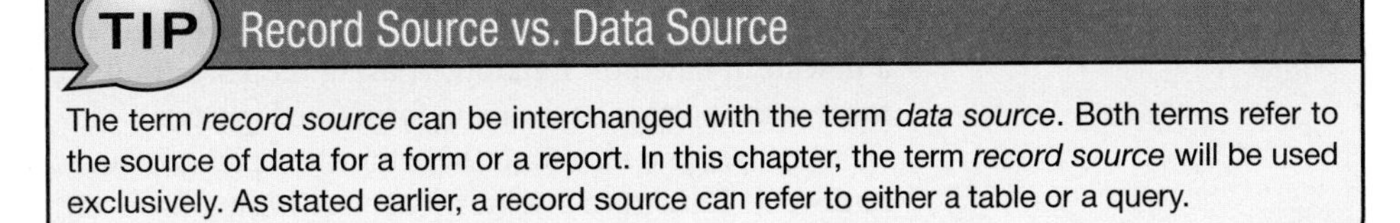

TIP Record Source vs. Data Source

The term *record source* can be interchanged with the term *data source*. Both terms refer to the source of data for a form or a report. In this chapter, the term *record source* will be used exclusively. As stated earlier, a record source can refer to either a table or a query.

For example, if a sales rep wants to create a form that only displays customers from a single state—where his customers reside—he should base the form on a query. Or, if a parts manager needs to review only parts with a zero on-hand quantity, he could create a form based on a query that only includes records with on-hand equal to zero.

Sketch the Form

It will help you to create the form in Access if you sketch the form first. A sketch may look similar to the form in Figure 2. After sketching the form, you will have a better idea of which form tool to use to create the form. After the form is created, use the sketch to determine which fields are required and what the order of fields should be.

Use the Form Tool

A **stacked layout form** displays fields in a vertical column, and displays one record at a time.

A **tabular layout form** displays records horizontally, with label controls across the top and the data values in rows under the labels.

Layout view is used to modify the design of a form.

As noted earlier, the Form tool is the most common tool for creating forms. Select a table or query from the Navigation Pane, and then click Form in the Forms Group on the Create tab, and Access creates a new form. You may need to modify the form slightly, but you can create a stacked layout form in a just one click. A ***stacked layout form*** displays fields in a vertical column, and displays one record at a time, as shown in Figure 3. Multiple Items and Datasheet forms, in contrast to stacked layout forms, are examples of tabular layout forms. A ***tabular layout form*** displays records horizontally, with label controls across the top and the data values in rows under the labels. When a new form is created using the Form tool, Access opens the form in Layout view ready for customizing. You can generate forms for your database using the Form tool, and then use ***Layout view*** to modify the design of a form. Figure 3 shows the Employees form in Layout view.

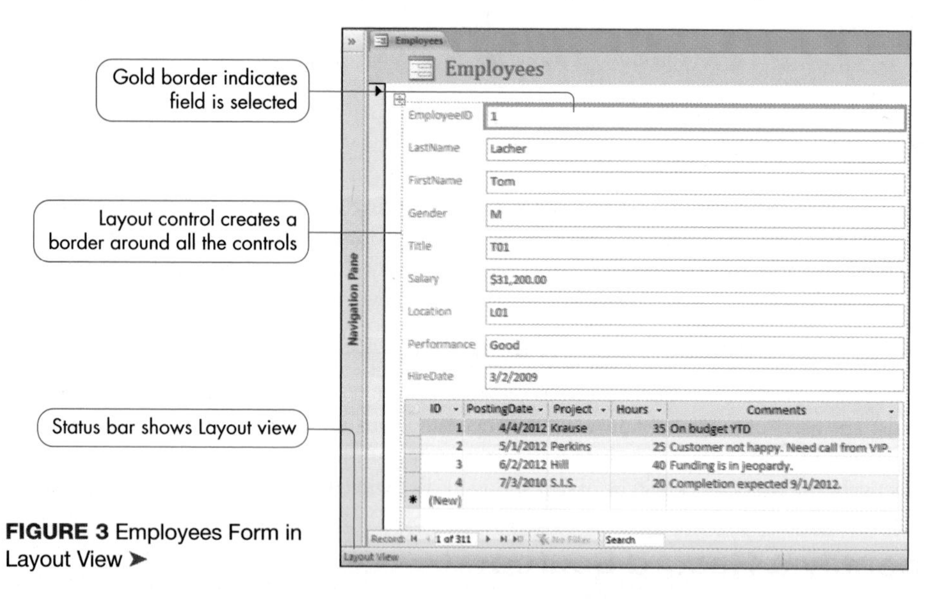

FIGURE 3 Employees Form in Layout View ➤

Work with a Subform

When you use the Form tool to create a form, Access will analyze the table relationships you created in the database and automatically add a subform to the main form. A subform displays records with foreign key values that match the primary key value in the main form. For example, assume you have a database that contains the tables Employees and Project Time, and a relationship exists between the two tables based on the EmployeeID field. If you create a new form based on Employees, using the Form tool, Access will add a Project Time subform to the bottom of the main form (see Figure 3).

At times, you may want the subform as part of your form; other times, you may want to remove it. To remove a subform control from a form, switch to Design view, click the subform control, and then press Delete. The subform is deleted!

Create a Split Form

A **split form** combines two views of the same record source—one section is displayed in a stacked layout and the other section is displayed in a tabular layout.

A ***split form*** combines two views of the same record source—one section is displayed in a stacked layout and the other section is displayed in a tabular layout. By default, the form view is positioned on the top and the datasheet view is displayed on the bottom; however, the orientation can be changed from horizontal to vertical in Layout view. If you select a record in the top half of the form, the same record will be selected in the bottom half of the form, and vice versa. For example, if you create a split form based on the Employees table, you can select an employee in the datasheet section and then see the employee's information in the *Form view* section (see Figure 4). If the selected employee is incorrect, click another employee in the datasheet section. The top and bottom halves are synchronized at all times.

To create a split form, first select a table or query in the Navigation Pane. Next, click the Create tab, click More Forms in the Forms group, and then select Split Form from the list of options. A new split form now appears. You can add, edit, or delete records in either section.

The **splitter bar** divides the form into two halves.

The ***splitter bar*** divides the form into two halves. Users can adjust the splitter bar up or down unless the form designer disables this option.

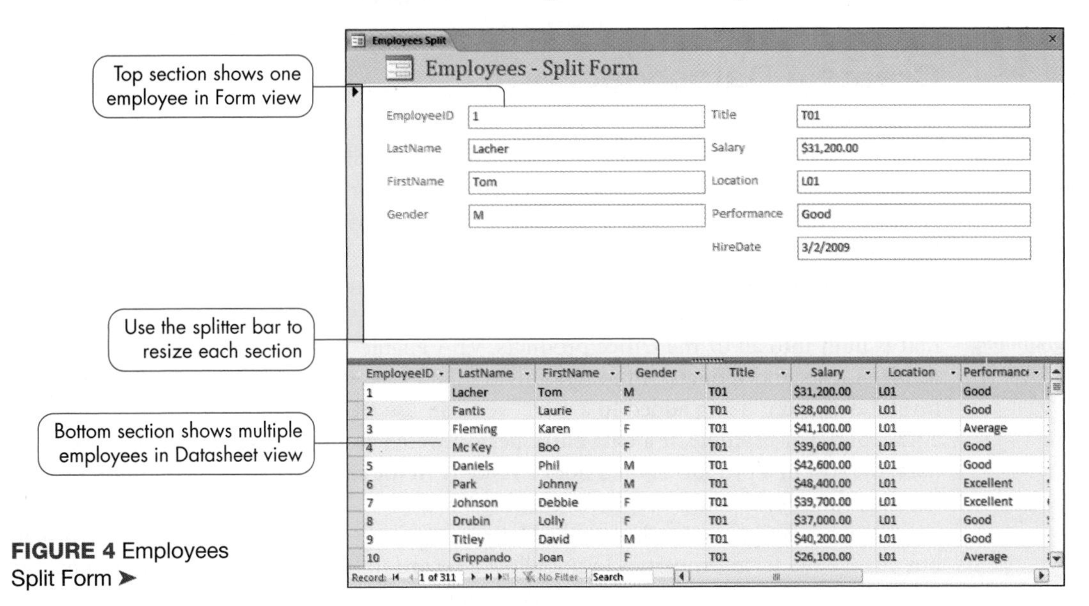

FIGURE 4 Employees Split Form ➤

Create a Multiple Items Form

A **Multiple Items form** displays multiple records in a tabular layout similar to a table's Datasheet view.

A ***Multiple Items form*** displays multiple records in a tabular layout similar to a table's Datasheet view. However, a Multiple Items form gives you more customization options than a datasheet, such as the ability to add graphical elements, buttons, and other controls. Figure 5 shows a Multiple Items form created from the Employees table. Compare this Multiple Items form to the Employees Datasheet form shown in Figure 6. The color scheme applied to the Multiple Items form could not be applied to the Datasheet form since the Datasheet form is much more limited in design and control options. To create a Multiple Items form, first select a table or query from the Navigation Pane. Next, click the Create tab, click More Forms in the Forms group, and then select Multiple Items from the list of options.

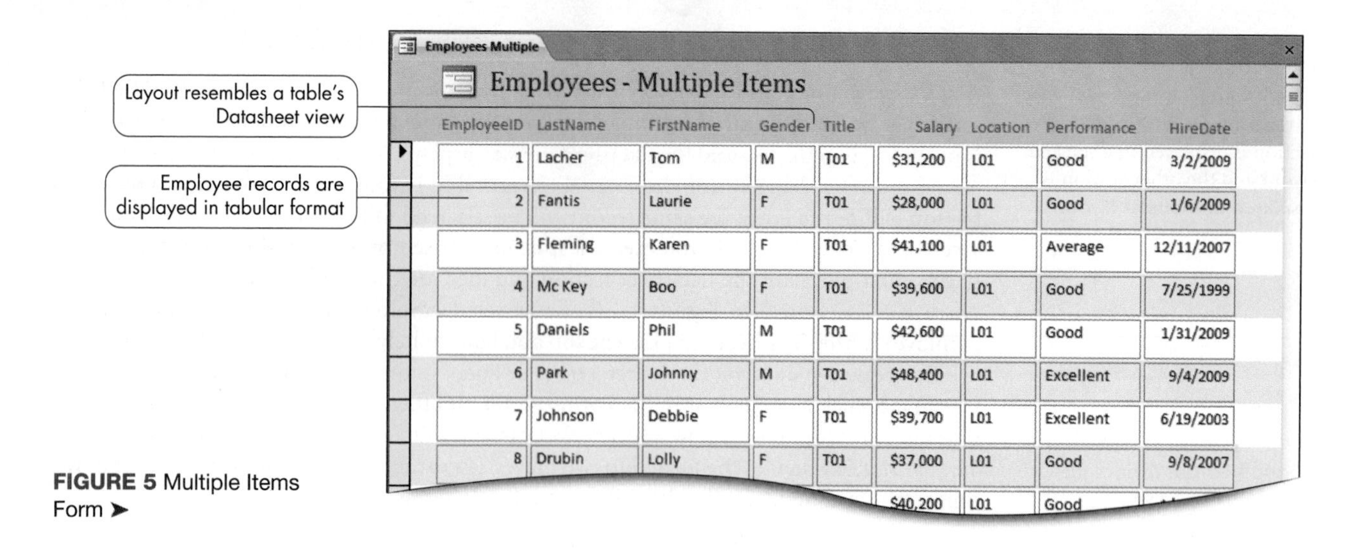
Layout resembles a table's Datasheet view
Employee records are displayed in tabular format
Employees Multiple
Employees - Multiple Items

EmployeeID	LastName	FirstName	Gender	Title	Salary	Location	Performance	HireDate
1	Lacher	Tom	M	T01	$31,200	L01	Good	3/2/2009
2	Fantis	Laurie	F	T01	$28,000	L01	Good	1/6/2009
3	Fleming	Karen	F	T01	$41,100	L01	Average	12/11/2007
4	Mc Key	Boo	F	T01	$39,600	L01	Good	7/25/1999
5	Daniels	Phil	M	T01	$42,600	L01	Good	1/31/2009
6	Park	Johnny	M	T01	$48,400	L01	Excellent	9/4/2009
7	Johnson	Debbie	F	T01	$39,700	L01	Excellent	6/19/2003
8	Drubin	Lolly	F	T01	$37,000	L01	Good	9/8/2007
					$40,200	L01	Good	

FIGURE 5 Multiple Items Form ➤

Create a Datasheet Form

A **Datasheet form** is a replica of a table or query's Datasheet view except that it still retains some of the form properties.

Visual Basic for Applications (VBA) is Microsoft's programming language that is built into all of the Office products.

A ***Datasheet form*** is a replica of a table or query's Datasheet view except that it still retains some of the form properties. A Datasheet form created from the Employees table is shown in Figure 6. To create a Datasheet form, first select a table or query from the Navigation Pane. Next, click the Create tab, click More Forms in the Forms group, and then select Datasheet from the list of options.

A datasheet form, like all Access forms, can be customized to add additional functionality using ***Visual Basic for Applications (VBA)***. VBA is Microsoft's programming language that is built into all of the Office products. VBA enables an advanced Access user to customize forms and reports. Although a field's data type and field properties help prevent invalid data from being added to a table, you can use VBA to enforce more complex data entry rules. For example, if a data entry person were entering new products into the database, the cost of a product should not be more than the sale price. If that condition existed, the data entry form could alert the user using VBA.

Database designers can also use the Datasheet form to display data in a table-like format, but change the form properties to not allow a record to be deleted. This would protect the data from accidental damage while still providing the users with the familiar Datasheet view.

Employees Datasheet
Layout is a replica of a table's Datasheet view

EmployeeID	LastName	FirstName	Gender	Title	Salary	Location	Performanc
1	Lacher	Tom	M	T01	$31,200.00	L01	Good
2	Fantis	Laurie	F	T01	$28,000.00	L01	Good
3	Fleming	Karen	F	T01	$41,100.00	L01	Average
4	Mc Key	Boo	F	T01	$39,600.00	L01	Good
5	Daniels	Phil	M	T01	$42,600.00	L01	Good
6	Park	Johnny	M	T01	$48,400.00	L01	Excellent
7	Johnson	Debbie	F	T01	$39,700.00	L01	Excellent
8	Drubin	Lolly	F	T01	$37,000.00	L01	Good
9	Titley	David	M	T01	$40,200.00	L01	Good
10	Grippando	Joan	F	T01	$26,100.00	L01	Average
11	Block	Leonard	M	T01	$26,200.00	L01	Excellent
12	Mills	Jack	M	T01	$44,600.00	L01	Average
13	Nagel	Mimi	F	T01	$46,200.00	L01	Average
14	Rammos	Mitzi	F	T01	$32,500.00	L01	Excellent
15	Vieth	Paula	F	T01	$40,400.00	L01	Good
16	Novicheck	Deborah	F	T01	$46,800.00	L01	Good
17	Brumbaugh	Paige	F	T01	$49,300.00	L01	Average
18	Abrams	Wendy	F	T01	$47,500.00	L01	Good
19	Harrison	Jenifer	F	T01	$44,800.00	L01	Excellent
20	Gander	John	M	T01	$38,400.00	L01	Average
21	Sell	Mike	M	T01	$43,500.00	L01	Excellent
22	Smith	Denise	F	T01	$45,200.00	L01	Average
				T01	$42,700.00	L01	

FIGURE 6 Datasheet Form ➤

Create Forms Using the Other Form Tools

The Form Design tool and the Blank Form tools can be used to create a form manually. Click one of these tools and Access will open a completely blank form. Click Add Existing Fields, on the Design tab, in the Tools group and add the necessary fields.

The Navigation option in the Forms group enables you to create user interface forms that have the look and feel of a Web-based form, and enable users to open and close the objects of a database. These forms are also useful for setting up an Access database on the Internet. For more information about Navigation forms, visit www.microsoft.com.

PivotTables and PivotCharts can also be converted to forms by selecting PivotChart or PivotTable in the More Forms option in the Forms group. After you create a PivotTable form or a PivotChart form, use the Layout view and Design view to customize the form.

The Modal Dialog Form tool can be used to create a dialog box. This feature is useful when you need to gather information from the user before working with another object. Dialog boxes are common in all Microsoft Office applications; creating a custom dialog box in Access can be useful when you need to collect information from the user.

REFERENCE Form Tools

Form Tool	Location	Use
Form	Create tab, Forms group	Creates a form with a stacked layout displaying all of the fields in the record source.
Form Design	Create tab, Forms group	Create a new blank form in Design view.
Blank Form	Create tab, Forms group	Create a new blank form in Layout view.
Form Wizard	Create tab, Forms group	Answer a series of questions and Access will create a custom form for you.
Navigation	Create tab, Forms group, Navigation button	Create user interface forms that can also be used on the Internet.
Split Form	Create tab, Forms group, More Forms button	Creates a two-part form with a stacked layout in one section and a tabular layout in the other.
Multiple Items	Create tab, Forms group, More Forms button	Creates a tabular layout form that includes all of the fields from the record source.
Datasheet	Create tab, Forms group, More Forms button	Creates a form that resembles the datasheet of a table or query.
PivotTable	Create tab, Forms group, More Forms button	The PivotTable form tool enables you to present data from a table or query using a multi-dimensional table format.
PivotChart	Create tab, Forms group, More Forms button	The PivotChart form tool enables you to present data from a table or query using a multi-dimensional chart format.
Modal Dialog	Create tab, Forms group, More Forms button	Creates a custom dialog box that forces the user to respond before working with another object.

Modifying a Form

After a form is generated by a Form tool, you will usually need to modify it. The most common form changes are add a field, remove a field, change the order of fields, change the width of a field, and modify label text. These changes, as well as adding a theme, can be made in a form's Layout view. Advanced changes, such as adding a calculated field or adding VBA code, can be made in a form's Design view.

Add a Field to a Form

To add a field to a form with a stacked layout, open the form in Layout view. Click Add Existing Fields in the Tools group on the Design tab to reveal the available fields from the form's record source. Drag the new field to the precise location on the form, using the orange line as a guide for the position of the new field. The other fields will automatically adjust to make room for the new field.

To add a field to a form with a tabular layout, follow the same steps for adding a field to a stacked layout form. The only difference is the orange line will appear vertically to help determine the insertion point of the new field.

Work with a Form Layout Control

A **layout control** provides guides to help keep controls aligned horizontally and vertically, and give your form a uniform appearance.

Whenever you use one of the form tools to create a new form, Access will add a layout control to help align the fields. In general, form layout controls can help you create and modify forms. A ***layout control*** provides guides to help keep controls aligned horizontally and vertically, and give your form a uniform appearance. However, there are times when a layout control is too restrictive and will keep you from positioning controls where you want them. In this case, you can remove the layout control and position the controls manually on the grid.

To remove a form layout control, switch to Design view, and then click anywhere inside the control you want to remove. On the Arrange tab, click Select Layout in the Rows & Columns group. (You can also click the Layout Selector, the small square with a cross inside, to select the layout.) Click Remove Layout in the Table group and the layout control is gone. All of the other controls are still on the form, but the rectangle binding them together is gone.

You can add a layout control to a form by first selecting all the controls you want to keep together. Then, click Stacked or Tabular in the Table group and the layout control appears.

Delete a Field from a Form

To delete a field in Layout view, click the text box control of the field to be deleted and note the orange border around the control. With the orange border showing, press Delete. The field's text box and label are both removed from the form and a space remains where the field used to be. Click the space, and then press Delete again, and the other fields will automatically adjust to close the gap around the deleted field.

Adjust Column Widths in a Form

When column widths are adjusted in a form with a stacked layout, all columns will increase and decrease together. Therefore, it is best to make sure that field columns are wide enough to accommodate the widest value in the table. For example, if a form contains first name, last name, address, city, state, ZIP, phone, and e-mail address, you will need to make sure the longest address and the longest e-mail address are completely visible (since those fields are likely to contain the longest data values).

To decrease column widths in a form with a stacked layout, open the form in Layout view. Click the text box control of the first field—usually on the right—to select it. Move the mouse over the right border of the field until the mouse pointer turns into a double arrow, then drag the right edge to the left until you arrive at the desired width. All the fields change as you change the width of the first field. Drag the same edge to the right to increase the width.

Add a Theme to a Form

An **Office Theme** is a defined set of colors, fonts, and graphics that can be applied to a form.

You can apply an Office Theme to a form in order to give the form a more professional finish. An ***Office Theme*** is a defined set of colors, fonts, and graphics that can be applied to a form. Click the Themes picker in the Themes group on the Design tab, select a theme from the Themes Gallery, and Access will apply the theme to your form. You can apply a theme to a single form or to all the forms in your database that share a common theme. Applying the same theme to all forms will provide a consistent look to your database; most users prefer a consistent theme when using Access forms. The same Office Themes found in Access are also available in Excel, Word, and PowerPoint. Therefore, you can achieve a uniformed look across all Office applications.

Sorting Records in a Form

When a form is created using a Form tool, the sort order of the records in the form is dependent on the sort order of the record source—a table or a query. Tables are usually sorted by the primary key, whereas queries can be sorted in a variety of ways.

Change the Sorting in a Form

To modify the sort order of a form, open the form in Form view, and then select the field you want to use for sorting. Next, click Ascending in the Sort & Filter group on the Home tab and the records will immediately be reordered based on the selected field.

You can also modify the sort order of a form by modifying the underlying query's sort order. The method enables you to create a more advanced sort order, based on multiple fields. To begin, switch to Design view, and then open the Property Sheet. Select the form by clicking the arrow under Selection type at the top of the Property Sheet, and then clicking Form. Next, locate the Record Source property on the Data tab, click in the property box, and then click Build to the right of the property box. Answer Yes to the message that appears. Access opens the underlying query in Design view. Add the sorting you want, close the query, and save the query when prompted. You will also need to save the form.

Remove Sorting in a Form

To remove the sort order in a form, switch to Form view, and then click Remove Sort in the Sort & Filter group on the Home tab. If the form's sort order was modified, clicking this command will reset the form to the original order.

HANDS-ON EXERCISES

1 Form Basics

It is your first day on the job at Santiago Coffee Shop. After talking with Alex about his data entry needs, you decide to create several sample forms with different formats. You will show each form to Alex to get his feedback and see if he has a preference. Remember to select the correct record source prior to creating each new form.

Skills covered: Use the Form Tool and Adjust Column Widths in a Form • Create a Split Form • Create a Multiple Items Form • Create a Datasheet Form and Delete a Field from a Form • Add a Field to a Form • Change the Sorting in a Form and Remove Sorting in a Form

STEP 1 USE THE FORM TOOL AND ADJUST COLUMN WIDTHS IN A FORM

Use the Form tool to create an Access form to help Alex manage his customers. This form will enable Tonya to add, edit, and delete records more efficiently than working with tables. Refer to Figure 7 as you complete Step 1.

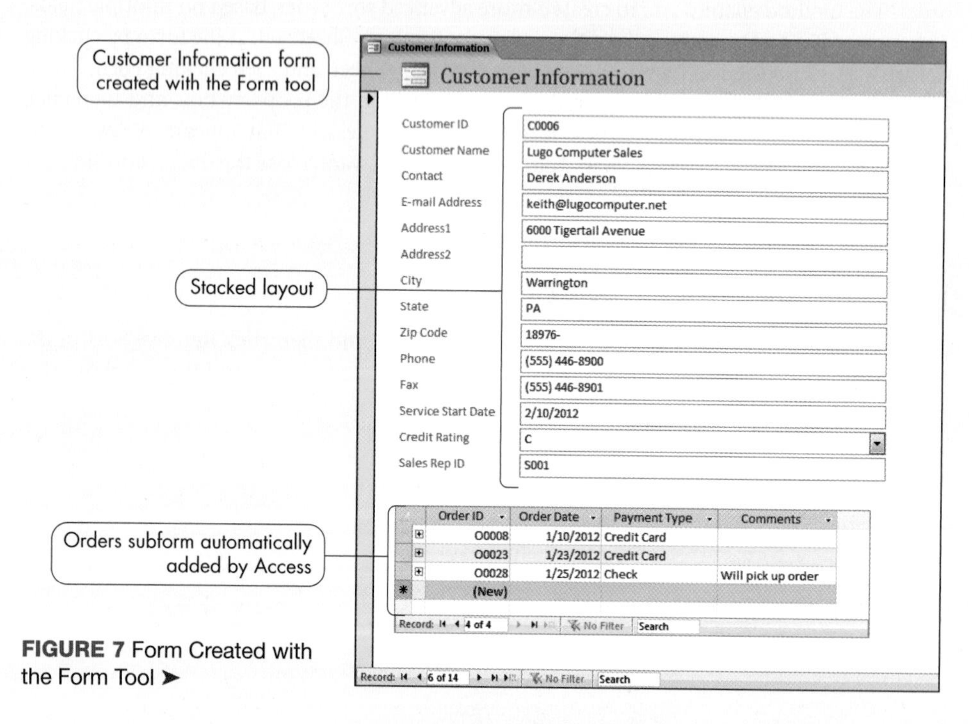

FIGURE 7 Form Created with the Form Tool ➤

a. Open *a04h1coffee*. Click the **File tab**, click **Save Database As**, and then type **a04h1coffee_LastnameFirstname**. Click Save.

> **TROUBLESHOOTING:** Throughout the remainder of this chapter and textbook, click Enable Content whenever you are working with student files.

> **TROUBLESHOOTING:** If you make any major mistakes in this exercise, you can close the file, repeat step a above, and then start over.

b. Click the **Customers table** in the Navigation Pane. Click the **Create tab**, and then click **Form** in the Forms group.

Access creates a new form with two record sources—Customers (with stacked layout, on top) and Orders (with tabular layout, below). Access found a one-to-many relationship between the Customers and Orders tables. The form opens in Layout view.

c. Click the top text box containing *C0001*. The text box is outlined with an orange border. Move the mouse to the right edge of the orange border until the mouse pointer changes to a double-headed arrow. Drag the right edge to the left until the text box is approximately 50% of its original size.

All the text boxes and the subform at the bottom adjust in size when you adjust the top text box. This is a characteristic of Layout view—enabling you to easily modify all controls at once.

TROUBLESHOOTING: You may need to maximize the Access window, or close the Navigation Pane, if the right edge of the text box is not visible.

d. Click the Arrange tab, and then click **Select Layout** in the Rows & Columns group.

All the controls are now selected.

TROUBLESHOOTING: Click any control in the top part of the form before you click Select layout.

e. On the Arrange tab, click **Control Padding** in the Position group. Select **Narrow** from the list of choices.

The space between the controls is reduced.

f. Click **Save** in the Quick Access Toolbar, and then type **Customer Information** as the form name in the **Save As dialog box**. Click **OK**.

g. Click the **Home tab**, and then click **View** in the Views group to switch to Form view, the view that most users will see. Advance to the sixth customer, *Lugo Computer Sales*, using the **Navigation bar** at the bottom of the form.

TROUBLESHOOTING: Two Navigation bars exist, one for the main form and one for the subform. Make sure you use the bottom one that shows 14 records.

h. Double-click the **Customers table** in the Navigation Pane.

Two tabs now appear in the main window. You will compare the table data and the form data while you make changes to both.

i. Verify the sixth record of the Customers table is *Lugo Computer Sales*, which corresponds to the sixth record in the Customer Information form. Click the tabs to switch between the table and the form.

j. Click the **Customer Information tab**, and then replace *Derek Anderson*, the contact for Lugo Computer Sales, with your name. Advance to the next record to save the changes. Click the **Customers tab** to see that the contact name changed in the table as well.

The contact field and the other fields on the Customer Information form are bound controls. Changing the data in the form automatically changes the data in the underlying table.

TROUBLESHOOTING: If the change to Derek Anderson does not appear in the Customers table, check the Customer Information form to see if the pencil appears in the left margin. If it does, save the record by advancing to the next customer, and then recheck to see if the name has changed.

k. Replace your name with **Derek Anderson**. Save the record by clicking on the record below *Lugo Computer Sales*. Click the **Customer Information tab**, and then find the sixth record. You should see the change you just made—Derek is back!

l. Switch to Layout view. Click the **Customers title** at the top of the form to select it, and then click again and change the title to **Customer Information**.

The Customer Information title, a label control, is an example of an unbound control; an unbound control does not have a connection to an underlying table.

m. Click **Save** in the Quick Access Toolbar to save the changes to the form's title. Close the form and the table.

> **TROUBLESHOOTING:** If you make a mistake that you cannot easily recover from, consider deleting the form and starting over. The Form tool makes it easy to start over again.

STEP 2 CREATE A SPLIT FORM

Use the Split Form tool to create a different form to show to Tonya. She may prefer to use a split form to add, edit, and delete records rather than the Customer Information form that you created in the previous step. Refer to Figure 8 as you complete Step 2.

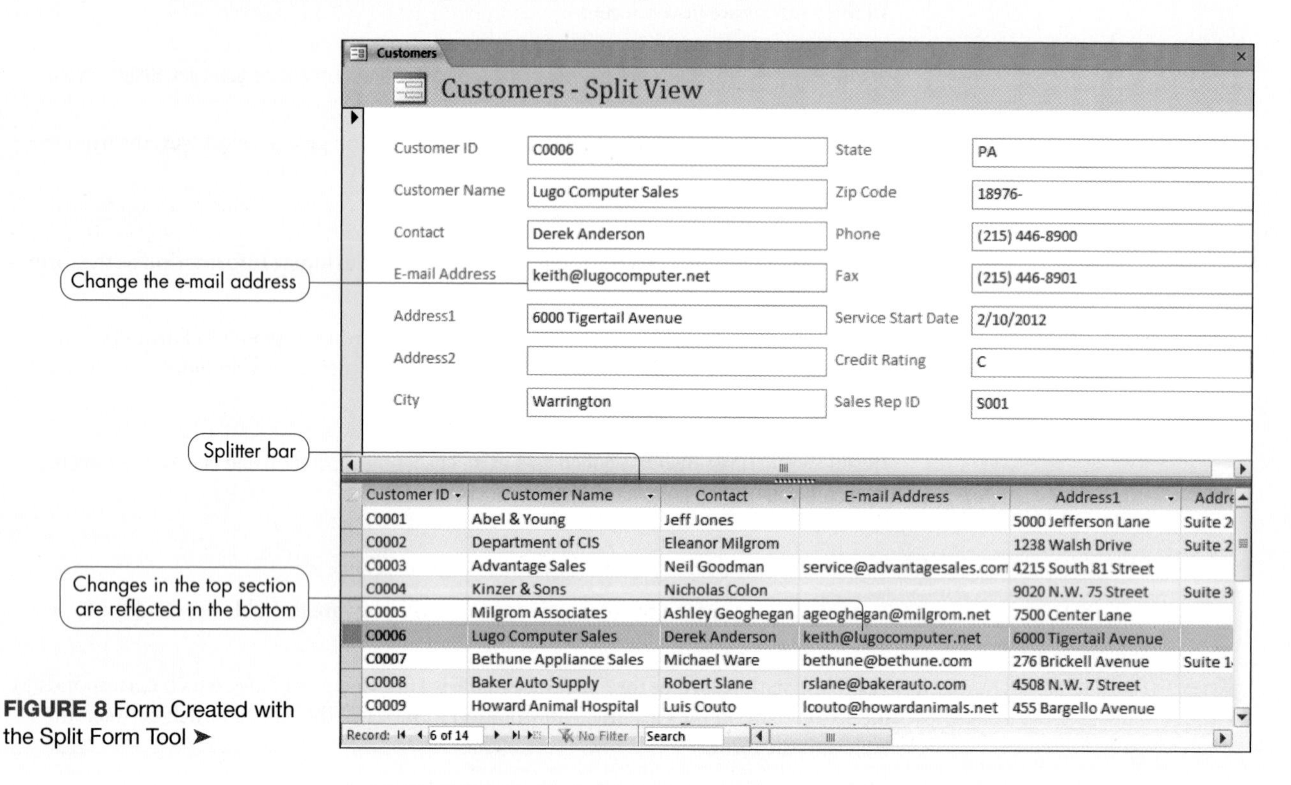

FIGURE 8 Form Created with the Split Form Tool ➤

a. Verify the Customers table is selected in the Navigation Pane. Click the **Create tab**, click **More Forms** in the Forms group, and then select **Split Form** from the list.

   Access creates a new form with a split view, one view in stacked layout and one view in tabular layout.

b. Switch to Form view. In the bottom portion of the split form, click **Lugo Computer Sales**, the sixth record. Notice the top portion now displays the information for Lugo Computer Sales.

c. Change *service@lugocomputer.net* to ***yourname*@lugocomputer.net** in the top portion of the form.

   The bottom portion reflects your change when you move to another field or advance to another record.

d. Click another record, and then click back on **Lugo Computer Sales**.

   The pencil disappears from the record selector box and the changes are saved to the table.

e. Click anywhere on the Coulter Office Supplies customer in the bottom portion of the form (record 14).

   The top portion shows all the information for this customer.

f. Modify the Contact, E-mail Address, and Address1 information in the top portion of the form, by typing **xyz** at the end of each cell. Save your changes by clicking anywhere in the bottom portion of the window.

   Notice the xyz characters appear in the bottom portion of the form.

g. Remove the xyz's from the Coulter Office Supplies record in the top section.

h. Switch to Layout view. Click the **Customers title** at the top of the form to select it, and then click **Customers** again and change the title to **Customers - Split View.**

i. Click **Save** on the Quick Access Toolbar, and then type **Customers - Split View** in the **Form Name box.** Click **OK.**

j. Move your mouse over the splitter bar, the border between the top and bottom portions of the window. When the pointer shape changes to a double-headed arrow, drag the splitter bar up until it almost touches the Sales Rep ID field.

k. Close the form and save the changes when prompted.

STEP 3 CREATE A MULTIPLE ITEMS FORM

You decide to use the Multiple Items tool to create a form for Alex to manage his products. Because of its tabular format, it will enable Alex and Tonya to view multiple records at one time. Refer to Figure 9 as you complete Step 3.

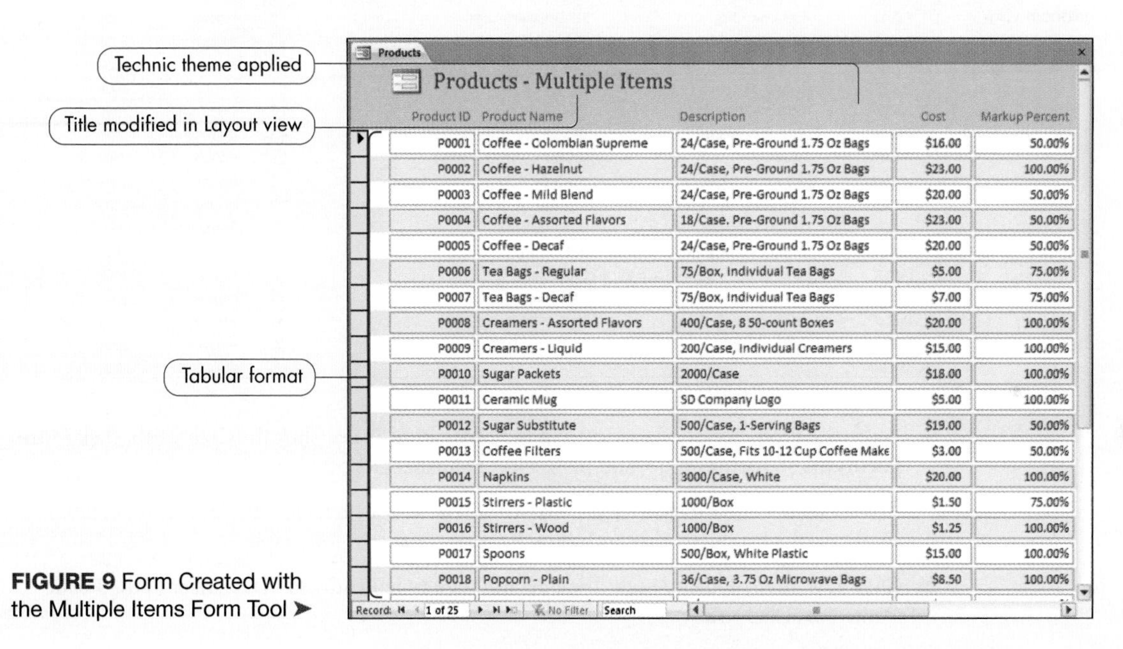

Product ID	Product Name	Description	Cost	Markup Percent
P0001	Coffee - Colombian Supreme	24/Case, Pre-Ground 1.75 Oz Bags	$16.00	50.00%
P0002	Coffee - Hazelnut	24/Case, Pre-Ground 1.75 Oz Bags	$23.00	100.00%
P0003	Coffee - Mild Blend	24/Case, Pre-Ground 1.75 Oz Bags	$20.00	50.00%
P0004	Coffee - Assorted Flavors	18/Case. Pre-Ground 1.75 Oz Bags	$23.00	50.00%
P0005	Coffee - Decaf	24/Case, Pre-Ground 1.75 Oz Bags	$20.00	50.00%
P0006	Tea Bags - Regular	75/Box, Individual Tea Bags	$5.00	75.00%
P0007	Tea Bags - Decaf	75/Box, Individual Tea Bags	$7.00	75.00%
P0008	Creamers - Assorted Flavors	400/Case, 8 50-count Boxes	$20.00	100.00%
P0009	Creamers - Liquid	200/Case, Individual Creamers	$15.00	100.00%
P0010	Sugar Packets	2000/Case	$18.00	100.00%
P0011	Ceramic Mug	SD Company Logo	$5.00	100.00%
P0012	Sugar Substitute	500/Case, 1-Serving Bags	$19.00	50.00%
P0013	Coffee Filters	500/Case, Fits 10-12 Cup Coffee Make	$3.00	50.00%
P0014	Napkins	3000/Case, White	$20.00	100.00%
P0015	Stirrers - Plastic	1000/Box	$1.50	75.00%
P0016	Stirrers - Wood	1000/Box	$1.25	100.00%
P0017	Spoons	500/Box, White Plastic	$15.00	100.00%
P0018	Popcorn - Plain	36/Case, 3.75 Oz Microwave Bags	$8.50	100.00%

FIGURE 9 Form Created with the Multiple Items Form Tool ➤

a. Click the **Products table** in the Navigation Pane. Click the **Create tab**, click **More Forms** in the Forms group, and then select **Multiple Items** from the list.

   Access creates a new multiple items form based on the Products table. The form resembles the datasheet of a table—both have a tabular layout.

b. Click **cell P0001**. Move the mouse over the bottom edge of cell P0001 until the pointer shape changes to a two-headed arrow. Drag the bottom edge up to reduce the height of the rows by 50%.

   Changing the height of one row affects the height of all the rows.

c. Click the **Products title** at the top of the form to select it, and then click again on **Products** and change the title to **Products - Multiple Items.**

d. Click the **Themes arrow** in the Themes group on the Design tab. Right-click the **Technic Theme** (near the bottom of the gallery), and then choose **Apply Theme to This Object Only**.

Hover over a theme and its name will display as a ScreenTip. The Technic theme is applied to the Products - Multiple Items form.

e. Close and save the form as **Products - Multiple Items**.

STEP 4 CREATE A DATASHEET FORM AND DELETE A FIELD FROM A FORM

You decide to use the Datasheet tool to create another form for Alex to manage his products. The Datasheet form is in tabular format and is similar to the Multiple Items form, but requires little or no maintenance, which Alex may like. Refer to Figure 10 as you complete Step 4.

Datasheet form based on the Products table

Field name modified

Datasheet form looks similar to Datasheet view

Products - Datasheet

Product ID	Product Name	Description	Refrig?	Brand	Year Introduce
P0001	Coffee - Colombian Supreme	24/Case, Pre-Ground 1.75 Oz Bags	☐	Discount	2008
P0002	Coffee - Hazelnut	24/Case, Pre-Ground 1.75 Oz Bags	☐	Premium	2008
P0003	Coffee - Mild Blend	24/Case, Pre-Ground 1.75 Oz Bags	☐	House	2008
P0004	Coffee - Assorted Flavors	18/Case. Pre-Ground 1.75 Oz Bags	☐	House	2008
P0005	Coffee - Decaf	24/Case, Pre-Ground 1.75 Oz Bags	☐	Discount	2008
P0006	Tea Bags - Regular	75/Box, Individual Tea Bags	☐	House	2008
P0007	Tea Bags - Decaf	75/Box, Individual Tea Bags	☐	House	2008
P0008	Creamers - Assorted Flavors	400/Case, 8 50-count Boxes	☐	Discount	2008
P0009	Creamers - Liquid	200/Case, Individual Creamers	☑	Premium	2008
P0010	Sugar Packets	2000/Case	☐	House	2008
P0011	Ceramic Mug	SD Company Logo	☐	House	2008
P0012	Sugar Substitute	500/Case, 1-Serving Bags	☐	Discount	2008
P0013	Coffee Filters	500/Case, Fits 10-12 Cup Coffee Maker	☐	House	2008
P0014	Napkins	3000/Case, White	☐	House	2008
P0015	Stirrers - Plastic	1000/Box	☐	Discount	2008
P0016	Stirrers - Wood	1000/Box	☐	Discount	2008
P0017	Spoons	500/Box, White Plastic	☐	House	2008
P0018	Popcorn - Plain	36/Case, 3.75 Oz Microwave Bags	☐	House	2008
P0019	Popcorn - Buttered	36/Case, 3.75 Oz Microwave Bags	☐	House	2008
P0020	Soup - Chicken	50 Envelopes	☐	Premium	2008
P0021	Soup - Variety Pak	50 Envelopes	☐	Premium	2008
P0022	Styrofoam Cups - 10 ounce	1000/Case	☐	House	2008
P0023	Styrofoam Cups - 12 ounce	1000/Case	☐	House	2008
P0024	Milk - 1 quart	Delivered Daily	☑	House	2008
P0025	Milk - 1 pint	Delivered Daily	☑	House	2008
* (New)			☐	House	2010

FIGURE 10 Datasheet Form ➤

a. Verify the Products table is selected in the Navigation Pane. Click the **Create tab**, click **More Forms** in the Forms group, and then select **Datasheet**.

Access creates a new datasheet form based on the Products table. The Tabular form looks similar to the Products table and could be easily mistaken for a table.

b. Click **Save** in the Quick Access Toolbar, and then type **Products - Datasheet** in the **Form Name box**. Click **OK**.

c. Widen the Navigation Pane so all object names are visible. Right-click the **Products - Datasheet form** in the Navigation Pane, and then choose **Layout View** from the list of options.

TROUBLESHOOTING: The View arrow does not contain the Layout view options.

d. Click anywhere in an empty area to deselect the controls.

e. Click the **Cost box**, the control on the right, to select it (you will see the orange border), and then press **Delete**. Click the blank space, and then press **Delete** to remove the blank space. Repeat the process to delete *MarkupPercent.*

You removed fields from the Products form and the other fields adjust to maintain an even distribution (after you remove the blank space).

f. Click the **Refrigeration Needed label** to select it. Change the label to the abbreviation **Refrig?**. Save the form, and then switch to Datasheet view.

g. Double-click the **Products table** in the Navigation Pane to open it.

   The Products - Datasheet form and the Products table now appear different because the Cost and MarkupPercent fields were deleted from the form.

h. Close the Products Datasheet form and the Products table.

STEP 5 ADD A FIELD TO A FORM

The form tools made it easy to create forms for Alex's company. But Alex decided he needs a Website field, so you need to modify the form. Refer to Figure 11 as you complete Step 5.

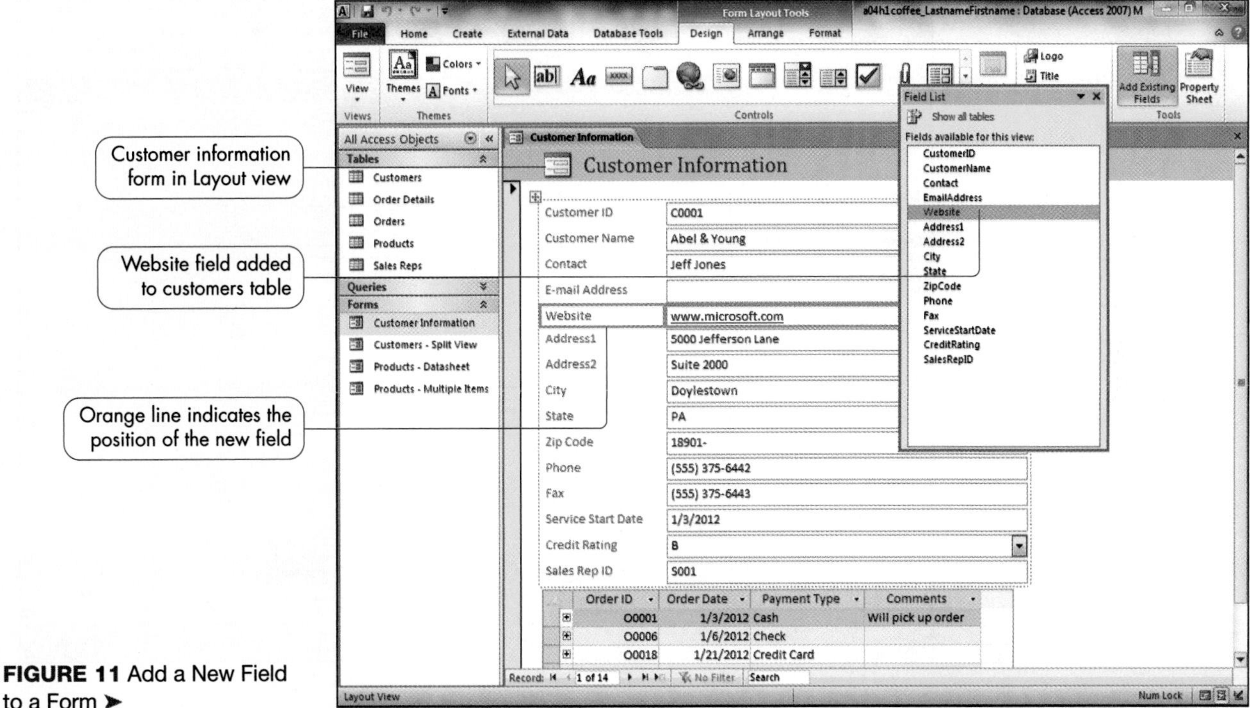

FIGURE 11 Add a New Field to a Form ➤

a. Right-click the **Customers table** in the Navigation Pane, and then click **Design View**.

   You will add the Website field to the Customers table.

b. Click the **Address1 field**, and then click **Insert Rows** in the Tools group.

   A new row is inserted above the Address1 field.

c. Type **Website** in the blank **Field Name box**, and then choose **Hyperlink** as the Data Type.

d. Close and save the Customers table.

e. Right-click the **Customer Information form** in the Navigation Pane, and then click **Layout View**.

   You will add the Website field to the Customer Information form.

f. Click **Add Existing Fields** in the Tools group to display the Field List pane (if necessary).

g. Drag the **Website field** from the Field List pane to the form, below the E-mail Address field, until an orange line displays between E-mail Address and Address1 and release the mouse.

   Access shows an orange line to help you place the field in the correct location.

h. Switch to Form view. Press **Tab** until you reach the **Website field**, and then type **www.microsoft.com** into the field.

i. Press **Tab** until the focus reaches the Orders subform to verify the tab order is correct.

j. Close and save the Customer Information form.

STEP 6 CHANGE THE SORTING IN A FORM AND REMOVE SORTING IN A FORM

Alex tested the Customer Information form and likes the way it is working. He asks you to change the sorting to make it easier to find customers with a similar Customer Name. Refer to Figure 12 as you complete Step 6.

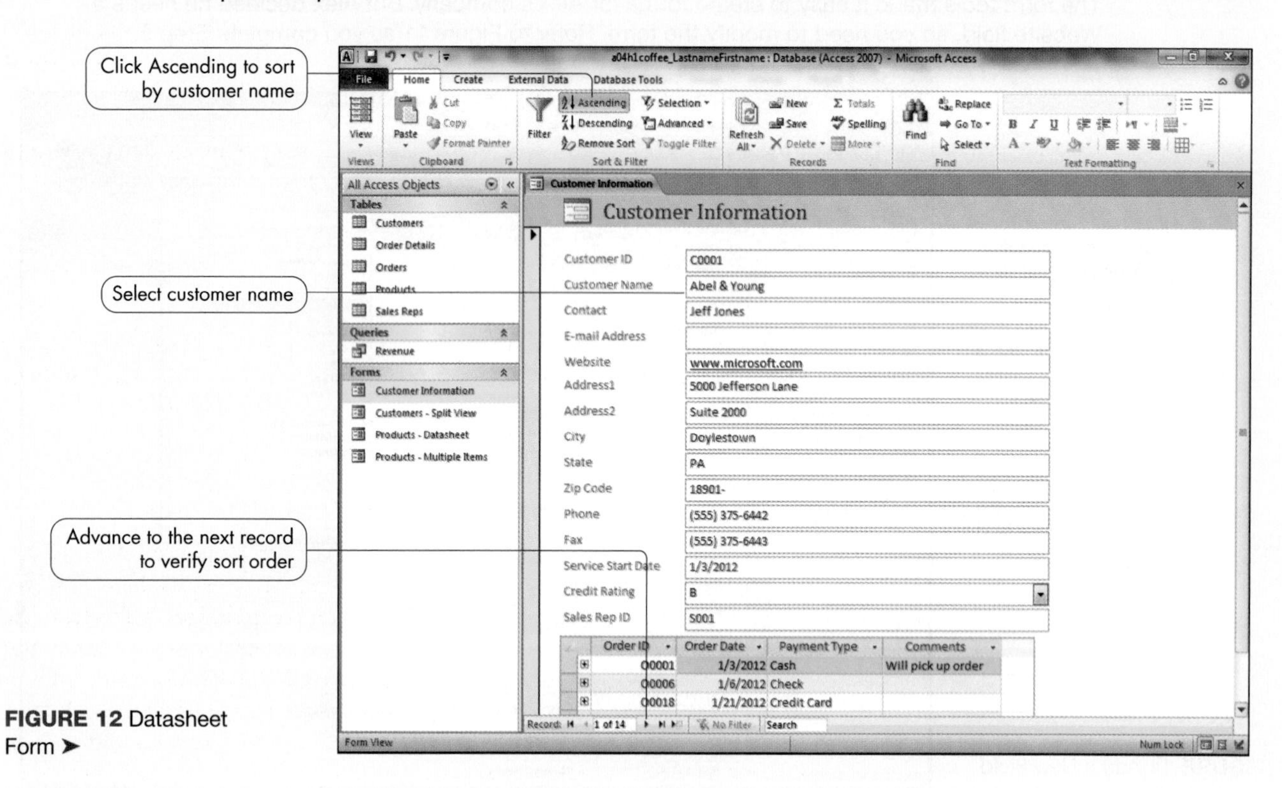

FIGURE 12 Datasheet Form ➤

a. Open the Customer Information form. Click **Next record** in the Navigation bar at the bottom several times to advance through the records.

Take note that the customers are in Customer ID order.

b. Click **First record** in the Navigation bar to return to customer Abel & Young.

c. Click the **Customer Name field**, and then click **Ascending** in the Sort & Filter group.

d. Click **Next record** in the Navigation bar at the bottom to advance through the records.

The records are now in Customer Name order.

e. Close the Customer Information form.

f. Click the **File tab**, and then click **Compact & Repair Database**.

g. Keep the database onscreen if you plan to continue with Hands-On Exercise 2. If not, close the database and exit Access.

Form Sections, Views, and Controls

As you work with the form tools to create and modify forms, you will often need to switch between the three form views in Access—Layout view, Form view, and Design view. Most of your design work will be done in Layout view; occasionally, you will switch to Design view to add a more advanced feature, such as a calculated field. Users of the form will only work in Form view. There should be no reason for a user to switch to Layout or Design view. Modifications to the form should be done by the designated form designer.

... you will often need to switch between the three form views in Access—Layout view, Form view, and Design view.

In this section, you will examine the different form sections. As you learn how to create forms, placing fields and labels in the right section will become second nature. You may have to use trial and error at first, switching between Form view and Layout view until the form is working correctly.

Controls are also covered in this section. You will learn the difference between bound and unbound controls. You will also learn how to add a calculated control.

Identifying Form Sections

Access forms, by default, are divided into three sections that can be viewed when you display a form in Design view. Each section can be collapsed or expanded as needed, but only in Design view.

Identify the Default Form Sections

Each form by default contains three main sections—*Form Header, Detail,* and *Form Footer.* These sections can vary depending on what type of form you create. Stacked layout forms will have different requirements than a tabular layout form. Form designers also have the option of removing certain sections from a form. Two additional sections—*Page Header* and *Page Footer*—are optional and can be added to a form as needed. These sections are visible in Design view and also during Print Preview and printing; however, page headers and footers are not visible in Form view or Layout view. Because these sections are less common in forms, they will not be explored further in this chapter. Use Microsoft Help for more information about the *Page Header* and *Page Footer* sections.

The **Form Header section** displays at the top of each form.

The ***Form Header section*** displays at the top of each form. This section will usually contain the form title, a logo or other graphic, and the current date and time. Column headings (labels) will also be located in this section for Multiple Item forms.

The **Detail section** displays the records in the form's record source.

The ***Detail section*** displays the records in the form's record source. Stacked forms will display one label and one text box for each field placed in the *Detail* section. Navigation controls enable the user to advance to the next, last, previous, and first record. Multiple Item forms will display multiple records (text boxes) in the *Detail* section, as many as can fit onto one screen.

The **Form Footer section** displays at the bottom of the form.

The ***Form Footer section*** displays at the bottom of the form. The Form Footer is commonly used to add totals for field values. For example, an invoice form would display the invoice subtotal, the shipping charges, the taxes, and the invoice total in the *Form Footer* section.

Modify the Default Form Sections

In Figure 13, three light grey section bars mark the top boundary of each form section. The top bar denotes the top boundary of the Form Header; the middle bar designates the top of the *Detail* section; and the bottom bar shows the top boundary of the Form Footer. The grid-like area under the bars shows the amount of space allotted to each section. If you decide that the allotted space for a particular section is not needed, you can collapse that section fully so that the section bars are touching. In Figure 13, the form has no space allocated to the Form Footer. The section remains in the form's design but will not take up space in Form view. If you want to remove the *Form Footer* section from the form, right-click the Form Footer bar, and then click Form Header/Footer from the list. When you remove the Form Footer, the *Form Header* section will also be removed. This may cause a problem since the title of the form usually resides in the Form Header.

To expand or collapse the space between sections, move your mouse over the bottom bar, and when the mouse pointer changes to a double-headed arrow, click and drag to expand or collapse the section. If you expand or collapse the space allotment for one section, the overall height of the form will be affected.

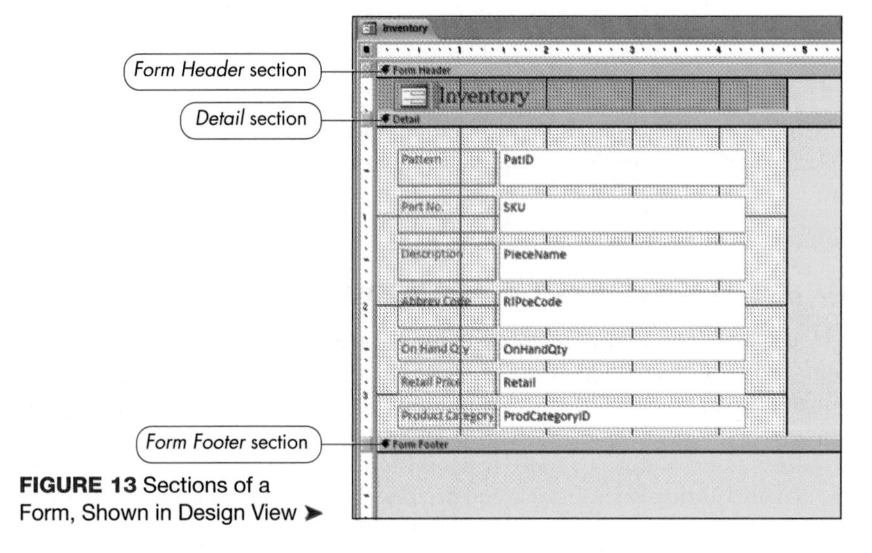

FIGURE 13 Sections of a Form, Shown in Design View ➤

Revising Forms Using Form Views

Access provides different views for a form, similar to the different views in tables and queries. Tables and queries have Design view and Datasheet view. Most forms have Layout view, Form view, and Design view. A Datasheet form has one additional view, the Datasheet view, but it does not have the Form view.

Switch Between Form Views

A variety of methods for switching between form views exist: click View in the Views group, click the View arrow, right-click a form in the Navigation Pane, right-click the form tab, or click one of the small view icons in the status bar at the bottom right of the form. Perhaps the quickest method for switching between views is clicking View. This will toggle the form between Layout view and Form view. Click the View arrow or right-click the form tab to switch to Design view. Each view is described in the sections below.

Edit Data in Form View

Use **Form view** to add, edit, and delete data in a form; the layout and design of the form cannot be changed in this view.

Use ***Form view*** to add, edit, and delete data in a form; the layout and design of the form cannot be changed in this view. Most users will only see Form view; if a form needs modification, the user will notify the database designer, who will make a change on the fly or during the next scheduled maintenance interval. Figure 14 shows a form in Form view. Users can print from this view by clicking the File tab and then selecting the Print option. However, printing from a form should be done with caution. A form with a stacked layout of 810 records could print as many as 810 pages (depending on how many records fit onto one page) unless you choose the Selected Record(s) option in the Print dialog box. The Selected Record(s) option will only print the current record or the number of records you selected.

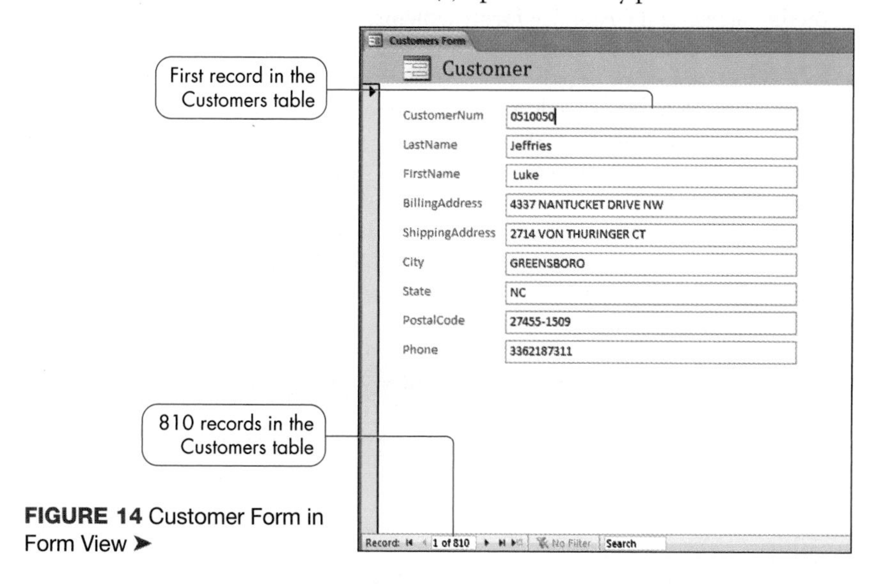

FIGURE 14 Customer Form in Form View ➤

Alter a Form in Layout View

Use Layout view to alter the form design while still viewing the data. You use Layout view to add or delete fields in a form, modify field properties, change the column widths, and enhance a form by adding a color scheme or styling. While you are working in Layout view, you can see the data as it would appear in Form view, but you cannot edit the data in Layout view. Seeing the data in Layout view makes it easier to size controls, for example, to ensure the data is visible (see Figure 15). It is good practice to test a form in Form view after making changes in Layout view.

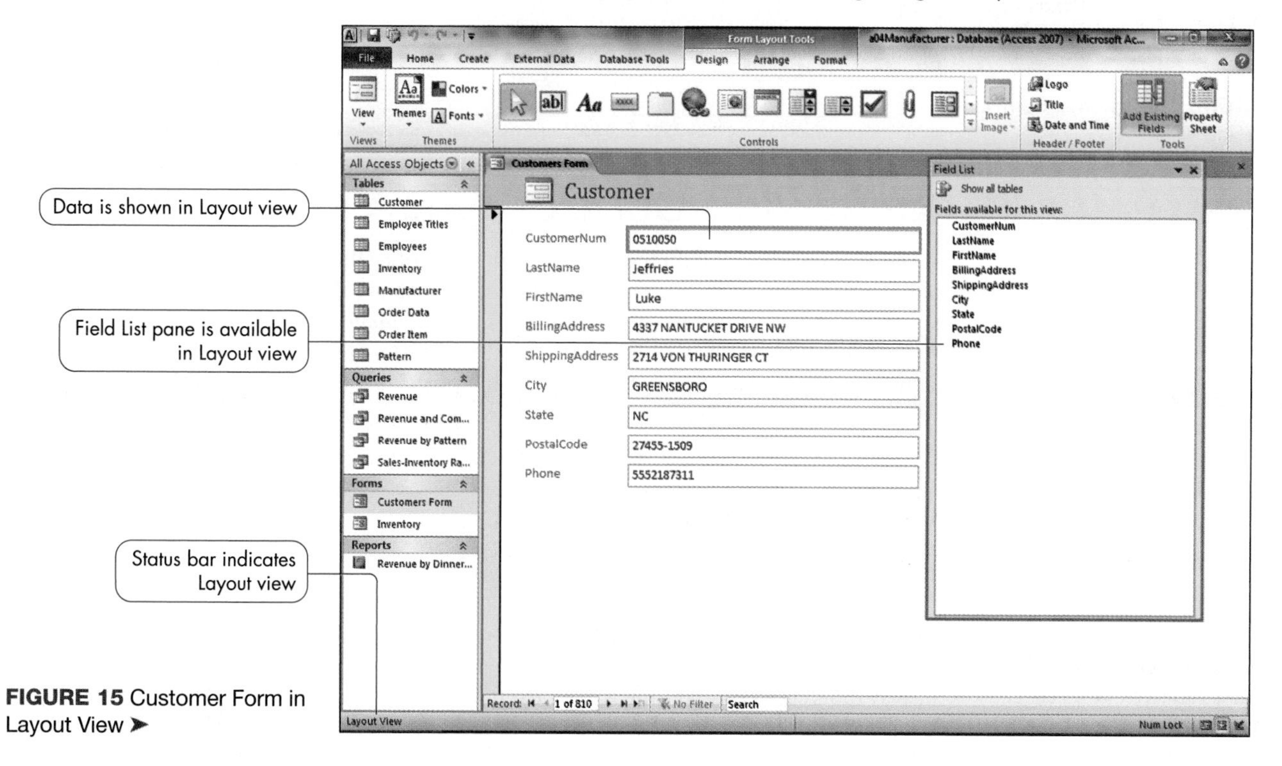

FIGURE 15 Customer Form in Layout View ➤

Perform Advanced Changes to a Form in Design View

Use **Design view** to perform advanced changes to a form's design.

Use ***Design view*** to perform advanced changes to a form's design. It provides you the most advanced method of editing an Access form. You can perform many of the same tasks in Design view as you can in Layout view—add and delete fields, change the field order, adjust field widths, modify labels, and customize form elements. But certain tasks cannot be done in Layout view, and Access displays a message telling you to use Design view. For example, changes to the form sections can only be made in Design view. After you finish making changes in Design view, it is best to switch to Form view to examine the results.

You need to experiment using both the Layout view and Design view to decide which view you prefer. Figure 16 displays the Customer form in Design view. The next section describes how to edit the finer details of a form.

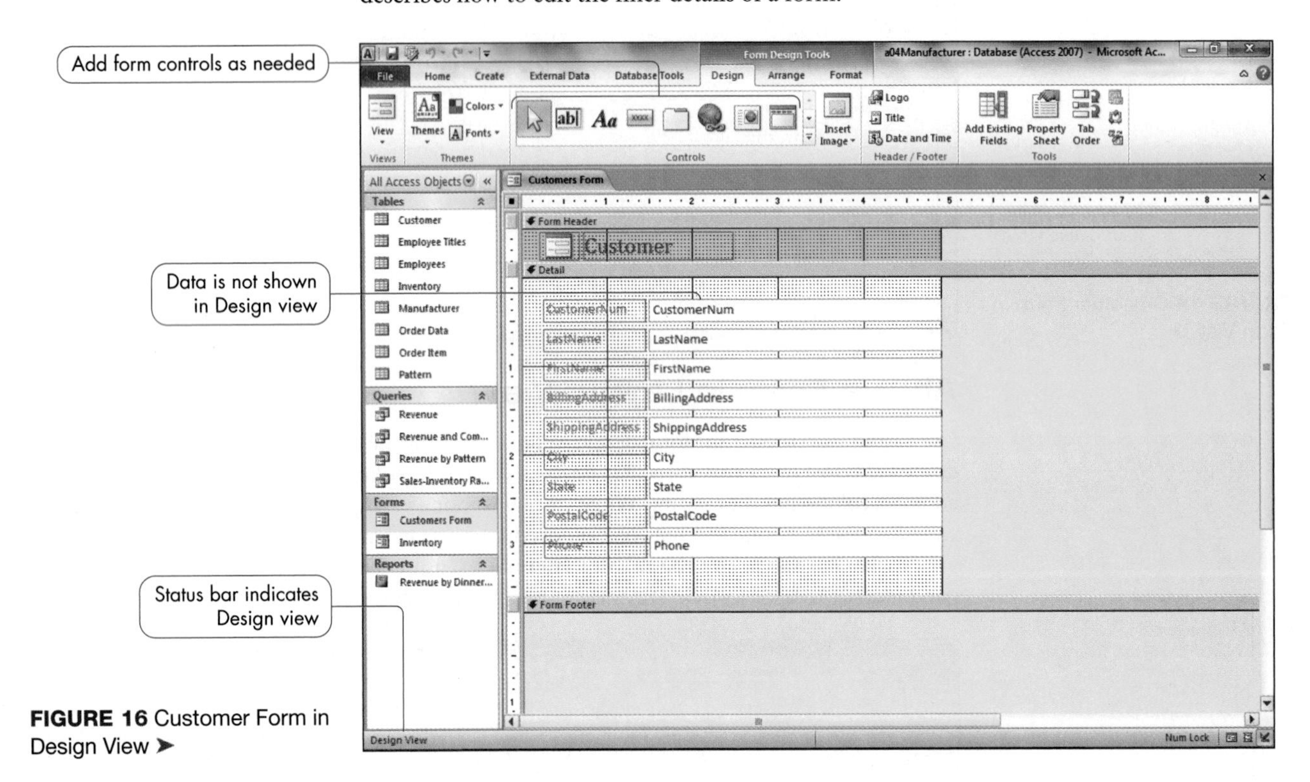

FIGURE 16 Customer Form in Design View ➤

Identifying Control Types in Forms

A **text box control** displays the data found in a form's record source.

A **label control** is a literal word or phrase to describe the data.

If you examine the fields on the form in Figure 16, notice that each field has a label on the left and a text box on the right. The ***text box control*** displays the data found in a form's record source (the Customers table in this example) and the ***label control*** is a literal word or phrase to describe the data. The position of the label and the text box can be interchanged; however, in most cases, the label is positioned to the left of the text box in a stacked layout. Although the term *text box* might imply *text only*, a text box can also display numeric data, currency, and dates.

Work with Controls

A **bound control** is a text box that is connected to a field in a table or query.

Label and Text Box objects are known as *controls*. They are among the many types of controls found in the Controls group on the Design tab when you are in the Design view of a form. Controls can be categorized as bound, unbound, or calculated.

A ***bound control*** is a text box that is connected to a field in a table or query. These controls display different data each time you switch to a new record. The most common way to add a bound control to a form is to drag a field from the Field List pane, and then drop it onto the form.

An **unbound control** is a label or other decorative design element, and is not connected to a source of data.

A **calculated control** contains an expression that generates a calculated result when displayed in Form view.

An ***unbound control*** is a label or other decorative design element, and is not connected to a source of data. These controls usually describe and decorate the data rather than display the data, and remain the same each time you switch to a new record. Unbound controls include labels, lines, borders, and images; they can be added to a form using the Controls group on the Design tab while in Design view. For example, a label that displays the title of the form is an unbound control.

A ***calculated control*** contains an expression that generates a calculated result when displayed in Form view. The expression can contain field names from the form's record source, constants, and functions. Use a text box, found in the Controls group, to create a calculated control.

Most forms include an unbound control (label) to describe each bound control (text box) on the form. In the form in Figure 17, each text box has a label describing it. As you add or delete fields from a form, be aware that many bound controls are connected to an unbound label. If you move the bound control, the label moves, too. Likewise, if you move the label, the bound control moves along with it. You can ungroup the controls and move them separately, but the default is that they are joined together.

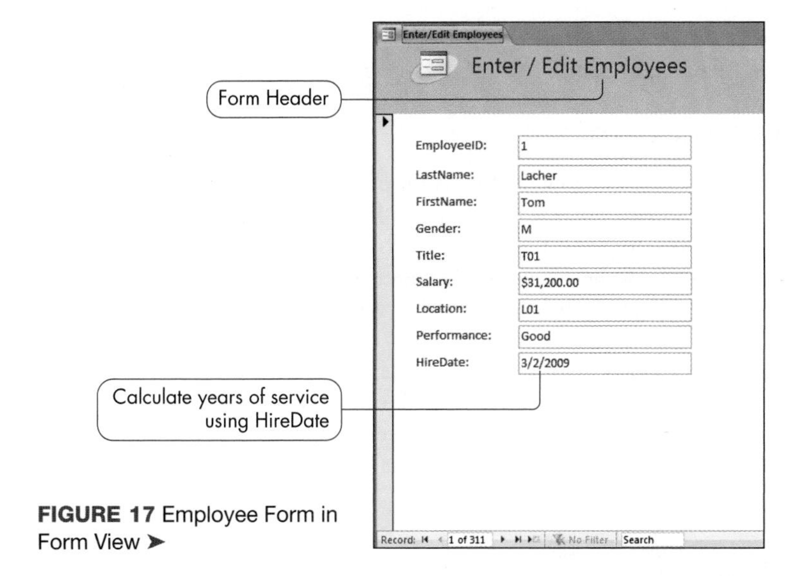

FIGURE 17 Employee Form in Form View ➤

Add a Calculated Control to a Form

Review the Enter/Edit Customers form in Figure 17 above. Users must manually calculate an employee's years of service using the HireDate field at the bottom of the form. Based on your knowledge of date arithmetic, you could calculate each employee's years of service using the expression:

= (Date( ) – HireDate) / 365

To add this expression to the form, you add a calculated field using a text box. Open the form in Design view, and then click Text Box in the Controls group on the Design tab. Place a text box at the desired location, and then enter the expression *=(Date() – HireDate)/365* into the control source property of the new text box. Format the control as needed. Figure 18 shows the Years of Service text box formatted as fixed with one decimal.

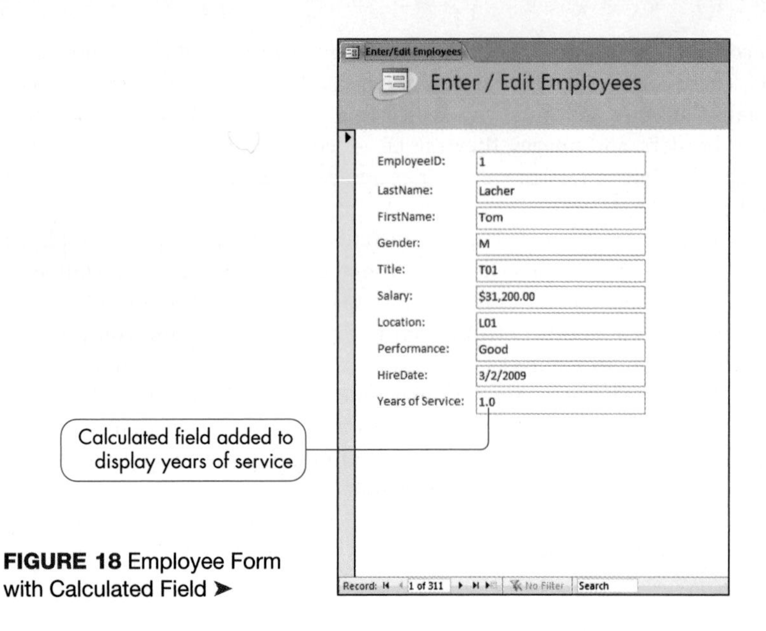

FIGURE 18 Employee Form with Calculated Field ➤

Add Styling to a Form

Modifying the font size of labels, changing the font color of labels, and adding a background color can enhance a form and also make it more usable. It is best to choose a familiar font family, such as Arial or Calibri, for both the form label controls and the text box controls. Apply bold to the labels in order to help the user distinguish labels from the text boxes. You should also consider left-aligning the labels to themselves and left-aligning the text box controls to themselves.

As illustrated in Figure 19, it is helpful to group like controls together and define the group visually by drawing a box around them using the Rectangle control. Similarly, separate the primary key field, such as the EmployeeID, from the rest of the form by providing a sufficient visual boundary. Also, the Years of Service field has been highlighted to help the user locate this information quickly.

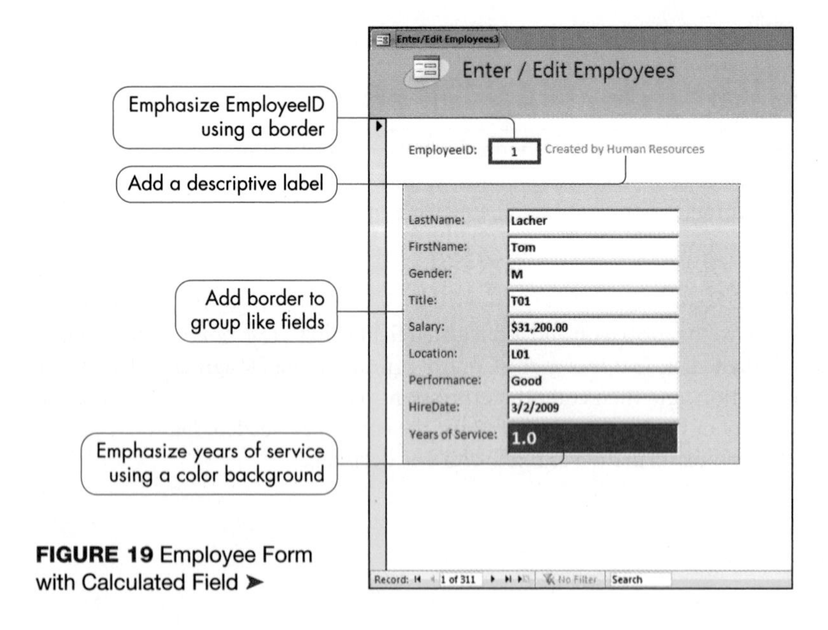

FIGURE 19 Employee Form with Calculated Field ➤

2 Form Sections, Views, and Controls

You already created several forms for the Santiago Coffee Shop; however, Alex would like some additional forms. After the new forms are created, you use the different views to make changes and test the forms.

Skills covered: Understand the Main Form Sections and Alter a Form in Design View • Edit Data in Form View • Work with Controls • Add a Calculated Control to a Form • Add Styling to a Form

STEP 1 UNDERSTAND THE MAIN FORM SECTIONS AND ALTER A FORM IN DESIGN VIEW

You have decided to use the Form tool to create a Revenue form. This form will enable Alex to track revenue for his company. You will use Design view to modify this form. Refer to Figure 20 as you complete Step 1.

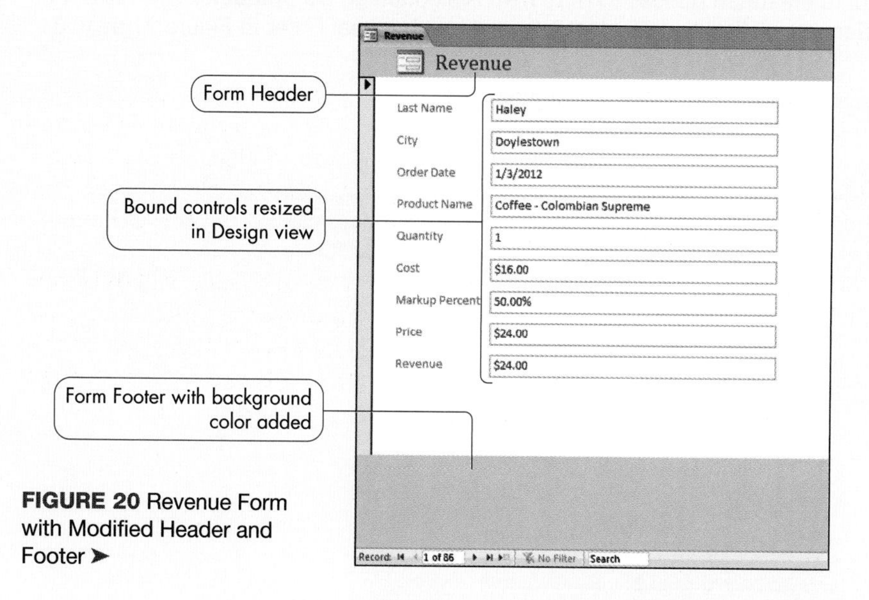

FIGURE 20 Revenue Form with Modified Header and Footer ➤

a. Open *a04h1coffee_LastnameFirstname* if you closed it at the end of Hands-On Exercise 1. Click the **File tab**, click **Save Database As**, and then type **a04h2coffee_LastnameFirstname**, changing *h1* to *h2*. Click **Save**.

b. Select **Revenue query** in the Navigation Pane. Click the **Create tab**, and then click **Form** in the Forms group.

   Access creates a new form based on the Revenue query. The form opens in Layout view, ready to edit.

c. Place the mouse on the right edge of the Last Name control so the mouse pointer changes to a double-headed arrow. Drag to the left to size the control section to 50% of its original size.

   Access simultaneously reduces the size of all the controls.

d. Switch to Design view.

   Notice the three sections of the form—*Form Header*, *Detail*, and *Form Footer*.

e. Place the mouse on the bottom edge of the Form Footer bar so the mouse pointer changes to a double-headed arrow. Drag the bar down until the size of the *Form Footer* section is **1"**, using the vertical ruler.

f. Switch to Form view.

With a white background, it is difficult to tell where the *Form Footer* section begins and ends.

g. Switch to Design view. Click **Property Sheet** in the Tools group. Click the **Selection type arrow**, and select **FormFooter**.

h. In the Property Sheet, click the **Format tab**, click the **Back Color arrow**, and then select **Background Light Header** from the list. Close the Property Sheet, and then switch to Form view.

With the new background color, the Form Footer is now evident. You will add content to the footer in a later step.

i. Switch to Design view.

j. Place the mouse on the top edge of the Detail bar so the mouse pointer changes to a double-headed arrow. Drag the bar down until the *Form Header* section is **3/4"**.

k. Click **Save** in the Quick Access Toolbar and save the form as **Revenue**. Close the form.

STEP 2 EDIT DATA IN FORM VIEW

You will use the Form tool to create an Access form to help Alex manage his products. This form will enable Tonya to make changes easily when product information changes. Refer to Figure 21 as you complete Step 2.

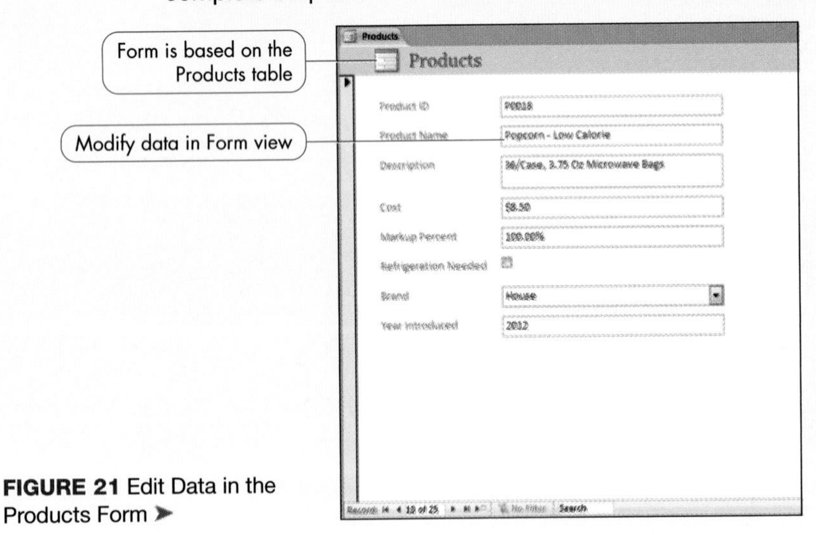

FIGURE 21 Edit Data in the Products Form ➤

a. Select the **Products table** in the Navigation Pane. Click the **Create tab**, and then click **Form** in the Forms group.

Access creates a new form based on the Products table.

b. Click anywhere in the subform at the bottom of the window, click the Layout Selector, and then press **Delete** to delete the subform. Click **View** in the Views group to switch to Form view.

c. Click **Next Record** in the Navigation bar to advance to the third record in the Products form.

Use Next Record to advance through the records.

d. Click in the **Product Name box**, and then change *Coffee - Mild Blend* to **Coffee - Light.**

e. Click **Last Record** in the Navigation bar to advance to the last record in the Products form. Click **Previous Record** to locate record 23.

Use Last Record to advance to the last record.

f. Click in the **Product Name box**, and change *Styrofoam Cups - 12 ounce* to **Heavy Paper Cups - 12 ounce.**

g. Click in the **Current Record box** in the Navigation bar, type **12**, and then press **Enter** to go to the 12th record in the Products form.

   Use the Current Record box to advance to a specific record.

h. Click in the **Product Name box**, and then change *Sugar Substitute* to **Splenda**.

i. Click in the **Search box** in the Navigation bar, and then type **pop** to locate any records with *pop* in any data value, in this case, record 18.

   Use the Search box to find a record with a value you type.

j. Click in the **Product Name box**, and then change *Popcorn - Plain* to **Popcorn - Low Calorie**.

k. Click **Save** in the Quick Access Toolbar and save the form as **Products**. Close the form.

STEP 3 WORK WITH CONTROLS

You make some enhancements to the Revenue form to increase its usability. Afterwards, Tonya and Alex test the form to determine if the changes are an improvement to the form. Refer to Figure 22 as you complete Step 3.

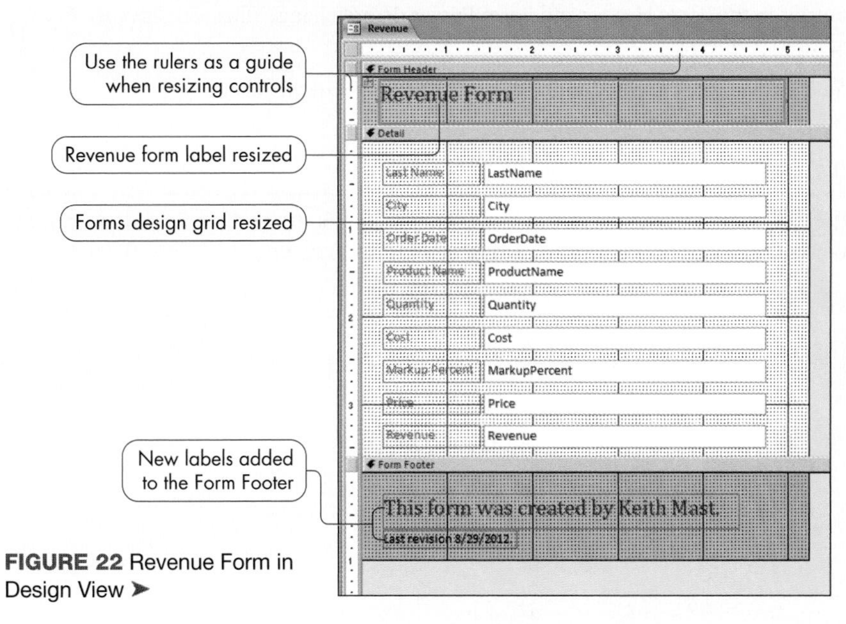

FIGURE 22 Revenue Form in Design View ➤

a. Right-click the **Revenue form** in the Navigation Pane, and then click **Design View**.

b. Click the **Revenue label** in the Form Header, and then click it again to edit it. Change the label to **Revenue Form**.

c. Click the **Form Logo** to the left of the Revenue Form label, and then press **Delete** to delete the image.

d. Click **Label** in the Controls group, and then click in the **Form Footer** at the 1/4" mark from both the horizontal and vertical rulers to insert a text box. Type **This form was created by *your name*.**

e. Click the **Revenue Form label** in the Form Header, and then click **Format Painter** in the Clipboard group on the Home tab. Click the new label in the Form Footer to apply the same format. Click the label, and then drag the bottom-right sizing handle down and to the right so the entire text is visible.

f. Click **Label** in the Controls group on the Design tab, and then add a second label under the first label in the Form Footer at the 1/4" mark on the horizontal ruler. Type **Last revision *today's date*.** Accept the default font.

g. Click the **Form Header bar**, and then open the Property Sheet if necessary. Change the Height property to **.65**.

   You can change the height of the Form Header by dragging it with the mouse or by modifying the Height property.

h. Click the **Revenue Form label** in the Form Header. Modify the following properties:
   - Change the Height property to **.5**.
   - Change the Width property to **4.75**. Close the Property Sheet.

i. Place the mouse on the right edge of the form's design grid so the mouse pointer changes to a double-headed arrow. Drag the grid to the left to change the form's width to **5.25"**.

   Use the horizontal ruler to locate the 5.25" mark.

> **TROUBLESHOOTING:** If other Text box controls are too wide, reduce their width first, and then reduce the grid to 5.25".

j. Switch to Form view. Advance through the records using the Navigation bar at the bottom.

   The controls in the Form Header and Form Footer do not change when you advance from one record to the next.

k. Click **Save** in the Quick Access Toolbar to save the changes to the form.

STEP 4 ADD A CALCULATED CONTROL TO A FORM

After reviewing the changes you made to the Revenue form, Alex asks you to add a calculated control. The new control will show the total cost of each order. Refer to Figure 23 as you complete Step 4.

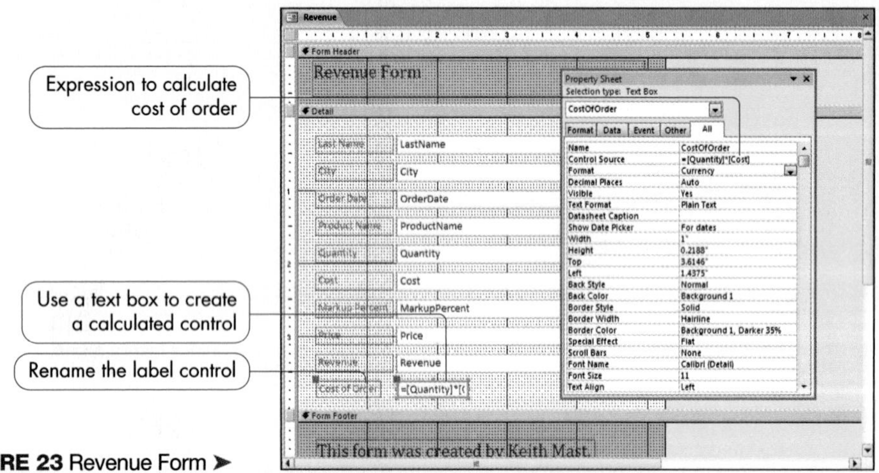

FIGURE 23 Revenue Form ➤

a. Switch to Design view.

b. Position the mouse on the top edge of the Form Footer bar until the mouse pointer changes to the double-arrow resizing shape. Drag the **Form Footer bar** down to increase the *Detail* section to **4"**.

c. Click **Text Box** in the Controls group, and then click just below the **Revenue text box** (the white rectangle) at the bottom of the *Detail* section.

d. Click in the **text box**, and then type =**[Quantity]*[Cost]** in place of *Unbound.* Press **Enter**.

   The expression you typed creates a calculated control that shows the total value of the current product.

e. Open the Property Sheet if necessary. Click the **All tab** in the Property Sheet, click in the **Name property box**, and then replace the existing text with **CostOfOrder**. Click the **Format property**, and then use the arrow to select **Currency** from the list of options.

f. Switch to Form view. Advance through the records using the Navigation bar at the bottom.

As you advance from one record to the next, the cost of each order is displayed in the calculated control.

TROUBLESHOOTING: If you see *#Name* in the calculated control, you have typed the expression incorrectly. Be sure you begin the expression with =.

g. Switch to Design view.

h. Click the label control for the new calculated control, and then replace the existing label caption with **Cost of Order**. Resize label control to fit new text, if necessary.

i. Click the calculated control, and then click the **Other tab** on the Property Sheet. Locate the Tab Stop property and change it to **No**.

j. Click **View** in the Views Group to switch to Form view. Press **Tab** to advance through the fields to test the tab stop change.

A calculated control does not require data entry. It is now skipped when Tab is pressed.

k. Save the form.

STEP 5 ADD STYLING TO A FORM

The users of the Santiago Coffee Shop database have asked you to add some styling to the new form. You discuss their ideas with Alex, and then decide to apply the suggested styles. Refer to Figure 24 as you complete Step 5.

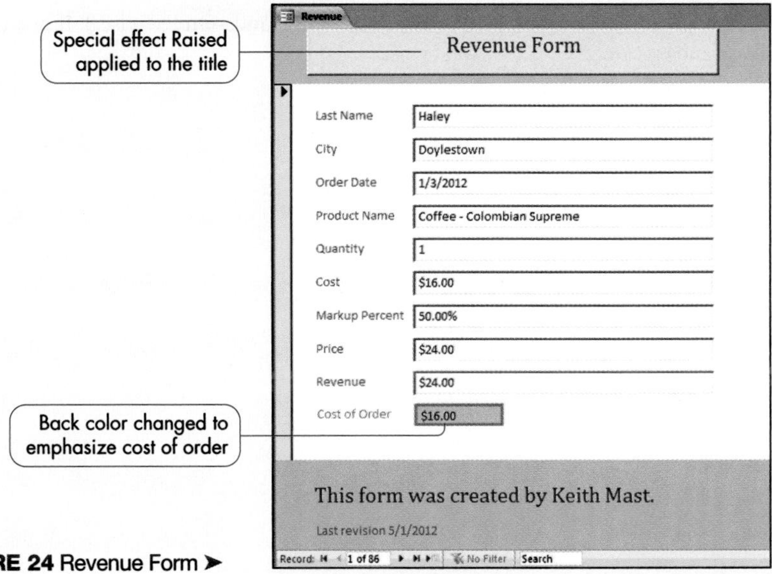

FIGURE 24 Revenue Form ➤

a. Switch to Design view.

b. Open the Property Sheet (if necessary), and then click the **Revenue Form label**.

c. Click the **Back Color arrow** on the Property Sheet Format tab, and then choose **Access Theme 2**.

The background color of the title changes to a light blue.

d. Click the **Special Effect arrow** on the Property Sheet Format tab, and then choose **Raised**.

The title now appears raised.

e. Click **Center** in the Font group on the Format tab on the Ribbon.

The form title is now centered within the control box.

f. Click just above the LastName box on the blank grid space, and then drag the mouse through all the fields, except Cost of Order.

All the text box fields are now selected as indicated with an orange border, except the Cost of Order field.

g. Click the **Special Effect arrow** on the Property Sheet Format tab, and then choose **Sunken.**

The fields now appear sunken.

h. Click the **Cost of Order box control**, click the **Border Width arrow** in the Property Sheet Format tab, and then click **2 pt**. Close the Property Sheet.

The border of the calculated control increases.

i. Click **Background Color arrow** in the Font group on the Format tab, and then select **Light Gray 2** (Standard Colors, first column, third row).

The background color of the calculated control is now gray to set it apart from the bound data entry fields.

j. Click the **Cost of Order label control**, click the **Font Color arrow** in the Font group, and then select **Light Gray 4** (Standard Colors, first column, fifth row).

The font color of the calculated control is now gray to set it apart from the bound data entry fields.

k. Switch to Form view. Compare your results to Figure 24, and then close and save the form.

l. Click the **File tab**, and then click **Compact & Repair Database**.

m. Keep the database onscreen if you plan to continue with Hands-On Exercise 3. If not, close the database and exit Access.

Report Basics

A **report** is a printed document that displays information from a database in a format that provides meaningful information to its readers.

By now, you know how to plan a database, create a table, establish relationships between tables, enter data into tables, and extract data using queries. You generated output by printing table and query datasheets. You also learned how to create several types of data entry forms. These forms can also be used for inquiries about the data in a database. In this section, you will learn how to create professional reports using the report-writing tools in Access. A ***report*** is a printed document that displays information from a database in a format that provides meaningful information to its readers.

Although you can print information from tables, queries, and forms, information printed from these database objects may not be in the best format. Most of the printed documents generated by Access will come from reports. Reports can be enhanced to help the reader understand and analyze the data. For example, if you print the Datasheet view from the Customers table, you will be able to locate the key information about each customer. However, using report tools, you can group the customers by sales rep, and then highlight the customers who have not placed an order in six months. This is an example of converting a list of customers into an effective business tool. To increase business, each sales rep could contact their customers who have not ordered in six months, and then review his or her findings with the sales manager. A sales report could be run each month to see if the strategy has helped produce any new business.

Most of the printed documents generated by Access will come from reports.

In this section, you will create reports in Access by first identifying a record source, then sketching the report, and finally choosing a Report tool. You will learn how to modify a report by adding and deleting fields, by resizing columns, and by adding a color scheme. You will also learn about the report sections, the report views, and controls on reports. After having worked through forms in the section above, you will discover that there are many similarities between forms and reports.

Creating Reports Using Report Tools

The **Report tool** is used to instantly create a tabular report based on the table or query currently selected.

Access provides five different report tools for creating reports. The report tools are found in the Reports group, as shown in Figure 25. Click one of these tools and Access will create an automatic report (or launch a wizard to guide you) using the table or query that is currently selected. The most common of the tools, the ***Report tool***, is used to instantly create a tabular report based on the table or query currently selected. The Blank Report tool is used to create a new blank report so that you can insert fields and controls manually and design the report. The Report Design tool is used to create a new blank report in Design view. In Design view, you can make advanced design changes to reports, such as adding custom control types and working with report sections. The Report Wizard tool will ask a series of questions and help you create a report based on your answers. The Labels tool is used to create a page of labels using one of the preformatted templates provided by Access. After you create a report using one of the report tools, you can perform modifications in Layout view or Design view.

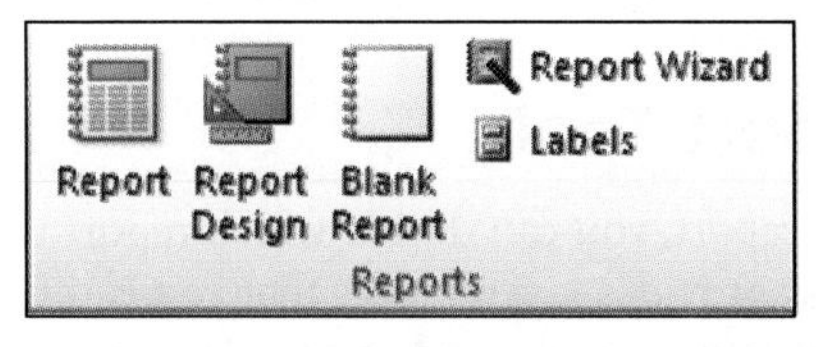

FIGURE 25 Report Tools in the Reports Group ➤

Before you create a report in Access, you should ask these questions:

- What is the purpose of the report?
- Who will use the report?
- Which tables are needed for the report?
- What fields, labels, and calculations need to be included?
- How will the report be distributed? Will users pull the information directly from Access or will they receive it through e-mail, fax, or the Internet?
- Will the results be converted to Word, Excel, HTML, or another format?

Sample reports include a telephone directory sorted by last name, a customer list grouped by sales rep, an employee list sorted by most years of service, a financial statement, a bar chart showing sales over the past 12 months, a shipping label, and a letter to customers reminding them about a past due payment.

Identify the Record Source

The first step in planning your report is to identify the record source. You may use one or more tables, queries, or a combination of tables and queries as the report's record source. Sometimes, a single table contains all of the records you need for the report. Other times, you will need to incorporate several tables. When multiple tables are needed to create a report, you can add all the necessary tables into a single query, and then base the report on that query. (As stated earlier, multiple tables in a query must be related, as indicated with join lines. Tables with no join lines usually indicate an incorrect record source.)

Reports can also contain graphics as well as text and numeric data. For example, you can add a company logo, or a watermark to indicate the information is confidential or just a draft. After you identify the record source, you also need to specify which graphic images are needed (and the location of the images).

Sketch the Report

In the *Forms* section, you learned that it is helpful to sketch an Access form before you launch Access. The same holds true for creating an Access report. Design the report and indicate the record source (table names or query name), the title, the format of the report (stacked or tabular), the fields, and the order of fields. It would also be helpful to indicate the grouping and totals needed for the report. Sketch the report first and you will be happier with the results. A sample sketch is shown in Figure 26.

Physicians Report - Draft

First Name	Last Name	Address	City	State	Zip Code	Phone Number	Specialization
Bonnie	Clinton	10000 SW 59 Court	Coral Springs	FL	33071	(954) 777-8889	Obstetrics
Warren	Brasington	9470 SW 25 Street	Coral Springs	FL	33071	(954) 888-7654	Hematology
James	Shindell	Avenue	Coral Springs	FL	33070	(954) 773-4343	General Medicine
Edward	Wood	Avenue	Coral Springs	FL	33072	(954) 555-5555	Cardiology
Michelle	Quintana	3990 NW 3 Street	Coral Springs	FL	33071	(954) 888-1221	Internal Medicine
Kristine	Park	9290 NW 59 Steet	Coral Springs	FL	33072	(954) 777-1111	Exercise Physiology
William	Williamson	108 Los Pinos Place	Coral Springs	FL	33071	(954) 888-4554	General Medicine
Holly	Davis	8009 Riviera Drive	Coral Springs	FL	33072	(954) 388-7676	Cardiology
Steven	Fisher	444 SW 190 Street	Coral Springs	FL	33070	(954) 777-3333	Internal Medicine
David	Tannen	50 Main Street	Coral Springs	FL	33171	(954) 777-2211	Hematology
Jeffrey	Jacobsen	490 Bell Drive	Coral Springs	FL	33070	(954) 388-9999	Internal Medicine
Patsy	Clark	200 Harding Blvd	Coral Springs	FL	33070	(954) 777-1087	Cardiology
Keith	Mast	102 SCC	E. Norriton	PA	19401	(610) 555-1212	General Medicine

FIGURE 26 Sketch of the Physicians Report ➤

Use the Report Tool

After you sketch the report, you can decide which report tool is appropriate to produce the desired report. Access provides several tools that you can use to create a report, as shown in Figure 27. Which one you select depends on the layout of the report, the record source, and the complexity of the report design.

The easiest way to create a report is with the Report tool. Select a table or query in the Navigation Pane, then click Report in the Reports group on the Create tab, and Access creates a tabular layout report instantly. A ***tabular layout report*** displays data horizontally across the page in a landscape view, as shown in Figure 27.

A **tabular layout report** displays data horizontally across the page in a landscape view.

A **stacked layout report** displays fields in a vertical column.

You can also create a ***stacked layout report*** in Access, although this type of report is less common. A stacked layout report displays fields in a vertical column. The number of records on one page depends on the number of fields in the record source. You can also force a new page at the start of each record.

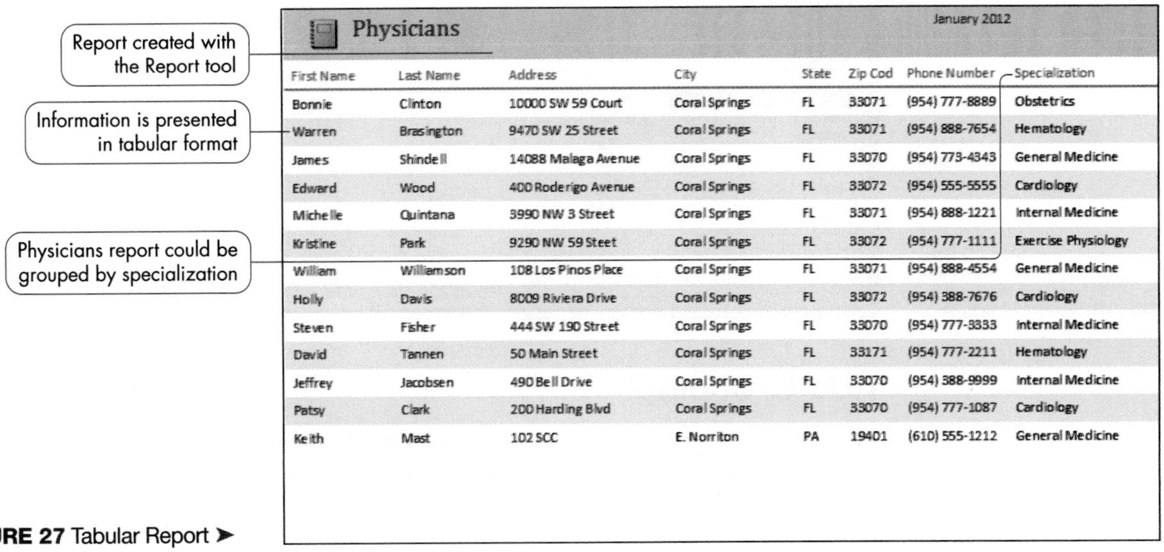

Report created with the Report tool

Information is presented in tabular format

Physicians report could be grouped by specialization

Physicians

January 2012

First Name	Last Name	Address	City	State	Zip Cod	Phone Number	Specialization
Bonnie	Clinton	10000 SW 59 Court	Coral Springs	FL	33071	(954) 777-8889	Obstetrics
Warren	Brasington	9470 SW 25 Street	Coral Springs	FL	33071	(954) 888-7654	Hematology
James	Shindell	14088 Malaga Avenue	Coral Springs	FL	33070	(954) 773-4343	General Medicine
Edward	Wood	400 Roderigo Avenue	Coral Springs	FL	33072	(954) 555-5555	Cardiology
Michelle	Quintana	3990 NW 3 Street	Coral Springs	FL	33071	(954) 888-1221	Internal Medicine
Kristine	Park	9290 NW 59 Steet	Coral Springs	FL	33072	(954) 777-1111	Exercise Physiology
William	Williamson	108 Los Pinos Place	Coral Springs	FL	33071	(954) 888-4554	General Medicine
Holly	Davis	8009 Riviera Drive	Coral Springs	FL	33072	(954) 388-7676	Cardiology
Steven	Fisher	444 SW 190 Street	Coral Springs	FL	33070	(954) 777-3333	Internal Medicine
David	Tannen	50 Main Street	Coral Springs	FL	33171	(954) 777-2211	Hematology
Jeffrey	Jacobsen	490 Bell Drive	Coral Springs	FL	33070	(954) 388-9999	Internal Medicine
Patsy	Clark	200 Harding Blvd	Coral Springs	FL	33070	(954) 777-1087	Cardiology
Keith	Mast	102 SCC	E. Norriton	PA	19401	(610) 555-1212	General Medicine

FIGURE 27 Tabular Report ➤

Use the Report Wizard

The Report Wizard.... uses six dialog boxes to collect information about your report.

You can also create a professional report with the Report Wizard. The ***Report Wizard*** asks you questions and then uses your answers to generate a report. The wizard uses six dialog boxes to collect information about your report.

The **Report Wizard** asks you questions and then uses your answers to generate a report.

Start the Report Wizard

After thinking through the structure, the layout, and the record source, you are ready to launch the Report Wizard. First, select the report's record source in the Navigation Pane, and then click Report Wizard in the Reports group on the Create tab. The wizard opens with the table or query (the record source) displayed in the first dialog box. Although you chose the record source before you started, the first dialog box enables you to select fields from additional tables or queries.

To demonstrate the Report Wizard, an Access database was created to track several health studies being conducted by a local physicians group. The studies are tracked using a StudyID code, S01, S02, S03, etc. The report that you need to create will list each volunteer alphabetically, grouped by study. See Figure 28 to review the fields in the Volunteers table—a key table in the Physicians database.

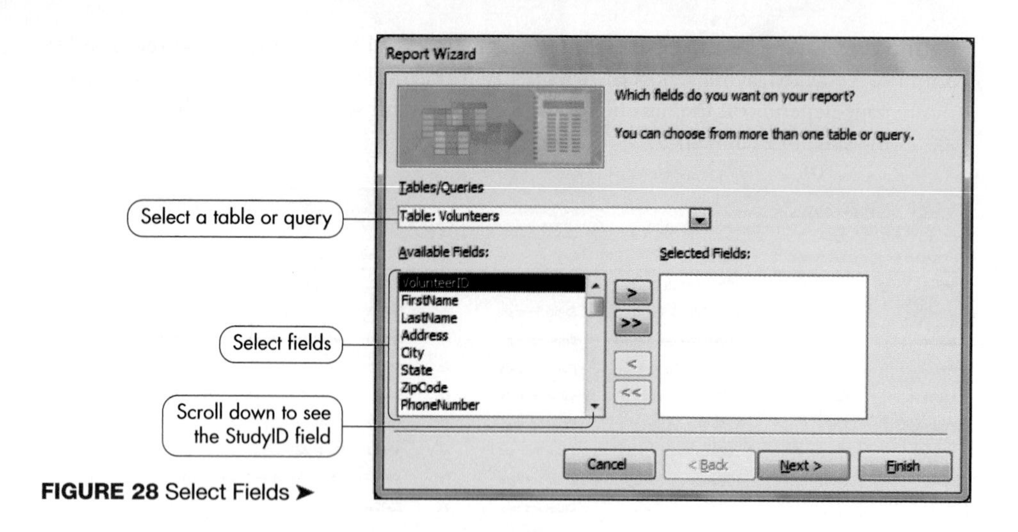

FIGURE 28 Select Fields ➤

Add Grouping

The next dialog box asks, "Do you want to add any grouping levels?" As we learned earlier in this chapter, grouping lets you organize and summarize your data. You can also add totals (sum, count, average) at the end of a group. In the sample report, Access correctly predicts that you want the data grouped by the study field (as shown in Figure 29). If you did not want to group the report by the StudyID field, you could click the < button to remove the group in step two of the Report Wizard. After you remove the unwanted grouping, select the field you want to group by, and then click the > button to add the new group. If you need a second or third grouping level, add those field names in order. The order in which you select the groups dictates the order of display in the report.

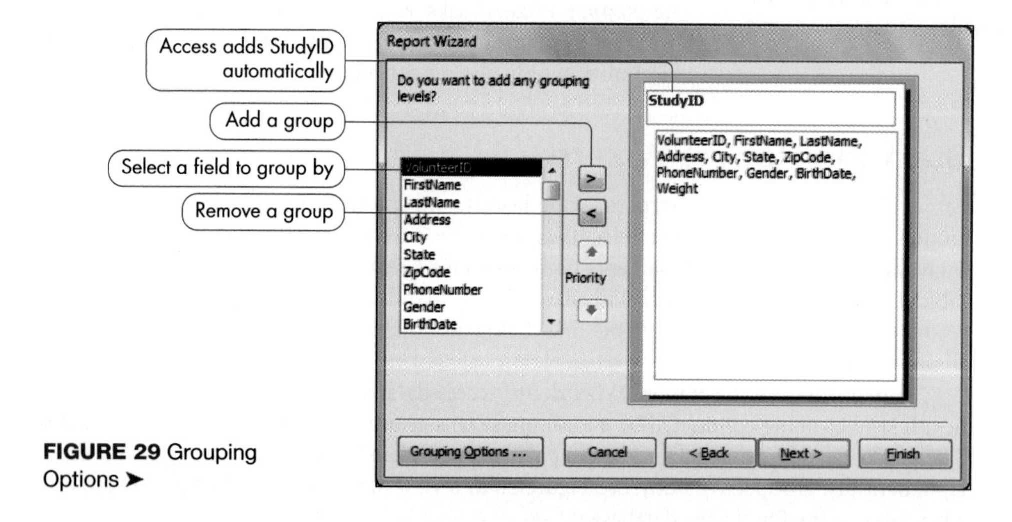

FIGURE 29 Grouping Options ➤

Add Sorting and Summary Options

The next dialog box asks, "What sort order and summary information do you want for detail records?" The summary information option will only appear if there is a numeric field in the selected fields (see Figure 30). Click Summary Options if you want to add aggregate functions (e.g., sum, average, minimum, and maximum) and to specify whether you want to see detail records on the report or only the aggregate results. Click OK or Cancel to return to the Report Wizard (see Figure 31). For the sort options, specify which field you want to sort by first, then second, third, and fourth. For each field, choose ascending order and/or descending order.

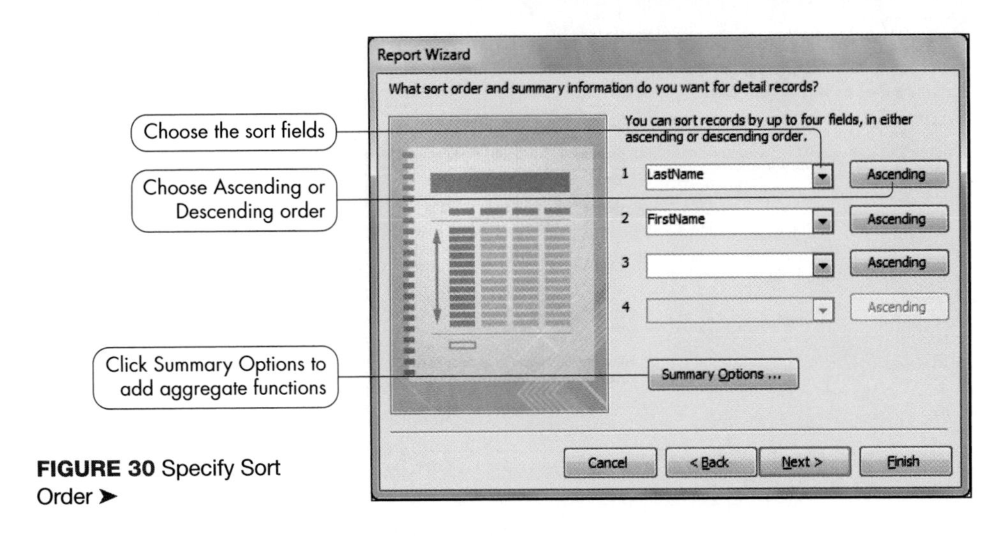

FIGURE 30 Specify Sort Order ➤

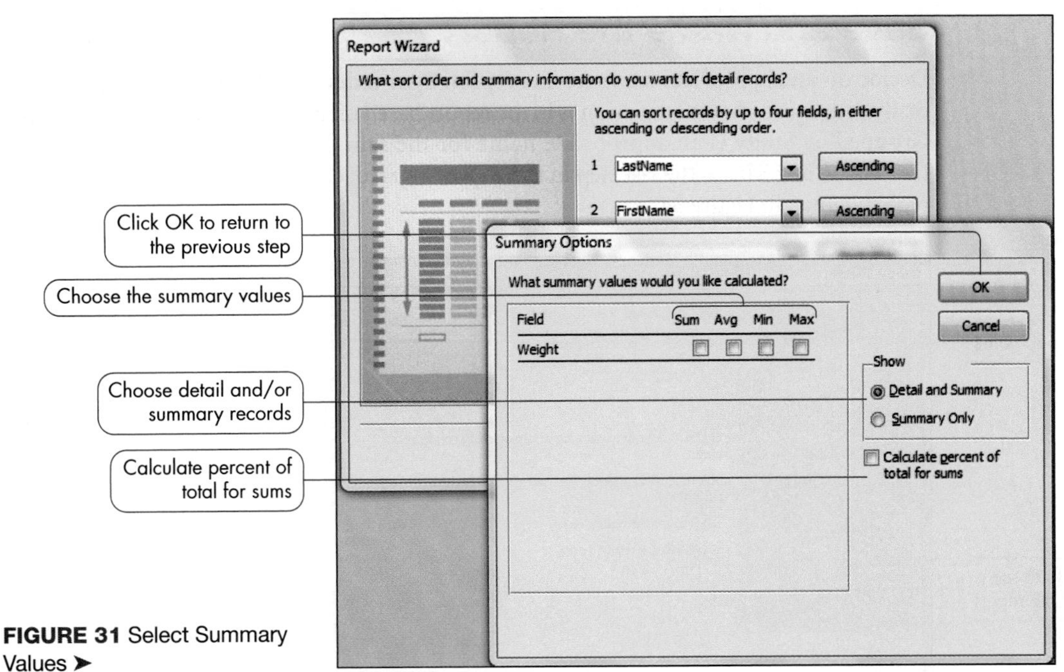

FIGURE 31 Select Summary Values ➤

Choose the Layout for the Report

The next dialog box will determine the report's appearance. First, you select the layout from three options—Stepped, Block, or Outline. Clicking an option will give you a general preview in the preview area. You can also select the orientation for the report, either Portrait or Landscape (see Figure 32). Select an appropriate format for the report.

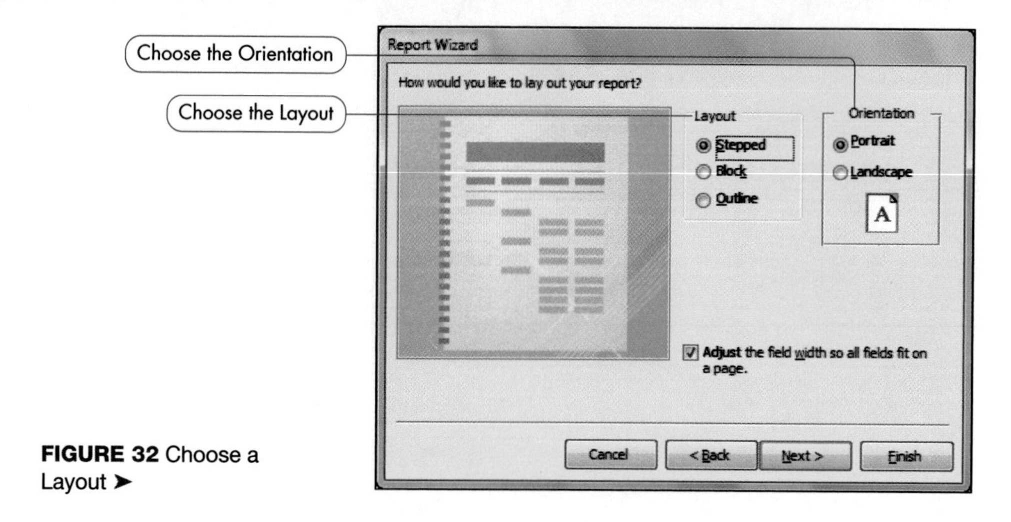

FIGURE 32 Choose a Layout ➤

Save and Name the Report

Decide on an appropriate name for the report. Type a descriptive report name so you can easily determine what information is in the report based on the title. For example, Volunteers Grouped by Study is an appropriate name for the sample report created in this section (see Figure 33). This is the last step in the Report Wizard; click Finish to see a preview of the report, shown in Figure 34.

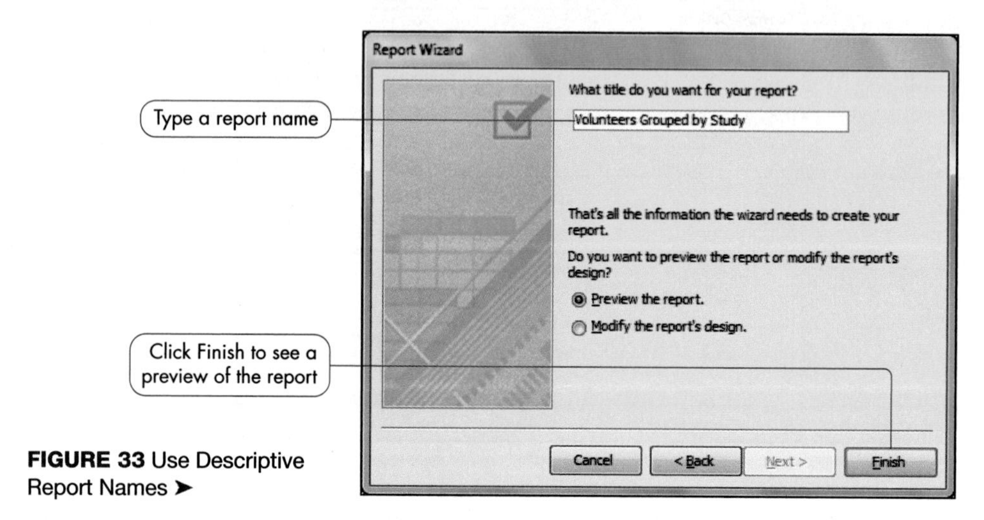

FIGURE 33 Use Descriptive Report Names ➤

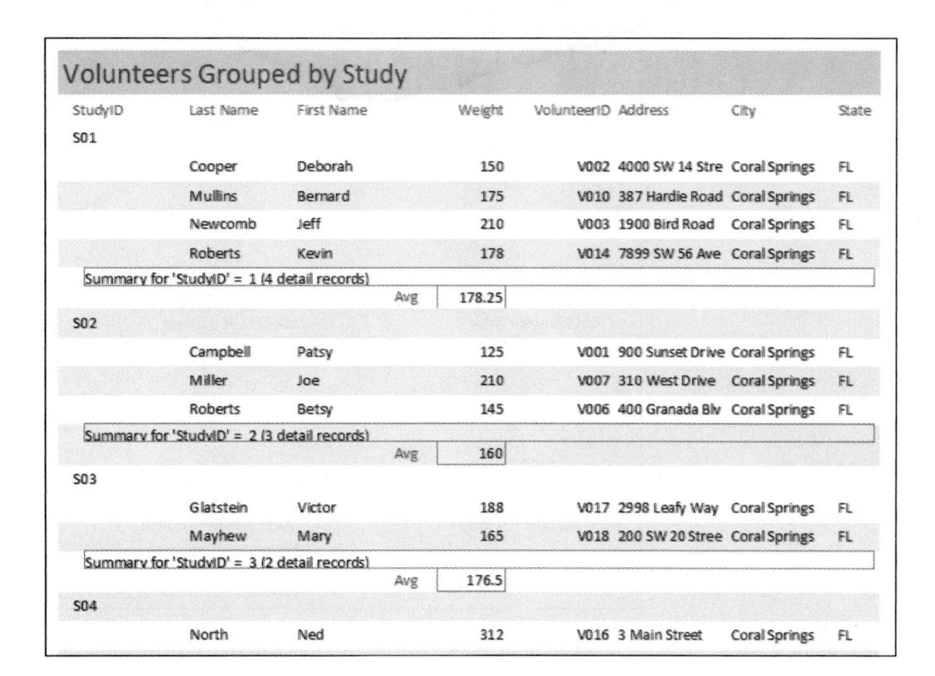

Volunteers Grouped by Study

StudyID	Last Name	First Name	Weight	VolunteerID	Address	City	State
S01							
	Cooper	Deborah	150	V002	4000 SW 14 Stre	Coral Springs	FL
	Mullins	Bernard	175	V010	387 Hardie Road	Coral Springs	FL
	Newcomb	Jeff	210	V003	1900 Bird Road	Coral Springs	FL
	Roberts	Kevin	178	V014	7899 SW 56 Ave	Coral Springs	FL
Summary for 'StudyID' = 1 (4 detail records)							
		Avg	178.25				
S02							
	Campbell	Patsy	125	V001	900 Sunset Drive	Coral Springs	FL
	Miller	Joe	210	V007	310 West Drive	Coral Springs	FL
	Roberts	Betsy	145	V006	400 Granada Blv	Coral Springs	FL
Summary for 'StudyID' = 2 (3 detail records)							
		Avg	160				
S03							
	Glatstein	Victor	188	V017	2998 Leafy Way	Coral Springs	FL
	Mayhew	Mary	165	V018	200 SW 20 Stree	Coral Springs	FL
Summary for 'StudyID' = 3 (2 detail records)							
		Avg	176.5				
S04							
	North	Ned	312	V016	3 Main Street	Coral Springs	FL

FIGURE 34 Volunteers Grouped by Study Report ➤

Use the Label Wizard

The **Label Wizard** enables you to easily create mailing labels, name tags, and other specialized tags.

A **mailing label** is a specialized report that comes preformatted to coordinate with name-brand labels, such as Avery.

The ***Label Wizard*** enables you to easily create mailing labels, name tags, and other specialized tags. A ***mailing label*** is a specialized report that comes preformatted to coordinate with name-brand labels, such as Avery. You then use the Label Wizard to create a label that fits the 5660 template. To begin, click Labels in the Reports group on the Create tab, and then select the manufacturer, the product number, and the label type. Next, choose the font type and size, and then add the fields to the label template, as shown in Figure 35. The Physicians Labels report is shown in Figure 36.

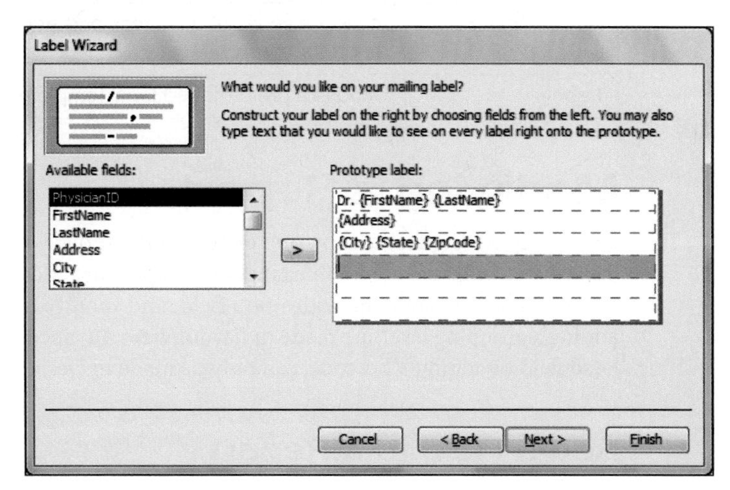

FIGURE 35 Create a Mailing Label ➤

Dr. Warren Brasington
9470 SW 25 Street
Coral Springs fl 33071

Dr. Patsy Clark
200 Harding Blvd
Coral Springs fl 33070

Dr. Bonnie Clinton
10000 SW 59 Court
Coral Springs FL 33071

Dr. Holly Davis
8009 Riviera Drive
Coral Springs FL 33072

Dr. Steven Fisher
444 SW 190 Street
Coral Springs fl 33070

Dr. Jeffrey Jacobsen
490 Bell Drive
Coral Springs fl 33070

Dr. Keith Mast
102 SCC
E. Norriton PA 19401

Dr. Kristine Park
9290 NW 59 Steet
Coral Springs fl 33072

Dr. Michelle Quintana
3990 NW 3 Street
Coral Springs fl 33071

FIGURE 36 Physicians Label Report ➤

Table 1 provides a summary of the five report tools and their usage.

TABLE 1 Report Tools and Their Usage

Report Tool	Usage
Report	Create a tabular report showing all of the fields in the record source.
Report Design	Create a new blank report in Design view. Add fields and controls manually.
Blank Report	Create a new blank report in Layout view. Add fields and controls manually.
Report Wizard	Answer a series of questions and Access will design a custom report for you.
Labels	Choose a preformatted label template and create a sheet of labels.

Modifying a Report

After a report is generated by one of the report tools, you will usually need to modify it. Similar to forms, the common changes to a report are add a field, remove a field, change the order of fields, change the width of a field, and modify the title. These changes, as well as adding a grouping level, are made in Layout view. Advanced changes, such as adding a calculated field or adding VBA code, can only be made in Design view.

Add a Field to a Report

Adding a field to a report with a tabular layout is similar to adding a field to a form with a tabular layout. Right-click a report in the Navigation Pane, and then click Layout view. Next, click Add Existing Fields in the Tools group on the Design tab to reveal the available fields in the report's record source. Drag the new field to a precise location on the report, using the vertical orange line as a guide for the position of the new field, and release the mouse. The other fields will automatically adjust to make room for the new field.

The process of adding a field to a report with a stacked layout is the same as a tabular layout. The only difference is the orange line will appear horizontally.

Delete a Field from a Report

To delete a field from the *Detail* section of a tabular report, first switch to the Layout view or Design view of the report. Next, click the text box of the field to be deleted and note the orange border around the field. With the orange border visible, press Delete. Repeat the process to delete the associated label from the Page Header. After the controls are deleted, click in the blank space, and then press Delete again. After the text box and label are removed from the report, the other fields automatically adjust to close the gap around the deleted field.

Work with a Report Layout Control

Whenever you use one of the report tools to create a new report, Access will add a layout control to help align the fields. Layout controls in reports work the same as layout controls in forms. As discussed earlier in this chapter, the layout control provides guides to help keep controls aligned horizontally and vertically, and give your report a uniform appearance.

There are times when you may want to remove the layout control from a report in order to position the fields without aligning them to each other. If you want to remove the layout control from a report, switch to Design view, and then click anywhere inside the control you want to remove. On the Arrange tab, click Select Layout in the Rows & Columns group. Click Remove Layout in the Table group and the layout control is gone. All of the other controls are still on the report, but the rectangle binding them together is gone.

You can add a layout control to a report by first selecting all the controls you want to keep together. Then, click Stacked or Tabular in the Table group and the layout control appears.

Adjust Column Widths in a Report

You can adjust the width of each column in a tabular report individually so that each column is wide enough to accommodate the widest value. For example, if a report contains first name, last name, address and city, and e-mail address, you will need to make sure the longest value in each field is completely visible. Scroll through the records to make sure this is the case.

To modify column widths in a tabular report, first switch to the Layout view or Design view of the report. Click the text box of the field you want to adjust. The field will have an orange border around it, indicating it is selected. Move the mouse to the right border of the selected field; when the mouse pointer turns to a double arrow, drag the edge to the right (to increase) or the left (to decrease) until you arrive at the desired width.

Add a Theme to the Report

You can enhance the report's appearance by applying one of the themes provided by Access. To apply a theme, switch to Layout view, and then click Themes in the Themes group on the Design tab. Scroll through the themes until you find a theme you like; hover over one of the options to see a quick preview of the current report using the current theme. Right-click a theme, and then choose Apply Theme to This Object Only (as shown in Figure 37). You can also apply the theme to all matching objects.

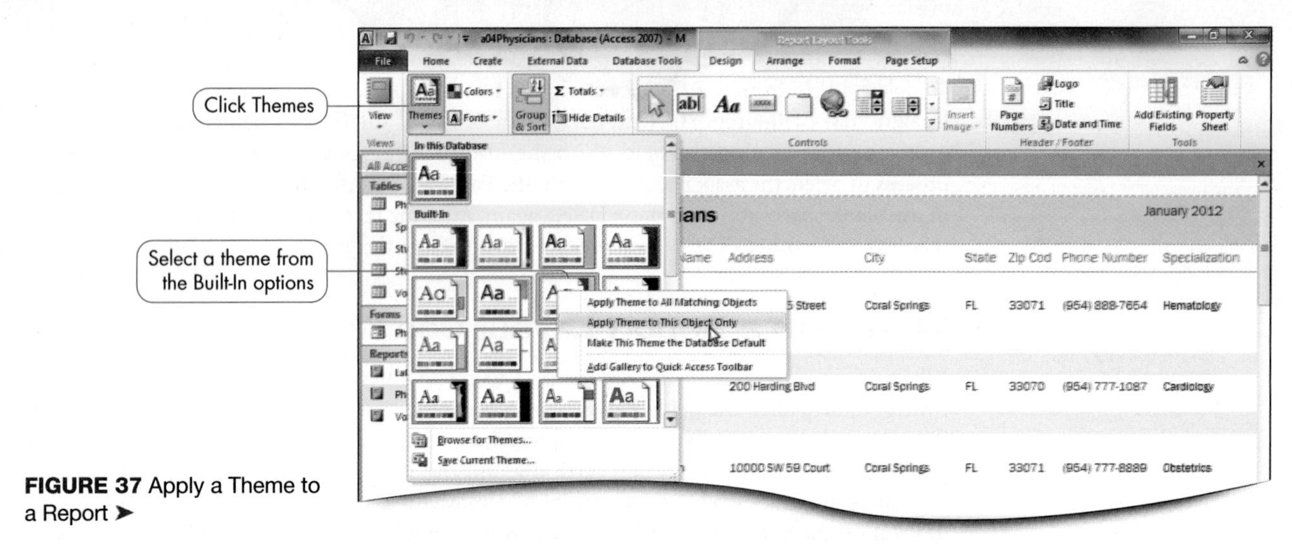

FIGURE 37 Apply a Theme to a Report ➤

Sorting Records in a Report

When a report is created using the Report tool, the sort order of the records in the report is initially dependent on the sort order of the record source—similar to the way records are sorted in a form. The primary key of the record source usually dictates the sort order. However, a report has an additional feature for sorting. While in Layout view or Design view, click Group & Sort in the Grouping & Totals group on the Design tab. The Group, Sort, and Total pane now appears at the bottom of the report. This section enables you to set the sort order for the report and override the sorting in the report's record source.

Change the Sorting in a Report

While working in the Layout view of a report, click Group & Sort to display the *Group, Sort, and Total* section, as shown in Figure 38. To sort the records in a report by last name, click Add a sort and select LastName from the list. The report records will instantly sort by LastName in ascending order. Next, you can set a second sort by clicking Add a Sort again. For example, you could add the FirstName sort after the LastName sort, as shown in Figure 38.

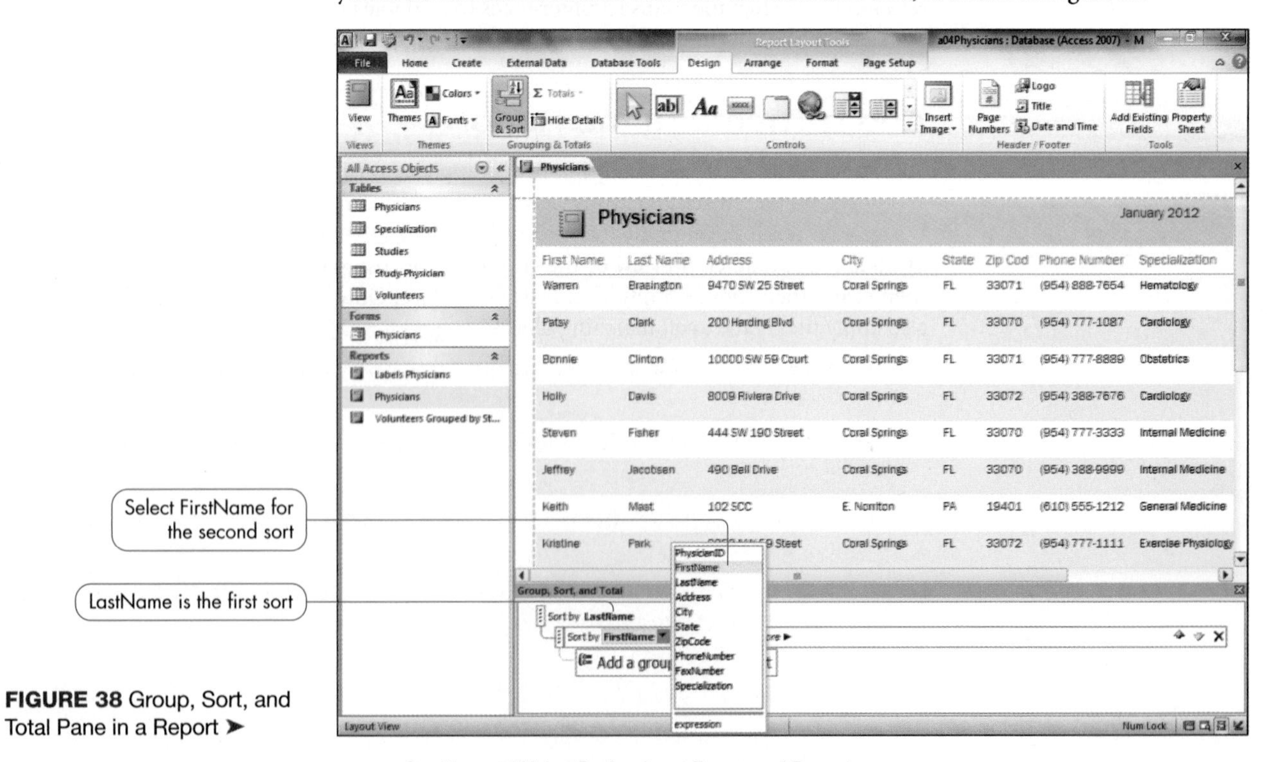

FIGURE 38 Group, Sort, and Total Pane in a Report ➤

HANDS-ON EXERCISES

3 Report Basics

You create a Products report using the Access Report tool to help Alex stay on top of the key data for his business. After Access creates the report, you modify the column widths so the entire report fits on one page (portrait or landscape, depending on the report). You also use the Report Wizard tool to create other reports for Alex.

Skills covered: Use the Report Tool • Add a Field to a Report • Delete a Field from a Report and Adjust Column Widths in a Report • Apply a Theme to the Report • Change the Sorting in a Report • Use the Report Wizard

STEP 1 USE THE REPORT TOOL

You use the Report tool to create an Access report to help Alex manage his product information. This report is especially useful for determining which products he needs to order to fill upcoming orders. Refer to Figure 39 as you complete Step 1.

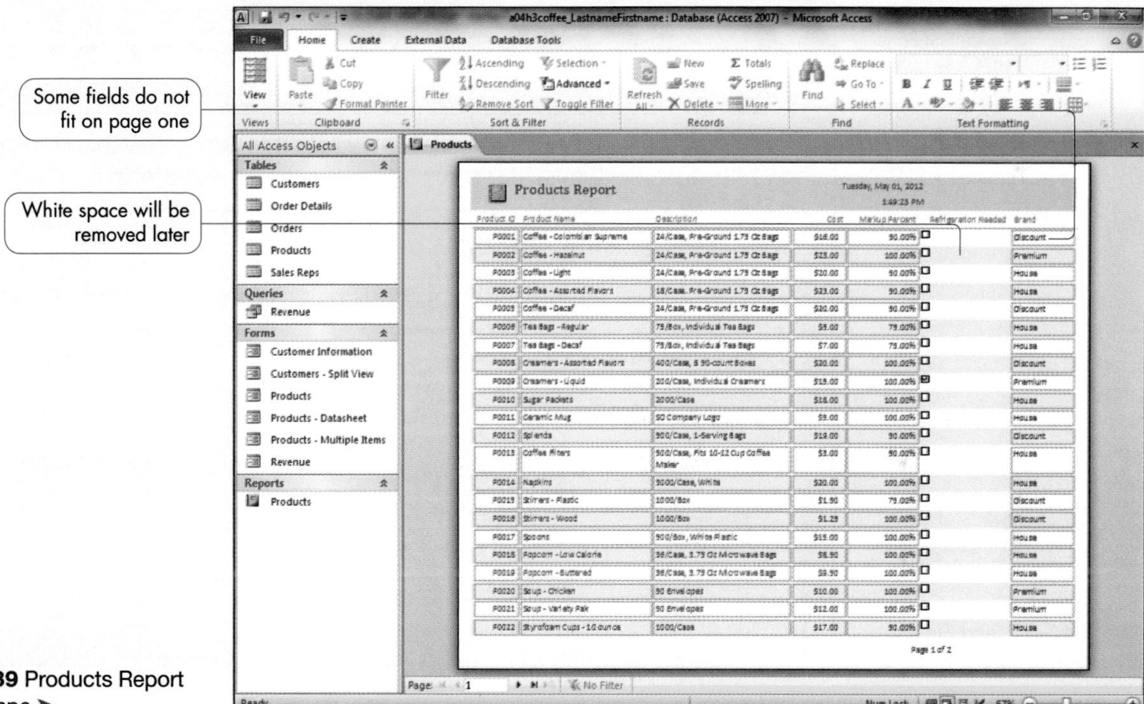

FIGURE 39 Products Report in Landscape ➤

a. Open *a04h2coffee_LastnameFirstname* if you closed it at the end of Hands-On Exercise 2. Click the **File tab**, click **Save Database As**, and then type **a04h3coffee_LastnameFirstname**, changing *h2* to *h3*. Click **Save**.

b. Select the **Products table** in the Navigation Pane. Click the **Create tab**, and then click **Report** in the Reports group.

   Access creates a new tabular layout report based on the Products table. The report opens in Layout view ready to edit.

c. Click the **Products title** at the top of the report to select it, and then click again on **Products** and change the title to **Products Report**.

d. Display the report in Print Preview.

   The report is too wide for the page; you will change the orientation to Landscape.

e. Click **Close Print Preview**.

f. Click the **Page Setup tab**, and then click **Landscape** in the Page Layout group.

   The report changes to Landscape orientation. Most of the columns now fit onto one page. You will make further revisions to the report later on so that it fits on one page.

g. Display the report in Print Preview.

h. Close and save the report as **Products**.

STEP 2 ADD A FIELD TO A REPORT

The Products report you created for Santiago Coffee looks very good (according to Alex). However, Alex asks you to add a new field to the Products table and incorporate that into the Products report. Refer to Figure 40 as you complete Step 2.

FIGURE 40 OnHand Field Added to the Report ➤

a. Open the Products table, and then click **View** in the Views group to switch to Design view.

   You need to add the OnHand field to the Products table.

b. Click the **MarkupPercent field**, and then click **Insert Rows** in the Tools group.

   A new blank row appears above the MarkupPercent field.

c. Type **OnHand** in the **Field Name box**, and then select **Number** as the Data Type. In the Field Properties at the bottom, change the Field Size to **Integer**.

d. Save the table. Click **View** to change to Datasheet view.

   The new OnHand column appears empty in each row. Next you will add sample data to the new field.

e. Type the following OnHand values starting at the top and continuing through the last row: **10, 10, 10, 10, 10, 10, 10, 25, 25, 55, 40, 55, 125, 75, 200, 200, 200, 75, 75, 42, 42, 175, 175, 22, 37.**

f. Close the Products table.

g. Open the Products report in Layout view.

h. Click the **Open/Close button** on the Navigation Pane to collapse the Navigation Pane so more of the report is visible. Close the Property sheet, if necessary.

i. Click **Add Existing Fields** in the Tools group on the Design tab. Drag the **OnHand field** from the Field List pane onto the Products report between the Cost and MarkupPercent fields. Close the Field List pane.

   Because of the tabular layout control, Access adjusts all the columns to make room for the new OnHand field.

j. Insert a space in the OnHand label control in the Report Header so that it reads *On Hand.*

   A space was added to make the heading more readable.

k. Display the report in Print Preview.

   The report is still too wide for a single page. Next, you will modify the column widths.

l. Save the report.

STEP 3 DELETE A FIELD FROM A REPORT AND ADJUST COLUMN WIDTHS IN A REPORT

The Products report now contains the new OnHand value that Alex requested, but the report is too wide to print on one page. In this step, you delete unnecessary fields and read just the remaining column widths. Refer to Figure 41 as you complete Step 3.

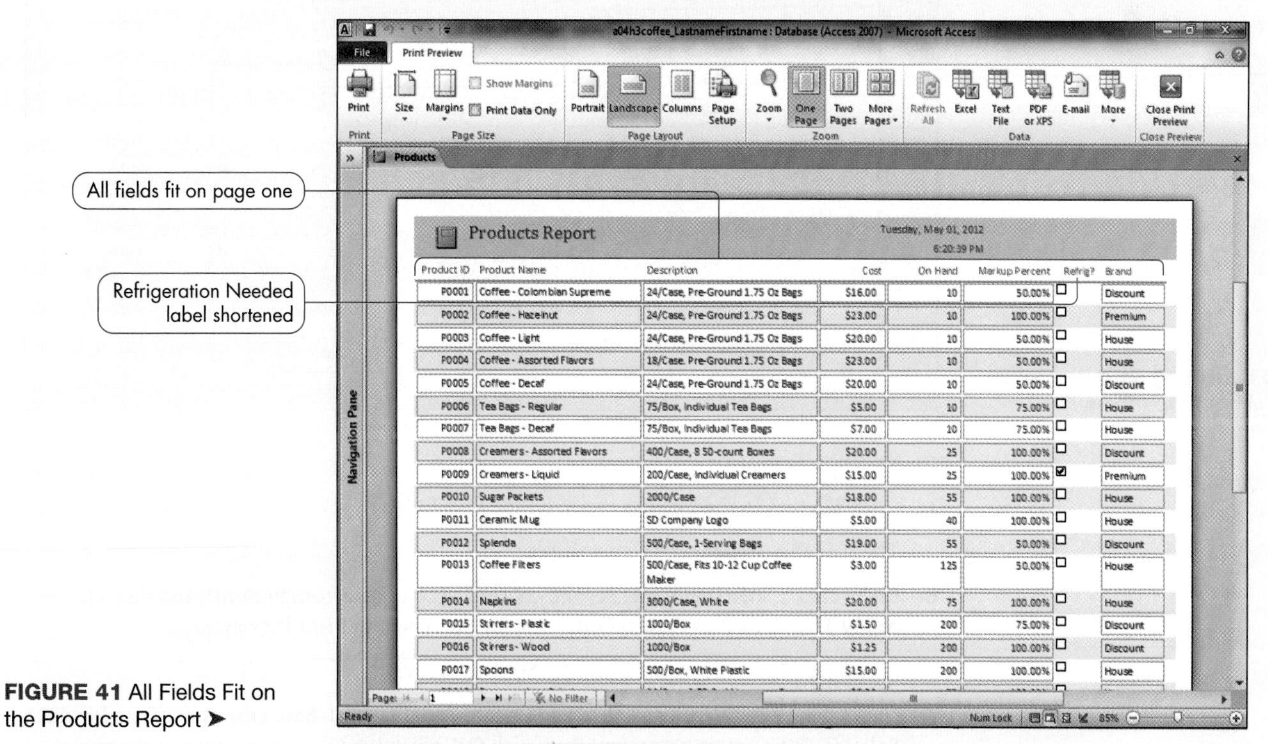

FIGURE 41 All Fields Fit on the Products Report ➤

a. Click **Close Print Preview.**

b. Scroll to the right, right-click anywhere on the **Year Introduced column**, and then click **Select Entire Column** from the shortcut menu. Press **Delete** to remove the column.

   The Year Introduced column is removed from the report.

c. Click the **ProductID column heading**, and then drag the right border to the left until the Product ID heading still fits, but any extra white space is removed.

d. Click the **Refrigeration Needed column heading**, and then rename the column **Refrig?**. Adjust the column width of the Refrig? column.

e. Adjust the width of the remaining columns until all fields fit on one page.

f. Display the report in Print Preview.

   This report now fits nicely onto one landscape page.

g. Click **Close Print Preview**, and then save the report.

STEP 4 APPLY A THEME TO THE REPORT

The Products report now contains the new OnHand value and the report fits nicely onto one landscape page. You create two color schemes for Alex and ask him to select one of them. Refer to Figure 42 as you complete Step 4.

Product ID	Product Name	Description	Cost	On Hand	Markup Percent	Refrig?
P0001	Coffee - Colombian Supreme	24/Case, Pre-Ground 1.75 Oz Bags	$16.00	10	50.00%	☐
P0002	Coffee - Hazelnut	24/Case, Pre-Ground 1.75 Oz Bags	$23.00	10	100.00%	☐
P0003	Coffee - Light	24/Case, Pre-Ground 1.75 Oz Bags	$20.00	10	50.00%	☐
P0004	Coffee - Assorted Flavors	18/Case. Pre-Ground 1.75 Oz Bags	$23.00	10	50.00%	☐
P0005	Coffee - Decaf	24/Case, Pre-Ground 1.75 Oz Bags	$20.00	10	50.00%	☐
P0006	Tea Bags - Regular	75/Box, Individual Tea Bags	$5.00	10	75.00%	☐
P0007	Tea Bags - Decaf	75/Box, Individual Tea Bags	$7.00	10	75.00%	☐
P0008	Creamers - Assorted Flavors	400/Case, 8 50-count Boxes	$20.00	25	100.00%	☐
P0009	Creamers - Liquid	200/Case, Individual Creamers	$15.00	25	100.00%	☑
P0010	Sugar Packets	2000/Case	$18.00	55	100.00%	☐
P0011	Ceramic Mug	SD Company Logo	$5.00	40	100.00%	☐
P0012	Splenda	500/Case, 1-Serving Bags	$19.00	55	50.00%	☐
P0013	Coffee Filters	500/Case, Fits 10-12 Cup Coffee Maker	$3.00	125	50.00%	☐
P0014	Napkins	3000/Case, White	$20.00	75	100.00%	☐

FIGURE 42 Products Report with Solstice Theme ➤

a. Switch to Layout view, if necessary.

b. Click **Themes** in the Themes group on the Design tab.

   The available predefined themes display.

c. Right-click a **Solstice theme** (second column, second row from bottom), and then choose **Apply Theme to This Object Only**. Display the report in Print Preview.

   Access reformats the report using the Solstice theme.

d. Click **Close Print Preview**. Click the **File tab**, and then click **Save Object As**. Type **Products Solstice** as the report name, and then click **OK**. Click the **File tab** to return to the report.

   You saved the report with one theme. Now, you will apply a second theme to the report and save it with a different name.

e. Switch to Layout view, and then click **Themes** in the Themes group to apply a different theme.

f. Right-click a **Module theme** (first column, seventh row), and then choose **Apply Theme to This Object Only**. Display the report in Print Preview.

   Compare the Solstice theme to the Module theme.

g. Click **Close Print Preview.** Click the **File tab**, and then click **Save Object As.** Type **Products Module** as the report name, and then click **OK.** Click the **File tab** to return to the report.

STEP 5 CHANGE THE SORTING IN A REPORT

Alex would like the Products Module report to be sorted by Product Name order (rather than ProductID order). You change the sort order and preview again to see the results. Refer to Figure 43 as you complete Step 5.

FIGURE 43 Products Report Sorted by Product Name ➤

a. Verify the Products Module report is in Layout view.

b. Click **Group & Sort** in the Grouping & Totals group.

   The Add a group and Add a sort options appear at the bottom of the report.

c. Click **Add a sort.**

   A new Sort bar appears at the bottom of the report.

d. Select **ProductName** from the list.

   The report is now sorted by ProductName.

e. Display the report in Print Preview.

f. Close Print Preview, and then save and close the report.

STEP 6 USE THE REPORT WIZARD

You decide to create the Sales by City report for Santiago Coffee. After discussing the report parameters with Alex, you decide to use the Report Wizard. Refer to Figure 44 as you complete Step 6.

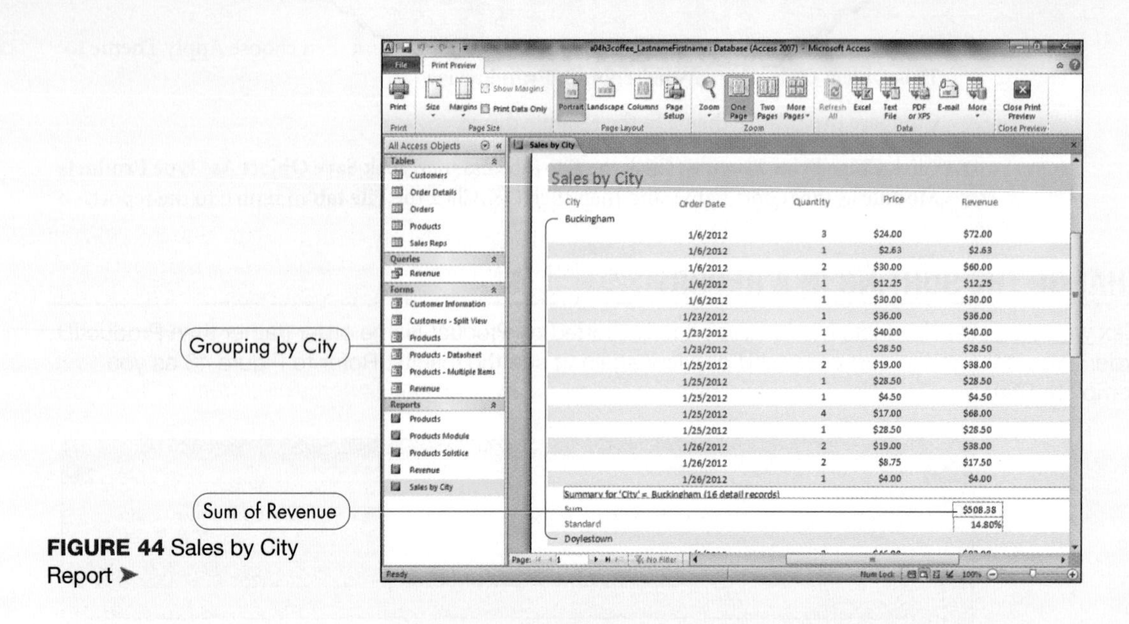

FIGURE 44 Sales by City Report ➤

a. Open the Navigation Pane, and then select the **Revenue query** in the Navigation Pane. Click the **Create tab**, and then click **Report Wizard** in the Reports group.

   The Report Wizard launches.

b. Click the >> **button** to add all the fields to the selected Fields box. Click **Cost**, and then click the < **button** to remove the Cost field. Also remove the MarkupPercent, Lastname, and ProductName fields. Click **Next**.

c. Select **City**, and then click the > **button** to add grouping by city. Click **Next**.

d. Select **OrderDate** for the sort order. Click **Summary Options**.

e. Click **Sum** to summarize the Revenue field. Click the **Calculate percent of total for sums check box** to show the relationship between each group and the whole. Click **OK**.

f. Click **Next**. Click **Next** again to accept the default layout.

g. Type **Sales by City** for the title of the report. Click **Finish**.

   The report is displayed in Print Preview mode. Some of the data values and labels cannot be seen. Next, you will adjust the controls.

h. Click **Close Print Preview**. In Layout view, adjust the controls so all the field values are visible, as shown in Figure 44. Widen the totals controls under the Revenue column. Click in the **Revenue total field**, open the Property Sheet, and then select the **Currency format**.

i. Display the report in Print Preview to verify your changes.

j. Close and save the report.

k. Click the **File tab**, and then click **Compact & Repair Database**.

l. Keep the database onscreen if you plan to continue with Hands-On Exercise 4. If not, close the database and exit Access.

Report Sections, Views, and Controls

You just created and modified reports in the previous section. In this section, you will learn about the various views you accessed while creating and modifying the reports. As you work with the report tools to create and modify reports, you will find the need to frequently switch between the four report views in Access—Layout view, Print Preview, Design view, and Report view. Most of your design work will be done in Layout view, but occasionally, you will need to switch to Design view to apply a more advanced feature, such as a calculated field. Users of the report will use Print Preview, Print, and occasionally Layout view. There should be no reason for a user to switch to Layout view or Design view. Modifications to the report should be done by the designated report designer.

To switch between the four views, click the View arrow in the Views group and select the desired view. Layout view and Print Preview are the most common views; Report view is useful for filtering a report based on a field value. You can also switch between views by right-clicking on the report tab or by right-clicking a report in the Navigation Pane. You can also click one of the small view icons in the bottom right of the Access window.

Even though reports have more default sections than forms, working with report sections will be similar to working with form sections.

In this section, you will learn how to identify report sections. You learned about the form sections earlier in this chapter; you can apply that knowledge as you learn about the report sections. Even though reports have more default sections than forms, working with report sections will be similar to working with form sections.

Controls are also covered in this section. Again, the overlap between forms and reports will become evident (and be helpful).

Identifying Report Sections

Access reports are divided into five main sections that can be viewed when you display a report in Design view. You need to become familiar with each section so you can manipulate reports to meet your needs.

Identify the Default Report Sections

In the forms section, you learned that Access divides forms into three main sections. For reports, Access creates five main sections—*Report Header, Page Header, Detail, Page Footer,* and *Report Footer* as shown in Figure 45. When in Design view, you can collapse or expand each section as needed, and delete any header or footer section.

The **Report Header section** prints once at the beginning of each report.

The ***Report Header section*** prints at the beginning of each report. This section will usually contain the report title, a logo or other graphic, and the date and time when the report was printed. You can remove this section by right-clicking on a section bar, and then clicking the Report Header/Footer option. Follow the same process to add the Report Header/Footer to a report. When you remove the Report Header, the Report Footer is also removed automatically.

The **Page Header section** appears once at the top of each page.

The ***Page Header section*** appears at the top of each page. Use this section to add or edit column headings on the top of each page. The Page Header will usually contain a horizontal line to separate the column headings from the data values. You can remove this section by right-clicking on a section bar, and then clicking the Page Header/Footer option. Follow the same process to add the Report Header/Footer to a report. If you remove the Page Header, the Page Footer is also removed automatically.

The *Detail* section prints one line for each record in the report's record source. Fields that are connected to the report's record source are known as *bound controls.* The *Detail* section can be hidden, if necessary, by clicking Hide Details in the Grouping & Totals group on the Design tab. For reports that only require summarized data, you will want to hide the details. Access makes it easy for you to show or hide detail levels. Click Hide Details again to redisplay hidden details.

Although the *Detail* section cannot be removed from a report, you can hide it from Print Preview, Layout view, and Design view to show only the headers and footers. This is relevant when the output only requires the totals of each category and not the details that make up the category.

The **Page Footer section** appears once at the bottom of each page.

The ***Page Footer section*** appears at the bottom of each page. Use this section to show page numbers at the bottom of each page. Totals should not be added to this section since the results will produce an error. You can remove this section by right-clicking on a section bar, and then clicking the Page Header/Footer option. Follow the same process to add the Report Header/Footer to a report. If you remove the Page Footer, the Page Header is also removed automatically.

The **Report Footer section** prints once at the bottom of the report.

The ***Report Footer section*** prints one time at the bottom of the report. The Report Footer is commonly used for displaying the grand total of certain columns. You can also display the count of all records in the *Report Footer* section. You can remove this section by right-clicking on a section bar, and then clicking the Report Header/Footer option. Follow the same process to add the Report Header/Footer to a report. If you remove the Report Footer, the Report Header is also removed automatically.

In Figure 45, each gray section bar marks the top boundary of a report section. The top bar denotes the top boundary of the Report Header. The bottom bar displays the top boundary of the Report Footer. The grid-like area under the bars shows the space allotted to that section. Notice that the report has no space allocated to the Report Footer. If you decide that the allotted space for a particular section is not needed, you can collapse that section fully so that the section bars are touching. The section remains in the report's design but will not be visible on the Print Preview or the printed page.

Similar to form sections, you can expand or collapse the space between report sections by moving your mouse over the section bar. When the mouse pointer shape changes to a double-headed arrow, drag to expand or collapse the section. A grid-like area appears as your mouse drags down. If you expand or collapse the space allotment for one section, the other sections may also be affected.

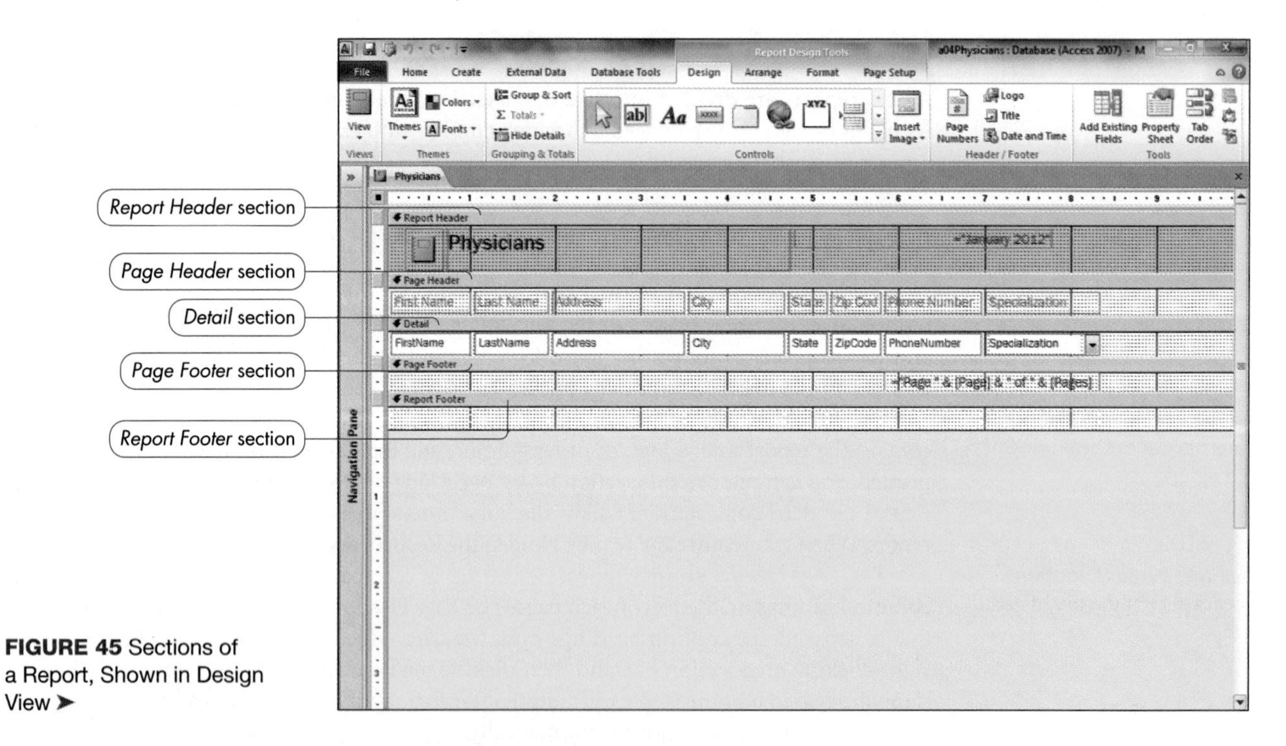

FIGURE 45 Sections of a Report, Shown in Design View ➤

Add a Group Header/Footer

In addition to the five main sections listed above, you can also add a custom *group header/footer* section to a report. For example, if you use the Report tool to create a report based on the Physicians table (as shown in Figure 46), you may want this report to be grouped by Specialization. It will be easier for users to locate a physician within a given specialization. Otherwise, you would have to search through the entire list to locate a doctor within a certain specialization.

To add a custom group to a report, open the report in Layout view, and then click Group & Sort in the Grouping & Totals group on the Design tab. The Group, Sort, and Total pane appears below the report. This section enables you to add a custom group. Click Add a Group, and then select the field that you want to group by. For a field to be a candidate for grouping, field values must repeat in the *Detail* section. For example, since specialization repeats in the *Detail* section, it could be used for grouping.

A **Group Header section**, when activated, will appear just above the *Detail* section in Design view, with the name of the field you are grouping.

Once you establish the custom group, a ***Group Header section*** will appear just above the *Detail* section in Design view, along with the name of the field you are grouping. If you select the Specialization field as a custom group, the section will be named *Specialization Header*, as shown in Figure 46. Click Print Preview in the Views group to view the data in the report; each time the grouping field value changes, the group header will print with the new value. For example, in a physicians report with five specializations, grouped by Specialization, the group header will print five times, once for each specialization, with the physicians printed under each specialization.

The **Group Footer section**, when activated, will appear just below the *Detail* section in Design view, but only when you select this option in the Group, Sort, and Total pane.

A ***Group Footer section*** appears just below the *Detail* section in Design view, but only when you select this option in the Group, Sort, and Total pane. Locate the group header in question, and then click the More option on that group header bar; then click the *without a footer* arrow and select the *with a footer* option. The group footer is useful for totaling the data at the end of each group. If a group of physicians is part of a major practice, it would be good to know how many physicians are assigned to each specialization. The group footer could display the count of physicians for each specialization.

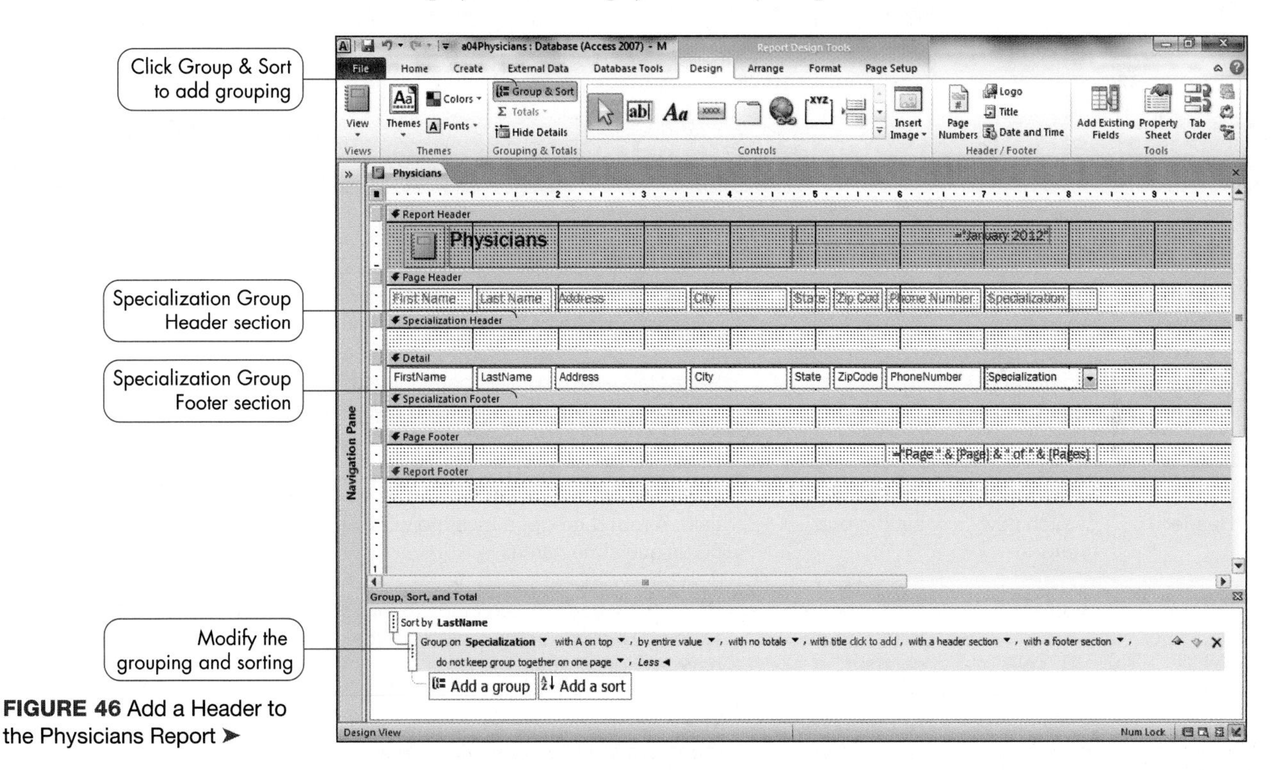

FIGURE 46 Add a Header to the Physicians Report ➤

Add Totals to a Group Footer/Report Footer

Often, reports require totals at the group level and/or at the grand total level. For example, the Physicians Report might contain a count of physicians in each Specialization group, and again at the end of the report. Figure 47 shows a report with a total number of customers for each sales rep and the total number of customers at the end of the report.

To add totals to a report, first create the group section required for the totals. For example, add the Sales Rep group to a Customers report. Next, in Layout view, click the field that contains the data you want to total, click Totals in the Grouping & Totals group on the

Design tab, and then select the appropriate option. Access will add a total after each group and again at the end of the report.

You remove a total from a report in the same way you add a total. First, select the field that contains the total, click Totals in the Grouping & Totals group, and then uncheck the option you want to remove.

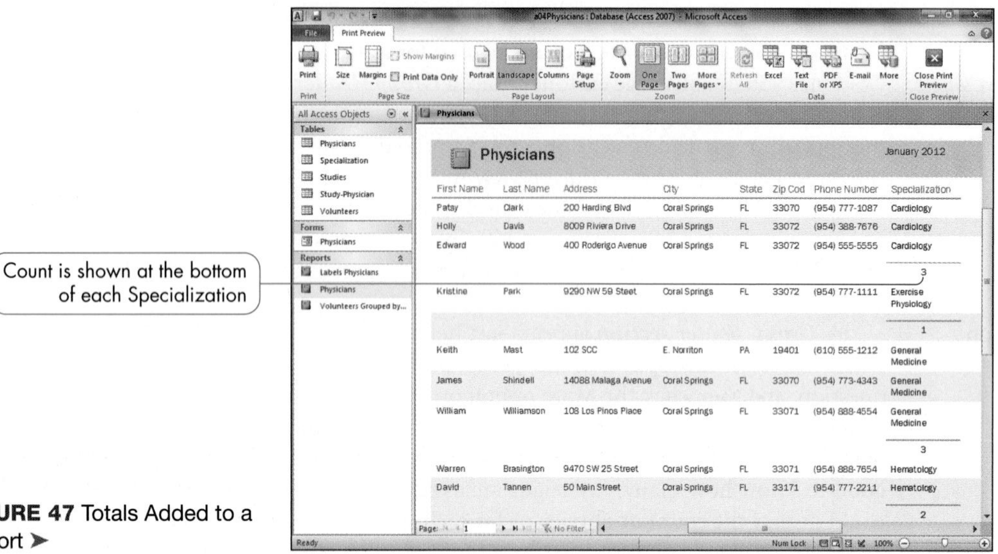
Count is shown at the bottom of each Specialization
Physicians
January 2012

FIGURE 47 Totals Added to a Report ➤

See the reference table below for a summary of each report section.

REFERENCE Report Sections

Section	Location	Frequency	Usage	Default
Report Header	Top of the report	Once	Holds the report title, the organization's name, the company logo, and the run date & time.	On
Page Header	Top of each page	Once per page	Page Headers generally contain the column headings. In a multi-page report, the labels repeat at the top of each page to provide continuity.	On
Group Header	At the start of each new group	At the start of each group	Prints the value of each unique instance for a grouped field. A report grouped by state would print up to 50 unique state names.	Off
Detail	Middle	Once per record in the record source	Repeats for each record in the record source. If there were 500 records in the record source, the report would have 500 detail lines.	On
Group Footer	At the end of each group	At the end of each group	This section generally mirrors the group header. For a report grouped by state, group footer could be used to show a count of the records in each state.	Off
Page Footer	Bottom of each page	Once per page	The Page Footer is generally used to print page numbers on the report.	On
Report Footer	End of the report	Once	Use the Report Footer to print grand totals or other aggregate information for the records.	On

TIP Report Footer Confusion

In Design view, the *Report Footer* section is located below the *Page Footer* section. However, in Print Preview, the Report Footer is positioned above the Page Footer. This may cause some confusion at first; however, the *Report Footer* section will be needed to produce grand totals at the end of a report.

Revising Reports Using Report Views

Access provides different views for a report similar to the different views in tables, queries, and forms. Tables and queries have Design view and Datasheet view. Forms have Layout view, Form view, and Design view. Reports have Layout view, Print Preview, Design view, and Report view. To switch between certain views, click View in the Views group, or click the View arrow, and then select a view from the list. Each view is described in the sections below.

Layout View

Use Layout view to alter the report design while still viewing the data. You should use Layout view to add or delete fields in the report, modify field properties, change the column widths, add grouping and sorting levels to a report, and to filter data by excluding certain records. Although Layout view appears similar to Print Preview, you will find sufficient variations between the two views, so that you will always need to verify the report in Print Preview to evaluate all the changes made in Layout view.

Print Preview

Print Preview enables you to see exactly what the report will look like when it is printed.

Print Preview enables you to see exactly what the report will look like when it is printed. Most users prefer to use Print Preview prior to printing the report. This enables you to intercept errors in reports before you send the report to the printer. You cannot modify the design in this view; switch to Layout view or Design view to modify the design. By default, Print Preview will display all the pages in the report. Figure 47 shows an Access report in Print Preview.

Design View

Design view displays the report's design without displaying the data. You can perform many of the same tasks in Design view as you can in Layout view—add and delete fields, add and remove sorting and grouping layers, rearrange columns, adjust column widths, and modify report elements. When a report is very long, Design view is useful because you can alter the design without needing to scroll through pages of data. However, after you make a change in Design view, it is best to switch to Layout view or Print Preview to examine the final output. You need to experiment using both the Layout view and Design view to decide which view you prefer. As with forms, some changes to reports can only be done in Design view. Figure 46 displays the Physicians report in Design view.

Report View

Report view enables you to see what the printed report will look like in a continuous page layout.

Report view enables you to see what a printed report will look like in a continuous page layout. Because Report view is similar to Layout view, but not used as frequently, this view will not be discussed further in this chapter.

TIP Always Preview Access Reports Before Printing

Because databases contain a great deal of information, Access reports may become very long, requiring many pages to print. Experienced Access users always use Print Preview prior to printing their reports. Some reports may require hundreds of pages to print—better to know that before sending it to the printer. Other reports may be formatted incorrectly and a blank page may print after each actual page. It would be better to correct this problem prior to sending it to the printer.

Identifying Control Types in Reports

If you examine the fields in a report, such as the one in Figure 47, you will notice that each field has a label (heading) at the top with a column of data values under the heading. As you learned in the forms section earlier in this chapter, a text box displays the data found in the record source and a label is a literal word or phrase to describe the data. The heading in Figure 47 is a label, and the data values are displayed using a text box.

The label and text box controls are among the many types of controls found on the Controls group on the Design tab when you are in the Design view of a report. As discussed earlier in the forms section, controls can be categorized as bound, unbound, or calculated.

Report Column Headings

The column headings in reports are based on the captions used in the source table or query. If captions do not exist in the source table or query, you may need to edit the label controls that represent the column headings. For example, the Products table contains the MarkupPercent field, which includes the caption Markup Percent. Markup Percent becomes the column heading in the Products report. If the caption was not used in the Products table, then you would have to add a space between Markup and Percent in the column label.

Work with Controls

Bound controls are text boxes that are connected to a field in a table or a query. These controls display different data for each new record that is printed. To add a bound control to a report, switch to Layout view, and then drag a field from the Field List pane onto the report.

Unbound controls are labels and other decorative design elements. These controls usually describe and decorate the data rather than display the data. These controls remain the same each time a new record is printed. Unbound controls include labels, lines, borders, and images. Add an unbound control to a report using the Controls group on the Design tab in the Design view of a report.

Calculated controls contain an expression that generates a calculated result when displayed in Print Preview. The expression can contain field names from the report's record source, constants, or functions. Use a text box, found in the Controls group on the Design tab, while in Design view to create a calculated control.

Add a Calculated Control to a Report

To add a calculated control to the report, switch to Design view, and then click Text Box in the Controls group on the Design tab. Place a text box at the desired location, then enter the expression to create the calculation. Format the control as needed.

In Hands-On Exercise 4, you will create a report, add sorting and grouping to refine the content, work with data aggregates, and add a new field to the report.

HANDS-ON EXERCISES

4 Report Sections, Views, and Controls

The reports you created for Alex are working nicely. Alex would like you to modify the layout of the new reports to make them more attractive. You suggest he add grouping to one of the reports.

Skills covered: Identify the Default Report Sections and Add a Group Header/Footer in Layout View • Add Totals to a Group Footer/Report Footer in Layout View • Work with Controls in Design View • Add a Calculated Control to a Report in Design View

STEP 1 IDENTIFY THE DEFAULT REPORT SECTIONS AND ADD A GROUP HEADER/FOOTER IN LAYOUT VIEW

Alex asks you to make several changes to the Monthly Revenue by Salesperson report. First, you update the Sales Rep table with the latest information. Refer to Figure 48 as you complete Step 1.

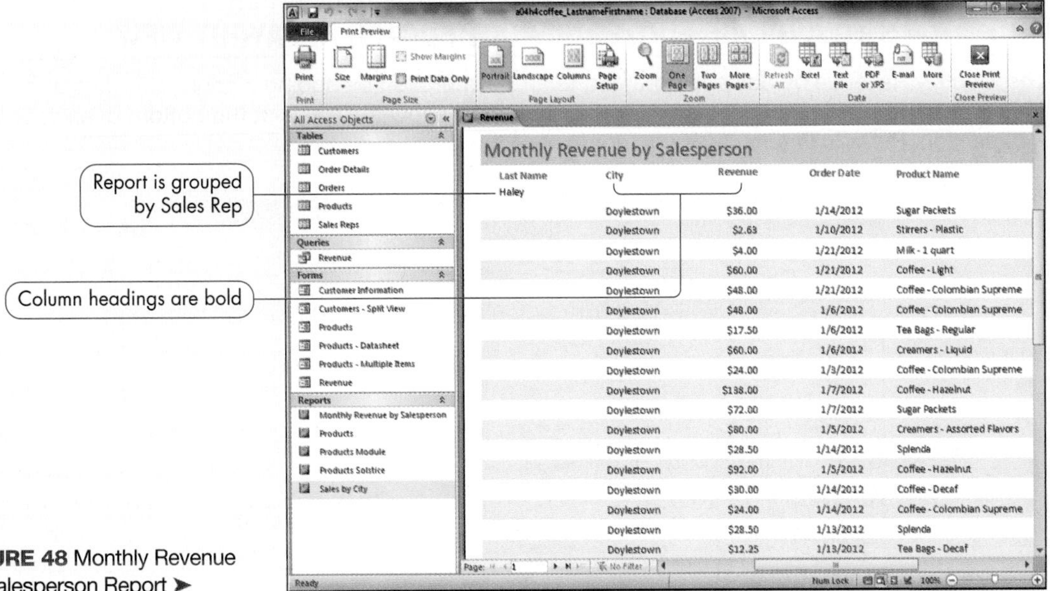

FIGURE 48 Monthly Revenue by Salesperson Report ➤

a. Open *a04h3coffee_LastnameFirstname* if you closed it at the end of Hands-On Exercise 3. Click the **File tab**, click **Save Database As**, and then type **a04h4coffee_LastnameFirstname**, changing *h3* to *h4*. Click **Save**.

b. Open the Sales Reps table. Add your first name and last name to sales rep S0002. Leave the other fields as they are. Close the table.

c. Open the Customers table. For all the customers in the city of Buckingham, change the Sales Rep ID to **003**. The leading *S* appears automatically due to the Format property. Close the table.

d. Select the **Revenue query** in the Navigation Pane, click the **Create tab**, and then click **Report Wizard** in the Reports group.

e. Add the **LastName**, **City**, **Revenue**, **OrderDate**, and **ProductName fields** to the Selected Fields list. Click **Next** four times to accept the default settings. The wizard now asks "What title do you want for your report?" Type **Monthly Revenue by Salesperson**.

   The completed report is displayed in Print Preview.

f. Close Print Preview, and then switch to Layout view.

Next, you will add the Last Name group.

g. Click **Group & Sort** in the Grouping and Sorting group. Click **Add a group**, and then select **LastName.** Close Group & Sort.

The report now contains the LastName group.

h. Select the **Last Name column heading**, and then click **Bold** in the Font group on the Format tab. Apply bold to the rest of the column headings.

i. Select the **Last Name column heading**, and then type **Sales Rep**.

j. Modify the report column widths so the column spacing is uniform (as shown in Figure 48).

k. Switch to Print Preview.

The report is now divided into Sales Rep groups.

l. Click **Close Print Preview**, and then save the report.

STEP 2 ADD TOTALS TO A GROUP FOOTER/REPORT FOOTER IN LAYOUT VIEW

The Monthly Revenue by Salesperson report can be improved by adding a count of orders and a total of the revenue field. You suggest to Alex that the report show the totals at the bottom of each *Sales Rep* section. Refer to Figure 49 as you complete Step 2.

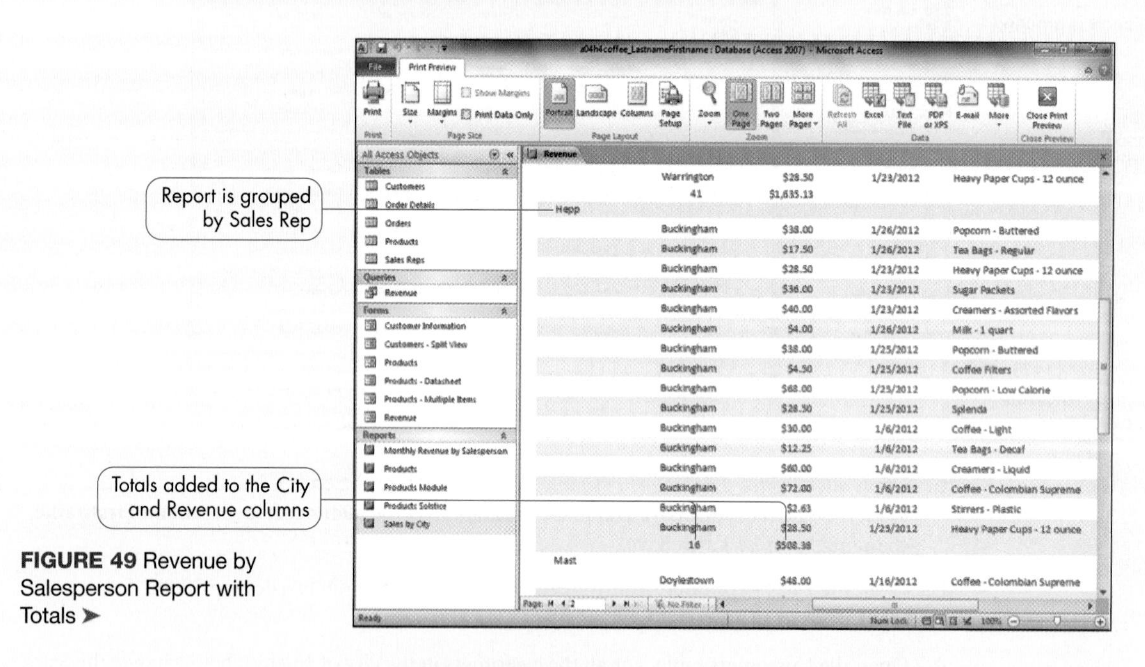

FIGURE 49 Revenue by Salesperson Report with Totals ➤

a. Verify the Monthly Revenue by Salesperson report is open in Layout view. Click the **Revenue field**, click **Totals** in the Grouping & Totals group, and then select **Sum** from the list.

A sum of revenue is now added to the group footer of each Sales Rep group.

b. Click the **View arrow** in the Views group, and then select **Print Preview.**

c. Advance to the next page to view the order count for each Sales Rep.

d. Click **Close Print Preview**, and then click the **City field**. Click **Totals** in the Grouping & Totals group, and then select **Count Records**.

e. Scroll down until the first totals control in the Revenue column is visible. Select the **totals calculated control box**, and then click **Property Sheet** in the Tools group. Click the **Format arrow** on the Format tab, and then choose **Currency** from the list.

   The totals are now formatted for currency.

f. Scroll down to the bottom of the report, and then click the **grand total calculated control box** under the Revenue column. Click the **Format arrow** on the Format tab, and then choose **Currency** from the list. Close the Property Sheet.

   The grand total is now formatted for currency.

g. Display the report in Print Preview. Advance through all the pages.

   The total revenue is now added to the group footer of each Sales Rep group.

h. Click **Close Print Preview**, and then scroll to the bottom of the report.

   The count of orders and the total revenue were automatically added to the Report Footer.

i. Switch to Design View.

   In Design view, you can see the seven sections of the Monthly Revenue by Salesperson report. The data is no longer visible.

j. Save the report.

STEP 3 WORK WITH CONTROLS IN DESIGN VIEW

Alex asks you to add Santiago Coffee Shop at the top of the Monthly Revenue by Salesperson report. You add a new label to the report section and make a few other formatting enhancements. Refer to Figure 50 as you complete Step 3.

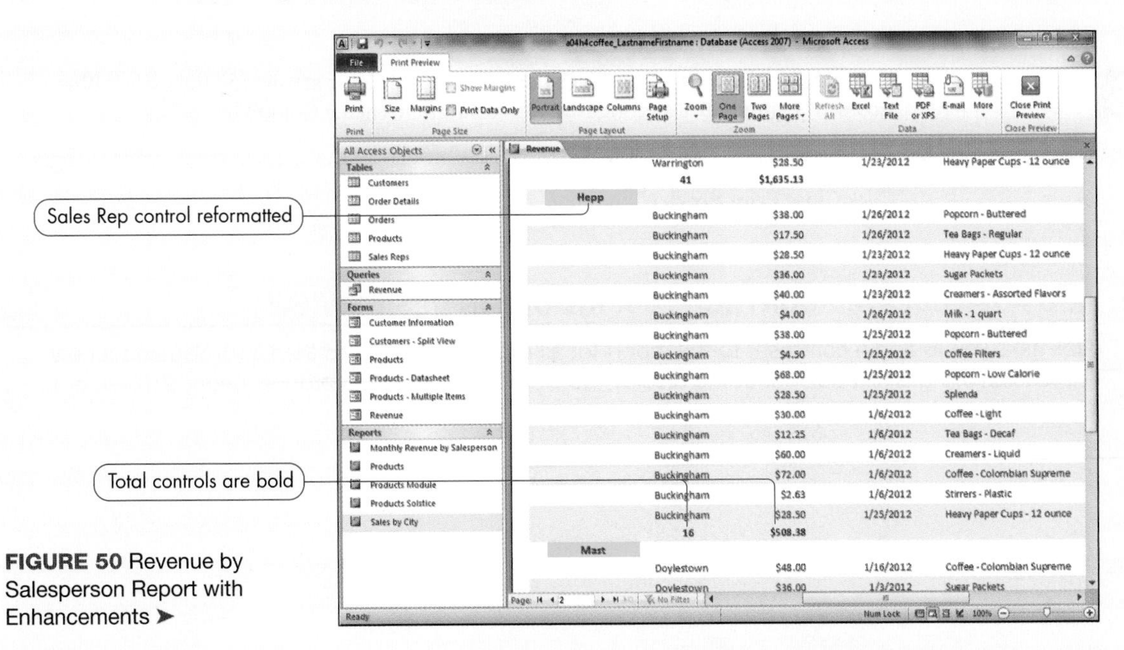

FIGURE 50 Revenue by Salesperson Report with Enhancements ➤

a. Click the **Monthly Revenue by Salesperson label** in the Report Header. Press ↓ to move the label down 1/4" to make room for another label.

When you move the title down using [↓], the *Report Header* section grows automatically.

b. Click **Label** in the Controls group on the Design tab, and then click just above the *M* in the Monthly Revenue title.

   The label control is ready for you to type a phrase.

c. Type **Santiago Coffee Shop** into the new label, and then press **Enter**.

   An orange border indicates the label control is still selected.

d. Click the **Format tab**, and then use the **Font group commands** to modify the new label:

   Font Size: **14**
   Font Color: **Dark Blue, Text 2, Darker 25%** (fifth row, fourth column)
   Style: **Italic**

e. Resize the new label using the bottom-right corner of the control box. Widen the box so the entire phrase is visible.

f. Click the **LastName text box** in the *LastName Header* section, and then modify the properties as follows:

   Font Size: **12**
   Font Color: **Dark Blue, Text 2** (first row, fourth column)
   Style: **Bold**
   Align: **Center**
   Background Color: **Yellow**

g. Resize the **LastName text box** using the bottom-right corner of the control box. Widen the field so the entire last name is visible when you switch to Layout view.

h. Click the **Count control** in the LastName Footer, and then click **Center** in the Font group. Hold down **Shift**, and then click the **Revenue Sum control** in the LastName Footer.

   Both controls are now selected.

i. Click **Bold** in the Font group.

j. Click the **Count control** in the Report Footer, hold down **Shift**, and then click the **Sum control** in the Report Footer.

   Both controls are now selected.

k. Click **Bold** in the Font group. Click the **Background Color arrow**, and then select **Blue, Accent 1, Lighter 80%** (second row, fifth column in Theme Colors).

l. Display the report in Print Preview. Advance through all the pages to review your changes.

m. Click **Close Print Preview**, and then save the report.

STEP 4 ADD A CALCULATED CONTROL TO A REPORT IN DESIGN VIEW

Alex asks you to add a comment to the report for all orders that are less than $10. You add a new expression using a text box control to display the word *minimum* if the order is under $10. Refer to Figure 51 as you complete Step 4.

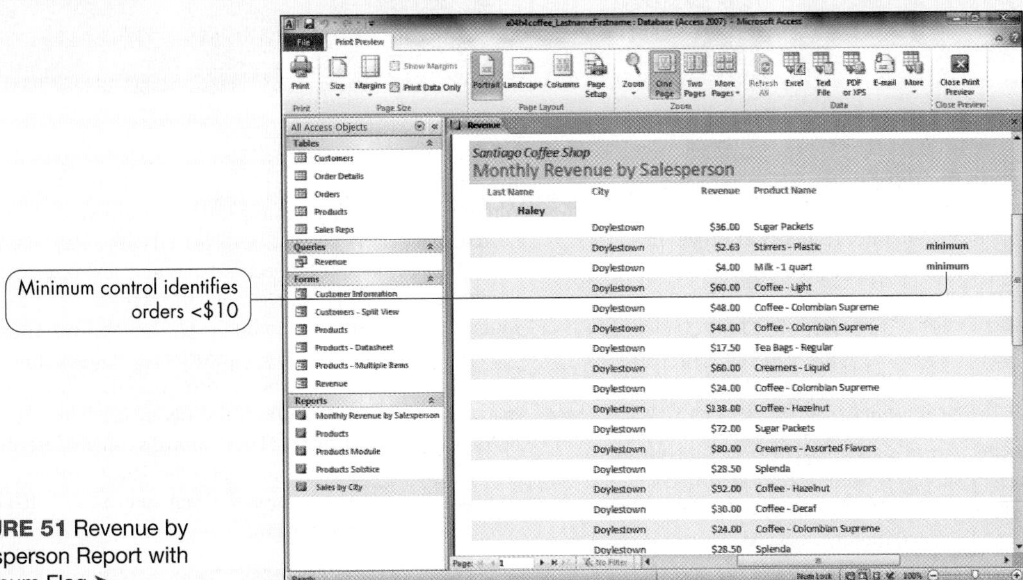

FIGURE 51 Revenue by Salesperson Report with Minimum Flag ➤

a. Switch to Design View if necessary. Click the **OrderDate box**, press **Delete**, and then delete the Order Date label. Drag the **Product Name box and label** to the **4 1/2"** mark on the horizontal ruler, moving the other labels and boxes, if necessary.

b. Click **Text Box** in the Controls group on the Design tab. Click in the **Detail section** to the right of the ProductName control.

   A new text box is created along with a label. The label overlaps the ProductName text box.

c. Click the new **Label control**, and then press **Delete**.

   The label control is deleted.

> **TROUBLESHOOTING:** If you delete the text box control, click Undo to restore the deleted control and delete only the Label control.

d. Click **Property Sheet** in the Tools group. Click the new text box, labeled *Unbound*, to select it.

e. Click the **All tab** in the Property Sheet pane. Type **MinimumOrder** in the **Name property box** and **="minimum"** in the **Control Source property box.** Change the Border Style property to **Transparent.**

f. Display the report in Print Preview.

   Minimum shows on all orders. You will now add an expression so that only orders less than $10 will show.

g. Click **Close Print Preview.** Verify the MinimumOrder control is selected.

h. Click the **Control Source**, and then press **Shift+F2** to expand the cell. Change the expression in the Control Source property to **=IIf(Revenue < 10, "minimum", "")**. Click **OK.**

   The second set of quote marks is an empty text string.

i. Display the report in Print Preview. Advance through all the pages to examine the minimum orders. Click **Close Print Preview.**

j. Click the **MinimumOrder control** in the *Detail* section, click **Bold** in the Font group on the Format tab, click the **Font Color arrow**, and then select **Red** under Standard Colors.

k. Display the report in Print Preview. Review the changes to the report, and then close and save the report.

l. Click the **File tab,** and then click **Compact & Repair Database.**

m. Exit Access.

n. Submit based on your instructor's directions.

CHAPTER OBJECTIVES REVIEW

After reading this chapter, you have accomplished the following objectives:

1. **Create forms using the form tools.** Access provides 16 different tools for creating forms. The form tools are found in the Forms group located on the Create tab, as shown in Figure 1. Click one of these tools and Access will create an automatic form using the table or query that is currently selected. The most common of these tools, the Form tool, is used to create stacked layout forms for customers, employees, products, and other primary tables. Once a form is created, you can customize the form using Layout and Design views.
2. **Modify a form.** After a form is generated by one of the form tools, you often need to modify it. Some common form changes are to add a field, remove a field, change the order of fields, change the width of a field, and modify label text. These changes, as well as adding a theme, can be made in a form's Layout view. Advanced changes, such as adding a calculated field or adding VBA code, can be made in a form's Design view.
3. **Sort records in a form.** When a form is created using a form tool, the sort order of the records in the form is dependent on the sort order of the record source. To modify the sort order of a form, open the form in Form view, and then select the field you want to use for sorting and click Ascending in the Sort & Filter group on the Home tab.
4. **Identify form sections.** Access forms, by default, are divided into three sections—Form Header, Detail, and Form Footer. These sections can vary depending on what type of form you create. Form designers also have the option of removing certain sections from a form. The *Form Header* section is displayed at the top of each form. This section will usually contain the form title, a logo or other graphic, and the date and time the report was printed. The *Detail* section displays the records in the form's record source. The *Form Footer* section is displayed at the bottom of the form. The Form Footer is commonly used to display totals for relevant field values.
5. **Revise forms using form views.** Access provides different views for a form, similar to the different views in tables and queries. Forms can be displayed in Layout view, Form view, and Design view. Use Layout view to alter the form design while still viewing the data. Use Design view to add or delete fields in a form, modify field properties, change the column widths, and enhance a form by adding a color scheme or styling.

   Most users will only see Form view; if a form needs modification, the user should notify the database designer. Use Design view to perform advanced changes to a form's design. It provides you the most advanced method of editing an Access form. You can perform many of the same tasks in Design view as you can in Layout view—add and delete fields, change the field order, adjust field widths, modify labels, and customize form elements.
6. **Identify control types in forms.** If you examine the elements on a form, you will notice that each field has a Label control box on the left and a Text Box control on the right. The text box displays the data found in the form's record source and the label is a literal word or phrase to describe the data. Although text box might imply text only, numeric data, currency, and dates can also be displayed with a text box.

   These two types of objects—Label and Text Box—are known as controls. They are among the many types of controls found in the Controls group on the Design tab when you are in Design view. Controls can be categorized as bound, unbound, or calculated. Bound controls are text boxes that are connected to a table or a query. Unbound controls are labels and other decorative design elements. These controls usually describe and decorate the data rather than display the data. Calculated controls contain an expression that generates a calculated result when displayed in Form view.
7. **Create reports using report tools.** Access provides five different report tools for creating reports. The report tools are found in the Reports group located on the Create tab, as shown in Figure 25. Click one of these tools and Access will create an automatic report using the table or query that is currently selected. The most common of the tools, the Report tool, is used to instantly create a tabular layout report based on the table or query currently selected. The Report Wizard will ask a series of questions and help you create the most appropriate report based on your answers. Use the Labels tool to create a page of labels using one of the preformatted templates provided by Access. After you create a report, you can perform modifications in Layout view and Design view.
8. **Modify a report.** After a report is generated by one of the report tools, you will usually need to modify it. The most common changes are to add a field, remove a field, change the order of fields, change the width of a field, and modify the title. These changes, as well as adding a grouping level, adding a sort order, and adding a theme, can be made in a report's Layout view or Design view. Advanced changes, such as adding a calculated field or adding VBA code, can be made in a report's Design view.
9. **Sort records in a report.** When a report is created using the Report tool, the sort order of the records in the report is initially dependent on the sort order of the record source. A report can be sorted while in Layout view or Design view by clicking Group & Sort in the Grouping & Totals group on the Design tab. The Group, Sort, and Total pane will appear at the bottom of the report. This section enables you to set the sort order for the report and override the sorting in the report's record source.
10. **Identify report sections.** Access reports are divided into five main sections, as shown in Figure 45. Each section can be collapsed or expanded as needed, but only in Design view. You can also remove any of the sections, except the *Detail* section, by right-clicking any section bar, and then clicking the *Header/Footer* section you wish to remove. The *Report Header* section prints once at the beginning of each report. The *Page Header* section appears once at the top of each page. The *Detail* section prints one line for each record in the report's record

source. The *Page Footer* section appears once at the bottom of each page. The *Report Footer* section prints once at the bottom of the report.

11. **Revise reports using report views.** Access provides different views for a report similar to the different views in tables, queries, and forms. Reports have Layout view, Print Preview, Design view, and Report view. To switch between views, click the View arrow in the Views group and select the Layout view or Design view. Use Layout view to alter the report design while still viewing the data. Print Preview enables you to see the closest approximation of what the report will look like when it is printed. Design view displays the report's layout without displaying the data. Report view enables you to see what the printed report will look like in a continuous page layout.

12. **Identify control types in reports.** If you examine the fields on a report, such as the one in Figure 47, you will notice that each field has a label (heading) at the top with a column of data values under the heading. A text box displays the data found in the record source and a label is a literal word or phrase to describe the data. The Label and Text Box controls are among the many types of controls found in the Controls group when you are in the Layout view or the Design view of a report. As discussed earlier, controls can be categorized as bound, unbound, or calculated. Bound controls are text boxes that are connected to a table or a query. Unbound controls are labels and other decorative design elements. Calculated controls contain an expression that generates a calculated result when displayed in Print Preview.

KEY TERMS

Bound control
Calculated control
Datasheet form
Design view
Detail section
Form
Form Footer section
Form Header section
Form tool
Form view
Group Footer section
Group Header section
Label control
Label Wizard
Layout control
Layout view
Mailing label
Multiple Items form
Page Footer section
Page Header section
Print Preview
Record source
Report
Report Footer section
Report Header section
Report tool
Report view
Report Wizard
Split form
Splitter bar
Stacked layout form
Stacked layout report
Tabular layout form
Tabular layout report
Text box control
Unbound control
Visual Basic for Applications (VBA)

MULTIPLE CHOICE

1. Which form tool does not place controls onto a form automatically?
   (a) Form Wizard
   (b) Form tool
   (c) Form Design tool
   (d) Datasheet tool

2. The Design view for a form enables you to do all of the following except:
   (a) Modify the form.
   (b) Add a new group.
   (c) View the data as it will be presented in the form.
   (d) Add a background color.

3. Which of the following guides you as you create a new report?
   (a) Report tool
   (b) Report Wizard
   (c) Blank Report tool
   (d) Report Design tool

4. Use the ____________ to see exactly what the printed report will look like before printing.
   (a) Report tool
   (b) Report Wizard
   (c) Report view
   (d) Print Preview

5. The easiest way to modify control widths in a form is in:
   (a) Layout view.
   (b) Form view.
   (c) Design view.
   (d) Report view.

6. What happens if you click a text box control in Layout view, and then press Delete?
   (a) The control is deleted from the report, but the other controls do not adjust to the empty space.
   (b) Nothing; you cannot change fields in Layout view.
   (c) The record is deleted from the report and from the database.
   (d) An error message appears stating that you should not attempt to delete records in a report.

7. The mouse pointer shape changes to a ____________ when you widen or narrow a column in Layout view.
   (a) single arrow
   (b) hand
   (c) two-headed arrow
   (d) four-headed arrow

8. Which of these is not a section in an Access form?
   (a) *Detail* section
   (b) *Group* section
   (c) *Form Header* section
   (d) *Form Footer* section

9. Which statement is true about controls?
   (a) Unbound controls are not used in reports.
   (b) Unbound controls are not used in the *Detail* section.
   (c) A calculated field is created with a text box control.
   (d) A form's title is usually created with the title control.

10. To organize your data in categories, you would use:
    (a) Sorting.
    (b) Grouping.
    (c) Queries.
    (d) Calculated fields.

1 National Conference

You are working on a database that will track speakers for a national conference. The data entry person entered information in the Speakers table incorrectly. He entered the first half of a new record correctly, but then jumped to a different record and overwrote the existing information with incorrect data. When you discovered the error, it took you a long time to find the correct information and correct both records. You decide that a form would help your co-workers enter data more accurately and help eliminate these types of errors. You create a form that will help the office staff add new speakers and sessions to the database as plans are finalized. After creating the form, you will customize it to be more user-friendly. If you have problems, reread the detailed directions presented in the chapter. This exercise follows the same set of skills as used in Hands-On Exercises 1 and 2 in the chapter. Refer to Figure 52 as you complete this exercise.

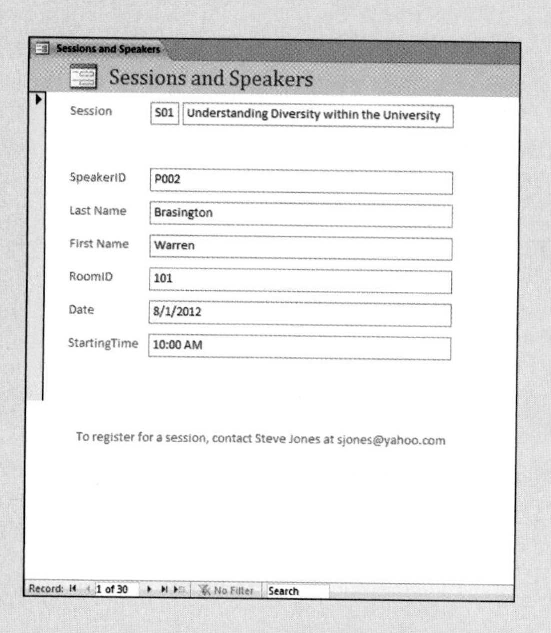

FIGURE 52 Sessions and Speakers Form in Form View ➤

a. Open *a04p1natconf*. Click the **File tab**, click **Save Database As**, and then type **a04p1natconf_LastnameFirstname**. Click **Save**.
b. Open the Speakers table, and then replace *Your_Name* with your name in the First Name and Last Name fields. Close the Speakers table.
c. Open the Sessions and Speakers query in Datasheet view, and then review the data.
d. Close the query; make sure it remains selected.
e. Click the **Create tab**, and then click **Form** in the Forms group to create a new form that opens in Layout view.
f. Click the **SpeakerID box.** Drag the right border of the first field to the left to shrink the column by 50%.
g. Right-click the **SessionID box**, and then select **Select Entire Row** from the list. Drag the **SessionID control** up to the first position.
h. Right-click the **SessionTitle box**, and then select **Select Entire Row** from the list. Drag the **SessionTitle** up to the second position.
i. Remove the stacked layout of the form as follows:
   - Switch to Design view.
   - Click the **SessionID label.**
   - Click **Select Layout** in the Rows & Columns group on the Arrange tab.
   - Click **Remove Layout** in the Table group.

j. Modify and reposition the controls as follows:
   - Switch to Layout view.
   - Click the **SessionID box.**
   - Drag the right border of the SessionID text box to the left to shrink the control to about 1/2" wide.
   - Click the **SessionTitle box.**
   - Drag the left border of the Understanding Diversity text box to the right to reduce the size of the control by 1/2".
   - Drag the **SessionTitle box** up and position it even with the SessionID control, as shown in Figure 52.
   - Rename the *SessionID* label as **Session:**
   - Delete the SessionTitle label.

k. Switch to Form view.

l. Click the **SessionID box.** Click **Ascending** in the Sort & Filter group. Click **Next Record** in the Navigation bar several times to verify the records are now ordered by SessionID.

m. Switch to Design view.

n. Add a message to the bottom of the form as follows:
   - Place the mouse on the bottom edge of the Form Footer bar so the mouse pointer changes to the double-arrow resizing shape. Drag the **Form Footer section** down to **2"**.
   - Click **Label** in the Controls group.
   - Click in the **Form Footer** on the 1" horizontal line, approximately 1/4" from the left edge.
   - Type **To register for a session, contact Steve Jones at sjones@yahoo.com.**
   - Compare the position of the new label to Figure 52.

o. Click **View** in the Views group to switch to Form view. Click **Next Record** in the Navigation bar to verify the new message appears on every record.

p. Save the form as **Sessions and Speakers.** Close the form and any other open objects.

q. Click the **File tab**, and then click **Compact & Repair Database.**

r. Close the database. Exit Access.

s. Submit based on your instructor's directions.

2 Comfort Insurance

The Human Resources department of the Comfort Insurance Agency has initiated its annual employee performance reviews. The reviews affect employee salary increases and bonuses. The employee data, along with forms and reports, are stored in an Access database. You need to prepare a report showing employee raises and bonuses by city. This exercise follows the same set of skills as used in Hands-On Exercises 1, 3, and 4 in the chapter. Refer to Figure 53 as you complete this exercise.

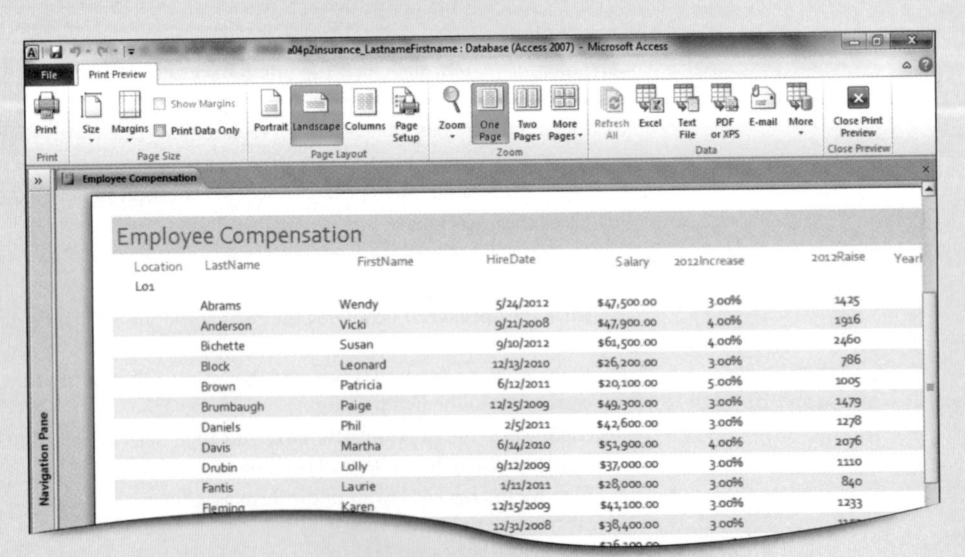

FIGURE 53 Employee Compensation Report with Totals ➤

a. Open *a04p2insurance*. Click the **File tab**, click **Save Database As**, and then type **a04p2insurance_LastnameFirstname**. Click **Save**.
b. Select the **Locations table**. Click the **Create tab**, and then click **Form** in the Forms group to create a new form that opens in Layout view.
c. Click the **LocationID text box** containing *L01*. Move the mouse to the right edge of the orange border until the mouse pointer changes to a double-headed arrow. Drag the right edge to the left to reduce the size of the text box to approximately 50% of its original size.
d. Click the subform at the bottom of the form, and then click the **Layout Selector** (the small square with a four-headed arrow inside). Press **Delete** to delete the subform.
e. Click **Themes** in the Themes group on the Design tab. Right-click a **Solstice theme** (second column, second row from bottom), and then choose **Apply Theme to This Object Only**.
f. Save the form as **Locations.** Close the form.
g. Select the **Locations table**. Click the **Create tab**, and then click **Report** in the Reports group to create a new tabular layout report in Layout view.
h. Click the **Locations label**, and then drag the right border of the label to the left to reduce the size of the control to **50%**.
i. Repeat the sizing process with the Zipcode label and the OfficePhone label. Adjust the other columns if necessary until there are no controls on the right side of the vertical dashed line.
j. Display the report in Print Preview. Verify that the report is only one page wide. Close and save the report using the name **Locations**.
k. Select the **Employee Query**. Click the **Create tab**, and then click **Report Wizard** in the Reports group to launch the Report Wizard. Respond to the questions as follows:
    - Click (>>) to add all the fields to the Selected Fields box. Click **Next**.
    - Accept grouping by Location. Click **Next**.
    - Select **LastName** for the first sort order and **FirstName** for the second. Click **Summary Options**.
    - Click **Sum** for Salary, **Avg** for 2012Increase, and **Avg** for YearsWorked. Click **OK**. Click **Next**.
    - Accept the Stepped layout. Change Orientation to **Landscape**. Click **Next**.
    - Type **Employee Compensation** for the title of the report. Click **Finish**.
    - The Report is displayed in Print Preview mode. Some of the columns are too narrow. Next, you will adjust the columns and summary controls.
l. Click **Close Print Preview**. Switch to Layout view.
m. Adjust the column widths so that all the data values are showing. Some of the columns will need to be reduced and some will need to be widened. Change the YearsWorked label to **Years.** Use Figure 53 as a guide.
n. Adjust the Summary controls at the bottom of the first Location (L01) so all the values are visible. Adjust the Summary controls in the Report Footer so all the values are visible. Align all the Summary controls with their associated detail columns.
o. Open the Property Sheet. Click the **Avg Of YearsWorked control**, and then select **Fixed** for the Format property and **0** for the Decimal Places property.
p. Click **Themes** in the Themes group. Right-click the **Module theme** (first column, fourth row from bottom), and then choose **Apply Theme to This Object Only**.
q. Display the report in Print Preview. Close the Navigation Pane, and then verify that the report is still one page wide. Compare your report to Figure 53. Adjust column widths if necessary.
r. Save and close the Employee Compensation report.
s. Click the **File tab**, and then click **Compact & Repair Database**.
t. Close the database. Exit Access.
u. Submit based on your instructor's directions.

MID-LEVEL EXERCISES

1 Hotel Chain

You are the general manager of a large hotel chain. You track revenue by categories: hotel rooms, conference rooms, and weddings. You need to create a report that shows which locations are earning the most revenue in each category. You also need to create a form that will enable you to enter and maintain member data for those guests who pay an annual fee in exchange for discounts and hotel privileges. Refer to Figure 54 as you complete this exercise.

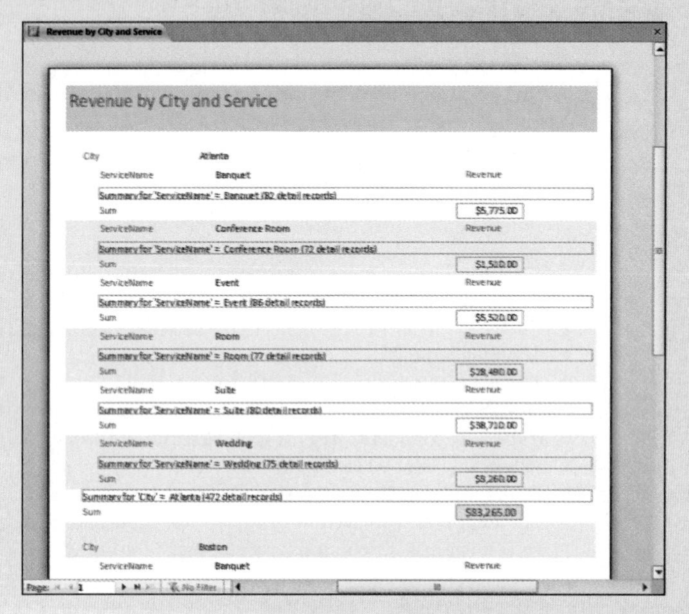

FIGURE 54 Revenue by City and Service, Summary Only ➤

a. Open *a04m1rewards.* Click the **File tab**, click **Save Database As,** and then type **a04m1rewards_LastnameFirstname.** Click **Save.**

b. Select the **Members table,** and then create a Multiple Items form. Save the form as **Maintain Members.**

c. Modify the form in Layout view as follows:
   - Reduce the row height by 50%.
   - Change the MemNumber label to **MemID,** and then reduce the MemNumber column width.
   - Adjust the column widths to eliminate extra white space.
   - Delete the form icon in the Form Header.

d. Switch to Design view, and then modify the form as follows:
   - Open the Property sheet, and then click the **Members title control** to change the Width property to **2.5".**
   - Add the special effect **Raised** to the **Members title control.**
   - Increase the Form Footer to **1/2".**
   - Add a new label control to the left side of the Form Footer.
   - Type **Form created by *your name.***
   - Reduce the width of the form to **12"** (reduce the e-mail column width, if necessary).
   - Add today's date to the right side of the Form Header using the **Date and Time command** in the Header/Footer group.

e. Switch to Form view. Verify that the controls in the *Header* and *Footer* sections remain constant as you advance through the records. Close and save the form.

f. Select the **Revenue query,** and then create a report using the Report Wizard. Answer the wizard prompts as follows:
   - Include all fields.
   - Add grouping by City and by ServiceName.
   - Add a Sum to the Revenue field.
   - Check the **Summary Only option.**

- Choose **Outline Layout**.
- Name the report **Revenue by City and Service**.

g. Scroll through all the pages to check the layout of the report while in Print Preview mode.

h. Switch to Design view, and then delete the NoInParty and PerPersonCharge controls in the *Detail* and *ServiceName Header* sections. Drag the remaining controls in the *ServiceName Header* section to the top of the section. Reduce the height of the *ServiceName Header* section as shown in Figure 54.

i. Open the Property Sheet, and then use the Width property to change the width of the Revenue control in the *Detail* section to **1.0"**, the width of the Sum of Revenue control in the ServiceName Footer to **1.0"**, the width of the Sum of Revenue1control in the City Footer to **1.0"**, and the width of the Revenue Grand Total Sum control in the Report Footer to **1.0"**.

j. Click each of the revenue controls while holding down **Shift**, and then set the Format property of all the selected controls to **Currency**.

k. Change the font size, font color, and background color of the Sum of Revenue1 control in the City Footer so the control stands out from the other controls.

l. Apply a different style to the Grand Total Sum control in the Report Footer.

m. Close and save the report.

n. Compact and repair the database.

o. Close the database. Exit Access.

p. Submit based on your instructor's directions.

2 Philadelphia National Bank

You are the manager of the loan department at Philadelphia National Bank (PNB). PNB issues mortgages, car loans, and personal loans to its customers. The bank's database contains the records of all of the customer loans. You need to create a form to manage the customer list. You also need to create a report that summarizes the loan payments by month. Refer to Figure 55 as you complete this exercise.

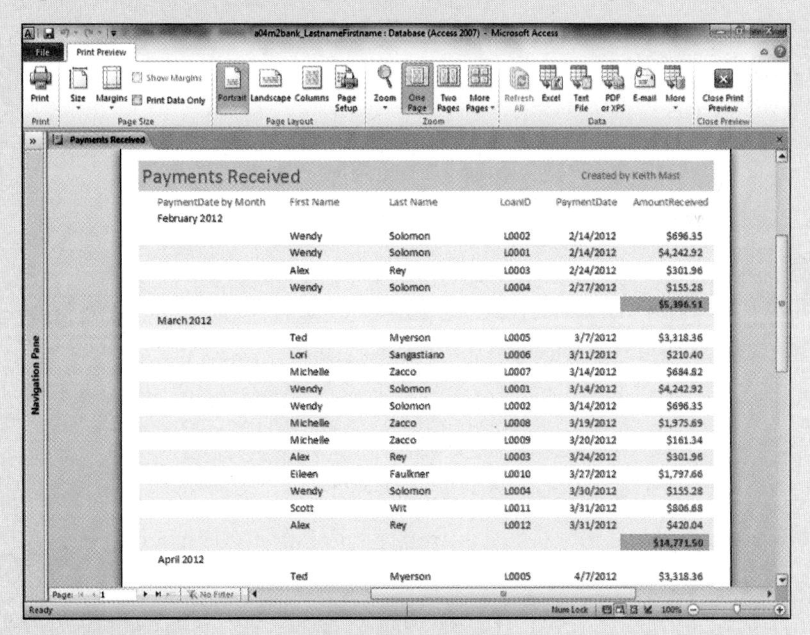

PaymentDate by Month	First Name	Last Name	LoanID	PaymentDate	AmountReceived
February 2012					
	Wendy	Solomon	L0002	2/14/2012	$696.35
	Wendy	Solomon	L0001	2/14/2012	$4,242.92
	Alex	Rey	L0003	2/24/2012	$301.96
	Wendy	Solomon	L0004	2/27/2012	$155.28
					$5,396.51
March 2012					
	Ted	Myerson	L0005	3/7/2012	$3,318.36
	Lori	Sangastiano	L0006	3/11/2012	$210.40
	Michelle	Zacco	L0007	3/14/2012	$684.82
	Wendy	Solomon	L0001	3/14/2012	$4,242.92
	Wendy	Solomon	L0002	3/14/2012	$696.35
	Michelle	Zacco	L0008	3/19/2012	$1,975.69
	Michelle	Zacco	L0009	3/20/2012	$161.34
	Alex	Rey	L0003	3/24/2012	$301.96
	Eileen	Faulkner	L0010	3/27/2012	$1,797.66
	Wendy	Solomon	L0004	3/30/2012	$155.28
	Scott	Wit	L0011	3/31/2012	$806.68
	Alex	Rey	L0012	3/31/2012	$420.04
					$14,771.50
April 2012					
	Ted	Myerson	L0005	4/7/2012	$3,318.36

FIGURE 55 Payments Received Report ➤

a. Open *a04m2bank*. Click the **File tab**, click **Save Database As**, and then type **a04m2bank_LastnameFirstname**. Click **Save**.

b. Create a form based on the Customers table. Access automatically adds the Loans subform to the bottom of the Customers form.

c. Close the form, but do not save it.

DISCOVER 

d. Open the Relationships window, and then find the relationship between Customers and Loans (this relationship caused the subform to appear in step b). Double-click the join line, and then make a note of which check boxes are checked in the Edit Relationships dialog box. Close the dialog box. Right-click the join line, select **Delete**, and then click **Yes** to confirm deletion. Save the relationship changes. Create the Customers form again and notice the subform is not there. Save the form as **Customers**, and then close it. Restore the relationships.

e. Open the Customers form in Layout view. Reduce the size of the text box controls by 50%, and then close and save the form.

f. Select the **Payments Received query**, and then create a report using the Report Wizard. Include all fields, view data by Payments, add grouping by PaymentDate, skip the sorting step, accept the default layout, and name the report **Payments Received**.

g. Switch to Design view, and then add a label to the right side of the Report Header that says **Created by *your name*.** Switch to Layout view.

h. Click the **AmountReceived field**, and then click **Totals** in the Grouping & Totals group. Select **Sum** from the list of options.

i. Add a different style to the AccessTotalsAmountReceived control so it stands out from the other controls. Add a light gray box around the AccessTotalsAmountReceived1 control.

j. Close the Navigation Pane, preview the report, and then adjust column widths as needed. Close and save the report.

k. Compact and repair the database.

l. Close the database. Exit Access.

m. Submit based on your instructor's directions.

CAPSTONE EXERCISE

Your boss asked you to prepare a schedule for each speaker for the national conference being hosted next year on your campus. She wants to mail the schedules to the speakers so that they can provide feedback on the schedule prior to its publication. You assure her that you can accomplish this task with Access.

Database File Setup

You need to copy an original database file, rename the copied file, and then open the copied database to complete this capstone exercise. After you open the copied database, you replace an existing employee's name with your name.

a. Open *a04c1natconf*.

b. Click the **File tab**, click **Save Database As**, and then type **a04c1natconf_LastnameFirstname**. Click **Save**.

c. Open the Speakers table.

d. Find and replace *Your_Name* with your name. Close the table.

Create a Form

You need to create a form to add and update Speakers. Use the Form tool to create the form, and then modify the form as explained.

a. Select the **Speakers table** as the record source for the form.

b. Use the **Form tool** to create a new stacked form.

c. Change the title to **Enter/Edit Speakers**.

d. Reduce the width of the text box controls to **50%**.

e. Delete the Sessions subform.

f. Add a new label control in the Form Footer that says **Contact Elaine Carey if you have questions about Speakers**.

g. View the form and data in Form view. Sort the records by LastName. Locate your record.

h. Save the form as **Edit Speakers**. Close the form.

Create a Report

You need to create a report based on the Speaker and Room Schedule query. You decide to use the Report Wizard to accomplish this task.

a. Select the **Speaker and Room Schedule query** as the record source for the report.

b. Activate the **Report Wizard** and use the following options as you go through the Wizard:
   - Select all of the available fields for the report.
   - View the data by Speakers.
   - Verify that LastName and FirstName will provide grouping levels.
   - Use **Date** as the primary sort field.
   - Accept the **Stepped** and **Portrait options**.
   - Name the report **Speaker Schedule**.
   - Switch to Layout view, and apply the **Module theme** to only this report.

c. Preview the report, and then adjust the column widths if necessary.

d. Close and save the report.

Add an Additional Field

You realize the session times were not included in the query. You add the field to the query and then start over with the Report Wizard.

a. Open the Speaker and Room Schedule query in Design view.

b. Add the **StartingTime field** in the Sessions table to the design grid. Run the query.

c. Close and save the query.

d. Start the Report Wizard again and use the following options:
   - Select the **Speaker and Room Schedule query**.
   - Select all of the available fields for the report.
   - View the data by Speakers.
   - Use the **LastName, FirstName fields** as the primary grouping level.
   - Use **Date** as the primary sort field.
   - Use **StartingTime** as the secondary sort field.
   - Select the **Stepped** and **Portrait options**.
   - Name the report **Speaker Schedule Revised**.
   - Switch to Layout view, and then apply the **Trek theme** to only this report.

e. Adjust the column widths in Layout View so that all the data is visible.

f. Increase the width of the StartingTime label control in the *Page Header* section in Design view, so that the entire phrase is visible. Add a space to the column heading labels as needed.

g. Close and save the report. Compact the database.

h. Close the database. Exit Access.

i. Submit based on your instructor's directions.

BEYOND THE CLASSROOM

Inventory Value

GENERAL CASE 

The owner of a bookstore asked for your help with her database. Her insurance company asked her to provide an inventory report listing the values of the books she has in stock. Open *a04b1books.* Click the File tab, click Save Database As, and then type **a04b1books_LastnameFirstname.** Click Save. Use the skills you learned in this chapter to create three stacked layout forms for Authors, Publishers, and Books. Delete any attached subforms. Next, create the inventory report that shows the inventory values for the books on hand. The database contains a query that you can use to create the report. Group the records by publisher name; alphabetize authors by last name and first name within groups. Name the report **Bookstore Inventory Value.** In Layout view, create a total value control for each publisher and create a grand total. Resize and reposition the total controls so they are visible and aligned with the correct column. Add Currency formatting where applicable, and then modify column headings as needed. Preview the report and verify that all the columns are correct, and then save and close the report. Compact and repair the database, and then close the database and close Access. Submit based on your instructor's directions.

Create Mailing Labels

RESEARCH CASE 

This chapter introduced you to Access reports. Use Access Help to search for mailing labels. Then put your new knowledge to the test. Open *a04b2arbor.* Click the File tab, click Save Database As, and then type **a04b2arbor_LastnameFirstname.** Click Save. It contains a query identifying volunteers who will be invited to this year's gala. Your challenge is to print the names and addresses as mailing labels in the format shown below. You already purchased Avery 5260 labels. Sort the labels by lastname, firstname. Name the report **Volunteer Invitation Labels.** After you create the labels, preview them and verify everything will fit onto the 5260 label template. Save and close the label report. Compact and repair the database, and then close the database and close Access. Submit based on your instructor's directions.

Label format:
Mr. (Dr., Ms., Mrs.,) John Doe, Jr.
Street Address
City, State Postal Code

Real Estate Development Report

DISASTER RECOVERY 

A co-worker is having difficulty with an Access report and asked you for your assistance. Open *a04b3property.* Click the File tab, click Save Database As, and then type **a04b3property_LastnameFirstname.** Click Save. The database contains the Sales Report query that was used to create the Sales by Agent report. The report is supposed to show each agent's total sales grouped by Subdivision. There should be totals for the sale price, the sales commissions, and the list price columns for each subdivision and each agent. The Percent of List should be averaged for each subdivision and each agent. Find and correct the errors. If you are unable to correct the errors, try creating the report again using the Report Wizard. Compact and repair the database, close the database, and then close Access. Submit based on your instructor's directions.

GLOSSARY

100% stacked column chart A chart type that places (stacks) data in one column per category, with each column having the same height of 100%.

3-D chart A chart that contains a third dimension to each data series, creating a distorted perspective of the data.

Absolute cell reference A designation that provides a permanent reference to a specific cell. When you copy a formula containing an absolute cell reference, the cell reference in the copied formula does not change, regardless of where you copy the formula. An absolute cell reference appears with a dollar sign before both the column letter and row number, such as B5.

Access A database program that is included in Microsoft Office.

Active cell The current cell in a worksheet. It is indicated by a dark border onscreen.

Area chart A chart type that emphasizes magnitude of changes over time by filling in the space between lines with a color.

Argument A variable or constant input, such as a cell reference or value, needed to complete a function. The entire group of arguments for a function is enclosed within parentheses.

Auto fill A feature that enables you to copy the contents of a cell or a range of cells or to continue a sequence by dragging the fill handle over an adjacent cell or range of cells.

AVERAGE function A predefined formula that calculates the arithmetic mean, or average, of values in a range.

Axis title A label that describes either the category axis or the value axis.

Backstage view Display that includes commands related to common file activities and that provides information on an open file.

Backup A copy of a file, usually on another storage medium.

Bar chart A chart type that compares values across categories using horizontal bars. In a bar chart, the horizontal axis displays values, and the vertical axis displays categories.

Border A line that surrounds a paragraph, a page, a table, or an image in a document, or that surrounds a cell or range of cells in a worksheet.

Breakpoint The lowest value for a specific category or series in a lookup table.

Bubble chart A chart type that shows relationships among three values by using bubbles to show a third dimension.

Category axis The chart element that displays descriptive group names or labels, such as college names or cities, to identify data.

Category label Text that describes a collection of data points in a chart.

Cell The intersection of a column or row in a worksheet or table.

Cell address The unique identifier of a cell, starting with the column letter and then the row number, such as A9.

Chart A visual representation of numerical data that compares data and helps reveal trends or patterns to help people make informed decisions.

Chart area A boundary that contains the entire chart and all of its elements, including the plot area, titles, legends, and labels.

Chart sheet A sheet within a workbook that contains a single chart and no spreadsheet data.

Chart title The label that describes the entire chart.

Circular reference A situation that occurs when a formula contains a direct or an indirect reference to the cell containing the formula.

Clip art An electronic illustration that can be inserted into an Office project.

Clipboard An Office feature that temporarily holds selections that have been cut or copied.

Clustered column chart A type of chart that groups or clusters similar data into columns to compare values across categories.

Color scale A conditional format that displays a particular color based on the relative value of the cell contents to other selected cells.

Column chart A type of chart that displays data vertically in columns to compare values across different categories.

Column index number The number of the column in the lookup table that contains the return values.

Column width The horizontal measurement of a column in a table or a worksheet. In Excel, it is measured by the number of characters or pixels.

Command A button or area within a group that you click to perform tasks.

Conditional formatting A set of rules that apply special formatting to highlight or emphasize cells that meet specific conditions.

Contextual tab A Ribbon tab that displays when an object, such as a picture or clip art, is selected.

Copy Duplicates a selection from the original location and places the copy in the Office Clipboard.

COUNT function A predefined formula that tallies the number of cells in a range that contain values you can use in calculations, such as numerical and date data, but excludes blank cells or text entries from the tally.

COUNTA function A predefined formula that tallies the number of cells in a range that are not blank; that is, cells that contain data whether a value, text, or a formula.

COUNTBLANK function A predefined formula that tallies the number of cells in a range that are blank.

Cut Removes a selection from the original location and places it in the Office Clipboard.

Data bar A conditional format that displays horizontal gradient or solid fill indicating the cell's relative value compared to other selected cells.

Data label A descriptive label that shows the exact value of the data points on the value axis.

Data point A numeric value that describes a single value on a chart.

Data series A group of related data points that appear in row(s) or column(s) in the worksheet.

Default A setting that is in place unless you specify otherwise.

Dialog box A window that opens when you are accomplishing a task that enables you to make selections or indicate settings beyond those provided on the Ribbon.

Dialog Box Launcher An icon in Ribbon groups that you can click to open a related dialog box.

Doughnut chart A chart type that displays values as percentages of the whole but may contain more than one data series.

Enhanced ScreenTip Provides a brief summary of a command when you place the mouse pointer on the command button.

Excel Software included in Microsoft Office that specializes in organizing data in worksheet form.

Exploded pie chart A chart type in which one or more pie slices are separated from the rest of the pie chart.

Field The smallest data element contained in a table, such as first name, last name, address, and phone number.

File A document or item of information that you create with software and to which you give a name.

Fill color The background color that appears behind data in a cell.

Fill handle A small black square at the bottom-right corner of a cell used to copy cell contents or text or number patterns to adjacent cells.

Filtering The process of specifying conditions to display only those records that meet the conditions.

Find Locates a word or phrase that you indicate in a document.

Folder A named storage location where you can save files.

Font A complete set of characters—upper- and lowercase letters, numbers, punctuation marks, and special symbols with the same design that includes size, spacing, and shape.

Format Painter A Clipboard group command that copies the formatting of text from one location to another.

Formula A combination of cell references, operators, values, and/or functions used to perform a calculation.

Formula AutoComplete A feature that displays a list of functions and defined names that match letters as you type a formula.

Formula Bar An element in Excel that appears below the Ribbon and to the right of the Insert command that shows the contents of the active cell so that you edit the text, value, date, formula, or function.

Freezing The process of keeping rows and/or columns visible onscreen at all times even when you scroll through a large dataset.

Function A predefined computation that simplifies creating a complex calculation and produces a result based on inputs known as arguments.

Function ScreenTip A small pop-up description that displays the arguments for a function as you enter it.

Gallery A set of selections that appears when you click a More button, or in some cases when you click a command, in a Ribbon group.

Gridline A horizontal or vertical line that extends from the horizontal or vertical axis through the plot area.

Group A subset of a tab that organizes similar tasks together.

HLOOKUP function A predefined formula that looks up a value in a horizontal lookup table where the first row contains the values to compare with the lookup value.

Horizontal alignment The placement of data or text between the left and right margins in a document, or cell margins in a spreadsheet.

Icon set A conditional format that displays an icon representing a value in the top third, quarter, or fifth based on values in the selected range.

IF function A predefined logical formula that evaluates a condition and returns one value if the condition is true and a different value if the condition is false.

Input area A range of cells to enter values for variables or assumptions that will be used in formulas within a workbook.

Key Tip The letter or number that displays over features on the Ribbon and Quick Access Toolbar.

Landscape Page or worksheet that is wider than it is tall.

Legend A key that identifies the color, gradient, picture, texture, or pattern assigned to each data series in a chart.

Library An organization method that collects files from different locations and displays them as one unit.

Line chart A chart type that displays lines connecting data points to show trends over equal time periods, such as months, quarters, years, or decades.

Live Preview An Office feature that provides a preview of the results of a selection when you point to an option in a list.

Logical test An expression that evaluates to true or false.

Lookup table A range that contains data for the basis of the lookup and data to be retrieved.

Lookup value The cell reference of the cell that contains the value to look up within a lookup table.

Margin The blank space around the sides, top, and bottom of a document or worksheet.

MAX function A predefined formula that finds the highest value in a range.

MEDIAN function A predefined formula that finds the midpoint value, which is the value that one-half of the population is above or below.

Microsoft Office A productivity software suite that includes word processing, spreadsheet, presentation, and database software components.

MIN function A predefined formula that finds the lowest value in a range.

Mini toolbar An Office feature that provides access to common formatting commands when text is selected.

Mixed cell reference A designation that combines an absolute cell reference with a relative cell reference. When you copy a formula containing a mixed cell reference, either the column letter or the row number that has the absolute reference remains fixed, whereas the other part of the cell reference that is relative changes in the copied formula. A mixed cell reference appears with the $ symbol before either the column letter or row number, such as $B5 or B$5.

Multiple data series Two or more sets of data, such as the values for Chicago, New York, and Los Angeles sales for 2010, 2011, and 2012.

Name Box An element in Excel that identifies the address or range name of the active cell in a worksheet.

Navigation Pane Located on the left side of the Windows Explorer window, providing access to Favorites, Libraries, Homegroup, Computer, and Network areas.

Nested function A function that contains another function embedded inside one or more of its arguments.

Nonadjacent range A collection of multiple ranges that are not positioned in a contiguous cluster in an Excel worksheet.

NOW function A predefined formula that uses the computer's clock to display the current date and time in a cell.

Nper The number of payment periods over the life of the loan.

Order of precedence A rule that controls the sequence in which arithmetic operations are performed.

Output area A range of cells that contains the results of manipulating values in an input area.

Page break An indication where data will start on another printed page. The software inserts automatic page breaks based on data, margins, and paper size. Users can insert additional page breaks.

Paste Places a cut or copied item in another location.

Picture A graphic file that is retrieved from the Internet, a disk, or CD and placed in an Office project.

Pie chart A chart type that shows each data point in proportion to the whole data series as a slice in a circular pie.

Plot area The region containing the graphical representation of the values in the data series.

PMT function A predefined formula that calculates the periodic payment for a loan with a fixed interest rate and fixed term.

Pointing The process of using the mouse pointer to select cells while building a formula. Also known as *semi-selection*.

Portrait Page or worksheet that is taller than it is wide.

PowerPoint A Microsoft Office software component that enables you to prepare slideshow presentations for audiences.

Print area The range of cells within a worksheet that will print.

Print order The sequence in which the pages are printed.

Pv The present value of the loan or an annuity.

Quick Access Toolbar Provides one-click access to commonly used commands.

Radar chart A chart type that compares aggregate values of three or more variables represented on axes starting from the same point.

Range A group of adjacent or contiguous cells in an Excel worksheet.

Range name A word or string of characters assigned to one or more cells. It can be up to 255 letters, characters, or numbers, starting with a letter.

Rate The periodic interest rate; the percentage of interest paid for each payment period.

Record A group of related fields, representing one entity, such as data for one person, place, event, or concept.

Relative cell reference A designation that indicates a cell's relative location within the worksheet using the column letter and row number, such as B5. When a formula containing a relative cell reference is copied, the cell references in the copied formula change relative to the position of the copied formula.

Replace Finds text and replaces it with a word or phrase that you indicate.

Ribbon The long bar of tabs, groups, and commands located just beneath the Title bar.

Row height The vertical measurement of a row in a table or a worksheet.

Semi-selection The process of using the mouse pointer to select cells while building a formula. Also known as *pointing*.

Sheet tab A visual item in Excel that looks like a folder tab that displays the name of a worksheet, such as *Sheet1* or *June Sales*.

Shortcut A link, or pointer, to a program or computer resource.

Sizing handles A series of faint dots on the outside border of a selected chart; enables you to adjust the size of the chart.

Sorting Listing records or text in a specific sequence, such as alphabetically by last name.

Sparkline A small line, column, or win/loss chart contained in a single cell.

Spreadsheet An electronic file that contains a grid of columns and rows to organize related data and to display results of calculations.

Spreadsheet program A computer application, such as Microsoft Excel, that people use to create and modify spreadsheets.

Stacked column chart A chart type that places stacks of data in segments on top of each other in one column, with each category in the data series represented by a different color.

Status bar The horizontal bar located at the bottom of an Office application containing information relative to the open file.

Stock chart A chart type that shows fluctuations in stock changes.

Structured reference A tag or use of a table element, such as a column heading, as a reference in a formula.

Subfolder A folder that is housed within another folder.

SUBTOTAL function A predefined formula that calculates an aggregate value, such as totals, for values in a range or database.

SUM function A predefined formula that calculates the total of values contained in two or more cells.

Surface chart A chart type that displays trends using two dimensions on a continuous curve.

Syntax The rules that dictate the structure and components required to perform the necessary calculations in an equation or evaluate expressions.

Tab Ribbon area that contains groups of related tasks.

Table Organizes information in a series of records (rows), with each record made up of a number of fields (columns).

Table array The range that contains the body of the lookup table, excluding column headings. The first column must be in ascending order to find a value in a range, or it can be in any order to look up an exact value.

Table style The rules that control the fill color of the header row, columns, and records in a table.

Template A predesigned file that incorporates formatting elements, such as a theme and layouts, and may include content that can be modified.

Text One or more letters, numbers, symbols, and/or spaces often used as a label in a worksheet.

Title bar A horizontal bar that appears at the top of each open window. The title bar contains the current file name, Office application, and control buttons.

TODAY function A predefined formula that displays the current date in a cell.

Toggle Commands such as bold and italic that enable you to switch from one setting to another.

Total row A table row that appears below the last row of records in an Excel table, or in Datasheet view of a table or query, and displays summary or aggregate statistics.

Trendline A line that depicts trends or helps forecast future data.

User interface A collection of onscreen components that facilitates communication between the software and the user.

Value A number that represents a quantity or an amount.

Value axis The chart element that displays incremental numbers to identify approximate values, such as dollars or units, of data points in the chart.

Vertical alignment The position of data between the top and bottom cell margins.

View The way a file appears onscreen.

VLOOKUP function A predefined formula that looks up a value and returns a related result from the lookup table.

Windows Explorer A Windows component that can be used to create and manage folders.

Word A word processing program that is included in Microsoft Office.

Workbook A collection of one or more related worksheets contained within a single file.

Worksheet A single spreadsheet that typically contains labels, values, formulas, functions, and graphical representations of data.

Wrap text A formatting option that enables a label to appear on multiple lines within the current cell.

X Y (scatter) chart A chart type that shows a relationship between two variables using their X and Y coordinates. Excel plots one variable on the horizontal X-axis and the other variable on the vertical Y-axis. Scatter charts are often used to represent data in educational, scientific, and medical experiments.

X-axis A horizontal border that provides a frame of reference for measuring data horizontally on a chart.

Y-axis A vertical border that provides a frame of reference for measuring data vertically on a chart.

Zoom slider Enables you to increase or decrease the size of file contents onscreen.

dex

references followed by "f" indicate illustrated
ɜs or photographs; followed by "t" indicates a